LINGVA LATINA

A College Companion

based on Hans Ørberg's *Latine Disco*, with Vocabulary and Grammar

LINGVA LATINA

A College Companion

based on Hans Ørberg's *Latine Disco*, with Vocabulary and Grammar

Jeanne Marie Neumann

Davidson College

Dedication
Jon et Conor, filiis iucundissimis medullitusque amatis.

ISBN 10: 1-58510-191-5
ISBN 13: 978-1-58510-191-7

Table of Contents

Preface

Ørberg's *Lingua Latina* series, conceived as a completely acquisition-based approach to learning Latin, offers an unparalleled resource for Latin learning, enabling the motivated student to acquire skill *in* reading Latin *by* reading Latin. *Lingua Latina* guides readers through an expanding world of Latin syntax while they enjoy a delightful story of a Roman family of the early imperial period. The reading mirrors "real" Latin in the way it unfolds the periodic structure and idiomatic features of the language, introducing early critical features: students meet the relative pronoun in Chapter 3, the passive voice in Chapter 6; by the time they get the full verbal paradigm of the present tense in Chapter 15-17, they have mastered the concept and workings of active and passive voice. Length of readings, number of vocabulary words and complexity of sentence structure increase as the chapters build on each other, all in support of a narrative that engages students from middle school through college (and beyond).

Lingua Latina offers a smooth and efficient path to acquisition of the language and immerses the student from the first in a true experience of Latin. The impetus of this book arose not from any flaw in Ørberg's method, but rather from the differing needs of some students and classrooms. In most colleges, students signing up for Latin commit to a two-term introductory experience, followed by a term (sometimes two) of reading ancient texts. Reading *Familia Romana* in a two-semester course in introductory Latin, meeting three times a week for two 13- or 14-week semesters becomes a Herculean task. The book, however, and its results both proved too good to abandon. There seems to me no better guide than *Lingua Latina* for students who want to learn Latin *through Latin*, even for those students without the time and inclination to move through it at the pace intended. *Est modus in rebus*, as Horace wrote long ago, and there is a middle ground between the complete nature method and the traditional paradigm method.

More than time constraints, however, inspired this book. Different students learn differently: *Alii aliis viis Romam perveniunt.* While *Latine Disco* is an excellent companion for some, for others, who want more grammatical structure, it works less well. Students clamored for us to keep the text, but make it suit their needs. This book, therefore, aims to strike a balance between a purely inductive method and the study of grammatical rules and paradigms. This balance addresses not only student need, but the instructor's proclivities as well. As such it may find immediate appeal with instructors and students using Ørberg at the college level; its benefits in the middle school, high school or home-school classroom may accrue more to the instructor than the students.

How does this book fit into the *Lingua Latina* series? What does it replace? This book replaces the *Latine Disco*, the *Grammatica Latina*, and the Latin-English Vocabulary. It does not replace the *Exercitia*.

What are the primary features of this book? The book provides a running **grammatical commentary** on the narrative of *Lingua Latina*. It differs from the *Latine Disco* in scope and aim. *Latine Disco* provides clear and concise information that students need to acquire an understanding of Latin at their own pace. This book builds from Ørberg's original *Latine Disco*; the presentation and formatting have been altered and more explication and examples are offered. To the degree possible, the **commentary corresponds to the reading sections** within each chapter, enabling students to study just the grammar for each section. Important and challenging structures are illustrated with several **examples** from the story. As the grammatical concepts build, they are collected and reviewed in **periodic recensiones**, facilitating an overview of the language and enabling students to know where to look for the places in the story where, e.g., they learned about accusative and infinitive construction. An overview is further facilitated by the index of the new grammar (**Res Grammaticae Novae**) that gives a synopsis, in categories, of the material covered in that chapter. In addition to the division by part of speech and definition of vocabulary at the end of each chapter and the full vocabulary at the back of the book, **vocabulary review** is enhanced by an appendix listing the vocabulary according to chapter but without meanings; students can quiz themselves on their grasp of vocabulary outside the context of the story. Finally, Ørberg's own mastery of the language shows through in his ability to write lucid, idiomatic Latin. Where appropriate, student attention is directed to *points of style* that highlight the way the language works syntactically or idiomatically.

This book, therefore, is designed for different audiences: university students, instructors of home-scholars, and independent learners whose learning style appreciates such a guide. *Lingua Latina* can be used to teach students Latin as early as age eight, yet the story engages adult readers as well. At the college level, however, introductory language courses do not have the luxury of gradual acquisition, the two years (or four semesters) recommended to learn to read Latin well from the book. The Ørberg text, however, can be highly effective for these students as well. Instead of reading discrete, even random, sentences chosen to illustrate the grammatical principles under consideration, *Lingua Latina* offers considerable practice in both grammar and a rich vocabulary in an engaging context of well-written Latin.

Home-schooling parents and instructors of students learning outside of the traditional classroom, especially those with little or no Latin training, can use this book for their own preparation. This book supplements that process, as a companion to *Lingua Latina*; the instructor will be the best judge of where and when it is a useful guide. For the most part, students should gradually learn the whole of Latin grammar by working out grammatical rules from their own observation as they begin to read actual Latin in the text, while their instructors can feel more confident in their grasp of the material and can use the added examples from *Familia Romana* to review and reinforce concepts or answer questions their charges present. In itself, this is not a text suited for pure inductive learning or for the very young student. This book might also help to confirm the Latin and the structures that are learned in the inductive method, facilitating the process in the more intense college classroom.

Jeanne M. Neumann
Davidson College

Acknowledgements

Amicis qui me librum hunc scribentem adiuverunt maximas gratias et ago et habeo, praecipue Jarrett Welsh, Keyne Cheshire, Megan Drinkwater et Gina Soter. Discipulis hic apud Collegium Davidsoniense Latine discentibus gratias quoque ago, praecipue Gregory Means et Angela Soper. Nam illi et menda typographica notaverunt et consilium quo liber melior et clarior fieret praebuerunt.

For the Instructor

Lingua Latina as a Two-Semester Course

What follows is a brief explanation of how we have adapted *Familia Rōmāna* to our introductory sequence at Davidson College. The constraints of two semesters propel the course forward quickly, with usually two class days devoted to each chapter. This pace makes "catch-up" cramming difficult, if not impossible. Therefore, the relative weight of each facet of evaluation reflects the philosophy of the course: daily use of a language is the only way to mastery. Daily work carries the greatest weight in the course (*id est*: quizzes, homework, tests and class preparation and participation), while the final exam accounts for a much smaller portion of the grade. Students should expect to spend one hour each day working on Latin skills: that means seven hours a week of work outside of class. We encourage students to break up this work into small, frequent encounters with the Latin throughout their day.

The pace of the course and presentation of the material both complicate and energize the instructor's presentation. The text can be used as a basis for asking questions in Latin. When students answer in Latin, they strengthen their grasp of the vocabulary and the syntax and their ability to stay in the target language. Longer, more difficult sentences can be paraphrased in Latin to facilitate understanding or broken down into smaller components. While the bulk of our classes are conducted in English, moving back and forth frequently between the two languages will help the students' Latin get strong enough to read the ever-lengthening stories and ever more complex sentences.

There follow two different sets of instructions for a course that aims to read *Familia Rōmāna* in two terms of three meetings a week. These are offered as examples of the approaches of two instructors at Davidson and represent the general guidelines offered to students. The approaches are quite different: the first has the students read the chapter before any instruction, either verbal or from the *Companion*, while the second introduces all major grammatical concepts before the students read the text.

There are many roads to Rome and other ways of using the *Companion* as a pedagogical aid. We offer our experience as examples.

One Approach

Assignment for Day One (the first of two class days spent on a given chapter):

- Look at the *marginalia* in *Familia Rōmāna* (*marginalia*: the material written in the margins of the *Lingua Latina* text).
- Read the entire chapter in Latin; each chapter is divided into three sections, marked by Roman numerals in the inside margins of the text. In Chapter II, for example, Section II begins with the words "*Estne Mēdus fīlius Iūliī?*" (p. 14). Each new section practices a different grammatical principle.
- Try not to translate each sentence into English but to understand the sentences in Latin (a challenge which grows easier with time).
- Study the *Grammatica Latina* at the end of each chapter in *Familia Rōmāna*.
- Study the pages in *College Companion*.
- If you cannot grasp the meaning of a vocabulary word from context, look it up in the Latin-English vocabulary at the end of the chapter or the back of this book. Vocabulary words recur frequently. If you need to look up a word more than once, or find the next day you cannot remember what it means, memorize the word by making a flash card. Carry the flash cards around with you and review frequently.
- Complete homework as assigned.

After the second day:

- Re-read the entire chapter, paying close attention to the forms and grammatical principles, and making sure you have a firm understanding of both the grammar and meaning of the chapter. At this reading, it should be much easier not to translate in your head from Latin to English.
- Review the *marginalia* and the vocabulary. In the margin of each chapter of *Familia Rōmāna* is a list of new vocabulary. Make sure you understand those words out of context. If you don't remember, find the word in the text *before* looking it up.
- Complete homework as assigned.
- Look ahead briefly to discover the emphasis of the next chapter.

A Second Approach

Day 1:

- Introduce the chapter (vocabulary and all major grammatical concepts) before students see anything.
- Homework: read *College Companion* and *Familia Rōmāna* narrative; study for quiz.

Day 2:

- Quiz on new vocabulary.
- Questions about the reading? (Have them marked by line # with notes.)
- Warm-up with Pensum A.
- "Conversational" Latin: Ask questions about the reading and their lives. Then other intense/fun drill/practice activities, all in Latin.
- Homework: carefully chosen Exercitia.

Both approaches are intense, but students enjoy and profit from the course.

To the Student

You will learn far more Latin more quickly and in a more interesting way if you first work with the book and the readings and the (very important) **marginalia** (that is, the words and images in the columns next to the reading) and then refer to this book to help you organize what it is you have encountered. By this method the book helps you confirm what you have already learned.

The value of the marginalia and the images in the *Familia Rōmāna* text cannot be overemphasized! The marginalia mark out new things you will learn and help you to understand the Latin quickly and visually. The illustrations will be valuable clues to what the Latin itself is saying.

Try *not* to translate into English as you read. Instead, keep images in your mind and work as much as you can in Latin. Only by increasing your stamina for reading and thinking within the Latin language will you gain proficiency in understanding.

A note on translations: You will find that translations accompany only a few of the illustrative sentences in this book. These translations demonstrate how a particular construction works in the English language in order to help you understand how Latin works, not to encourage translation into English. Remember, the goal is Latin!

The more actively you engage, the more you will learn. Quiz yourself by going back into earlier chapters and randomly picking a word. Do you know what that word means without reading it in context? If not, reread the surrounding sentences and see whether context prods your memory. If not, look the word up. Do you recognize its case (if appropriate)? Could you reconstruct the nominative from that case? If the word is a verb, recount to yourself all you know about it (the amount you will know will depend on how far into the course you have proceeded). Try to write short synopses of the reading in Latin. Read out loud. Send a classmate an email in Latin! The more you engage different senses, the faster you will learn and the more you will retain.

Before you start

Orthography

Latin was written (orthography) as it sounded. Therefore, the spelling of Latin changed with natural variations of pronunciation that occurred over time and place. So, for example, Cicero would have written *equos* for "the horse," while Caesar Augustus would have written *ecus*; we find this same word in our Latin texts as *equus* because editors of Latin texts generally adopt the spelling of the first century AD, when variations in orthography had leveled out. We still find variation in the treatment of the semi-vowels *u/v* and *i/j*, however (on these semi-vowels, see below under pronunciation).

Latin Pronunciation

Latin was spoken through many countries over many hundreds of years. When you think how much pronunciation varies in different regions of our own country during our own time, the very thought of how to "correctly" pronounce Latin becomes daunting. We actually know quite a bit about how upper-class educated Romans living in Rome during a relatively short time span spoke Latin because Roman writers themselves have given us various hints. This pronunciation is called the "Restored Pronunciation." Even though the Restored Pronunciation may be the way Horace recited his *Odes*, for example, or Virgil his *Aeneid*, we should not feel constrained to try to duplicate it. In our own language, English, we don't feel we need to research how Shakespeare might have spoken in order to read *Hamlet*. Elizabethan actors might be amazed at our renditions, but we aren't talking to them. Our goal is to be faithful to the principles of the language and to be understood by others. But—you may object that we can't really appreciate the beauty of a Latin poem unless we hear it as the Romans did. If that were true, we would need more than sounds to appreciate Latin literature—we would need the full spectrum of cultural values that comprise aesthetic appreciation.

So, how to pronounce Latin? If we are faithful to a few principles, we can read with confidence and feeling and understand and be understood by others. In order to utter Latin well, we must understand the quantities of vowels and syllables, know where to put the accent, and how to enunciate. Thus, while the guide below will suggest pronunciations that mirror some of the things we know about ancient pronunciation, if you pay attention to quantities, accent and enunciation, you will be understood whether you pronounce *c* hard (i.e. like "k") as the Romans did or soft, as Ecclesiastical Latin.

But first, let's look at the alphabet.

The Alphabet

The Latin alphabet can be most simply divided into vowels and consonants. That broad division has subdivisions as well. The Latin alphabet has 23 letters; it lacks the English *w*; *y* and *z* were Greek imports, as were *ch, ph, th*.

Vowels

- Latin has both single vowels and diphthongs (two vowels that form one sound).
- Vowels can be either "long" or "short." A long vowel is pronounced for twice the length of time. Compare the "a" in "father" and "aha." We hold the "a" sound twice as long in "father." Long vowels in this book are marked by a bar over the vowel called a "macron" (i.e. *ā, ē, ī, ō, ū*). The Latin vowels are:
- a
  - ▷ short: *a* as the first *a* in "aha": *amat*
  - ▷ long: *ā* as in "father": *ālā, pānis*
- e
  - ▷ short: *e* as in "let": *et, bene*
  - ▷ long: *ē* as in "prey": *mē*
- i
  - ▷ short: *i* as in "fit: *in, nimis*[1]
  - ▷ long: *ī* as *ee* in "feet": *hīc, līberī*
- o
  - ▷ short: *o* as in "hot": *post, modo*
  - ▷ long: *ō* as in bone: *pōnō*
- u
  - ▷ short: *u* as in "full": *num, sumus*
  - ▷ long: *ū* as in "fool": *ūna, tū*
- y (represents the Greek *upsilon*)
  - ▷ short: *y* as French *u* in "lune": *Syria*
  - ▷ long: *ȳ* as French *u* in "pur": *Lȳdia*
- Diphthongs, being two vowels together, take twice as long to pronounce as single short vowels and so are considered long. They are:
- *ae* as *ie* in "die": *Graecia, laetus, paene*
- *oe* as *oi* in "boil": *foedus, poena*
- *au* as *ou* in "loud": *aut, nauta*
- *eu* as *e+u* combined into one syllable (ĕh-oo): *Eurōpa, heu, heus, neu, seu.* (But the endings *-us, -um, -unt* form separate syllables after *e*: *de|us, me|us, e|um, e|unt, aure|us*.)
- *ui* in *cui, huic, cuius, huius* as *u+i* combined into one syllable

---

1   The sound as in f*i*t, h*i*t does not occur in the modern Romance languages, suggesting that short *i* had more of an *ee* sound, but held for a shorter time.

Semi-vowels (glides)

Latin has two letters called "glides," which represent either a vowel or a consonant sound depending on the letters around them. These letters are represented in our book as *i* and *u/v*:

- *i*: The father of our family is Iulius, the same as the English Julius. The "j" and "i" of his name represent the same letter in Latin, which was always represented by "i" by the Romans. <u>Sound</u>: Before a consonant "i" represents the vowel sound "i" and before a vowel the consonant sound "y."
- *u/v*: The word for slave shows you the other glide in Latin. The word for slave is *servus*, in the plural it's *servi*. The "v" and "u" are actually the same letter and work the same way as "i" and "j." <u>Sound</u>: Before a consonant "u" represents the vowel sound "u" and before a vowel the consonant sound "w."

Consonants

Most consonants are the same as, or very similar to English.

- *b* as in English: *bibit, ab*
- *bs* and *bt* as *ps* and *pt*: *absunt, obtulit, urbs*
- *c* always hard as in "cat" (= *k*, without aspiration): *canis, centum, circus, nec*
- *ch, ph, th* as *k, p, t* with aspiration: *pulcher, amphitheātrum*
- *d* as in English: *dē, dedit, ad*
- *f* as in English: *forum, flūmen*
- *g* as in English "get" (never as in "gem"): *gallus, gemma, agit*
- *gn* as *ngn* in "willingness": *signum, pugna, magnus*
- *h* as in English (tending to disappear): *hīc, homō, nihil*
- *l* as in English: *lūna, gladius, male, vel*
- *m* as in English: *mē, domus, tam*
- In the unstressed endings -*am*, -*em*, -*um* it tended to disappear.
- *n* as in English: *nōn, ūnus*; before *c, g, q* as in "ink": *incola, longus, quīnque*
- Before *s* it tended to disappear: *mēnsa, īnsula*
- *p* as in English (without aspiration): *pēs, populus, prope*
- *ph* as English *p* with aspiration: see above under *ch*
- *qu* as English *qu* in "quick": *quis, aqua, equus*
- *r* rolled or trilled: *rēs, ōra, arbor, cūr*
- *s* as in English "gas" (never voiced as in "has"): *sē, rōsa, is*
- *t* as in English (without aspiration): *tē, ita, et*
- *th* as English *t* with aspiration: see above under *ch*
- *t* is always hard (not like *t* in nation)
- *v* as English *w*: *vōs, vīvus*
- *x* as in English (= *ks*): *ex, saxum*
- *z* as English *z* in "zone": *zōna*

Thus, very generally, the sound of Latin consonants can be compared to those of English:

- Like English: *d, f, l, m* & *n* (initial and medial)[2], *p, qu, z*
- Like English + variations (see above): *bs, bt, gn*
- Always a hard sound: *c, g, s, t, x*
- Softer than English: *h,* final *m, n*
- Different: *r* (trilled) *v* (like *w*)

Now, we return to our guidelines for pronunciation of quantities, accentuation, and enunciation. In Chapter XVIII you will get an excellent lesson in the concepts below, in Latin.

1. Syllables:
   a. A word has as many syllables as it has vowels and/or diphthongs:
      i. *Est, nōn, sunt*
      ii. *Rō ma, Nī lus, quo que*
      iii. *Flu vi us, op pi dum, īn su la*
      iv. *Brun di si um, Hi spā ni a*
   b. Note that in the examples above:
      i. A consonant goes with the following vowel: *Rō ma*
      ii. Two consonants are divided: *op pi dum*
         a. Some consonants stay together:
      ~ *ch, ph, th, qu*
      ~ *l* or *r* preceded by *b, d, g, p, t, c* and *f*
2. Vowel quantity:
   a. A long vowel takes twice the time to pronounce as a short vowel.
3. Syllable quantity:
   a. A syllable is either :
      i. open (ends in a vowel)
      ii. closed (ends in a consonant)
   b. Long/Heavy syllables:
      i. Closed syllables
      ii. Open syllables with long vowel/diphthong
   c. Short/Light syllables:
      i. Open syllables with a short vowel
4. Accent:
   a. The last three syllables of a Latin word determine accent.
   b. These syllables are called:
      i. ultima (for *syllaba ultima*: the last syllable)
      ii. penult (for *syllaba paene ultima*: almost the last syllable)
      iii. antepenult (for *ante paene ultimam syllabam*: "before the almost the last")
   c. The accent, or stress, of a Latin word depends on the length of the second to last, or penultimate, syllable.

---

2   I.e. beginning a word (initial) and in the middle of a word (medial)

    d. The penult (penultimate) syllable is accented when long/heavy (closed or has long vowel or diphthong).

    e. Otherwise the accent moves to the antepenult.

    f. Examples:

        i. *Rōma in Italiā est. Italia in Eurōpā est. Graecia in Eurōpā est. Italia et Graecia in Eurōpā sunt. Hispānia et Italia et Graecia in in Eurōpā sunt.*

5. Enunciation: this last principle sounds easy, but most people who feel nervous about saying a word correctly try to say it as fast as possible. Some tips:

   ▷ Speak slowly and say what you see.

   ▷ Doubled consonants (two consonants in a row) are both pronounced.

   ▷ Long vowels take twice the time to pronounce as short vowels.

Parts of Speech with Examples

[The chapter in brackets gives the first introduction of the part of speech.]

Noun (substantive) [Chapter I]:

1. names a person, place or thing
2. properties:
    a. gender: masculine, feminine, or neuter (neither masculine or feminine)
    b. number: singular or plural
    c. case: different endings depending on the role of the word in the sentence

    Exempla Latīna:

      Rōma
      Fluvius
      Oppidum

Adjective [Chapter 1]:

1. qualifies a noun
2. stands on its own as a substantive
3. has (like nouns) gender, number, and case
4. has (unlike nouns) all three genders (can stand in agreement with any noun)
5. matches (agrees) with its noun in gender, number, and case

    Exempla Latīna:

      magnus (fluvius)
      parva (īnsula)
      parvum (oppidum)

Pronoun [Chapter II]:

1. points to, or stands for, a noun without naming it, e.g.: "he," "whom," "they"
2. has (like nouns) gender, number and case

   Exempla Latīna:

Quis	*Cuius*
Quae	*Quid*

Verb [Chapter I]:

1. shows action, state of being
2. properties:
   a. person: 1st (I/we), 2nd (you), 3rd (he, she, it/they)
   b. number: singular, plural
   c. tense: time frame of the verb:
      i. present (continuing action in the present)
      ii. imperfect (continuing action in the past)
      iii. future (projected action)
      iv. perfect (completed action)
      v. pluperfect (action completed before another completed action)
      vi. future perfect (action to be completed before a projected action)
   d. voice:
      i. active (subject is the agent of the verb)
      ii. passive (subject is the recipient of the action of the verb)
   e. mood: expresses the speakers attitude to the verb
      i. indicative (states a fact, asks a question)
      ii. infinitive (the unbounded, "to" form of the verb)
      iii. imperative (gives a command)
      iv. subjunctive (various uses)

   Exempla Latīna:

   est, sunt
   pulsat [Chapter III]
   cantat [Chapter III]

Participle [Chapter XIV]:
   1. shares qualities of *verbs* and *adjectives*
   2. like a *verb*, a participle has
      a. tense (present, past, future)
      b. voice (active, passive)
   3. like an *adjective*, a participle has
      a. gender
      b. number
      c. case
          Exempla Latīna:
              dormiēns (*puer*)
              canentem (*gallum*)
              stantem (*servum*)

Adverb [Chapter I]:
   1. qualifies a
      a. verb
      b. adjective
      c. another adverb
          Exempla Latīna:
              nōn
              ubi (interrogative adverb)
              num (interrogative adverb)

Preposition [Chapter I]:
   1. determines the relationship between two nouns
          Exempla Latīna:
              in (*Italiā*)
              sine (*rōsīs*)[Chapter V]
              cum (*Aemiliā*)[Chapter V]

Conjunction [Chapter 1]:
   1. joins words, phrases or clauses
          Exempla Latīna:
              sed
              et

Interjection: an exclamation for emphasis [Chapter XXII]:
          Exempla Latīna:
              heus!

Syntactic Terms

[Examples are underlined]

Subject: the focus of the sentence. To find the subject, ask "who" with the verb.

- Julia is singing. Who is singing? Julia (subject)

  Exempla Latīna:

  <u>Rōma</u> in Italiā est.
  <u>Iūlia</u> cantat [Chapter III].

Predicate: the action or state of being in the sentence and its modifier. To find the verb, look for the action or state of being in the sentence.

- *Rōma in Italiā <u>est</u>*: *est* is the verb/predicate (state of being)
- *Iūlia <u>cantat</u>*: *cantat* is the action (action)

Predicate nominative: a noun used with a copulative (linking) verb to **restate** the subject.

- *Corsica <u>īnsula</u> est.*
- *Tūsculum <u>oppidum</u> Rōmanum est.*

Predicate adjective: an adjective used with a copulative (linking) verb to **qualify** the subject.

- *Fluvius <u>magnus</u> est.*
- *Oppidum <u>parvum</u> est.*

Transitive verb: a verb which is completed by a direct object.

  Exempla Latīna:

  Mārcus nōn <u>videt</u> Quīntum [Chapter III].
  Mārcus puellam <u>pulsat</u> [Chapter III].

Intransitive verb: a verb which is not completed by a direct object (which is in the accusative case). In both examples below, the dative case completes the verb, which is intransitive.

  Exempla Latīna:

  Germānī Rōmānīs nōn <u>parent</u> [Chapter XII].
  Iūlius servīs <u>imperat</u>.

Direct object: a word in the accusative case that receives the action of the verb.

  Exempla Latīna:

  Mārcus nōn videt <u>Quīntum</u> [Chapter III].
  Mārcus <u>puellam</u> pulsat [Chapter III].

Indirect object: a word in the dative case that tells "to or for whom" the action of the verb is performed.

  Exempla Latīna:

  Pater fīliō suō magnum mālum dat [Chapter VII].
  Dominus servīs māla et pira dat.

I. Imperium Rōmānum

Rēs Grammaticae Novae

1. Getting Started: The Roman Empire
2. Using This Book
   a. Pay Attention to Endings
   b. Be Aware of Latin's Flexible Word Order
   c. Concentrate on Meaning and Context
   d. Be Patient: Keep Reading:
      conjunctions *quoque* and *sed*
   e. Answers Often Explain Questions: *-ne?* and *ubi?*
   f. Look to Context for Word Meaning
3. Morphology
   a. Verbs: Singular/Plural
   b. Antonyms
   c. Adjectives and Substantives
   d. Interrogatives: *num, quid*
   e. Numbers: *mille*
4. Points of Style: Latin Concision

Lectiō Prīma (Section I)
Getting Started: The Roman Empire

In the first chapter we take you almost 2,000 years back into the past, to the time when the Roman Empire was at the height of its power, extending from the Atlantic Ocean to the Caspian Sea and from Scotland to the Sahara. We give you a few geographical facts as background for the sketches from life in ancient Rome which follow.

On the map of the Roman Empire facing the first page of the text you will find all the geographical names occurring in the chapter. After locating the names *Rōma, Italia, Eurōpa, Graecia,* etc., you will understand what is said about the situation of the city of *Rōma* in the first sentence: *Rōma in Italiā est,* and about *Italia* and *Graecia* in the next two: *Italia in Eurōpā est. Graecia in Eurōpā est.* This is said once more in a single sentence: *Italia et Graecia in Eurōpā sunt.* The meaning of *et* should be quite clear, but can you tell why it is now *sunt* instead of *est?* If not, look in the margin, and read the next two sentences as well. Have you discovered when to use *est* and when *sunt*? If so, you have learned the first rule of grammar: that a singular subject is joined with a singular verb and a plural subject with a plural verb.

If you read *Lingua Latina* heeding the following suggestions, you'll learn Latin well and easily.

1. Pay Attention to Endings (e.g. -*a*, -*ā*)

Did you also notice the slight difference between *Italia* and *Italiā*, and what little word produces the long -*ā*? This difference is pointed out and explained in the first marginal note:

> Italia
> in Italiā

2. Be Aware of Latin's Flexible Word Order (e.g. *est, sunt*)

Another thing worth noticing: *est* and *sunt* come at the end of the sentence; but you will see that it is not always so, *Rōma est in Italiā* is also correct. The word order is less rigid in Latin than in English.

3. Concentrate on Meaning and Context (e.g. the negation *nōn*)

Is it really possible, you may ask, to understand everything by just reading the text? It certainly is, provided that you concentrate your attention on the meaning and content of what you are reading. It is sufficient to know where *Aegyptus* is, to understand the statements *Aegyptus in Eurōpā nōn est, Aegyptus in Āfricā est* (l.5). There can be no doubt about the meaning of *nōn* (a so-called **negation**).

4. Be Patient: Keep Reading (e.g. *quoque* and *sed*)

Often a sentence is understood only when seen together with other sentences. In the sentence *Hispānia quoque in Eurōpā est* (ll.2-3) you will not understand *quoque* until you read in context: *Italia et Graecia in Eurōpā sunt. Hispānia quoque in Eurōpā est.* (The two preceding sentences might have been: *Italia in Eurōpā est. Graecia quoque in Eurōpā est.*) If you are still in doubt, just go on reading till the word recurs: *Syria nōn est in Eurōpā, sed in Asiā. Arabia quoque in Asiā est* (l.7). Now you will certainly understand *quoque*—and in the meantime you have learned the word *sed* almost without noticing it.

5. Answers often Explain Questions: (e.g. -*ne*...? and *ubi*...?)

In the next paragraph a number of questions are asked, and each question is followed by an answer. It is often necessary to read the answer before you can be quite sure of the meaning of the question. The first question is: *Estne Gallia in Eurōpā?* The particle -*ne* attached to *est* marks the sentence as a question (our question mark [?] was unknown to the ancient Romans). The answer is *Gallia in Eurōpā est.* The next question *Estne Rōma in Galliā?* is answered in the negative: *Rōma in Galliā nōn est.* (Latin has no single word for "yes" or "no," the sentence—or part of it—must be repeated with or without *nōn*).

In the question *Ubi est Rōma?* the word *ubi* is intelligible only when you get the answer: *Rōma est in Italiā.*

6. Look to Context for Word Meaning

After the short survey of the location of the principal Roman provinces, you are told about various localities: *Rhēnus* and *Nīlus, Corsica* and *Sardinia, Tūsculum* and *Brundisium.* You will find these names on the map, and the text will tell you what they represent. If you are still in doubt about the meaning of the words *fluvius, īnsula* and *oppidum,* turn back to the picture heading the chapter.

Verbs: Singular/Plural

Note that these words occur in two different forms: *Nīlus* alone is called *fluvius,* but *Nīlus* and *Rhēnus* together are called *fluviī.* In similar circumstances you will notice the use of the forms *īnsula* and *īnsulae,* and *oppidum* and *oppida.* In the section GRAMMATICA LATINA in LINGUA LATINA you will learn that the forms *fluvius, īnsula* and *oppidum* are called *singulāris,* while *fluviī, īnsulae* and *oppida* are called *plūrālis*—in English **singular** and **plural**.

Lectiō Altera (Section II)
Antonyms [↔]

As you read on you will see that *Nīlus* is referred to not only as *fluvius,* but as *fluvius magnus,* unlike *Tiberis,* which is described as *fluvius parvus.* In the same way *Sicilia* is referred to as *īnsula magna* as opposed to *Melita* (the modern Malta), which is called *īnsula parva.* In the margin *magnus* and *parvus* are represented as opposites (sign [↔], "the opposite of"); this will help you to understand the meaning of the words, but note the changing endings. Further examples are seen when *Brundisium* is called *oppidum magnum* and *Tūsculum oppidum parvum,* and when the same words occur in the plural: *fluviī magnī, īnsulae magnae, oppida magna.*

Adjectives and Substantives

A word which shows this variation between the endings *-us, -a, -um* in the singular and *-ī, -ae, -a* in the plural is called an **adjective** (Latin *adiectīvum,* "added word") because it is added to a **noun** (**substantive**), which it qualifies. Other nouns occurring in this chapter are:

prōvincia	*littera*
imperium	*vocābulum*
numerus	

Adjectives occuring in this chapter are:

magnus, -a, -um	*Rōmānus, -a, -um*
parvus, -a, -um	*Latīnus, -a, -um*
Graecus, -a, -um	*prīmus, -a, -um*

Plural adjectives found in this chapter are:

multī, -ae, -a	*paucī, -ae, -a*

Note: The endings of the adjectives depend on the nouns that they qualify; so *prōvincia magna* but *imperium magnum.*

More Interrogatives: *num, quid*

The question <u>Num</u> Crēta oppidum est? (l.49) must of course be answered in the negative: *Crēta oppidum <u>nōn</u> est*. *Num* is an **interrogative** (i.e. asking) particle, like *-ne*, but a question beginning with *num* implies a negative answer. The next question is <u>Quid</u> est Crēta? Here, again, only the answer, *Crēta <u>īnsula</u> est*, makes the meaning of the question quite plain.

Compare:

Est<u>ne</u> Crēta oppidum?	Is Crete a town? (I really don't know, so I'm asking.)
<u>Num</u> Crēta oppidum est?	Crete isn't a town, is it? (I suspect Crete is not a town and expect you to answer "no.")

Remember the other interrogatives in this chapter:

<u>Quid</u> est Crēta?	What is Crete?
<u>Ubi</u> est Crēta?	Where is Crete?

More about Endings

We have seen a final *-a* modified to *-ā* after *in*. We now see that *in* also makes *-um* change to *-ō*:

in imperi<u>ō</u> Rōmān<u>ō</u> (l.58)	in capitul<u>ō</u> prīm<u>ō</u> (l.73)
in vocābul<u>ō</u> (l.72)	

You will learn more about these forms in *-ā* and *-ō* in Chapter V.

Lectiō Tertia (Section III)
Mīlle

Mīlle, the word for "a thousand," is an **indeclinable** adjective; indeclinable means its endings never change. So:

mīlle numerī   mīlle vocābula   mīlle litterae

Points of Style: Latin Concision

Latin is a concise language. It can often express in a few words what requires several words in other languages. One of the reasons is that Latin has fewer particles (small uninflected words) than most modern languages; thus you will find nothing corresponding to the English articles "a" and "the" as in "a river," "the river," etc.

Recensiō (Review)

Remember:

1. Pay Attention to Endings.
2. Be Aware of Latin's Flexible Word Order.
3. Concentrate on Meaning and Context.
4. Be Patient: Keep Reading.
5. Answers often Explain Questions
6. Look to Context for Word Meaning

Vocābula Disposita/Ordināta

Nōmina

1st

grammatica, -ae	grammar
īnsula, -ae	island
littera, -ae	letter
prōvincia, -ae	province
syllaba, -ae	syllable

2nd

capitulum, -ī	chapter
exemplum, -ī	example, model
fluvius, -ī	river
imperium, -ī	command, empire
numerus, -ī	number
ōceanus, -ī	ocean
oppidum, -ī	town
pēnsum, -ī	task
vocābulum, -ī	word

Verba

est	he/she/it is
sunt	they are

Adiectīva

1st-2nd (us, -a, -um)

Graecus, -a, -um	Greek
Latīnus, -a, -um	Latin
magnus, -a, -um	big, large, great
multī, -ae, -a (*pl.*)	many, a great many
parvus, -a, -um	little, small
paucī, -ae, -a (*pl.*)	few, a few
prīmus, -a, -um	first
Rōmānus, -a, -um	Roman, of Rome
secundus, -a, -um	second, favorable
tertius, -a, -um	third

Numerī

ūnus	one, only
duo	two
trēs	three
sex	six
mīlle	one thousand

3rd (you will learn about these later)

plūrālis (numerus)	plural
singulāris (numerus)	singular

Adverbia
nōn — not

Praepositiōnēs
in (*prp. + abl.*) — in, on, at
(*prp. + acc.*) — into, to, against

Coniunctiōnēs
et — and, also
sed — but
quoque — also, too

Vocābula Interrogātīva
-ne? *enclitic added to the emphatic word at the beginning of a question the answer to which may be either "yes" or "no." It can be used in both direct and indirect questions.*
num? — if, whether
quid? *n. (v. quis)* — what, anything; *adv.* why
ubi? *interrog. adv.* — where

II. Familia Rōmāna

Rēs Grammaticae Novae

1. Gender: Masculine, Feminine, Neuter
2. Nouns
    a. Ending in -*us*
    b. Ending in -*a*
    c. Ending in -*um*
    d. Ending in -*er*
    e. Genitive
3. Adjectives
    a. *cēterī, ae, a*
    b. Possessive
    c. Numbers
4. Pronouns: *quis, quae, quid*
5. Adverbs: Interrogative *quot*
6. Conjunctions
7. *Ecce*
8. Points of Style: Enumerations

The Roman Family

We now introduce you to the people whose daily lives we will follow in the rest of the text. The picture shows them dressed in their best clothes, except for the four who are relegated to the margin—clearly they are not on the same level as the rest of the family. Be sure to remember their names, for you will soon become so well acquainted with these persons that you will almost feel like a friend visiting a real Roman family 2,000 years ago. And the remarkable thing about it is that you can understand their language!

Lectiō Prīma (Section I)

Gender: Masculine, Feminine, Neuter

Note that the names of these people end in either -*us* (masculine) or -*a* (feminine); none of them end in -*um* (neuter). You will see that the ending -*us* is characteristic of male persons:

7

> *Iūlius*   *Dāvus*
> *Mārcus*   *Mēdus*
> *Quīntus*

and -*a* of female persons:

> *Aemilia*   *Syra*
> *Iūlia*   *Dēlia*

This also applies to nouns that denote persons. Nouns referring to males generally end in -*us*:

> *fīlius*   *servus*
> *dominus*

A smaller number of masculine nouns end in -*r* instead of -*us*, e.g.:

> *vir*   *puer*

Nouns denoting females end mostly in -*a*:

> *fēmina*   *domina*
> *puella*   *ancilla*
> *fīlia*

No persons are denoted by words ending in -*um*.

Although male names end in *us* or *r*, and female names in *a*, Latin groups nouns by **gender,** not "sex." The word gender comes from the Latin *genus*, which means group or category. The three genders, or categories, are:

> **neuter** (Latin *neutrum,* "neither," i.e. neither masculine nor feminine)
>
> > *oppidum*   · *imperium*
> > *vocābulum*
>
> **masculine** (Latin *masculīnum*)
>
> > *fluvius*   *titulus*
> > *numerus*   *liber*
>
> **feminine** (Latin *fēminīnum,* from *fēmina*)
>
> > *īnsula*   *prōvincia*
> > *littera*   *familia*

Genders (in Latin)

> masculine (m.): -*us, er* (*ir*)
> feminine (f.): -*a*
> neuter (n.): -*um*

Nouns: Genitive

The word *familia* refers to the whole household, including all the slaves, *servī* and *ancillae*, who belong to the head of the family as his property. *Iūlius* is the father, *pater*, of *Mārcus, Quīntus* and *Iūlia*, and the master, *dominus*, of *Mēdus, Dāvus, Syra, Dēlia*, etc. To express these relationships we need the **genitive** (Latin *genetīvus*), a form of the noun ending in:

Singular: *-ī* (m./n.) and *-ae* (f.)

> *Iūlius est pater Mārcī et Quīntī et Iūliae.*
> *Titulus capitulī secundī est "Familia Rōmāna." (ll.87-88)*

Plural: *-ōrum* (m./n.) and *-ārum* (f.)

> *Iūlius est dominus multōrum servōrum et multārum ancillārum.*
> *In Graeciā et in Italiā magnus numerus oppidōrum est. (l.56)*

English has the ending *-s* or "of" to express the idea in the genitive: *mater Iūliae* = "Julia's mother" or "the mother *of* Julia."

genitive: "of," "s"

	m./n.	f.
sing.	*-ī*	*-ae*
pl.	*-ōrum*	*-ārum*

Conjunctions

Particles like *et* and *sed* are called **conjunctions** (Latin *coniūnctiōnēs*, from *coniungere*, "join together") because they join words and sentences.

Instead of *et* you often find the conjunction *-que* attached after the second word. *-Que* is called an **enclitic** because it "leans on" (from the Greek ἐνκλίνω) the word in front of it and cannot stand on its own. The mark "-" in front of it signals an enclitic. Both *et* and *-que* mean "and":

> *Dēlia Mēdusque = Dēlia et Mēdus. (l.9)*
> *fīliī fīliaeque = fīliī et fīliae (l.22)*

Conjunctions

> *sed*
> *...-que = et...*

Interrogatives: *Quis, Quae, Quid*

Among the new words in Chapter II are the interrogative words *quis* and *quae*, which are used to ask questions about persons (English "who"):

> *Quis est Mārcus?*   masculine *quis* (plural *quī*)
> *Quae est Iūlia?*   feminine *quae* (plural *quae*)

In Chapter I you met the neuter interrogative *quid* (English "what"):

> *Quid est Creta?*   neuter singular.

The genitive of the interrogative for all genders is *cuius* (English "whose"):

> *Cuius servus est Dāvus? Dāvus servus Iūliī est. (l.35)*

	m.	f.	n.
	quis?	*quae?*	*quid?*
gen.	*cuius?*		

Quot

Most words in Latin change endings, for example *fīlius* (one son) and *fīliī* (more than one son). Some words, however, never change form. They are called **invariable** or **indeclinable**: they always look the same. *Quot* ("how many") is an **invariable** interrogative adverb that asks questions about number:

> *Quot līberī sunt in familiā? In familiā Iūliī sunt trēs līberī.*
> *Quot fīliī et quot fīliae? Duo fīliī et ūna fīlia.*
> *Quot servī...?...centum servī. (ll.37-39)*

quot? 1, 2, 3...

Numerī

Like *mīlle* (Chapter I) and most numerals, *centum* (100, *l.*39) is invariable; that is, it does not change its ending (or "decline," the usual term for a change of ending). The numbers one (*ūnus*), two (*duo*), and three (*trēs*), however, do decline, that is, they change endings:

- *ūnus* has the familiar endings *-us -a -um*
- the feminine of *duo* is *duae* (*duae fīliae*) and the neuter *duo*
- the neuter of *trēs* is *tria* (*tria oppida*); *trēs* refers to both masculine and feminine nouns.

m.	f.	n.
ūnus	*ūna*	*ūnum*
duo	*duae*	*duo*
trēs	*trēs*	*tria*

Lectiō Altera (Section II)

Genitive (continued)

The number can also be indicated by the noun *numerus* combined with the genitive plural:

> *Numerus līberōrum est trēs. (ll.43-44)*
> *Numerus servōrum est centum. (l.43)*

As *centum* must be said to be *magnus numerus,* the following sentences are easily understood:

> *Numerus servōrum est magnus.*
> *In familiā magnus numerus servōrum est.*

It appears that *magnus numerus servōrum* is equivalent to *multī servī*. In the same way *parvus numerus līberōrum* has the same meaning as *paucī līberī.* You will also find the expressions *magnus numerus oppidōrum* and *fluviōrum* meaning *multa oppida* and *multī fluviī.*

> *magnus numerus...ōrum = multī...ī/multa...a*
> *magnus numerus...ārum = multae...ae*

Adjective: *cēterī, ae, a*

The Romans knew only the northern part of the continent of Africa, where there is only one big river, the Nile:

> *In Āfricā ūnus fluvius magnus est: Nīlus.* (*l.58*)

It goes on:

> <u>*Cēterī*</u> *fluviī Āfricae parvī sunt.* (*l.59*)

The adjective *cēterī -ae -a,* "the other(s)," recurs several times; thus the enumeration of the first three of the thirty-five *capitula* is concluded with *cētera*:

> *In Linguā Latīnā sunt multae pāginae et multa capitula: capitulum prīmum, secundum, tertium, cētera.* (*l.86*)

The sentence might have read *et cētera,* the Latin expression which gives us the abbreviation "etc.").

> *cēterī, -ae, -a*

Points of Style: Enumerations

The following rules apply to enumerations in Latin:

1. *et* put between all items: *Mārcus <u>et</u> Quīntus <u>et</u> Iūlia*
2. no conjunction used at all: *Mārcus, Quīntus, Iūlia*
3. *-que* added to the last item: *Mārcus, Quīntus Iūlia<u>que</u>*

enumeration:

1. *A et B et C*
2. *A, B, C*
3. *A, B C-que*

Lectiō Tertia (Section III)
Adjectives: Possessive

The conversation at the end of the chapter shows that instead of the genitive the adjectives *meus, -a, -um* and *tuus, -a, -um* are used to refer to what belongs to the person speaking or the person spoken to (like English "my" and "your").

The adjective always has the same gender (m. f. or n.) number (sing. or pl.) and case (e.g. nominative, genitive) as the noun it modifies. So, Julius says "*Delia est ancilla mea*" (*l.71*)—*mea* is an adjective agreeing with *ancilla*, so it is feminine nominative singular.

> *meus, -a, -um*
> *tuus, -a, -um*

ecce: →

On page 16 you come across the word *ecce* (illustrated with an arrow in the margin). It is used when you point to or call attention to something; in this case it is pointing to the two books.

Nouns Ending in -*er*: *puer, puerī, liber, librī*

Notice the form of an ancient book: a scroll with the text written in columns. The Latin word for such a scroll is *liber*. *Liber*, like *puer* (also in this chapter), ends in -*er* instead of in -*us*. Notice that some nouns (like *puer*) keep an *e* throughout, while others (like *liber*) have *e* only in the nominative (and vocative)[1]. The plural of *liber* is *librī*, while the plural of *puer* is *puerī*. These nouns are always masculine.

Notā Bene[2]: Look to the **genitive** to determine what happens to the *e*:

> *puer, puerī*   (there will be an *e* throughout)
> *liber, librī*   (the *e* is found only in the nominative)

	nominative	genitive
	liber	*librī*
	puer	*puerī*

Recensiō: Grammatical Terms

Decline: Nouns, adjectives, and pronouns change endings, depending on their use in the sentence; that is, they are said to **decline**.

Enclitic: An **enclitic** is a word that cannot stand on its own; it attaches itself to the word it follows.

Gender: Nouns, adjectives and pronouns fall into three categories called **genders**: masculine, feminine and neuter.

Invariable: A word is called **invariable** or **indeclinable** if it never changes endings.

Vocābula Disposita/Ordināta

Nōmina

1st

ancilla, -ae	female slave, servant
domina, -ae	mistress
familia, -ae	domestic staff, family
fēmina, -ae	woman
fīlia, -ae	daughter
pāgina, -ae	page
puella, -ae	girl

2nd

dominus, -ī	master
fēminīnum, -ī (genus)	feminine
fīlius, -ī	son
genetīvus, -ī (cāsus)	genitive
liber, -brī	book
līberī, -ōrum	children
masculīnum, -ī (genus)	masculine
neutrum (genus)	neuter

---

1   Vocative, Chapter IV

2   *Notā Bene* means "note well" or "take note—this is important!"

puer, -erī	boy
servus, -ī	slave, servant
titulus, -ī	title
vir, -ī	man, husband
3rd (you will learn more about these nouns in Chapter IX)	
māter, (*f.*)	mother
pater, (*m.*)	father

Adiectīva

1st-2nd (us, -a, -um)

antīquus, -a, -um	old, ancient, former
centum (*invariable*)	a hundred
cēterī, -ae, -a (*pl.*)	the other(s), the rest
duo, duae, duo	two
meus, -a, -um	my, mine
novus, -a, -um	new
trēs, tria	three
tuus, -a, -um	your, yours

Pronōmina

quis? quae? quid?	who, what
quī?, m (*pl.*)	what, which
cuius? (*gen. sing.*)	whose

Adverbia

quot?, *indecl.*	how many, (as many) as

Coniunctiōnēs

-que	**and,** *enclitic added to the second word of a pair of words in order to link them together*

III. Puer Improbus

Rēs Grammaticae Novae

1. Verbs
    a. The Latin Verb
    b. Transitive/Intransitive
    c. Implied Subject
2. Nouns: Subject/Object
3. Pronouns
    a. Personal Pronouns: Accusative Case
    b. Relative and Interrogative Pronouns
4. Adverbs: Interrogatives *cūr, quia*
5. Conjunctions: Negatives
6. Points of Style: Writing Relative Sentences

Sibling Quarrel

Now that you have been introduced to the family, you are going to watch some of their doings. We begin with the children—they were very much the same in ancient times as they are today. So we are not surprised to learn that Julius and Aemilia's children cannot always get on together. Here little Julia is the first to suffer, because her singing annoys her big brother. Peace is not restored until Mother and Father step in.

The chapter is divided up into three scenes (*scaena prima, secunda, tertia*).

Lectiō Prīma (Section I)
The Latin Verb

Several of the new words in this chapter are **verbs**. A verb (Latin *verbum*) is a word that expresses an action or a state: that someone does something or that something exists or takes place. The first Latin verb you come across is *cantat* in the opening sentence: *Iūlia cantat*. Other verbs are *pulsat, plōrat, rīdet, videt, vocat, venit*, etc. They all end in *-t*—like *est*, which is also a verb—and mostly come at the end of the sentence.

Verbs

-at	cantat, pulsat, plōrat
-et	rīdet, videt, respondet
-it	venit, audit, dormit

Verbs: Transitive/Intransitive

Verbs like *pulsat, videt, vocat*, which can be used with an object in the accusative, are called **transitive**. Verbs without an object, e.g. *rīdet, plōrat, dormit*, are **intransitive** verbs.

> *Iūlia plōrat* (intransitive: no object) *et Aemiliam vocat* (transitive: accusative object). (*l.9*)
> *Mārcus nōn videt Quīntum* (transitive). (*l.11*)
> *Mārcus puellam pulsat* (transitive) *-et rīdet!* (intransitive). (*l.12*)

Notā Bene: You need to pay attention to whether a word is transitive in Latin—which will not always be the same as its English equivalent!

Nouns: Subject/Object

The first of the two words in the sentence *Iūlia cantat* denotes the person who performs the action. Other sentences of the same kind are:

| *Iūlia plōrat.* (*l.9*) | *Aemilia venit.* (*l.21*) |
| *Mārcus rīdet.* (*l.10*) | *Pater dormit.* (*l.37*) |

But it is not always as simple as this. Take, for instance, the sentence that is illustrated by the little drawing in the margin: *Mārcus Iūliam pulsat* (*l.8*). Here we are told not only who performs the action, but also at whom the action is aimed. The same pattern is seen in the following sentences, also illustrated by pictures:

| *Quīntus Mārcum videt.* (*l.11*) | *Mārcus Quīntum pulsat.* (*l.14*) |
| *Quīntus Mārcum pulsat.* (*l.13*) | *Iūlia Aemiliam vocat.* (*l.19*) |

Subject: The person who performs the action is called the **subject** of the verb. The subject has one of the well-known endings *-us* and *-a*; these forms are called **nominative** (Latin *nōminātīvus*).

Object: The person toward whom the action is directed, the **object**, takes the ending *-um* or *-am*. The forms *-um* and *-am* are called **accusative** (Latin *accūsātīvus*).

In other words: *Iūlia* is changed to *Iūliam* when we are told that Marcus hits her, just as *Mārcus* becomes *Mārcum* when he is the victim. In similar circumstances *puella* changes to *puellam*, and *puer* to *puerum*, and qualifying adjectives get the same ending:

> *Mārcus parvam puellam pulsat.* (*l.59*)
> *Iūlius puerum improbum verberat.* (*l.64*)

> **subject object   verb**
> *Mārcus Iūliam   pulsat*

	m.	f.
nominative:	*-us*	*-a*
accusative:	*-um*	*-am*

Lectiō Altera (Section II)

Personal Pronouns: Accusative Case

Instead of accusative nouns in *-am* and *-um* you sometimes find the *eam* and *eum*, e.g.:

> *Iūlia plōrat quia Mārcus <u>eam</u> pulsat.* (*ll.27-28*)
> *Cūr Iūlius Quīntum nōn audit? Iūlius <u>eum</u> nōn audit, quia dormit.* (*ll.42-43*)

On page 20 you will notice the marginal note "*<u>eam</u>: Iūli<u>am</u>*" means that here *eam* stands for *Iūliam*.

A word of this kind, which takes the place of a name or noun, is called a **pronoun** (Latin *prōnōmen*, from *prō* "instead of" and *nōmen* "name" or "noun").

Corresponding to *eum* and *eam* the pronoun *mē* is used when a person is speaking about him- or herself, and *tē* is used about the person spoken to (in English "me" and "you"):

> *Aemilia: "Quis <u>mē</u> vocat?"*
> *Quīntus: "Iūlia <u>tē</u> vocat."* (*ll.24-25*)

	m.	f.
acc.	*eum*	*eam*
	mē	
	tē	

Implied Subject

In English we use the pronouns "he" and "she": Where is Julius? Why doesn't *he* come? But in Latin, these pronouns are not needed. When the identity of the subject is known, because the context shows who it is, it need not be repeated (or replaced by a pronoun) in a following sentence:

> *"Ubi est Iūlius? Cūr nōn <u>venit</u>?"* (*ll.35-36*)

Similarly:

> *Iūlius eum nōn audit, quia <u>dormit</u>.* (*l.43*)

> *"Cūr māter Mārcum verberat?" "Mārcum <u>verberat</u>,*
> *quia puer improbus est."* (*ll.58-59*)

Adverbs: Interrogatives *cūr* and *quia*

The interrogative adverb *cūr* is used to ask about the cause ("why?", Latin *causa*). A question introduced by *cūr* calls for an answer with the **causal conjunction** *quia* ("because"):

> *<u>Cūr</u> Iūlia plōrat? Iūlia plōrat, <u>quia</u> Mārcus eam pulsat.* (*ll.26-28*)
> *<u>Cūr</u> Mārcus Iūliam pulsat? <u>Quia</u> Iūlia cantat.* (*ll.30-31*)

question: *cūr...?*

answer: ... *quia* ...

Conjunctions: Negative

The conjunctions *et* and *sed* are not combined with a negation; instead of *et nōn* and *sed nōn* the conjunction *neque* (*ne-que*) is used, i.e. *-que* attached to the original negation *nē* (= *nōn*):

> *Iūlius dormit neque Quīntum audit.*   in English "and not"
> *Iūlius venit, neque Aemilia eum videt.*   in English "but not"
>
> *ne-que = et nōn (sed nōn)*

Lectiō Tertia (Section III)

Pronouns: Relative and Interrogative

In the sentence *Puer quī parvam puellam pulsat improbus est* (*l.63*) *quī* is the **relative** pronoun, which refers to *puer*. More examples:

> *Puer quī rīdet est Mārcus.* (*l.70*)
> *Puella quae plōrat est Julia.* (*l.71*)

As a relative pronoun *quem* is used in the masculine and *quam* in the feminine:

> *Puer quem Aemilia verberat est Mārcus.* (*ll.75-76*)
> *Puella quam Mārcus pulsat est Iūlia.* (*ll.72-73*)

The examples show that *quī* and *quem* (m.) refer to a masculine noun, and *quae* and *quam* (f.) to a feminine noun.

In Chapter IV (*l.75*) you will meet *quod*, which refers to a neuter noun:

> *baculum, quod in mēnsā est.*

At the end of the chapter (page 23) you find sentences with both the **interrogative** and the **relative** pronoun, e.g.:[1]

> *Quis est puer quī rīdet?*   Who (interrogative) is the boy
>   who (relative) is laughing? (*l.69*)

In the feminine the two pronouns are identical:

> *Quae est puella quae plōrat?*   Who (interrogative) is the girl
>   who (relative) is crying? (*l.70*)

The interrogative pronoun *quis* is *quem* in the accusative:

> *Quem vocat Quīntus? Quīntus Iūlium vocat.*

Points of Style: Writing Relative Sentences

Consider these sentences

- (from Chapter II) *Iūlius est vir Rōmānus. Iūlius est pater Mārcī.*
  These two independent sentences have equal value. Their common lexical link is *Iūlius*. Substituting the relative for one *Iūlius*, we can make two different complex sentences:

  Iūlius, quī est vir Rōmānus, est pater Mārcī.
  Iūlius, quī est pater Mārcī, est vir Rōmānus.

---

1   See the explanation (page ix) of when—and why—sentences will be translated.

In the first sentence, Julius's being a Roman man is made subordinate to his being the father of Marcus, while in the second, his being Marcus's father is the subordinate, or dependent, idea.

- (from Chapter III) *Iūlius eum audit. Iam nōn dormit pater.* (*l.48*)

Pater, quī eum audit, iam nōn dormit.	Father, who hears him, is no longer sleeping.
Iūlius, quī iam nōn dormit, eum audit.	Julius, who is no longer sleeping, hears him.

Since *pater* and *Iūlius* both refer to the same person, we can substitute a relative pronoun for one of the occurrences. The meaning of the sentence changes a bit, depending on how the clauses are combined. The first one suggests (as did the original two independent clauses) that Julius is no longer sleeping because he hears Marcus wailing and that wakes him up. The second implies that he hears Marcus because he is no longer sleeping.

relative pronoun: connects a clause

puer quī ...
puella quae...

	m.	f.	n.
nom.	*quī*	*quae*	*quod*
acc.	*quem*	*quam*	*quod*

interrogative pronoun: asks a question

nom.	*quis*
acc.	*quem*

Recensiō: Qu- words

quis? quae? quod?	who, what? (interrogative pronoun)
quī, quae	who (interrogative pronoun, plural)
quia	because (conjunction)
quot	how many? (interrogative adverb)

New Grammatical Terms

Subject: The person (or thing) that performs the action of the verb is called the **subject**, represented in Latin by the nominative case.

Object: The person (or thing) that completes the meaning of the verb is called the **direct object**, represented in Latin by the accusative case.

Transitive: A verb is **transitive** if an accusative direct object completes its meaning.

Intransitive: A verb is **intransitive** if its meaning is complete without an accusative direct object.

Implied Subject: If the subject is not directly stated but needs to be supplied from the ending of the verb, it is called an **implied subject**.

Pronoun: A **pronoun** takes the place of a noun.

Vocābula Disposita/Ordināta

Nōmina

1st

mamma, -ae	mommy
persōna, -ae	character, person
scaena, -ae	scene, stage

2nd

accūsātīvus, -ī (cāsus)	accusative
nōminātīvus, -ī (cāsus)	nominative
verbum, -ī	word, verb

Verba

-at (1)

cantat	sing
interrogat	ask, question
plōrat	cry
pulsat	strike, hit, knock (at)
verberat	beat, flog
vocat	call, invite

-et (2)

respondet	answer
rīdet	laugh, make fun of
videt	see

-it (4)

audit	hear, listen
dormit	sleep

Adiectīva

1st-2nd (-us, -a, -um)

improbus, -a, -um	bad, wicked
īrātus, -a, -um	angry
laetus, -a, -um	glad, happy
probus, -a, -um	good, honest, proper

Pronōmina

eam	her
eum	him
mē	me
quae (f.)	who, which, she who
quam (acc. sing. f.)	whom, which, she whom
quem (acc. sing. m.)	who, which, he whom
qui (m.)	who which, he who
tē	you

Adverbia

cūr?	why
iam	now, already
hīc	here

Coniunctiōnēs
   neque   and not, nor, neither
   quia   because
Alia ("other")
   ō!   oh!

IV. Dominus et Servī

Rēs Grammaticae Novae

1. Verbs
   a. Conjugations
   b. Imperative
2. Nouns: Vocative Case
3. Adjectives
   a. Numbers
   b. Possessives: *eius/suus, meus/tuus*
4. Pronouns: Nominative, Genitive Case

We now leave the children for a while and turn to the grown-ups. There is a worried look on Julius's face; it turns out that a sum of money is missing. Who is the thief? The problem is not solved until the end of the chapter, of course—and by then the culprit has already decamped! Later (in Chapters VI and VIII) you will find out where he is hiding and what he does with the money. But right now you must set to work to discover who is the thief.

Lectiō Prīma (Section I)

Verbs: Conjugations

The stem of a Latin verb ends in one of the long vowels -*ā*, -*ē*, -*ī*, or in a consonant. The verbs are therefore divided into four classes, called **conjugations**:

1st conjugation: *ā*-verbs, with stems ending in -*ā*: *vocā-, cantā-, pulsā-*.

2nd conjugation: *ē*- verbs, with stems ending in -*ē*: *tacē-, vidē-, habē-*.

3rd conjugation: consonant-verbs, with stems ending in a consonant: *pōn-, sūm-, discēd-*.

4th conjugation: *ī*-verbs, with stems ending in -*ī*: *venī-, audī-, dormī-*.

To these stems the different verbal endings are added (a vertical stroke [|] is here used to mark the division between stem and ending).

When -*t* is added:
- the last vowel of the stem becomes short: *voca|t, vide|t, veni|t*
- in the consonant-verbs a short -*i*- is inserted before the -*t*: *pōn|it, sūm|it, discēd|it.*

21

conjugations

ā-stems	*vocā-*
ē-stems	*vidē-*
consonant -stems	*pōn-*
ī-stems	*venī-*

This verbal form is called the **indicative** (Latin *indicātīvus*, "stating," "declaring"). The **indicative** makes a statement or asks a question.

Verbs: Imperative

The form of the verb used to give orders is called the **imperative** (Latin *imperātīvus*, from *imperat*). The Latin imperative (singular, giving an order to one person) consists of the shortest form of the verb called the **stem**, without any ending, e.g. *vocā! tacē! venī!*, or a short *-e* is added when the stem ends in a consonant, as in *pōne!* (the stem is *pōn-*). Examples:

> *Dāvum voca!* (*l.24*)   *Tacē, serve!* (*l.37*)
> *Venī!* (*l.27*)   *Saculum tuum in mēnsā pōne!* (*l.60*)

imperative

> *vocā! vidē! venī! pōne!*

In the following examples, the first verb is an **imperative** (gives an order), the second, **indicative** (makes a statement or asks a question).

vocā: call!	*voca|t*	he, she, it calls
vidē: see!	*vide|t*	he, she, it sees
pōn|e: put!	*pōn|it*	he, she, it puts
audī: listen!	*audi|t*	he, she, it listens

Pronouns: Genitive

The genitive of *is* (which you will learn in Section II) is *eius* (cf. English "his," her"):

> *In sacculō eius* (: *Iūliī*) *est pecūnia.* (*l.1*)

Possessives: *meus, -a, -um/tuus, -a, -um*

The adjectives *meus, -a, -um* (my), *tuus, -a, -um* (yours) and *suus, -a, -um* (his own, her own, its own) are called **possessive adjectives**. The possessive adjective *eius* serves to replace the genitive (for all three genders: masculine, feminine, and neuter).

Possessives: *eius/suus*

English has one set of possessives for the 3rd person: *his, her, its*. Latin has two:

> the genitive pronoun   *eius*
> the possessive adjective   *suus, a, um*

Compare the following two sentences:

> *Dāvus sacculum eius sūmit.*   Davus takes *his* (someone else's) bag.
> *Dāvus sacculum suum sūmit.*   Davus takes *his own* bag. (*l.74*)

Both *eius* and *suus, -a, -um* mean *his, her, its,* but they are not interchangeable. To understand the difference, compare the two examples (*ll.61-62*):

> *Dāvus sacculum suum in mēnsā pōnit.*
> *Iam sacculus eius in mēnsā est.*

In the first sentence—*Dāvus sacculum suum in mēnsā pōnit*—the subject is Davus and the money also belongs to Davus; therefore "his" (or "his own") is expressed by the adjective *suum*. When the "his" (or "hers" or "its") refers back to the subject of the sentence, Latin uses the possessive adjective *suus, -a, -um*. In English the word "own" is sometimes added to make the meaning plain: "his/her own."

In the second sentence— *Iam sacculus eius in mēnsā est*—the subject is *sacculus*, and "his" is expressed by the genitive of the pronoun: *eius*.

Look at another example:

> *Iūlius pecuiam suam sūmit.*   Julius takes his (own) money.

Note that "his own" is feminine, because it modifies *pecūniam*, even though it is translated "his" and refers to Julius. An adjective always has the same gender, number, and case as the noun it modifies.

In other words, when:
- referring to something that belongs to the subject of the sentence, the **adjective** *suus, -a, -um* is used: *Iūlius servum suum vocat.*
- referring to something that does not belong to the grammatical subject of the sentence, the **pronoun** *eius* is used: *Servus eius abest.*

Recensiō: Possessive Adjectives and Possessive Pronouns

Compare the following examples:

Ubi est sacculus tuus?	Where is *your* bag? (*l.58*)
Ecce sacculus meus.	Here is *my* bag. (*l.59*)
Sūme sacculum tuum.	Take *your* bag. (*l.73*)
Dāvus sacculum eius sūmit.	Davus takes *his* (someone else's) bag.
Dāvus sacculum suum sūmit.	Davus takes *his own* bag. (*l.74*)

Nouns: Vocative in *-e*

When one person uses another's name as a form of address, s/he uses the **vocative** case, the case of "calling" (Latin *vocātīvus*, from *vocat*). We have already seen the characters in our story addressing each other in Chapter III:

> *Mamma!* (*l.60*)
> *Mater! Mārcus Quīntum pulsat.* (*ll.16-17*)
> *Fū, puer!* (*l.45*)
> *St, puerī!* (*l.39*)
> *Pater! Pa-ter!* (*l.41*)

In each of these cases, the vocative has the same form as the nominative.

For nouns that end in *-us*, however, the vocative has a different form. In addressing a man in Latin the nominative ending in *-us* is replaced by a special form, the **vocative**, ending in *-e*. Medus calls Davus crying: *"Dāve!"* (*l.25*), and when Davus greets his master he says: *"Salvē, domine!"* and Julius answers: *"Salvē, serve!"* (*ll.34-35*).

> *Dāvus* (nom.)   →   *Dāve* (voc.)
> *dominus* (nom.)   →   *domine* (voc.)
> *servus* (nom.)   →   *serve* (voc.)

Numbers (*numerī*): 1-10

Of the following cardinal numbers, only one, two, and three decline (see Chapter X); the rest are indeclinable adjectives:

1. *ūnus*: I	6. *sex*: VI
2. *duo*: II	7. *septem*: VII
3. *trēs*: III	8. *octō*: VIII
4. *quattuor*: IV	9. *novem*: IX
5. *quīnque*: V	10. *decem*: X

Lectiō Altera (Section II)

Pronouns: Nominative

In the second of the two clauses *Mēdus discēdit, quia is pecūniam dominī habet* (*ll.76-77*) the nominative *Mēdus* is replaced by the pronoun *is,* which is the nominative corresponding to the accusative *eum* (English "he" and "him"). In English the pronoun is always used. In Latin the nominative of this pronoun:

- is used only when it carries a certain emphasis (here Medus is contrasted with Davus)
- is omitted when the subject is not emphasized ("implied subject," Cap. II)
  Mēdus nōn respondet, quia abest (next section, *l.85*).

In English we must mark emphasis by inflection (voice) or underlining (for example) the stressed word:

Medus does not answer because he is not there.	*Mēdus nōn respondet, quia abest.*
Medus leaves because he has the master's money.	*Mēdus discēdit, quia is pecūniam dominī habet.*

Lectiō Tertia (Section III)

The final reading in this chapter offers further practice of the material introduced in the first two readings. Notice in particular the emphasis of *is*:

> *Dāvus bonus servus est. Is nōn habet pecūniam meam.* (*ll.81-82*)
> *Mēdus nōn venit, quia is habet pecūniam tuam.* (*ll.92-93*)
> *Iūlius īrātus est—is nōn rīdet!* (*l.94*)

Recensiō: Grammatical Terms

Stem: the form of the verb without its endings: *Thema*

Conjugation: one of the four groups of verbs: *Coniūgatiō*

Indicative: the form of the verb that asks a question or makes a statement: *Indicātīvus*
Imperative: the form of the verb that gives an order: *Imperātīvus*
Nominative: the case of the subject: *Nōminātīvus*
Accusative: the case of the direct object: *Accusātīvus*
Genitive: the case of possession: *Genitīvus*
Vocative: the case of calling, or address: *Vocātīvus*

Vocābula Disposita/Ordināta

Nōmina
1st

mēnsa, -ae	table
pecūnia, -ae	money

2nd

baculum, -ī	stick
indicātīvus, -ī (modus)	indicative
imperātīvus,- -ī (modus)	imperative
nummus, -ī	coin, sesterce
sacculus, -ī	purse
vocātīvus, -ī (cāsus)	vocative

Verba
-ā (1)

abest	be absent
accūsat	accuse
adest	be present
imperat (+ *dat.*)	command, order, rule
numerat	count
salūtat	greet

-ē (2)

habet	have, hold, consider
pāret (+ *dat.*)	obey
tacet	be silent

consonant (3)

discēdit	go away, depart
pōnit	place, put, lay down
sūmit	take

Adiectīva
1st-2nd (-us, -a, -um)

bonus, -a, -um	good
decem	ten
novem	nine
nūllus, -a, -um	no, none
octō	eight
quattuor	four

quīnque	five
septem	seven
suus, -a, -um	his, her, their (own)
vacuus, -a, -um	empty

Pronōmina

eius	his (*gen. s. of* is, ea, id)
is, ea, id	him, her, it, that

Adverbia

rūrsus	again
tantum	so much, only

Coniunctiōnēs

quod	because, that

Alia

salvē	hello, good morning (*sing.*)

V. Vīlla et Hortus

Rēs Grammaticae Novae

1. Verbs
   a. Indicative and Imperative Plural
   b. *rīdet/rīdent*
   c. *agit/agunt*
2. Nouns
   a. Accusative Case (plural)
   b. Case Uses: Prepositions with the Ablative
3. Adjectives in *-er*
4. Pronouns: *is, ea, id*

The Roman Villa

We have made the acquaintance of what is evidently a prosperous Roman family, to judge from the splendid villa in which they live. The plan on page 33 and the pictures of various parts of the house will give you an impression of the layout of this typical Roman villa. Characteristic features are the atrium with its opening in the roof and pool for rainwater, and the peristyle, the inner courtyard lined with rows of columns.

Lectiō Prīma (Section I)

Accusative Case (Plural)

In Chapter III you learned the accusative singular in *-um* and *-am*; we now learn the **accusative plural** ending in *-ōs* and *-ās*. The plural *fīliī* becomes *fīliōs* when it is the object of the verb: *Iūlius duōs fīliōs habet*; similarly, *fīliae* changes to *fīliās*. E.g.:

> *is multōs servōs habet* (l.6)
> *ea multās ancillās habet* (ll.7-8)

The accusative of masculine and feminine nouns always ends:

- in *-m* in the singular and
- in *-s* in the plural

Neuter nouns have the same ending in the accusative as in the nominative (sing. *-um*, pl. *-a*):

> *In vīllā sunt duo ōstia.* (nominative, *l.25*)
> *Vīlla duo ōstia et multās fenestrās habet.* (accusative, *l.26*)

accusative sing. and pl.

	m.	f.	n.
sing.	*-um*	*-am*	*-um*
pl.	*-ōs*	*-ās*	*-a*

Prepositions with the Ablative Case

Prepositions, from Latin *praepositiōnēs*, "placing in front," are words that link the noun they are with to another word in the sentence. Since the first chapter, you have been using the preposition *in*:

> *Rōma in Italiā est.* (*Chap. I, l.1*)
> *Germānia in imperiō Rōmanō nōn est.* (*Chap. I, ll.58-59*)
> *Quot servī sunt in familiā tuā?* (*Chap. II, l.74*)
> *In sacculō meō* (*Chap. IV, l.15*)

In this chapter you learn more prepositions. Like *in*, the prepositions *ab, cum, ex* and *sine* cause the following nouns to take the ending *-ō* (m./n.) or *-ā* (f.) and in the plural *-īs*:

> *in ātriō*   *cum līberīs*
> *ex hortō*   *sine rosīs*
> *ab Aemiliā*

The forms in *-ō, -ā* and *-īs* are called **ablative** (Latin *ablātīvus*). The prepositions *ab, cum, ex, in, sine* are said to "take" the ablative.

ab, cum, ex, in, sine + *-ō, -ā, -īs*

ablative	m./n.	f.
sing.	*-ō*	*-ā*
pl.	*-īs*	*-īs*

Adjectives in *-er*

You learned in Chapter II that not all masculine nouns end in *-us*; some, like *puer* and *liber*, end in *-er*. Not all adjectives end in *-us, -a, -um*. Some, like *pulcher, pulchra, pulchrum*, end in *-er*:

> *Syra nōn est fēmina pulchra, neque pulcher est nāsus eius.* (*l.17*)
> *Cum rosīs pulchrīs.* (*l.61*)
> *Rosae pulchrae sunt.* (*l.63*)

Notā Bene: *pulcher, pulchra, pulchrum*, like *liber, librī*, has an *e* only in the nominative singular.

Pronoun *is, ea, id*

New forms of the pronoun *is* (masculine) are now introduced: feminine *ea*, neuter *id*; plural *iī* (= *eī*), *eae, ea*.

sing.	m.	f.	n.
nom.	*is*	*ea*	*id*
acc.	*eum*	*eam*	*id*
gen.	*eius*	*eius*	*eius*
abl.	*eō*	*eā*	*eō*
pl.			
nom.	*iī*	*eae*	*ea*
acc.	*eōs*	*eās*	*ea*
gen.	*eōrum*	*eārum*	*eōrun*
abl.	*iīs*	*iīs*	*iīs*

Notā Bene:

- In the accusative and ablative this pronoun shows the same endings as the noun it represents; remembering the accusatives *eum* and *eam* you will identify forms like *eō, eā* (abl. sing.), *eōs, eās* (acc. pl.) and *iīs* (= *eīs*, abl. pl.).
- The genitive plural is *eōrum, eārum* (thus for *dominus servōrum* you find *dominus eōrum*).
- The genitive singular has a special form *eius*, which is the same for all three genders: you have already had *sacculus eius* (: *Iūliī*), now you find *nāsus eius* (: *Syrae*). (These genitives correspond to the English possessive pronouns "his/her/its/their").

Verbs: Indicative Plural

Lastly, you learn the plural form of verbs:

(1) **Indicative:** when the subject is in the plural or more than one person, the verb ends, not in *-t* only, but in *-nt* (cf. *est* and *sunt*):

> *Mārcus et Quīntus Iūliam vocant.*
> *Puerī rīdent.*
> *Multī servī in ūnō cubiculō dormiunt.* (*l.40*)

Lectiō Altera (Section II)

Verbs: Imperative Plural

(2) **Imperative:** when two or more people are ordered to do something, the plural form of the imperative ending in *-te* is used:

> *Mārce et Quīnte! Iūliam vocāte!* (*l.51*)   *Audīte!* (*l.67*)
> *Tacēte, puerī!* (*l.72*)

Notā Bene: In the consonant-verbs (3rd conjugation) a short vowel is inserted before these plural endings:

- *-i-* before the imperative ending *-te*
  > *Discēdite, puerī!* (imperative) (*cf. l.73*)

- *-u-* before the indicative ending *-nt*:
  Puerī discēd<u>u</u>nt. (indicative) (*ll.75-76*)
- Even in the *ī*-verbs (4th conjugation) *-u-* is inserted before *-nt*:
  Puerī veni<u>u</u>nt. (indicative)

Imperative and Indicative

		sing.	pl.
1. *ā*	imp.	*vocā*	*vocā|te*
	ind.	*voca|t*	*voca|nt*
2. *ē*	imp.	*vidē*	*vidē|te*
	ind.	*vide|t*	*vide|nt*
3. con.	imp.	*pōn|e*	*pōn|ite*
	ind.	*pōn|it*	*pōn|unt*
4. *ī*	imp.	*audī*	*audī|te*
	ind.	*audi|t*	*audi|unt*

Verbs

rīdet/rīdent

Julia's remark *"puerī <u>mē</u> rīdent"* (*l.70*) shows that *rīdet*, which is usually an intransitive verb, can take an object in the sense "laugh at": *puerī Iūli<u>am</u> rīdent.*

rīdet alone	*puerī rīdent*	the boys are laughing
rīdet + acc.	*puerī me rīdent*	the boys are laughing at me

agit/agunt

The consonant-verb *agit, agunt* denotes action in general: *Quid agit Mārcus? Quid agunt puerī?* (English "do"). The imperative of this verb is often put before another imperative to emphasize the command, somewhat like our English "Come on!," "Get going!" e.g. *Age! venī, serve! Agite! venīte, servī!*

age! agite! + imp.

Recensiō: Prepositions with the Ablative

in

> *Iūlius <u>in magnā vīllā</u> habitat.* (*l.1*)
> *Vīlla Iūliī <u>in magnō hortō</u> est.* (*l.12*)
> *<u>In hortīs</u> sunt rosae et līlia.* (*l.13*)

ex

> *Discēdite <u>ex peristȳlō</u>.* (*l.73*)
> *Puerī aquam sūmunt <u>ex impluviō</u>.* (*l.83*)

ab

> *Puerī Iūliam audiunt, neque iī <u>ab Aemiliā</u> discēdunt.* (*l.56*)
> *Iūlia plōrat et cum ūnā rosā <u>ab iīs</u> discēdit.* (*l.71*)

cum

> *Iūlius in vīllā suā habitat <u>cum magnā familiā</u>.* (*l.9*)
> *Pater et māter habitant <u>cum Mārcō et Quīntō et Iūliā</u>.* (*ll.9-10*)
> *In Italiā sunt multae vīllae <u>cum magnīs hortīs</u>.* (*ll.12-13*)

sine

> *Aemilia <u>sine</u> <u>virō</u> <u>suō</u> <u>Iūliō</u> in vīllā est. (ll.44-45)*
> *In oppidō Tūsculō est <u>sine</u> <u>Aemīliā</u>. (ll.45-46)*
> *Puella <u>sine</u> <u>rosīs</u> pulchra nōn est. (ll.63-64)*

Vocābula Disposita/Ordināta

Nōmina

1st

aqua, -ae	water
fenestra, -ae	window
rosa, -ae	rose
vīlla, -ae	country house, villa

2nd

ablātīvus, -ī (cāsus)	ablative
ātrium, -ī	main room, hall
cubiculum, -ī	bedroom
hortus, -ī	garden
impluvium, -ī	water basin
līlium, -ī	lily
nāsus, -ī	nose
— ōstium, -ī	door, entrance
peristȳlum, -i	peristyle

Verba

-ā (1)

amat/amant	love
dēlectat/dēlectant	delight, please
habitat/habitant	dwell, live

consonant (3)

agit/agunt	drive, do, perform
carpit/carpunt	gather, pick, crop

Adiectīva

1st-2nd (us/er, -a, -um)

foedus, -a, -um	ugly, hideous
pulcher, -chra, -chrum	beautiful, fine
sōlus, -a, -um	alone, lonely

Pronōmina

is, ea, id	he, she it

Adverbia

etiam	also, even, yet

Praepositiōnēs

ab (*prp. + abl.*)	from, of, since, by
cum (*prp. + abl.*)	with
ex (*prp. + abl.*)	out of, from, of, since
sine (*prp. + abl.*)	without

VI. Via Latīna

Rēs Grammaticae Novae

1. Verbs
   a. *it/eunt*
   b. Passive Voice
2. Nouns
   a. Case Uses
      i. Accusative: Prepositions with the Accusative Case
      ii. Ablative:
         1. Preposition *ab/ā* + Ablative
         2. Ablative of Agent and Means/Instrument
   b. Constructions of Place
3. Correlative: *tam/quam*

Roman Roads

Road communications were highly developed in the ancient Roman world. The different parts of the Roman Empire were connected by an excellent network of highways. On the map on page 40 of Lingua Latina you see the most important Roman roads in Italy, among them the famous Via Appia, running southward from Rome and continuing all the way to Brundisium.

Running almost parallel to the Via Appia is the Via Latina, which passes the town of Tusculum mentioned in the first chapter. Julius's villa stands in the neighborhood of this town, so that anyone going from there to Rome must follow the Via Latina. Therefore it is not surprising to find Medus walking along this road. You will soon discover what it is that attracts him to the city.

Lectiō Prīma (Section I)

Prepositions with the Accusative Case

In Chapter V you met some common **prepositions** that take the ablative (see *recensiō* at the end of Chapter V). Most other prepositions take the **accusative**, e.g.:

ad	*ad vīll**am***	to the farmhouse (*l.19*)
ante	*ante lectīc**am***	in front of the litter chair (*l.33*)
apud	*apud e**um** = cum eō*	with him (*l.37*)
circum	*Circum Rōm**am** est mūrus antīquus.*	Around Rome is an ancient wall. (*ll.14-15*)
inter	*inter Rōm**am** et Capu**am***	between Rome and Capua (*ll.3-4*)
per	*per port**am***	through the gate (*l.76*)
post	*post lectīc**am***	behind the litter chair (*l.33*)
prope	*prope Rōm**am***	near Rome (*l.8*)

Prepositions *ad* and *ab/ā* (continued)

Ad indicates motion **to** a place—it is the opposite of *ab* (followed by the <u>abl</u>ative) which indicates motion away **from** a place.

The corresponding interrogative adverbs are *quō* and *unde*:

> *Quō it Iūlius? <u>Ad</u> vīll<u>am</u> it.*
> *<u>Unde</u> venit? <u>Ab</u> oppid<u>ō</u>.*

quō?   ad + acc.

unde?   ab + abl.

Instead of *ab* we often find the shortened form *ā* before a consonant, but never before a vowel or *h-*:

<u>ā</u> <u>v</u>īllā	*<u>ab</u> <u>a</u>ncillā*
<u>ā</u> <u>d</u>ominō	*<u>ab</u> <u>o</u>ppidō*

ab + vowel and *h-*

ā/ab + cons. (except *h-*)

Verbs: *it/eunt*

The verb "to go" belongs to the fourth conjugation, but is **irregular**, as you can see from the difference between *audiunt* (they hear) and *eunt* (they go). An **irregular** verb is one whose endings don't follow the standard pattern of the four conjugations; the verb "is" (*est/sunt*) is also irregular.

Iūlius ab oppidō ad vīllam suam <u>it</u>.	Julius is going from the town to his farmhouse. (*l.20*)
Dominus et servī ab oppidō ad vīllam <u>eunt</u>.	The master and slaves are going from the town to the farmhouse. (*ll.20-21*)

> *Quō it Iūlius? (l.35)*
> *<u>Ad</u> vīll<u>am</u> it. (l.35)*
> *Iūlius et Cornēlius ad vīllās suās <u>eunt</u>. (l.57)*

Correlatives: *Tam/Quam*

Quam is an interrogative adverb:

> <u>*Quam*</u> *longa est via Flāminia?*   <u>How</u> long is the via Flaminia? (*ll.11-12*)

Tam answers the question posed in *quam*; together they are called correlatives. **Correlatives** are adverbs that respond to each other. In Latin pairs of correlatives often resemble *tam/quam* in that one starts with "t" and the other with "qu" and the rest of the word is the same. *Tam...quam* is best translated into English as "as...as":

> <u>*Quam*</u> *longa est via Flāminia?*
>
> *Via Latīna nōn* <u>*tam*</u> *longa est* <u>*quam*</u> *via Appia.*
>   The Via Latina is not as long as the Via Appia. (*ll.10-11*)
>
> *Tiberis fluvius nōn* <u>*tam*</u> *longus est* <u>*quam*</u> *fluvius Padus.* (*l.13*)
>
> *Circum oppidum Tūsculum mūrus nōn* <u>*tam*</u> *longus est* <u>*quam*</u> *circum Rōmam.* (*ll.16-17*)
>
> *Saccī quōs Syrus et Lēander portant magnī sunt, sed saccus quem Syrus portat nōn* <u>*tam*</u> *magnus est* <u>*quam*</u> *saccus Lēandri.* (*ll.27-29*)

Lectiō Altera (Section II)

Nouns: Constructions of Place with Names of Cities and Towns

I. Accusative (place to which) and Ablative (place from which or separation)

Motion **to** or **from** a town mentioned by name is expressed by the name of the town in the accusative or ablative respectively **without a preposition**. In Latin therefore we speak of traveling *Rōmā—Brundisium* (from Rome to Brundisium), or, if going in the opposite direction, *Brundisiō—Rōmam* (from Brundisium to Rome).

The **accusative** shows the place toward which one moves:

> *Rōmam it.*   He is going to Rome. (*l.50*)
> *Cornēlius nōn Rōmam, sed Tūsculum it.* (*ll.54-55*)

It is the fundamental function of the **ablative** (with or without a preposition) to denote "place **from** which." In this function it is called **ablative of separation** (*ablātīvus* means "taking away"):

> *Tūsculō venit.*   He is coming from Tusculum. (*l.49*)
> *Is nōn Tūsculō, sed Rōmā venit.* (*ll.53-54*)

Otherwise, prepositions are used:

> *Iūlius ab oppidō ad vīllam suam it.* (*l.20*)
> *Dominus et servī ab oppidō ad vīllam eunt.* (*ll.20-21*)

II. Locative Case (place in which)

To indicate **where** something or somebody is, the preposition *in* followed by the ablative is most often used:

> <u>*in*</u> *Italiā*
> <u>*in*</u> *oppidō*
> <u>*in*</u> *hortō*

The following examples show, however, that *in* is no more used with names of towns than *ad* and *ab*:

> *Cornēlius Tūsculī habitat. (l.59)*
> *Mēdus Rōmae est. (l.47)*

Instead of "*in*" the name takes the ending *-ī* or *-ae* according as the nominative ends in *-um/-us* or *-a*. This form, which here has the same ending as the genitive, is called **locative** (Latin *locātīvus*, from *locus*, "place"):

Ubi habitat Cornēlius? Is Tūsculī habitat.	Where does Cornelius live? He lives in Tusculum. (*ll.58-59*)
Rōmam it, quia Lȳdia Rōmae habitat.	He is going to Rome because Lydia lives in Rome. (*ll.77-78*)

locative (= genitive) *-ī*, *-ae*

> *quō? Tūsculum Rōmam*
> *unde? Tūsculō Rōmā*
> *ubi? Tūsculī Rōmae*

Verbs: Passive Voice (*vōx passīva*)

All the verbs you have been using so far are in the **active voice** (the subject does the acting), e.g.:

> *Dāvus et Ursus portant Iūlium.*
> *Syrus saccum portat. (l.25)*

We can express the same idea differently using the **passive voice** (the subject receives the action):

> *Iūlius ab Ursō et Dāvō portātur. (l.62)*
> *Saccus ā Syrō portātur.*

Active Voice:
- Subject does the acting
- endings *-t, -nt*

Passive Voice:
- Subject acted upon
- endings *-tur, -ntur*
- The person or thing performing the action goes into the ablative (see next section)

In addition to the examples in the text and GRAMMATICA LATINA in LINGUA LATINA, consider the following sentences from earlier chapters changed into the passive:

- 1st conjugation
  Puer parvam puellam pulsat (Chap. II, l.29) → *Parva puella ā puerō pulsātur.*
- 2nd conjugation
  Quīntus Mārcum videt (Chap. II, l.11) → *Mārcus ā Quīntō vidētur.*

- 3rd conjugation
  Dāvus sacculum in mēnsā pōnit (Chap. IV, l.61) → *Sacculus ā Dāvō in mēnsā pōnitur.*
- 4th conjugation
  Puerī Iūliam audiunt (Chap. V, l.56) → *Iūlia ā puerīs audītur.*

	active	passive
1.	voca|t	vocā|tur
	voca|nt	voca|ntur
2.	vide|t	vidē|tur
	vide|nt	vide|ntur
3.	pōn|it	pōn|itur
	pōn|unt	pōn|untur
4.	audi|t	audī|tur
	audi|unt	audi|untur

Ablative Case (Agent and Means/Instrument)

Consider the following sentence:

Mārcus Iūliam pulsat.   Marcus hits Julia.

If we make that sentence passive, we get:

Iūlia pulsātur ā Mārcō.   Julia is hit by Marcus.

In the second sentence, Marcus is no longer the grammatical subject, but he is still the actor, or **agent**, of the verb. In the passive voice, the name of the person by whom the action is performed, the **agent**, is in the ablative preceded by *ab* or *ā* (*ā Mārcō*). This construction is called the **ablative of personal agent**, that is, when the agent is a person, not a thing or an animal:

Iūlius ab Ursō et Dāvō portātur.
    Julius is (being) carried by Ursus and Davus. (*l.62*)

Saccī quī ā Syrō et Lēandrō portantur magnī sunt.
    The bags which are being carried by Syrus and Leander are big. (*ll.65-66*)

Dominus ā servō malō timētur. (*ll.73-74*)
Verba Mēdī ā Lydiā laetā audiuntur. (*l.95*)

When the action is performed by something other than a person—an animal or an inanimate object—the source of the action is expressed by the simple ablative without the prepositon *ab/ā*. The simple ablative here indicates **means** or **cause**. This construction, called the **ablative of means** (also **ablative of instrument**—Latin *ablātīvus īnstrūmentī*) is very common both in passive and active sentences: e.g.

Cornēlius equō vehitur.	Cornelius is being transported by a horse. (or, more idiomatically, "he is riding a horse") (*ll.68-69*)
Iūlius lectīcā vehitur.	Julius is being carried in a litter chair. (*l.69*)
Lȳdia verbīs Mēdī dēlectātur.	Lydia is delighted by Medus's words. (*l.91*)

Iūlius lectīcā vehitur.
Dominus servum baculō verberat.
Servī saccōs umerīs portant.
Mēdus viā Latīnā Rōmam ambulat.

Sometimes the agent/ means is left unexpressed, e.g.:

Domini vehuntur.   Masters are carried (or "travel"). (*l.70*)

In the sentence *Mēdus Lȳdiam amat et ab eā amātur* (*ll.78-79*) the two constructions are combined.

Vocābula Disposita/Ordināta

Nōmina
   1st

amīca, -ae	girlfriend
lectīca, -ae	litter, sedan
— porta, -ae	gate
via, -ae	road, way, street

   2nd

actīvum, -ī (verbum)	active
amīcus, -ī	friend
equus, -ī	horse
inimīcus, -ī	(personal) enemy
locātīvus (cāsus)	locative
mūrus, -ī	wall
passīvum (verbum)	passive
saccus, -ī	sack
umerus, -ī	shoulder

   3rd (you will learn about this family of nouns later)

praepositiō (*f.*)	preposition

Verba
   -ā (1)

ambulat, ambulant, -ātur, -antur	walk
intrat, intrant, -ātur, -antur	enter
portat, portant, -ātur, -antur	carry

   -ē (2)

timet, timent, -ētur, -entur	fear, be afraid (of)

   consonant (3)

vehit, vehunt, vehitur, vehuntur	carry, convey, pass ride, sail, travel

   Irregular

it/eunt	go

Adiectīva
    1st-2nd (us/er, -a, -um)

duodecim	twelve
fessus, -a, -um	tired, weary
longus, -a, -um	long
malus, -a, -um	bad, wicked, evil

Adverbia

ante	in front of, before
autem	but, however
itaque	therefore
nam	for
post	behind, after, later
procul	far (*often combines with preposition* ab)
prope	near, nearly
quam	how, as, than
tam	so, as

Praepositiōnēs

ā (*prp. + abl.*)	from, of, since, by
ad (*prp. + acc.*)	to, toward, by, at, till
ante (*prp. + acc.*)	in front of, before
apud (*prp. + acc.*)	beside, near, by
circum (*prp. + acc.*)	round
inter (*prp. + acc.*)	between, among, during
per (*prp. + acc.*)	through, by, during
post (*prp. + acc.*)	behind, after, later
procul ab (+ *abl.*)	far from
prope (*prp. + acc.*)	near, nearly

Vocābula Interrogātīva

quō?	where (to)?
unde?	from where? whence?

VII. Puella et Rosa

Rēs Grammaticae Novae

1. Verbs
   a. Imperative of *esse*
   b. *salvē/salvēte*
   c. Compound Verbs
2. Nouns: Case Uses
   a. Accusative Case: Prepositions
   b. Genitive with *plēnus*
   c. Dative Case
      i. Dative Case *is, ea, id*
      ii. Dative Case: Interrogative and Relative Pronoun
      iii. Dative with Compound Verbs
   d. Ablative: Prepostion *ex/ē* + the Ablative Case
3. Pronouns
   a. Reflexive Pronoun
   b. Demonstrative Pronouns: *hic, haec, hoc*
4. Adverbs: Interrogative *num* & *nōnne*
5. Point of Style: *et ... et/neque...neque/nōn sōlum... sed etiam*

Julius Returns, with Gifts

Syra comforts a weeping Julia, who is concerned about the appearance of her nose. When Julius comes back from town, he usually brings something with him for the family, so in this chapter you find out what is in the two sacks that Syrus and Leander have been carrying.

Lectiō Prīma (Section I)

Reflexive Pronoun

The examples *Puella sē in speculō videt et sē interrogat* (*ll.*8-9) show that the pronoun *sē* (acc.) is used when referring to the subject in the same sentence; *sē* is called the **reflexive** pronoun (English "himself/herself/themselves"). Reflexive means it "bends back" toward the subject.

Puella sē in speculō videt et sē interrogat.
The girl looks at herself in the mirror and asks herself. (*ll.8-9*)

Puella Syram in speculō videt et eam interrogat.
The girl looks at Syra in the mirror and asks her (Syra).

Iūlia Syram post sē in speculō videt, i.e. post Iūliam. (*l.15*)

When to use what:

When the pronoun refers back to the subject of the sentence:

- use the **reflexive** *sē* (acc.): himself/herself/themselves

When the pronoun refers to a person or thing **other than** the subject of the sentence:

- use the personal pronoun *eum/eam/eōs/eās*: him/her/them

Recensiō: sē vs. *suus, -a, -um*

Sē is a pronoun and takes the place of a noun that refers back to the (3rd person) subject of the sentence.

Iūlia Syram post sē in speculō videt. (*l.15*) = *Iūlia Syram post Iūliam in speculō videt.*

Suus, a, um is a possessive adjective and modifies a noun that belongs to the (3rd person) subject of the sentence.

Aemilia virum suum amat. (*l.4*) = *Aemilia virum Aemiliae amat.*

Accusative Case: Prepositions

Compare the sentences:

Iūlius in vīllā est.
Iūlius in vīllam intrat.

In the first sentence *in* takes the ablative (*vīllā*), as we have seen so often; in the second it is followed by the accusative (*vīllam*). The examples show that *in* takes the accusative when there is motion **into** a place. Therefore we read:

Syra in cubiculum intrat. (*l.14*)
"Venī in hortum, Iūlia!" (*l.17*)

Place where:

ubi? in + ablative
in vīllā, in hortō, in cubiculō

Place to which:

quō? in + accusative
in vīllam, in hortum, in cubiculum

Interrogative *num* & *nōnne*

A question introduced with *num* calls for a negative answer; therefore Julia asks: *"Num nāsus meus foedus est?"* (*l.20*). The *num* shows she wants a "no!" answer. The opposite effect is obtained by *nōnne*: when Syra asks *"Nōnne fōrmōsus est nāsus meus?"* (*l.26*) she certainly expects the answer to be "yes." Nevertheless Julia says:

"Immō foedus est!" The word *immō* serves to stress a denial (English "no," "on the contrary").

question:	answer:
nōnne...est?	*...est*
num...est?	*...nōn est*

Verbs: Imperative of the Verb *esse*

The imperative of *est* is *es!* (i.e. the stem without an ending; plural *este!*):

> *"Tergē oculōs! Es laeta!"* (l.23)

es|t: imp. *es! es|te!*

Lectiō Altera (Section II)

Preposition *Ex/ē* + the Ablative Case

The example *Iūlia ē cubiculō exit* shows the shorter form *ē* of the preposition *ex*. The same rule applies to the use of *ex* and *ē* as to *ab* and *ā*:

- before vowels and *h-* only *ex* and *ab* are used
- *ē* and *ā* are only used before consonants, never before vowels or *h-*
- *ex* and *ab* can also be used before consonants

Examples with *ex* and *ē*:

- *ē/ex vīllā* (before a consonant use either *ē* or *ex*)
- *ex ātriō* (before a vowel use only *ex*)
- *ex hortō* (before an "h" use only *ex*)

Dative Case

I. Nouns

When we are told that Julius gives something to a member of the family, the name of this person ends in *-ō* (*Mārcō, Quīntō, Syrō, Lēandrō*) or in *-ae* (*Aemiliae, Iūliae, Syrae, Dēliae*). This form, ending in *-ō* in the masculine (and neuter) and in *-ae* in the feminine, is called **dative** (Latin *datīvus*, from *dat*, "gives"):

> *Iūlius Syrō et Lēandrō māla dat*

In the plural the dative ends in *-īs* like the ablative:

> *Iūlius servīs māla dat*
> *Iūlius ancillīs māla dat*

dative	m./n.	f.
sing.	*-ō*	*-ae*
pl.	*-īs*	*-īs*

Summary of Dative Endings

	masc. sing.	masc. pl.	fem. sing.	fem. pl.	neut. sing.	neut. pl.
nom.	-us	ī	-a	-ae	-um	-a
acc.	-um	-ōs	-am	-ās	-um	-a
gen.	ī	-ōrum	-ae	-ārum	ī	-ōrum
dat.	-ō	īs	-ae	īs	-ō	īs
abl.	-ō	īs	-ā	īs	-ō	īs
voc.	-e					

II. *is, ea, id*

The dative of the pronoun *is, ea, id* is *eī* in the singular

　　Iūlius eī (: *Quīntō/Iūliae*) *mālum dat.*

In the plural the dative of the pronoun *is ea id* is *iīs* (or *eīs*):

　　Iūlius iīs (: *servīs/ancillīs*) *māla dat.*

The forms are the same for all three genders.

Summary of *is, ea, id* and Reflexive Pronoun *se*

	singular masc.	fem.	neut.	plural masc.	fem.	neut.	reflexive pronoun
nom.	i|s	e|a	i|d	i|ī	e|ae	e|a	
acc.	e|um	e|am	i|d	e|ōs	e|ās	e|a	sē
gen.	e|ius	e|ius	e|ius	e|ōrum	e|ārum	e|ōrum	(Chap. X)
dat.	e|ī	e|ī	e|ī	i|īs	i|īs	i|īs	sibi
abl.	e|ō	e|ā	e|ō	i|īs	i|īs	i|īs	sē

Salvē/Salvēte

The greeting *Salvē!* expresses a wish for good health. It was understood as an imperative, so it has a plural form in *-te*: "*Salvēte, fīliī!*" (*l.31*)

　　sing.　*salvē!*
　　pl.　　*salvē|te!*

Demonstrative Pronouns: *hic, haec, hoc*

Referring to things close to him, Julius says e.g. *hic saccus* (*l.43*) and *hoc mālum* (*ll.90-91*), and Julia says *haec rosa* of the flower that she is holding (*l.85*). The **demonstrative** (or pointing) pronoun *hic, haec, hoc* (English "this") is treated in Chapter VIII.

Plēnus + the Genitive Case

Note the **genitive** after *plēnus* ("full of..."):

　　Hic saccus plēnus mālōrum est. (*ll.43-44*)
　　Oculī Iūliae plēnī sunt lacrimārum. (*l.79*)

　　plēnus + gen.

Verbs: Dative with Compound Verbs

Compound verbs have often prepositions as their first element, like _ad-est_ and _ab-est_. In this chapter you find _in-est_, _ad-venit_, _ad-it_, _ex-it_, in the next _ab-it_. Often the same preposition is put before a noun in the same sentence:

> Quid _inest in_ saccīs? (_l.39_)
> Iūlius _ad_ vīllam _ad_venit. (_l.30_)
> Iūlia _ē_ cubiculō _ex_it. (_ll.82-83_)

compounds with prepositions:

> ad-, ab-, ex-, in-

Lectiō Tertia (Section III)

Dative Case (continued): Interrogative & Relative Pronoun

The dative (sing.) of the interrogative and relative pronoun is _cui_ (see _ll.101-104_):

> _Cui_ Iūlius mālum dat? (_l.101_)
> Puer/puella _cui_ Iūlius mālum dat est fīlius/fīlia eius. (_ll.101-102_)

The genitive of the interrogative and relative will be met in Chapter VIII.

Point of style: _et...et/neque....neque/nōn sōlum...sed etiam_

Note the repetition of the conjunctions _et_ and _neque_ (_ll.50, 57_):

_et_ Mārcus _et_ Quīntus māla habent.	English "both...and"
Servī _neque_ māla _neque_ pira habent.	English "neither...nor"

Instead of _et...et_ we often find _nōn sōlum...sed etiam_:

nōn sōlum māla, _sed etiam_ pira. (_l.56_)	English "not only...but also"

_et...et_

neque...neque

nōn sōlum...sed etiam

Recensiō: Interrogative Words

Quis? Quid?	Who? What?
Ubi?	Where? In what place?
Quot?	How many?
Cūr?	Why?
Unde?	Whence? From what place?
Quō?	Where? To what place?
_-ne?_	Asks a question with no expectations.
Nōnne?	Expects a "yes" answer.
Num?	Expects a "no" answer.

Vocābula Disposita/Ordināta

Nōmina

    1st

lacrima, -ae	tear

    2nd

datīvus, -ī (cāsus)	dative
mālum, -ī	apple
oculus, -ī	eye
ōsculum, -ī	kiss
ōstiārius, -ī	doorkeeper
pirum, -ī	pear
sōlum, -ī	soil, ground, floor
speculum, -ī	mirror

Verba

    -ā (1)

dat, dant, -ātur, -antur	give
exspectat, exspectant, -ātur, -antur	wait (for), expect
lacrimat, -ant, -ātur, -antur	cry

    -ē (2)

tenet, tenent, -ētur, -entur	hold, keep (back)
terget, tergent, -ētur, -entur	wipe

    consonant (3)

claudit, claudunt, -itur, -untur	shut, close
currit, currunt, -itur, -untur	run
vertit, vertunt, -itur, -untur	turn

    -ī (4)

advenit, adveniunt	arrive
aperit, aperiunt, -ītur, -iuntur	open, disclose

    Irregular

adit, adeunt	go to, approach
exit, exeunt	go out
inest, insunt	be in

Adiectīva

    1st-2nd (us/er, -a, -um)

fōrmōsus, -a, -um	beautiful
plēnus, -a, -um (+ *gen./abl.*)	full (of)

Pronōmina

hic, haec, hoc	this
sē, sibi	himself, herself

Adverbia

immō	no, on the contrary
illīc	there[1]

---

1   Accent on the ultima: *illíc*; originally the word was *illíce*, with accent on the long penult; when the *e* dropped, the accent was retained.

Coniunctiōnēs
    et...et   both...and
    neque...neque   neither...nor

Praepositiōnēs
    ē (*prp. + abl.*)   out of, from, of, since

Vocābula Interrogātīva
    nōnne?   not?

VIII. Taberna Rōmāna

Rēs Grammaticae Novae

1. Nouns
   a. 3rd Conjugation "i-stems"
   b. Case Uses
      i. Ablative of Price (*ablātīvus pretiī*)
      ii. Ablative of Means/Instrument
         (*ablātīvus instrūmentī*) (continued)
      iii. Dative (continued)
2. Adjectives
   a. Interrogative Adjective
   b. Pronoun vs. Interrogative Adjective
   c. Correlatives: *tantus/quantus*
3. Pronouns
   a. Relative Pronoun Without an Antecedent
   b. Demonstratives *hic, haec, hoc/ ille, illa, illud*
   c. Inflection
4. Adverbs
   a. *quam*
5. Points of Style: *convenit*

Daily Life: Shopping

In the ancient world people did their shopping over open counters lining the streets. Passers-by could simply stand on the pavement in front of a shop and buy what they wanted. We can be sure that the shopkeepers gave their customers every encouragement.

Lectiō Prīma (Section I)

Pronouns

In this chapter we pay particular attention to some important **pronouns:**
- the **interrogative** pronoun: *quis, quae, quid* (introduced in Chapter II)
- the **relative** pronoun: *quī, quae, quod* (introduced in Chapter III)

- the **demonstrative** pronouns

  is, ea, id (introduced in Chapter III)
  hic, haec, hoc (introduced in Chaper VII)
  ille, illa, illud

Relative Pronoun Without an Antecedent (*Quī = Is quī*)

Instead of saying "he who, etc." or "whoever" Latin sometimes has just "who," e.g.:

> *Quī tabernam habet, tabernārius est = is quī...:*
> Whoever has a store is a store keeper. (*ll.3-4*)

> *Quī magnam pecūniam habent ōrnāmenta emunt = Iī quī...:*
> Those who have a lot of money buy jewelry. (*ll.16-17*)

> *Quae nūllam aut parvam pecūniam habent ōrnāmenta aspiciunt tantum, nōn emunt.* (*ll.14-15*)

> *Pecūniōsus est quī magnam pecūniam habet.* (*l.35*)

When the relative pronoun is used without an antecedent, a demonstrative pronoun may be understood, that is, *quī* can equal *is quī*.

Demonstrative Pronouns

The demonstrative pronoun *hic, haec, hoc* points to something that is near the speaker (compare the adverb *hīc,* "here") and represents the English "this." In the first reading we meet only the feminine singular, nominative, accusative, ablative:

> *haec taberna?* (*l.2*)
> *in hāc viā* (*l.11*)
> *ad hanc tabernam* (*l.16*)

Ablative of Means/Instrument (*ablātīvus instrūmentī*) (continued)

You learned the ablative of means or instrument in Chapter VI (in conjunction with the passive voice). Here are more examples of the **ablative of instrument** (without prepositions):

Fēminae ōrnāmentīs dēlectantur.	Women are delighted by adornments. (*ll.12-13*)
Gemmīs et margarītīs ānulīsque ōrnantur.	They are adorned by jewels and pearls and rings. (*l.24*)
Lȳdia tabernam Albīnī digitō mōnstrat.	Lydia points to the store of Albinus with her finger. (*l.43*)

Interrogative Adjective

In Chaper II, you learned the interrogative pronoun, which asks the question "who, what?" The interrogative adjective is used before nouns:

quī servus?	what/which slave?
quae ancilla?	what/which slave-woman?
quod oppidum?	what/which town?
Quī vir et quae fēmina? (*l.26*)	
Quod ōrnāmentum? (*ll.30-31*)	

Notā Bene: The interrogative pronoun looks the same as the interrogative adjective (and relative pronoun) *except* in the nominative masculine and neuter singular:

> *quis, quid*   nominative m/n singular interrogative <u>pronoun</u>
> *quī, quod*   nominative m/n singular interrogative <u>adjective</u>

Recensiō: Interrogative Pronoun vs. Interrogative Adjective

Quis clāmat?	Who is shouting? (pronoun)
Quī puer clāmat?	What boy is shouting? (adjective)
Quae ōrnāmentum accipit?	Who receives the jewelry? (pronoun)
Quae fēmina ōrnāmentum accipit?	What woman receives the jewelry? (adjective)
Quid vēndit tabernārius?	What does the tabernarius sell? (pronoun)
Quod ōrnāmentum vēndit tabernārius?	What piece of jewelry does the tabernarius sell? (adjective)

Notā Bene:
- You will sometimes find *quis* (i.e. the form of the interrogative **pronoun**) used instead of *quī* (the form of the interrogative **adjective**) before a noun in questions of identity: <u>*Quis* servus?</u> *Mēdus.*
- While we here use *quae* for the nominative feminine singular of the interrogative pronoun, when you read ancient authors you will usually find *quis* used for both masculine and feminine.

3rd Conjugation "i-stems"

So far you have learned verbs that end in a long vowel (ā, ē, ī,) or a consonant. The final group of verbs have a stem ending in a short ĭ and is grouped with the third conjugation. In this chapter we see the verbs *accipit* and *aspicit*, which have plural forms in *-iunt*:

> Stem: *accipi-*; *accipit*; *accip<u>iunt</u>*
> Stem: *aspici-*; *aspicit*; *aspic<u>iunt</u>*

The short ĭ appears only before an ending beginning with a vowel, such as *-unt*: *accipiunt, aspici<u>unt</u>*; otherwise these verbs behave like consonant-verbs and are regarded as belonging to the 3rd conjugation.

The imperatives of "i-stems" (introduced in Section II of *Lingua Latina*) in *-e*, *-ite* are just like consonant stems:

> *accip<u>e</u>! accip<u>ite</u>!*
> *aspic<u>e</u>! aspic<u>ite</u>!*

You will learn more about i-stem verbs in Chapter XII. When you have learned all the forms of the verb it will be easy to distinguish the consonant and i-stems of the third declension. Until then, they will be listed separately in the vocabulary.

Lectiō Altera (Section II)

Demonstrative Pronouns

In this reading we meet more forms of *hic, haec, hoc*:

hae margarītae (l.49)	*hic ānulus (l.69)*
hī ānulī (l.53)	*hunc ānulum(l.76)*
in hīs ānulīs (l.55)	*huius (ānulī) (l.75)*

We are also introduced to the demonstrative *ille, illa, illud*, which refers to something that is further away from the speaker and is respresented by the English "that":

illam tabernam (l.41)	*illum (ānulum) (l.76)*
illa ōrnāmenta (l.42)	*illīus ānulī (l.75)*
ille ānulus (l.70)	

Like *hic, haec, hoc* and *ille, -a, -ud* most pronouns have the endings *-īus* in the genitive and *-ī* in the dative in all three genders (but the *i* is short or consonantal in *eius, cuius, huius, cui, huic*).

The neuter ending *-ud* in *illud* is also found in *alius, -a, -ud (l.33)* and is like the *-od* in *quod*.

See the paradigms for *hic haec hoc, ille illa illud*, and *is, ea, id* in the *recensiō* at the end of the chapter .

Correlatives: *tantus/quantus*

In Chapter VI you learned the correlatives *tam...quam* (as...as). When talking about size, the adjectives *tantus* and *quantus* are used (instead of *tam magnus* and *quam magnus*). So *tantus...quantus* stands for *tam magnus quam. Tantus...quantus* ("as big as") are correlative adjectives, as *tam...quam* are correlative adverbs (*l.75*). That is, they respond to one another:

Digitus quārtus nōn tantus est quantus digitus medius.	The fourth finger is not <u>as big as</u> the middle finger. (*ll.126-128*)
Pretium illīus ānulī tantum est quantum huius.	The price of that ring is <u>as great as</u> that of this one. (*l.75*)

Tantus and *quantus* can also be used alone:

Tanta gemma sōla octōgintā sēstertiīs cōnstat.	Such a large gem alone costs 80 sesterces. (*ll.64-65*)
Quantum est pretium illīus ānulī?	How much is the price of that ring? (*ll.72-73*)

Remember, you have already learned (in Chapter IV) *tantum* as an adverb meaning "only."

Quae nūllam aut parvam pecūniam habent ōrnāmenta aspiciunt tantum, nōn emunt.	Those (women) who have no or little money only look at jewelry, they don't buy. (*ll.14-19*)

Quam

Quam is also used in exclamations and means "how":

"*Ō, quam pulchra sunt illa ōrnāmenta!*"	Oh, how beautiful those ornaments are! (*ll.41-42*)

Recensiō: Quam

- relative pronoun: feminine accusative singular
  Puella quam Aemilia videt est Iūlia.
- interrogative pronoun: feminine accusative singular
  Quam videt Aemilia?
- interrogative adjective: feminine accusative singular
  Quam puellam videt Aemilia?
- adverb correlating with *tam* (= as)
  Estne via Latīna tam longa quam Via Aurelia?
- adverb in questions and exclamations (= how)
  Quam pulchra est vīlla Iūliī!

Ablative of Price (*ablātīvus pretiī*)

With the verbs *emit, vēndit* and *cōnstat* (verbs of buying and selling, etc.) the price is in the ablative, called *ablātīvus pretiī* ("ablative of price"). Examples:

Hic ānulus centum nummīs cōnstat.   This ring costs 100 coins. (*l.59*)

Albīnus...Mēdō ānulum vēndit sēstertiīs nōnāgintā. (*ll.116-117*)

Dative (continued)

In the last example *Mēdō* is **dative** with *vēndit*. The dative now occurs also with *ostendit* (ll.46, 52, 58, 83) and *mōnstrat* (l.130). Being transitive, these verbs have an object in the accusative, which is often called the **direct object** to distinguish it from the dative, which is called the **indirect object**. Examples:

Albīnus Lȳdiae margarītās ostendit.
Albinus shows Lydia the pearls. (*ll.46-47*)

Shows what?	pearls, accusative direct object
Shows to whom?	Lydia, dative indirect object

Albīnus iīs trēs ānulōs ostendit.
Albinus shows them three rings. (*l.52*)

Shows what?	three rings, accusative direct object
Shows to whom?	them, dative indirect object

Lȳdia, quae Rōmae habitat, Mēdō viam mōnstrat.
Lydia, who lives in Rome, points out the road to Medus. (*ll.129-130*)

Shows what?	road, accusative direct object
Shows to whom?	Medus, dative indirect object

Points of Style: *Convenit*

Latin is not English. While we all know this, it presents one of the biggest obstacles to understanding the language, especially if you try to put a Latin thought into English! The use of *convenit* in the following examples illustrates important principles to bear in mind. Consider the following two sentences:

Tanta gemma ad tam parvum ānulum nōn convenit.	Such a big gem does not suit such a small ring. (*l.81*)
Hic ānulus ad digitum tuum nōn convenit.	This ring does not fit your finger. (*l.121*)

Note that:

1. The syntax of the two languages works differently. In English, both "suit" and "fit" are transitive verbs and take a direct object. In Latin, *convenit* is intransitive and (here) is followed by *ad* + the accusative.

2. The same word often needs to be translated by different English words in different contexts. The concept, if kept in Latin, is perfectly clear: one thing does not "come together well" (*convenit*) with something else (*ad* + the accusative). In English, however, we say "a gem does not suit a ring" rather than "does not come together with." In the second sentence, however, we are more likely to use "fit" for *convenit*.

You will find that you can often understand the Latin more fluently if you *don't* translate but understand the concept behind the vocabulary and apply that concept to its context. When moving between the two languages, remember to be flexible in your vocabulary and to let go of the expectation that other languages "should" act like English.

Lectiō Tertia (Section III)

Demonstrative Pronouns

In the final reading we continue to see more forms of the demonstratives *hic* and *ille*:

huic tabernāriō (*l.97*)	*haec ōrnāmenta* (*l.105*)
illī tabernāriī (*l.100*)	*hōs ānulōs* (*l.105*)
illae viae (*l.102*)	*hās gemmās* (*l.105*)
in illīs tabernīs (*ll.103-104*)	*hōrum ōrnāmentōrum* (*l.107*)

Notā Bene: As you can see, with a few exceptions, their declension is already familiar to you. The stem of *hic, haec, hoc* is just *h-*, cf. the plural *hī hae, hōs hās, hōrum hārum, hīs,* but in the singular (and in n. pl. nom./acc.) a *-c* is added. Again, full paradigms are below in the *recensiō* and in the GRAMMATICA LATINA in LINGUA LATINA.

In the GRAMMATICA LATINA you will find that not only *ille, -a, -ud,* but also *is, ea, id* is used as an adjective. *Is, ea, id* can be used as a weaker form of *hic* (English "this") or *ille* (English "that"):

    is servus   *ea ancilla*   *id ōrnāmentum*

Pronouns Multiplied (examples)

Note the use of both the interrogative and relative pronouns in the same sentence in the following examples:

> *Quae sunt illae viae in quibus illae tabernae sunt?*
> Which (interrogative) are those roads in which (relative)
> there are those stores? (*ll.102-104*)

> *Et quae sunt illa ōrnāmenta quae in illīs tabernīs parvō pretiō emuntur?*
> And which (interrogative) are those jewels which (relative)
> are sold for such a small price in those stores? (*ll.103-104*)

Recensiō: Pronouns

Personal: takes the place of a noun

is, ea, id

	sing.			pl.		
	masc.	fem.	neut.	masc.	fem.	neut.
nom.	i|s	e|a	i|d	i|ī	e|ae	e|a
acc.	e|um	e|am	i|d	e|ōs	e|ās	e|a
gen.	e|ius	e|ius	e|ius	e|ōrum	e|ārum	e|ōrum
dat.	e|ī	e|ī	e|ī	i|īs	i|īs	i|īs
abl.	e|ō	e|ā	e|ō	i|īs	i|īs	i|īs

Demonstrative: points out as closer or further away

Hic, haec, hoc

[1]	sing.			pl.		
	masc.	fem.	neut.	masc.	fem.	neut.
nom.	hic	haec	hoc	hī	hae	haec
acc.	hunc	hanc	hoc	hōs	hās	haec
gen.	huius	huius	huius	hōrum	hārum	hōrum
dat.	huic	huic	huic	hīs	hīs	hīs
abl.	hōc	hāc	hōc	hīs	hīs	hīs

Ille, illa, illud

[2]		masc.	fem.	neut.	masc.	fem.	neut.
	nom.	ill|e	ill|a	ill|ud	ill|ī	ill|ae	ill|a
	acc.	ill|um	ill|am	ill|ud	ill|ōs	ill|ās	ill|a
	gen.	ill|īus	ill|īus	ill|īus	ill|ōrum	ill|ārum	ill|ōrum
	dat.	ill|ī	ill|ī	ill|ī	ill|īs	ill|īs	ill|īs
	abl.	ill|ō	ill|ā	ill|ō	ill|īs	ill|īs	ill|īs

Interrogative: Asks a question

Quis, quid

	sing.			pl.		
	masc.	fem.	neut.	masc.	fem.	neut.
nom.	quis/quī	quae	quid/quod	quī	quae	quae
acc.	quem	quam	quid/quod	quōs	quās	quae
gen.	cuius	cuius	cuius	quōrum	quārum	quōrum
dat.	cui	cui	cui	quibus	quibus	quibus
abl.	quō	quā	quō	quibus	quibus	quibus

Relative: Connects a dependent clause to a sentence

Qui, quae, quod

	sing.			pl.		
	masc.	fem.	neut.	masc.	fem.	neut.
nom.	quī	quae	quod	quī	quae	quae
acc.	quem	quam	quod	quōs	quās	quae
gen.	cuius	cuius	cuius	quōrum	quārum	quōrum
dat.	cui	cui	cui	quibus	quibus	quibus
abl.	quō	quā	quō	quibus	quibus	quibus

Vocābula Disposita/Ordināta

Nōmina

1st

gemma, -ae	precious stone, jewel
līnea, -ae	string, line
margarīta, -ae	pearl
taberna, -ae	shop, stall

2nd

ānulus, -ī	ring
collum, -ī	neck
digitus, -ī	finger
ōrnāmentum, -ī	ornament, jewel
pretium, -ī	price, value
sēstertius, -ī	sesterce (coin)
tabernārius, -ī	shopkeeper

3rd

prōnōmen, prōnōminis (*n.*)	pronoun

Verba

-ā (1)

clāmat, clāmant, -ātur, -antur	shout
cōnstat, cōnstant, -ātur, -antur	be fixed, cost
mōnstrat, mōnstrant, -ātur, -antur	point out, show
ornat, ornant, -ātur, -antur	equip, adorn

consonant (3)
cōnsistit, cōnsistunt	stop, halt
emit, emunt, -itur, -untur	buy
ostendit, ostendunt, -itur, -untur	show
vēndit, vēndunt, -itur, -untur	sell

ĭ-stem (3)
aspicit, aspiciunt, -itur, -untur	look at, look
accipit, accipiunt, -itur, -untur	receive

-ī (4)
abit, abeunt	go away
convenit, conveniunt	come together, meet

Adiectīva

1st-2nd (us/er, -a, -um)
alius, alia, aliud	another, other
gemmātus, -a, -um	set with a jewel
medius, -a, -um	mid, middle
pecūniōsus, -a, -um	wealthy
quantus, -a, -um	how large, (as large) as
quārtus, -a, -um	fourth
tantus, -a, -um	so big, so great

Numerī (indecl. unless otherwise noted)
nōnāgintā	ninety
octōgintā	eighty
vīgintī	twenty

Pronōmina
ille, illa, illud	that, the one, he

Adverbia
nimis	too, too much
satis	enough, rather

Coniunctiōnēs
aut	or

IX. Pāstor et Ovēs

Rēs Grammaticae Novae

1. Verbs
   a. *ēst/edunt*
   b. *dūc/dūcite*
   c. Assimilation
2. Nouns: 3rd Declension (Consonant and *i*-Stem)
   a. Declensions
   b. Gender
   c. 3rd Declension
   d. Case Uses
      i. Prepositions *suprā* and *sub*
3. Pronouns: *ipse, ipsa, ipsum*
4. Conjunction: *dum*

The Italian Landscape

We leave the family at the villa for a while and join a shepherd and his dog guarding sheep.

Lectiō Prima (Section I)
Third Declension Nouns

By studying the landscape above the chapter you will learn a great many new Latin nouns. In the words *campus, herba, rīvus, umbra, silva, caelum* you see the familiar endings -*us*, -*a* and -*um*. The remaining words, *collis, pāstor, canis, mōns, sōl*, etc., have quite different endings, not only in the nominative, but also in the other **cases**, the word we use to refer to the inflected forms of nouns, adjectives, and pronouns (nominative, accusative, genitive, dative, and ablative).

The nominative singular of 3rd declension nouns varies. In the **nominative** singular, 3rd declension nouns have either:

- no ending

  pāstor
  sōl
  arbor

- or end in *-is*

  ovis   *pānis*
  canis   *collis*

- or end in *-ēs*

  nūbēs

- or end in just *-s*

  mōns
  *dēn*s

  ▷ This final *-s* causes changes in the stem, which can be seen in the genitive singular, e.g.:

    ○ When the stem (genitive singular) of *mōns* and *dēns* ends in *-t* (*mont|is, dent|is*)

    ○ When *-s* is added to a stem ending in *-t*, the *-t* drops and the vowel lengthens (*mont|s* and *dent|s*➔ *mōns, dēns*)

We can see from the example of *mōns* and *dēns* that the nominative of a 3rd declension word might look quite different from the rest of the cases. The **endings**, however, are regular:

- in the singular they have the following endings:

  -em in the accusative
  -is in the genitive
  -ī in the dative
  -e in the ablative

- in the plural they have the following endings:

  -ēs in the nominative and accusative
  -um or *-ium* in the genitive
  -ibus in the dative and ablative

Or, schematically:

	sing.	pl.
nom.	*-/-(i)s*	*-ēs*
acc.	*-em*	*-ēs*
gen.	*-is*	*-(i)um*
dat.	*-ī*	*-ibus*
abl.	*-e*	*-ibus*

Notā Bene: There are two possible endings to the genitive plural (*-um* and *-ium*) because there are two different kinds of third declension nouns: **consonant-stems** (end in *-um* in the genitive plural) and **i-stems** (end in *-ium* in the genitive plural). The two types differ only in the genitive plural.

Consonant-Stems

- nouns with no ending in the nominative, e.g. *pāstor* have *-um* in the genitive plural

I-Stems
  • nouns in -*is*, -*es*, and some in -*s* have -*ium* in the genitive plural

Examples of all these endings are shown with the nouns *ovis* and *pāstor* (*ll.3-7, 11-18*).

Gender

The 3rd declension nouns in this chapter are masculine or feminine, but since the endings are the same for the two genders you cannot determine the gender of such nouns until they are combined with adjectives of the 1st and 2nd declensions (like *magnus, -a, -um*). By looking at the noun/adjective combinations below, you can determine the gender of each noun:

pāstor fessus	*ovis alba*
parvus collis	*magna vallis*
magnus mōns	*multae arborēs*

From the above you can see that *pāstor, collis* and *mōns* are masculine and that *ovis, vallis* and *arbor* are feminine.

Words **declined** (i.e. inflected) in this way are said to belong to the **3rd declension** (Latin *dēclīnātiō tertia*), whereas the **1st declension** (*dēclīnātiō prīma*) comprises words in -*a* (like *fēmina*), and the **2nd declension** (*dēclīnātiō secunda*) words in -*us* and -*um* (like *servus* and *oppidum*).

In the GRAMMATICA LATINA section of LINGUA LATINA you will find examples of these three declensions. Take advantage of this opportunity to review the case-forms of *īnsula* (1st declension), *servus* and *verbum* (2nd declension), and then study the new 3rd declension (examples: *pāstor* and *ovis*).

Ēst/edunt

The verb in the sentence *Ovēs herbam edunt* (*l.8*) is a consonant-verb, as shown by the plural ending -*unt*; but the singular is irregular: *Pāstor pānem ēst* (only in Late Latin does the "regular" form *edit* appear). The macron (long mark) over the *ēst* in *ēst* will distinguish "he, she eats" from *est* "he, she is."

sing.	*ēst*
pl.	*edunt*

Dūc/eūcite

Also note the short imperative *dūc!* (without -*e*) of the consonant-verb *dūcit, dūcunt*.

imp.	*dūc! dūc|ite!*

Suprā/sub

New prepositions are *suprā*, which takes the accusative, and *sub*, which takes
the ablative (when motion is implied *sub* takes the accusative).

> *suprā* + acc.   above
>
> *sub* + abl. (acc.)   below

> > *Sōl in caelō est suprā campum.* (*l.25*)
> > *Caelum est suprā terram.* (*l.26*)
> > *Sub arbore autem umbra est.* (*l.30*)
> > *Sub arboribus sōl nōn lūcet.* (*l.52*)

Lectiō Altera (Section II)

Dum

So far the conjunctions you have met join two things—either words, phrases, or
independent clauses (a set of words with a subject and a verb that makes complete
sense by itself):

et	and	*sed*	but
et...et	both...and	*aut*	or
-que	and (enclitic)	*quod*	because
neque	and not, but not	*quia*	because
neque...neque	neither...nor		

We will now meet a different kind of conjunction. A **temporal conjunction**
joins to the main clause a clause that explains the time relationship between
the ideas in the two clauses. The temporal conjunction *dum* expresses
simultaneousness, that is, that the actions in the two clauses happen at the same
time (English "while"):

> *Dum pāstor in herbā dormit, ovis nigra abit.* (*l.39*)

Dum ("while") shows that the action in the main clause ("the black sheep
goes away") is happening at the same time (simultaneously) as the action in the
subordinate clause ("the shepherd sleeps in the grass").

After *exspectat, dum* means "until":

- *Ovis cōnsistit et exspectat dum lupus venit.* (*ll.69-70*)

Ipse, ipsa, ipsum

The demonstrative pronoun *ipse* is used for emphasis like English "himself/
herself/itself": *Ubi est lupus ipse?* (*ll.54-55*). It is declined like *ille* apart from the
neuter sing. in *-um* (not *-ud*): *ipse, -a, -um.*

nom.	*ips|e*	*ips|a*	*ips|um*	*ips|ī*	*ips|ae*	*ips|a*
acc.	*ips|um*	*ips|am*	*ips|um*	*ips|ōs*	*ips|ās*	*ips|a*
gen.	*ips|īus*	*ips|īus*	*ips|īus*	*ips|ōrum*	*ips|ārum*	*ips|ōrum*
dat.	*ips|ī*	*ips|ī*	*ips|ī*	*ips|īs*	*ips|īs*	*ips|īs*
abl.	*ips|ō*	*ips|ā*	*ips|ō*	*ips|īs*	*ips|īs*	*ips|īs*

Ubi est lupus ipse?	Where is the wolf itself (or "himself")? (*l.54-55*)
Ovis vestīgia lupī in terrā videt, neque lupum ipsum videt.	The sheep sees the tracks of the wolf in the earth, but she does not see the wolf itself. (*l.55-56*)
Ubi est ovis ipsa?	Where is the sheep herself (or "itself")? (*l.65*)

Assimilation

The meaning of verbs can be modified or clarified when they are augmented by **prefixes**. The final consonant of the prefix sometimes undergoes a sound change because of the initial consonant of the simple verb with which it is joined. So, for example, when *ad* and *in* enter into compounds with *currit* and *pōnit,* they change to *ac-* and *im-*: *ac-currit, im-pōnit.* Such a change, which makes one consonant like or similar to another (*m* is a labial consonant like *p*), is called **assimilation** (from Latin *similis,* "similar," "like").

Recensiō: Grammatical Terms

Case (*cāsus*): The various forms a noun/adjective/pronoun takes depending on its function in a sentence are called cases. The cases are nominative, accusative, genitive, dative, ablative, vocative.

Declension (*dēclīnātiō*): a family of nouns/adjectives is called a declension. You have learned the first three of five declensions of nouns.

Decline (*dēclīnāre*): When we recite the paradigm of a noun, adjective, or pronoun by giving each of the cases, we are said to decline the word.

Temporal conjunction (*coniunctiō temporālis*): a temporal conjunction joins two clauses in a sentence by showing the time relation between them, that is, whether the action in one clause happens before, after, or at the same time as the other.

Independent clause: A group of words with a subject (expressed or implied) and verb expressing a complete thought is called an independent clause ("The shepherd sleeps.").

Dependent clause: A group of words with a subject (expressed or implied) and verb that does not express a complete thought is called a dependent clause ("While the shepherd sleeps...").

Assimilation: When a prefix is added to a verb, the initial consonant of the verb may cause the final consonant of the prefix to adapt in sound to its neighbor; that is to say, it undergoes assimilation.

Vocābula Disposita/Ordināta

Nōmina

1st

herba, -ae	grass, herb
silva, -ae	wood, forest
terra, -ae	earth, ground, country
umbra, -ae	shade, shadow

2nd

caelum, -ī	sky, heaven
campus, -ī	plain
cibus, -ī	food
lupus, -ī	wolf
modus, -ī	manner, way
rīvus, -ī	brook
vestīgium, -ī	footprint, trace

3rd

arbor, arboris (*f.*)	tree
canis, canis (*m./f.*)	dog
clāmor, clāmōris (*m.*)	shout, shouting
collis, collis (*m.*)	hill
dēclīnātiō, dēlīnātiōnis (*f.*)	declension
dēns, dentis (*m.*)	tooth
mōns, montis (*m.*)	mountain
nūbēs, nūbis (*f.*)	cloud
ovis, ovis (*f.*)	sheep
pānis, pānis (*m.*)	bread, loaf
pāstor, pāstōris (*m.*)	shepherd
sōl, sōlis (*m.*)	sun
timor, timōris (*m.*)	fear
vallis, vallis (*f.*)	valley

Verba

-ā (1)

bālat, -ant, -ātur, -antur	bleat
dēclīnat, -ant, -ātur, -antur	decline, inflect
errat, -ant, -ātur, -antur	wander, stray
lātrat, -ant, -ātur, -antur	bark
ululat, -ant, -ātur, -antur	howl

-ē (2)

iacet, -ent	lie
lūcet, -ent	shine

Consonant/ĭ (3)

accurrit, -unt	come running
bibit, -unt	drink
dūcit, -unt, -itur, -untur	guide, lead, draw, trace
impōnit, -unt, -itur, -untur	place (in/on), put

petit, -unt, -itur, -untur	make for, aim at, attack, seek, ask for, request
quaerit, -unt, -itur, -untur	look for, seek, ask (for)
relinquit, -unt, -itur, -untur	leave
-ī (4)	
reperit, -iunt, -ītur, -iuntur	find
Irregular	
ēst, edunt	eat

Adiectīva
1st-2nd (us/er, -a, -um)

| niger, -gra, -grum | black |
| albus, -a, -um | white |

Numerī (indecl. unless otherwise noted)

| ūndēcentum | ninety-nine |

Pronōmina

| ipse, ipsa, ipsum | myself, yourself, etc; the very, the actual |

Adverbia

| suprā | above |
| procul | far (from), far away |

Praepositiōnēs

| suprā (*prp. + acc.*) | above |
| sub (*prp. + abl./acc.*) | under, near |

Coniunctiōnēs

| dum | while, as long as, till |
| ut | like, as |

X. Bēstiae et Hominēs

Rēs Grammaticae Novae

1. Verbs
   a. Infinitive Active
   b. Infinitive Active in *-se*
   c. Infinitive Passive
   d. Verbs and Expressions That Take an Infinitive
      i. *potest/possunt*
      ii. *necesse est*
      iii. *vult/volunt, audet/audent*
   e. Accusative and Infinitive Construction
2. Nouns
   a. 3rd Declension Masculine and Feminine
   b. 3rd Declension Neuter
   c. *nēmō*
   d. Case Uses
      i. Dative of Interest
      ii. Ablative of Manner (*ablātīvus modī*)
3. Conjunctions
   a. *cum*
   b. *quod*
4. Points of Style
   a. *alius...alius*
   b. active and passive

The Story

After reading about the physical characteristics of animals, humans, and gods, we rejoin Marcus, Quintus, and Julia in the garden.

Lectiō Prīma (Section I)

3rd Declension Masculine and Feminine

In this chapter several new 3rd declension nouns are introduced.

- Some of them have peculiar forms in the nominative singular: in *leō* an *-n* is dropped: gen. *leōn|is.*
- In *homō* this is combined with a vowel change: gen. *homin|is.*
- The *-s* ending produces the spelling *-x* for *-cs* in *vōx*: gen. *vōc|is.*
- The *-s* ending also produces the loss of *d* in *pēs*: gen. *ped|is.*

From now on the nominative and genitive of new nouns will be found in the margins of your *Lingua Latina* text, as well as in the vocabulary list at the end of each chapter in this book:

leō leōn|is m. lion	*vōx vōc|is* f. voice
homō homin|is m. person	*pēs ped|is* m. foot

This way of listing a noun (nominative, genitive, gender, meaning) is called the *lexical entry*, since that is the way the word will be listed in a lexicon (dictionary).

Conjunctions

Cum

You have already learned the preposition *cum*, which takes the ablative and means "with." *Cum* is also a **temporal** conjunction (referring to time) meaning when:

> <u>*Cum*</u> *avis volat, ālae moventur* When a bird flies, (its) wings move (literally: are moving). (*l.15*)

It is easy to distinguish between *cum* preposition and *cum* conjunction. Look at the following sentences:

> *Iūlius in vīllā suā habitat* <u>*cum*</u> *magnā familiā.* (*Chap. V, l.9*)
> *Aemilia* <u>*cum*</u> *Mārcō, Quīntō Iūliāque in peristȳlō est.* (*Chap. V, l.47*)
> *Etiam līnea* <u>*cum*</u> *margarītīs ōrnāmentum est.* (*Chap. VIII, ll.8-9*)
> <u>*Cum*</u> *homō ambulat, pedēs moventur.* (*Chap. X, l.15*)
> <u>*Cum*</u> *piscis natat, cauda movētur.* (*Chap. X, ll.15-16*)

Quod

You have learned *quod* as the neuter singular of both the relative pronoun *quī, quae, quod* and the interrogative adjective. *Quod* is also a causal conjunction with the same meaning as *quia* (because):

> *Hominēs ambulāre possunt,* <u>*quod*</u> *pedēs habent.* (*ll.23-24*)

means the same as:

> *Hominēs ambulāre possunt,* <u>*quia*</u> *pedēs habent.*

It is easy to distinguish between *quod* pronoun, *quod* interrogative adjective and *quod* conjunction. Look at the following sentences:

> *Iūlius ambulat ad* <u>*ōstium*</u>, <u>*quod*</u> *ab ōstiāriō aperītur.* (*Chap. VII, l.33*)
>
> *Lȳdia ōrnāmentum pulchrum in collō habet.* <u>*Quod ōrnāmentum?*</u> (*Chap. VIII, ll.30-31*)

Ōrnāmentum quod Lȳdia habet est līnea margarītārum. (*Chap. VIII, ll.31-32*)

Hominēs volāre nōn possunt, quod ālās nōn habent. (*Chap. X, ll.23-25*)

Neque avēs neque nīdī avium ab aquilā reperīrī possunt, quod rāmīs et foliīs occultantur. (*Chap. X, ll.89-91*)

Potest/possunt

The verb *potest*, which first appears in the sentence *Canis volāre nōn potest* (l.21), denotes ability (English "is able to," "can"). It is a compound with *est*: *pot-est*; the first element *pot-* (meaning "able") is changed before *s* by assimilation to *pos-*: *Hominēs ambulāre pos-sunt* (*l.23*). More examples:

Pāstor duōs pedēs habet, itaque pāstor ambulāre potest. (*ll.22-23*)
Homō sub aquā spīrāre nōn potest. (*ll.47-48*)
Nēmō enim sine cibō vīvere potest. (*ll.59-69*)
Hominēs deōs neque vidēre neque audīre possunt. (*ll.38-39*)
Piscēs numerārī nōn possunt. (*l.45*)
Avēs canere possunt, piscēs nōn possunt: piscēs vōcēs nōn habent. (*ll.85-86*)

sing. *pot-est*

pl. *pos-sunt*

Infinitive Active

Volāre and *ambulāre* are the first examples of the basic verb form which is called the **infinitive** (Latin *īnfīnītīvus*); the infinitive in English is expressed by "to" with the verb. The Latin infinitive active ends in *-re*. In *ā-*, *ē-* and *ī-*verbs (1st, 2nd and 4th conjugations), this ending is added directly to the stem:

volā|re: to fly
vidē|re: to see
audī|re: to hear

In consonant-verbs of the 3rd conjugation a short *e* is inserted before the ending:

pōn|ere: to put
sūm|ere: to take

The infinitive of i-stem verbs of the 3rd conjugation is indistinguishable from that of consonant stems:

accip|ere: to receive
fac|ere: to do, make

From now on the infinitive will be the form of new verbs shown in the margin of *Lingua Latina* and in the vocabulary of this book, so that you can always tell which of the four conjugations the verb belongs to: 1. *-āre*; 2. *-ēre*; 3. *-ere*; 4. *-īre*.

Lectiō Altera (Section II)
Infinitive Active in *-se*

The original ending of the infinitive was *-se,* but an intervocalic *-s-,* i.e. an *-s-* between vowels, was changed to *-r-,* so *-se* became *-re* after a vowel (eg. *amāre* < *amā|se*). The ending *-se* was kept only in the following infinitives, because it was added directly to the stems *es-* and *ed*:

> *esse* (*est sunt*)
> *ēsse* (*ēst edunt,* with assimilation *ds* > *ss*)
> *posse* (*potest possunt,* Chap. XI)

Examples:

> *Quī spīrat mortuus esse nōn potest.* (*ll.108-109*)
> *Mārcus et Iūlia Quīntum vīvum esse vident.* (*l.122*)
> *Ēsse quoque hominī necesse est.* (*l.59*)
> *nēmō enim gemmās ēsse potest.* (*l.64*)
> *Gemmae edī nōn possunt.* (*l.64*) (*Notā Bene* the passive infinitive *edī* of *ēsse*).

infinitive *-se*:

> *es|se*
> *ēs|se* (< *ed|se*); passive *edī*

Infinitive Passive

The sentence *Hominēs deōs vidēre nōn possunt* becomes in the passive: *Deī ab hominibus vidērī nōn possunt. Vidērī* (to <u>be</u> seen) is the **passive infinitive** corresponding to the active *vidēre* (to see). In the passive, *ā-, ē-* and *ī-*verbs have the ending *-rī* in the infinitive, e.g.:

> *numerā|rī* (*l.45*)
> *vidē|rī* (*l.39*)
> *audī|rī* (*l.39*)

Consonant-verbs have only *-ī,* e.g.:

> *em|ī: Sine pecūniā cibus emī nōn potest.* (*l.62*)

infinitive

active	passive
āre→ārī: vocā|re	*vocā|rī*
ēre→ērī: vidē|re	*vidē|rī*
ĕre→ī: pōn|ere	*pōn|ī*
īre→īrī: audī|re	*audī|rī*

More examples:

> *Aemilia fīlium suum ā Iūliō <u>portārī</u> videt.* (*l.126*)
>
> *Sed Mārcus eum spīrāre nōn videt, neque enim anima <u>vidērī</u> potest.* (*ll.109-110*)

Deī ab hominibus neque <u>vidērī</u> neque <u>audīrī</u> possunt. (*ll.38-39*)

Gemmae edī nōn possunt. (*l.64*)

Necesse est + the Infinitive and Dative of Interest

We have seen the infinitive occurs as object of:

potest possunt

It occurs after other verbs and expressions as well, for example, in this section of the reading, *necesse est*. *Necesse est* is an **impersonal** expression, that is, one without a subject ("it is necessary"); the person for whom it is necessary to do something is in the dative (**dative of interest**). Examples:

Spīrāre necesse est hominī. (*l.58*)
Necesse est cibum habēre. (*l.60*)

3rd Declension Neuter Nouns

You also meet the first **neuter** nouns of the 3rd declension. The declension of these nouns will be taken up in the next chapter, but for now, here are the nominative/accusative. Remember, the nominative and accusative of neuter nouns (and adjectives) are always the same:

flūmen
mare
animal

Like all neuter nouns, in the nominative and accusative plural these nouns end in *-a*:

flūmin<u>a</u>
mari<u>a</u>
animāli<u>a</u>

Nēmō

Homō combined with the negation *nē* forms the pronoun *nēmō* (< *nē* + *homō*, "nobody").

Lectiō Tertia (Section III)

Vult/volunt, audet/audent + infinitive

In addition to *potest/possunt* and *necesse est*, an infinitive also occurs after:

vult volunt   the irregular verb that denotes will
audet audent   a verb that denotes courage

Examples:

Iūlia cum puerīs lūd<u>ere</u> <u>vult</u>, neque iī cum puellā lūd<u>ere</u> <u>volunt</u>. (*ll.74-76*)
Canis avem ... cap<u>ere</u> <u>vult</u>, neque <u>potest</u>. (*ll.83-84*)
Quī volāre vult neque potest, ad terram cadit! (*ll.129-130*)
Fēminae quae pecūniam fac<u>ere</u> <u>volunt</u> ōrnāmenta sua vēndunt. (*ll.67-68*)
Avēs can<u>ere</u> nōn <u>audent</u>. (*l.88*)
Mārcus ipse in arborem ascend<u>ere</u> nōn <u>audet</u>! (*ll.96-97*)

Notā Bene: The form *vult* (he, she wants) lacks a vowel; the verb is irregular.

Accusative and Infinitive Construction

The object of verbs of perception, like *vidēre* and *audīre*, can be combined with an infinitive to express what someone is seen or heard to be doing (active infinitive) or what is being done to someone (passive infinitive). There are several ways of rendering the accusative and infinitive construction in English:

Puerī puellam canere audiunt (*l.80*):

The boys see (that) the girl is singing.
The boys see the girl sing/that the girl sings.
The boys see (that) the girl does sing.

Mārcus Quīntum ad terram cadere videt (*l.104*):
Marcus sees (that) Quintus is falling to the ground.
Marcus sees Quintus fall to the ground/that Quintus falls to the ground.
Marcus sees (that) Quintus does fall to the ground.

Aemilia fīlium suum ā Iūliō portārī videt (*l.126*):
Aemilia sees (that) her son is being carried by Julius.
Aemilia sees her son being carried by Julius.

Aemilia Quīntum ā Iūliō in lectō pōnī aspicit (*l.131*):
Aemilia sees (that) Quintus is being put onto the bed by Julius.
Aemilia sees Quintus being put onto the bed by Julius.

Notā Bene: The word "that" is optional in English translation and supplied; there is no Latin equivalent to "that" in any of the sentences above.

Ablative of Manner (*Ablātīvus Modī*)

Besides **means** and **cause**, the simple ablative can also denote **manner** (*ablātīvus modī*), e.g.:

magnā vōce clāmat (*l.112*)
"leō" dēclīnātur hōc modō... (*l.169*)

Points of Style

1. *Alius...alius*: In line 9 we read *"aliae bēstiae sunt avēs, aliae piscēs."* Repeating a form of *alius, alia, aliud* signals the idiom which represents the English "some...others." So:
   a. *Aliae bēstiae sunt avēs, aliae piscēs*: some creature are birds, others fish.
   b. *Alius librīs dēlectātur, alius ornamentīs*: one person is delighted by books, another by jewelry.
   c. *Aliī alia dicunt*: Different people say different things/some say one thing, others say another.
2. *Cauda movet/movētur*: Another example of how Latin differs from English can be seen in this chapter. In lines 16-17 we find *"cum piscis natat, cauda movētur"* (when a fish swims, its tail moves). In line 79, we see *"Canis pilam capit et caudam movet"* (the dog catches the ball and wags its tail). In English the first use is intransitive, the second transitive. Latin, however, expresses the same idea using the passive and active voices, respectively.

Notā Bene: Remember, the infinitive will be given in the vocabulary of this book, so that you can always tell which of the four conjugations the verb belongs to: 1. *-āre*; 2. *-ēre*; 3. *-ere*; 4. *-īre*.

Vocābula Disposita/Ordināta

Nōmina

1st

āla, -ae	wing
anima, -ae	breath, life, soul
aquila, -ae	eagle
bēstia, -ae	beast, animal
cauda, -ae	tail
fera, -ae	wild animal
pila, -ae	ball

2nd

asinus, -ī	ass, donkey
deus, -ī	god (*pl.* deī/diī/dī)
folium, -ī	leaf
īnfīnītīvus (modus)	infinitive
lectus, -ī	bed, couch
nīdus, -ī	nest
nūntius, -ī	message, messenger
ōvum, -ī	egg
petasus, -ī	hat with a brim
pullus, -ī	young (of an animal)
rāmus, -ī	branch, bough

3rd

āēr, āēris (*m.*)	air
animal, animālis (*n.*)	animal, living being
avis, avis (*f.*)	bird
flūmen, flūminis (*n.*)	river
homō, hominis (*m.*)	human being, person
leō, leōnis (*m.*)	lion
mare, maris (*n.*)	sea
mercātor, mercātōris (*m.*)	merchant
pēs, pēdis (*m.*)	foot
piscis, piscis (*m.*)	fish
pulmō, pulmōnis (*m.*)	lung
vōx, vōcis (*f.*)	voice

Verba

-āre (1)

natat, natāre	swim
occultat, occultāre	hide
spīrat, spīrāre	breathe
volat, volāre	fly

-ēre (2)

audet, audēre	dare, venture
movet, movēre	move, stir
sustinet, sustinēre	support, sustain, endure

-ĕre (3)

Consonant-stem

ascendit, ascendere	climb, go up, mount
cadit, cadere	fall
canit, canere	sing (of), crow, play
lūdit, lūdere	play
vīvit, vīvere	live, be alive

i-stem

capit, capere	take, match, capture
facit, facere	make do, cause
parit, parere	give birth to, lay

Irregular

necesse est	it is necessary
potest, possunt	be able
vult, volunt	want, be willing

Adiectīva

1st-2nd (us/er, -a, -um)

crassus, -a, -um	thick, fat
ferus, -a, -um	wild
mortuus, -a, -um	dead
perterritus, -a, -um	terrified
vīvus, -a, -um	living, alive

3rd (you will learn about these in Chapter XII)

tenuis, -e	thin

Pronōmina

nēmō	no one

Adverbia

ergō	therefore, so

Coniunctiōnes

cum	when
enim	for
quod	because

XI. Corpus Hūmānum

Rēs Grammaticae Novae

1. Verbs
   a. Infinitive in Indirect Statement
   b. *Posse*
2. Nouns
   a. 3rd Declension Neuter
   b. Case Uses
      i. Accusative in Indirect Statement
      ii. Ablative of Respect
      iii. Preposition: *de* + ablative
3. Possessive Adjectives
4. Conjunctions *atque/ neque (ac/nec)*

Roman Medicine

The art of healing was naturally far more primitive in the ancient world than it is today, although not all the doctors of antiquity were so incompetent as the zealous physician who treats poor Quintus. Blood-letting was used then as a kind of panacea.

Lectiō Prīma (Section I)
Third Declension Neuter Nouns

Among the names of parts of the body there are a number of neuter nouns of the 3rd declension. Like all neuters, these nouns have:
- the same form in the nominative and accusative
- the plural nominative/accusative ending in -*a*

In the other cases they have the well-known endings of the 3rd declension. These nouns are all consonant-stems, like *flūmen, -in|is*:

ōs, ōr|is	*cor, cord|is*
crūs, crūr|is	*iecur, iecor|is*
corpus, corpor|is	*caput, capit|is*
pectus, pector|is	*viscer|a, -um*

Notā Bene:
- a final -*s* is changed into *r* when endings are added
- *u* can become *o* in the stem, as in *corpus*, *pectus*, and *iecur*
- *caput, capit|is* and *cor, cord|is* are irregular
- *viscer|a, -um* is only used in the plural

3rd Declension *i*-stem Nouns

In Chapter X we met the 3rd declension neuter nouns *mar|e mar|is* and *animal* -*āl|is*. There are not many of these nouns; they differ from neuter consonant stems in that they have:
- -*ia* in the nom./acc. plural
- -*ium* in the gen. plural
- -*ī* in the abl. singular

The complete declension patterns (or **paradigms**) are shown below and on page 83 of *Lingua Latina*.

	sing.	pl.	sing.	pl.
nom.	mar|e	mar|ia	animal	animāl|ia
acc.	mar|e	mar|ia	animal	animāl|ia
gen.	mar|is	mar|ium	animāl|is	animāl|ium
dat.	mar|ī	mar|ibus	animāl|ī	animāl|ibus
abl.	mar|ī	mar|ibus	animāl|ī	animāl|ibus

Lectiō Altera (Section II)

Indirect Statement (Accusative and Infinitive Construction)

In sentences like *Iūlius puerum videt* and *Iūlius puerum audit* we have seen that an infinitive may be added to the accusative *puerum* to describe what the boy is doing or what is happening to him, e.g.:

> *Iūlius puerum vocāre audit.*
> *Iūlius puerum perterritum esse videt.*

Such a construction is called an **accusative and infinitive construction** (*accūsātīvus cum īnfīnītīvō*); in these constructions the accusative is logically the subject of the infinitive ("subject accusative"). You will find this construction with:
- verbs of perception (e.g. *vidēre, audīre* and *sentīre*)
  > *Medicus puerum dormīre videt.* (*l.59*)
  > *cor eius palpitāre sentit.* (*l.112*)
- verbs of speaking (e.g. *dīcere*) and thinking (e.g. *putāre*)
  > *Medicus "puerum dormīre" dīcit.* (*ll.63-64*)
  > *Syra eum mortuum esse putat.* (*l.108*)
- *iubēre*
  > *Dominus servum venīre iubet.*
  > *Medicus Quīntum ōs aperīre atque linguam ostendere iubet.* (*ll.69-70*)
  > *gaudēre* (and with other verbs expressing **mood**)
  > *Syra Quīntum vīvere gaudet* (= *Syra gaudet quod Quīntus vīvit*) (*l.118*)

- *necesse est* (and other **impersonal** expressions)
  Necesse est puer<u>um</u> dormī<u>re</u>. (l.128)

The **accusative and infinitive construction** reports a person's words or thoughts as an **indirect statement**, e.g.:

- Direct statement: *"Puer dormit."*
- Indirect statement: *Medicus "puer<u>um</u> dormī<u>re</u>" dīcit.*

In your text, single quotation marks are used to mark indirect speech, but not reported thoughts or perceptions, e.g. when Syra sees the unconscious Quintus:

- Indirect statement: *Syra e<u>um</u> mortu<u>um</u> <u>esse</u> putat. (l.108)*

In English indirect statement is generally expressed by a clause beginning with "that": "says/thinks/believes that…"

Conjunctions

Atque/ac

The conjunction *atque* has the same function as *et* and *-que*; the shortened form *ac* is often found (see *Chap. XII, l.59*):

- before consonants
- but not before vowels or *h-*

In the following sentences, *ac* could be substituted for *atque*:

> *Quīntus oculōs claudit atque dormit. (l.41)*
> *Medicus ad lectum adit atque puerum aspicit. (ll. 56-57)*

But in this sentence, *ac* could not be substituted because *horret* begins with *h*:

> *Quīntus sanguinem dē bracchiō fluere sentit atque horret. (ll.100-101)*

Neque/nec

Nec, the shortened form of *neque*, is used before consonants as well as vowels:

> *Itaque pedem aegrum habet nec ambulāre potest. (l.54)*

De + ablative

Like *ab*, the preposition *dē* expresses motion "from" (mostly "down from") and takes the ablative:

> *dē arbor<u>e</u> (ll.53-54)*   *dē bracchi<u>ō</u> (l.99)*

Ablative of Respect

The ablative in *ped<u>e</u> aeger* (l. 55) specifies the application of the term *aeger*. It is called **ablative of respect**, as it answers the question "in what respect?"

> *Nēc modo pede, sed etiam capite aeger est. (l.55)*
> Quintus is sick "in his foot" and "in his head."

Lectiō Tertia (Section III)

Posse

We saw in Chapter X that the infinitive of *est sunt* is *esse*; similarly, the infinitive of *potest possunt*, which is formed from *pot- + est sunt* is *posse* (*pot + esse*)

> *Aemilia nōn putat medic<u>um</u> puerum aegrum sānāre <u>posse.</u> (ll.134-135)*

Possessive Adjectives

In Chapter II you learned the possessive adjectives *meus, -a, -um* and *tuus, -a, -um*, and in Chapter IV the reflexive possessive *suus, -a, -um*. Here we see the plural possesive adjectives *noster, tra, trum* (English "our"):

> *Iam fīlius noster nōn modo pede, sed etiam bracchiō aeger est.* (*ll.131-132*)
> *Ille medicus crassus fīlium nostrum sānāre nōn potest.* (*ll.133-134*)

In Chapter XII you will find several examples of the **possessive adjectives** *noster, tra, trum* ("our") and *vester, tra, trum* ("your").

Vocābula Disposita/Ordināta

Nōmina
   1st

gena, -ae	cheek
lingua, -ae	tongue, language
vēna, -ae	vein

   2nd

bracchium, -ī	arm
capillus, -ī	hair
cerebrum, -ī	brain
culter, cultrī	knife
labrum, -ī	lip
medicus, -ī	doctor
membrum, -ī	limb
pōculum, -ī	cup

   3rd

auris, auris (*f.*)	ear
caput, capitis (*n.*)	head
color, colōris (*m.*)	color
cor, cordis (*n.*)	heart
corpus, corporis (*n.*)	body
crus, cruris (*n.*)	leg
frōns, frontis (*f.*)	forehead
iecur, iecoris (*n.*)	liver
ōs, oris (*n.*)	mouth
pectus, pectoris (*n.*)	chest
sanguis, sanguinis (*m.*)	blood
venter, ventris (*m.*)	stomach
viscera, viscerum (*n. pl.*)	internal organs

Verba
   -āre (1)

aegrotat, aegrōtāre	be ill
palpitat, palpitāre	beat, throb
putat, putāre	think, suppose
sānat, sānāre	heal, cure

spectat, spectāre	watch, look at
stat, stāre	stand
-ēre (2)	
deterget, dētergēre	wipe off
dolet, dolēre	hurt, feel pain, grieve
gaudet, gaudēre	be glad, be pleased
horret, horrēre	bristle, shudder (at)
iubet, iubēre	order, tell
sedet, sedēre	sit
-ĕre (3)	
appōnit, appōnere	place (on), serve
arcessit, arcessere	send for, fetch
dīcit, dīcere	say, call, speak
fluit, fluere	flow
tangit, tangere	touch
-īre (4)	
revenit, revenīre	come back
sentit, sentīre	feel, sense, think
irregular	
potest, posse	be able

Adiectīva

1st-2nd (us/er, -a, -um)

aeger, gra, grum	sick, ill
hūmānus, -a, -um	human
noster, nostra, nostrum	our, ours
ruber, rubra, rubrum	red
sānus, -a, -um	healthy, well
stultus, -a, -um	stupid, foolish

Adverbia

bene	well
male	badly, ill
modo	only, just

Praepositiōnēs

dē (*prp. + abl.*)	(down) from, of, about
īnfrā (*prp. + acc.*)	below
super (*prp. + acc.*)	on (top of), above

Coniunctiōnēs

atque	and, as, than
nec	and/but not, nor, not

XII. Mīles Rōmānus

Rēs Grammaticae Novae

1. Verbs
   a. *ferre*
   b. Irregular Imperatives
   c. 3rd Conjugation Vowel Stems
2. Nouns
   a. *tria nōmina*
   b. 4th Declension
   c. *plūrāle tantum*
   d. Case Uses
      i. Dative of Possession
      ii. Dative with Intransitive Verbs
      iii. Partitive Genitive
      iv. Accusative of Extent of Space
3. Adjectives
   a. 3rd Declension Adjectives
   b. Comparison of Adjectives
4. *Mīlle/Mīlia*

The Roman Army

The military played an important part in the Roman world. Above this chapter you find a picture of a *mīles Rōmānus*. The word "military" is derived from *mīles*, whose stem ends in -*t*: gen. *mīlit|is* (so also *pedes -it|is* and *eques -i|tis*).

Lectiō Prīma (Section I)

Dative of Possession

In the sentence *Mārcō ūna soror est* (*l.*6), *Mārcō* is dative. This **dative of possession** with *esse* is used to express to whom something belongs. These two sentences are different ways of expressing the same thing:

Mārcus ūnam sorōrem habet	Marcus has one sister.
Mārcō ūna soror est.	Marcus has one sister, or, in "Latin-ese": there is to Marcus one sister.

In the second sentence, *ūna soror* is nominative, and the dative *Mārcō* tells us "to whom" or "for whom" there is a sister. In English we would still say "Marcus has one sister." Here are more examples:

> *Quod nōmen est patrī? Eī nōmen est Iūlius.* (*ll.9-10*)
> *Aemiliae est ūnus frāter, cui "Aemilius" nōmen est.* (*l.17*)
> *Virō Rōmānō tria nōmina sunt.* (*ll.10-11*)
> *Fīliīs nōmina sunt "Mārcus Iūlius Balbus" et "Quīntus Iūlius Balbus."*
> (*ll.12-13*)

Tria Nōmina: Praenōmen, Nōmen, Cognōmen

Roman men often had three names, called the *tria nōmina*. *Iūlius* is a *nōmen*, or **family name**: male members of this family are called *Iūlius* and female members *Iūlia*. Besides the family name in *-ius* Roman men have a first or personal name, the *praenōmen* (the number of *praenōmina* is quite small: see the list in the margin of page 86 in *Lingua Latina*), and a surname, the *cognōmen*, which is common to a branch of the family. The *cognōmen* is often descriptive of the founder of the family, e.g. *Longus, Pulcher, Crassus; Paulus* means "small" and *Balbus* "stammering."

Irregular Verb: *Ferre*

In the verb *fer|re*, the infinitive ending *-re* is added directly to the consonant-stem; the original *-se* ending (encountered in Chapter X) became *-re* by assimilation to the *r* in *fer*. The endings *-t* and *-tur* are also added directly to the stem:

Infinitive:
> *fer|re*

Singular:
> *fer|t*
> *fer|tur*

Plural:
> *fer|unt*
> *fer|untur*

The imperative has no *-e*:
> *fer!*
> *fer|te!*

E.g.:

> *Mīles est vir quī scūtum et gladium et pīlum fert.* (*ll.33-34*)
> *Aemilius pīlum tantum fert.* (*l.42*)
> *Gladius eius brevis et levis est — brevior et levior quam is quī ab equite fertur.* (*ll.56-57*)
> *Gladiī ... ā Germānīs feruntur.* (*ll.57-58*)
> *Hispānī et Gallī ... et alia arma et arcūs sagittāsque ferunt.* (*ll.90-91*)

Irregular Imperatives

Like *fer!*, a few other verbs have a short imperative:

> *es!* of *esse* (pl. *es|te!*)
> *dūc!* of *dūcere* (pl. *dūc|ite!*)
> *dīc!* of *dīcere* (pl. *dīc |ite!*)
> *fac!* of *facere* (pl. *faci |te!* —*facere* is an *i*-stem: *faci|unt*)

3rd Declension Adjectives

All the adjectives learned so far, e.g. *alb|us -a -um*, follow the 1st and 2nd declensions: the 1st in the feminine (*alb|a*) and the 2nd in the masculine and neuter (*alb|us, alb|um*). A few adjectives, like *niger -gr|a -gr|um*, have *-er*, not *-us*, in the nom. sing. m., (cf. nouns like *liber -br|ī, culter -tr|ī*). Thus:

> *aeger, aegra, aegrum*   *noster, nostra, nostrum*
> *pulcher, pulchra, pulchrum*   *vester, vestra, vestrum*
> *ruber, rubra, rubrum*

There are also **adjectives of the 3rd declension,** one of which (*tenuis*) you met in Chapter X. Some others are:

> *brevis, breve*   *trīstis, trīste*
> *gravis, grave*   *fortis, forte*
> *levis, leve*

In the masculine and feminine these adjectives are declined like *ovis*, **except:**
- *-ī* (not *-e*) in the ablative singular

	sing. masc./fem.	pl. masc./fem.
nom.	*brev|is*	*brev|ēs*
acc.	*brev|em*	*brev|ēs*
gen.	*brev|is*	*brev|ium*
dat.	*brev|ī*	*brev|ibus*
abl.	*brev|ī*	*brev|ibus*

In the neuter they are declined like *mare*:
- *-e* in the nom./acc. singular
- *-ī* in the abl. singular
- *-ia* in the nom./acc. plural
- *-ium* in the gen. plural

	sing. neut.	pl. neut.
nom.	*brev|e*	*brev|ia*
acc.	*brev|e*	*brev|ia*
gen.	*brev|is*	*brev|ium*
dat.	*brev|ī*	*brev|ibus*
abl.	*brev|ī*	brev|ibus

So in the nominative singular we have *gladius brevis*, *hasta brevis* and *pīlum breve*.

Examples:

> *Itaque trīstis est Aemilia. (l.20)*
>
> *Cūr tam brev<u>is</u> est gladi<u>us</u>? Quod gladi<u>us</u> brev<u>is</u> nōn tam grav<u>is</u> est quam gladi<u>us</u> long<u>us</u>. (ll.50-53)*
>
> *Pīl<u>um</u> nostr<u>um</u> brev<u>e</u> et lev<u>e</u> est. (l.134)*
>
> *Mīlitēs Rōmānī fortēs sunt. (ll.118-119)*
>
> *Pīla eōrum brevia et levia sunt, nōn longa et gravia ut Germānōrum. (ll.136-137)*

Lectiō Altera (Section II)

Nouns: 4th Declension

The noun *exercitus* here represents the **4th declension** (*dēclīnātiō quārta*). All the forms are shown in lines 80-89. This declension does not comprise nearly so many words as the first three.

In the singular:

- the accusative has *-um*
- the genitive *-ūs*
- the dative *-uī*
- the ablative *-ū*

In the plural:

- the nominative and accusative end in *-ūs*
- the genitive in *-uum*
- the dative and ablative in *-ibus*.

	sing.		pl.	
nom.	*-us*	*manus*	*-ūs*	*manūs*
acc.	*-um*	*manum*	*-ūs*	*manūs*
gen.	*-ūs*	*manūs*	*-uum*	*manuum*
dat.	*-uī*	*manuī*	*-ibus*	*manibus*
abl.	*-ū*	*manū*	*-ibus*	*manibus*

4th declension nouns are regularly **masculine**, e.g.:

arcus	*metus*
equitātus	*passus*
exercitus	*versus*
impetus	

manus is **feminine** (*du<u>ae</u> manūs*)

Dative with Intransitive Verbs

Intransitive verbs are those that are not completed by an accusative direct object. The verbs *imperāre* and *pārēre* (first introduced in Chapter IV) are intransitive and take the dative (persons whom you command and whom you obey are in the dative). In the following sentences *exercituī* and *ducī* are datives:

Dux exercituī imperat. (l.82)
Exercitus ducī suō pāret. (l.82)
nec Rōmānīs pārent (ll.75-76)
Hispānī et Gallī iam exercitibus nostrīs pārent. (ll.88-89)

Notā Bene: Verbs that are transitive in English are not always transitive in Latin. It can be helpful to memorize intransitive verbs with a dative pronoun (*eī*) to help you remember that they do not take an accusative direct object, e.g.:

imperāre eī
parēre eī

Adjectives: Comparison

A comparison like *Via Latīna nōn tam longa est quam via Appia* can also be expressed *Via Appia longior est quam via Latīna*. *Longior* is a **comparative adjective** (Latin *comparātīvus*, from *comparāre*, "compare") and *quam* here means "than" (as opposed to "as" in *tam...quam* "as...as").

The comparative
- ends in *-ior* in the masculine and feminine (*gladius/hasta longior*)
- ends in *-ius* in the neuter (*pīlum longius*)
- follows the 3rd declension:
  ▷ gen. *-iōr|is*; plural - *iōr|um*
  ▷ nom./acc. pl. *-iōr|ēs* (m./f.) and *-iōr|a* (n.)
  ▷ abl. sing. *-e* (<u>not</u> *-ī*): *-iōr|e*

	sing. masc./fem.	pl. masc./fem.	sing. neut.	pl. neut.
nom.	*brevior|*	*brevior |ēs*	*brevius*	*brevior |a*
acc.	*brevior |em*	*brevior |ēs*	*brevius*	*brevior |a*
gen.	*brevior |is*	*brevior |um*	*brevior|is*	*brevior |um*
dat.	*brevior |ī*	*brevior |ibus*	*brevior|ī*	*brevior|ibus*
abl.	*brevior |e*	*brevior |ibus*	*brevior|e*	*brevior|ibus*

Examples:

Gladius equitis longior et gravior est quam peditis. (ll.53-54)
The sword of the cavalryman is longer and heavier than that [i.e., the sword] of the foot-soldier.

Gladius peditis brevis et levis est — brevior et levior quam is quī ab equite fertur. (ll.56-57)

Etiam gladiī quī ā Germānīs feruntur longiōrēs et graviōrēs sunt quam Rōmānōrum ac pīla eōrum longiōra et graviōra quam nostra sunt. (ll.57-59)

Comparative

sing.	masc./fem.	neut.
nom.	*-ior*	*-ius*
acc.	*-iōrem*	*-ius*
gen.	*-iōris*	
dat.	*-iōrī*	
abl.	*-iōre*	
pl.		
nom./acc.	*-iōrēs*	*-iōra*
gen.	*-iōrum*	
dat./abl.	*-iōribus*	

Genitive Case: Partitive

So far you have encoutered the following uses of the genitive case:
- possession (Chap. II)   *Iūlius domius Mēdī est.*
- with *numerus* (Chap. II)   *Numerus servōrum est centum.*
- with *plēnus* (Chap. VII)   *Hic saccus plēnus mālōrum est.*

In this chapter we see the genitive expressing the whole of which a part (*pars part|is* f.) is taken. It is called **partitive genitive**:

> *Prōvincia est pars imperiī Rōmānī, ut membrum pars corporis est. (ll.64-65)*

Lectiō Tertia (Section III)

Verbs: 3rd Conjugation Vowel Stems

Besides consonant-stems (like *pōn|ere, sūm|ere, dīc|ere*) the 3rd conjugation includes some verbs whose stems end in short *u* or *i*.

U-Stems: The inflection of *u*-stems does not differ from that of consonant-stems., e.g.:

> *flu|ere : fluit, fluunt*
> *metu|ere: metuit, metuunt*

I-Stems: *I*-stems, too, largely agree with consonant-stems, but they are characterized by having *i* before vowel endings, e.g. *-unt*. In Chapter VIII you saw the i-stems *accipiunt* and *aspiciunt*. In this chapter we also see:

> *capi|unt*
> *iaci|unt*
> *fugi|unt*

Notā Bene: *i* changes into *e*
- before *r*, e.g. in the infinitive: *cape|re, iace|re, fuge|re*, stem *capi-, iaci-, fugi-*
- and in final position: *cape! iace! fuge!* (imperative)

Plūrāle Tantum

Here you read about the equipment of a Roman soldier and the layout of a
· Roman army camp: *castra*. This noun is neuter **plural**, called *plūrāle tantum* ("plural
only," cf. "barracks," "entrails," "arms"). Other *plūrāle tantum* nouns:

> *līberī, -ōrum*   *arma, -ōrum*
> *viscera, -um*

Accordingly, though only one camp is meant, you read:

> *castra sunt* (*l.94*)   *in castrīs* (*l.97*)
> *vāllum castrōrum* (*l.101*)

Notā Bene: *Plūrāle tantum* nouns take plural verbs.

Mīlle/mīlia

The common Roman linear measures were:
* *pēs*, "foot" (29.6 cm)
* *passus* = 5 *pedēs* (1.48 m)

In Chapter I you learned *mīlle* (one thousand). *Mīlle passūs* (4th decl.), or "1,000
feet," equals "Roman mile" of 1.48 km, a little less than an English mile ("mile" is
derived from *mīlia*). In the singular, *mīlle* is an **indeclinable adjective**; the plural is
expressed by the **noun** *mīlia -ium* n., e.g. *duo mīlia* (2,000) which is followed by a
partitive genitive:

> *mīlle passūs* (adjective agrees with *passūs*)
> *duo mīlia passuum* (noun + genitive)
> *sex mīlia mīlitum*.
> *Ūnus passus est quīnque pedēs, ergō mīlle passūs sunt*
> *quīnque mīlia pedum*. (*ll.96-97*)

Long distances were given in *mīlia passuum* ("Roman miles").

> *1,000 = mīlle + noun*
> *more than 1,000 = mīlia + partitive genitive*

Accusative of Extent of Space

The accusative without a preposition is used to indicate extent ("how long?"
"how high?"), e.g.:

Gladius duōs pedēs longus est.	The sword is two feet long. (*l.49*)
Aemilius in castrīs habitat mīlle passūs ā fīne imperiī	Aemilius lives in a camp one mile from the boundary of the empire. (*l.93*)
Prope decem pedēs altum est, et duo mīlia passuum longum.	It is almost ten feet high and two miles long. (*ll.102-103*)

Recensiō: 3rd Declension Ablative Singular in -ī and -e

Ends in *-e*
* consonant-stem nouns of all genders:
  > *pastor* (m.) abl.: *pastōre*
  > *vōx* (f.) abl.: *vōce*
  > *nōmen* (n.) abl.: *nōmine*

- masculine and feminine *i*-stem nouns:
    mōns (m.) abl.: *monte*
    nūbēs (f.) abl.: *nūbe*
- comparative adjectives of all genders
    brevior, brevius (from *brevis, breve*): abl.: *breviōre*
    longior, longius (from *longus, longa, longum*): abl.: *longiōre*

Ends in *-ī*
- neuter *i-stem* nouns
    mare (n.) abl.: *marī*
- positive adjectives of all genders
    brevis, breve: abl.: *brevī*
    gravis, grave: abl.: *gravī*

Vocābula Disposita/Ordināta

Nōmina
1st
fossa, -ae	ditch, trench
hasta, -ae	lance
patria, -ae	native country/town
sagitta, -ae	arrow

2nd
adiectīvum (nomen)	adjective
avunculus, -ī	(maternal) uncle
arma, -ōrum (*n. pl.*)	arms
bellum, -ī	war
castra, -ōrum (*n. pl.*)	camp
comparātīvus, -ī (gradus)	comparative
gladius, -ī	sword
pīlum, -ī	spear, javelin
pugnus, -ī	fist
scūtum, -ī	shield
vāllum, -ī	rampart

3rd
cognōmen, -inis (*n.*)	surname
dux, ducis (*m.*)	leader, chief, general
eques, equitis (*m.*)	horseman
frāter, frātris (*m.*)	brother
fīnis, fīnis (*m.*)	boundary, limit, end
hostis, hostis (*m.*)	enemy
lātus, lāteris (*n.*)	side, flank
mīles, mīlitis (*m.*)	soldier
mīlia, mīlium (*n.*)	thousand
nōmen, nōminis (*n.*)	name
pars, partis (*f.*)	part, direction
pedes, peditis (*m.*)	footsoldier

praenōmen, parenōminis (*n.*)	first name
soror, sorōris (*f.*)	sister
4th	
arcus, arcūs	bow
equitātus, equitātūs	cavalry
exercitus, exercitūs	army
impetus, impetūs	attack, charge
metus, metūs	fear
passus, passūs	pace
versus, versūs	line, verse

Verba

-āre (1)

pugnat, pugnāre	fight
mīlitat, mīlitāre	serve as a soldier
expugnat, expugnāre	conquer
oppugnat, oppugnant	attack

-ere (3)

Consonant-stem

incolit, incolunt	inhabit
dividit, dividunt	divide
metuit, metuere	fear
dēfendit, dēfendere	defend

i-stem

iacit, iacere	throw, hurl
fugit, fugere	run away, flee

Irregular

fert, ferre	carry, bring, bear

Adiectīva

1st-2nd (us/er, -a, -um)

altus, -a, -um	high, tall, deep
armātus, -a, -um	armed
barbarus, -a, -um	foreign, barbarian
vester, -tra, -trum	your, yours

3rd

brevis, -e	short
fortis, -e	strong, brave
gravis, -e	heavy, severe, grave
levis, -e	light, slight
trīstis, -e	sad

Praepositiōnēs

contrā (*prp. + acc.*)	against

Coniunctiōnēs

ac	and, as, than

XIII. Annus et Mēnsēs

Rēs Grammaticae Novae

1. Verbs
   a. Preterite (Imperfect) Tense
   b. *dīcitur* + Nominative Infinitive
   c. Infinitive *velle*
2. Nouns
   a. Case Uses
      i. Ablative of Time When
      ii. Accusative of Duration of Time
   b. 5th Declension
   c. *māne* (noun/adverb)
3. Adjectives
   a. Names of the Months
   b. Comparison of Adjectives
      i. Positive
      ii. Comparative
      iii. Superlative
   c. Numerals
      i. Cardinals
      ii. Ordinals
      iii. Fractions
4. Conjunction: *vel*

Roman Calendar

Today we still use a version of Roman calendar, as it was reformed by Julius Caesar in 46 B.C., with twelve months and 365 days (366 in leap years). Before this reform, only four months—March, May, July and October—had 31 days, while February had 28, and the other months only 29. This made a total of 355 days. It was therefore necessary at intervals to put in an extra month. The Julian calendar was revised under Pope Gregory XIII in 1582 (creating the Gregorian calendar).

As you learn from the reading, in the oldest Roman calendar March was the first month of the year. This explains the names *September, Octōber, November* and *December*, which are clearly formed from the numerals *septem, octō, novem, decem*. The fifth month in the old calendar was called *Quīntīlis* (from *quīntus*), but after the death of Julius Caesar it was renamed *Iūlius* in memory of him. In the year 8 B.C., the following month, which until then had been called *Sextīlis* (from *sextus*), was given the name of the Roman emperor *Augustus*.

Lectiō Prīma (Section I)

Fifth Declension Nouns

The noun *diēs*, gen. *diēī*, here represents the **5th declension** (Latin *dēclīnātiō quīnta*). Only a few nouns belong to the 5th declension. The complete paradigm is shown below and on page 101 in *Lingua Latina*.

- 5th declension nouns have stems in *ē*, which is kept before all endings (but shortened in *-em*).
- Most 5th declension nouns have *-iēs* in the nominative, like:
    diēs
    merīdiēs
    faciēs
    glaciēs
- A few have a consonant before *-ēs* (and short *e* in gen./dat. sing. *-ēi*), e.g. the common word *rēs*, gen. *reī* ("thing," "matter"), which turns up in the next chapter.
- The nouns of this declension are feminine except for *diēs* (and *merī-diēs*) which is masculine. (In special senses and in late Latin *diēs* is feminine).

	sing.	pl.
nom.	di|ēs	di|ēs
acc.	di|em	di|ēs
gen.	di|ēī	di|ērum
dat.	di|ēī	di|ēbus
abl.	di|ē	di|ēbus

Recensiō: Declensions

You have now learned all **five declensions**. The classification is based on the (original) final stem-vowel:

1st declension: *a*-stems, e.g. *āla*, gen. sing. *-ae*

2nd declension: *o*-stems, e.g. *equus, ōvum*
- the "u" in the ending of these nouns was originally an "o"
    equus < equo\|s
    ōvum < ōvo\|m, gen. sing. *-ī* (*<-oi*)

3rd declension: consonant-stems and *i*-stems, e.g. *sōl, ovi\|s*, gen. sing. *-is*

4th declension: *u*-stems, e.g. *lacu\|s*, gen. sing. *-ūs*

5th declension: *ē*-stems, e.g. *diē\|s, rē\|s*, gen. sing. *-ēī, -eī*

Māne

The neuter noun *māne* is **indeclinable** (also used as an adverb: Chap. XIV, 1.55).

Prīma pars diēī est māne, pars postrēma vesper. (ll.35-36)
Nox est tempus ā vesperō ad māne. (l.37)

Calendar: Names of the Months

The names of the months are **adjectives**: *mēnsis Iānuārius*, etc.
- They are often used alone without *mēnsis*.
- Most of the months are 1st/2nd declension (e.g. *Iānuārius, -a, -um*).
- 3rd declension:
    Aprīlis, is
    September, Octōber, November, December

    o Nominative masculine singular: *-ber* (without *-is*), gen. *-br|is*.
    o Ablative in *-ī*: *(mense) Aprīlī, Septembrī, Octōbrī*, etc.

Expressions of Time

To express **time when** the ablative (*ablātīvus temporis*) without a preposition is used:

mēnse Decembrī	in the month of December
illō tempore	at that time
hōrā prīmā	at the first hour

Tempore antīquō Mārtius mēnsis prīmus erat. (ll.17-19)
Nocte sōl nōn lūcet. (l.46)
Vēre campī novā herbā operiuntur. (l.92)
"Quandō sōl altissimus est?" "Hōrā sextā vel merīdiē." (ll.107-108)

Time **how long** (duration) is expressed by the accusative:

centum annōs vīvere (ll.10-11)

Numerals

Of the Latin **numerals** you already know the **cardinals** 1-10:

ūn|us, -a, -um	*sex*
du|o, -ae, -o	*septem*
tr|ēs, -ia	*octō*
quattuor	*novem*
quīnque	*decem*

and the **ordinals** 1st-4th. In numbering the months the first twelve ordinals are needed:

prīm|us, -a, -um	*septim|us, -a, -um*
secund|us, -a, -um	*octāv|us, -a, -um*
terti|us, -a, -um	*nōn|us, -a, -um*
quārt|us, -a, -um	*decim|us, -a, -um*
quīnt|us, -a, -um	*ūndecim|us, -a, -um*
sext|us, -a, -um	*duodecim|us, -a, -um*

The ordinals are also combined with *pars* to form **fractions**:

⅓ *tertia pars*
¼ *quārta pars*
⅕ *quīnta pars* etc.
Notā bene: ½ *dīmidia pars*

Verbs: Preterite (Imperfect) Tense

The forms *erat erant* are used instead of *est sunt* when the past is concerned. Compare the sentences:

Tunc (= *illō tempore*) *Mārtius mēnsis prīmus erat.*
Nunc (= *hōc tempore*) *Mārtius mēnsis tertius est.*

Erat erant is called the **imperfect tense,** or *preterite* while *est sunt* is the **present tense** ("tense" comes from Latin *tempus*). The past tense of other verbs comes later (Chapter XIX).

Comparison of Adjectives

Consider the following examples:

Februārius brevis est.
Februārius brevior est quam Iānuārius.
Februārius mēnsis annī brevissimus est.

Brevis (**positive degree**)
- simply describes or limits the noun "February"
- ends in:
   -*us, -a, -um* (e.g. *longus, -a, -um*)
   -*is, -e* (e.g., *brevis, -e*)
   (other endings will be learned later)

Brevior (**comparative degree**) of *brevis*
- it compares February with January
- ends in:
   -*ior, -ius* (e.g. *longior, longius, brevior, brevius*)

Brevissimus (**superlative degree**) (Latin *superlātīvus*) of *brevis*:
- compares February with all the other months of the year
- ends in:
   -*issimus, -a, -um* (e.g. *longissimus, -a, -um, brevissimus, -a, -um*)

Quam

Lines 25-30 illustrate the three degrees as well as different uses of *quam*:

Quam (=how) *longus* (positive degree) *est mēnsis November?*
November trīgintā diēs longus est. December ūnum et trīgintā diēs habet.

Iānuārius tam longus est quam (=as…as) *December, sed Februārius brevior* (comparative degree) *est: duodētrīgintā aut ūndētrīgintā diēs tantum habet.*

Februārius brevior (comparative degree) *est quam* (= than) *cēterī ūndecim mēnsēs: is mēnsis annī brevissimus* (superlative degree) *est.*

Vel

The conjunction *vel* is originally the imperative of *velle*; it implies a free choice between two expressions or possibilities:

> *duodecim mēnsēs vel trecentōs sexāgintā quīsque diēs* (l.7)
> *centum annī vel saeculum* (l.9)
> *hōra sexta vel merīdiēs* (l.43)

Vel is distinct from *aut*, which is put between mutually exclusive alternatives:

> *duodētrīgintā aut ūndētrīgintā diēs* (l.28)

Lectiō Altera (Section II)
Roman Calendar: Divisons of the Month

Three days in each month had special names; they are all feminine plurals:

kalendae	the 1st
īdūs	the 13th (*īdūs -uum* 4th decl.)
nōnae	the 5th (the 9th day before *īdūs*: inclusive reckoning)

In March, May, July and October (the four months that originally had 31 days):

īdūs was the 15th
nōnae consequently the 7th

The following mnemonic may help:

> In March, July, October, May
> The IDES fall on the fifteenth day,
> The NONES the seventh; all besides
> Have two days less for Nones and Ides.

To these names (*kalendae*, *īdūs* and *nōnae*), the names of the months are added as adjectives. Thus:

January 1st	*kalendae Iānuāriae*
January 5th	*nōnae Iānuāriae*
January 13th	*īdūs Iānuāriae*

Ablative of Time When

Dates are given in the ***ablātīvus temporis***, e.g.:

kalendīs Iānuāriīs	"on January 1st"
īdibus Mārtiīs	"on March 15th"

Other dates were indicated by stating the number of days before the following *kalendae, nōnae* or *īdūs*. The Romans counted inclusively; that is, they counted the beginning and ending day, e.g.; since April 21st (Rome's birthday) is the 11th day before *kalendae Māiae* (inclusive reckoning), it should therefore be:

> *diēs ūndecimus ante kalendās Māiās*

but *ante* being illogically put first, it became a set phrase with all the words in the accusative:

> *ante diem ūndecimum kalendās Māiās*
> usually shortened *a. d. XI kal. Māi*

Dīcitur + **Nominative and Infinitive**

Note the passive *dīcitur* with an infinitive and the *nominative* case:

Lūn*a* "nov*a*" *esse* dīc*itur*. (*l.52*, "is said to be…")

Compare the same thought using the active verb (*dīcunt*) with the accusative and infinitive construction you learned in Chapter XI:

(*Hominēs*) lūn*am* "nov*am*" *esse* dīc*unt*.

When used with a predicate nominative *dīcitur* is closer in meaning to "is called."

Diēs prīmus mēnsis Iānuāriī <u>dīcitur</u> "kalendae Iānuāriae." (*ll.56-57*)

Item "īdūs Februāriae" dīcitur diēs tertius decimus mēnsis Februāriī. (*ll.64-65*)

Diēs octāvus ante kalendās Iānuāriās, quī <u>dīcitur</u> "ante diem octāvum kalendās Iānuāriās," est diēs annī brevissimus. (*ll.72-74*)

Lectiō Tertia (Section III)

Velle

The infinitive of *vult volunt* has the irregular form *velle*, as appears from the acc. + inf. in:

Aemilia puerum dormīre <u>velle</u> putat. (*l.140*)

Recensiō: **Expressions of Time and Space: Ablative and Accusative**

The ablative represents a point in space or time:

- Space: Where?

    Diēs est dum sōl <u>in caelō</u> est. (*l.35*)

    <u>In Germāniā</u> hiemēs frīgidiōrēs sunt quam <u>in Italiā</u>. (*ll.95-96*)

- Time: When? During what time?

    <u>Aestāte</u> diēs longī sunt, sōl lūcet, āēr calidus est. (*l.87*)

    <u>Hōc</u> annī <u>tempore</u> diēs nōn tam calidī sunt quam aestāte et noctēs frīgidiōrēs sunt. (*ll.120-121*)

The accusative represents movement through a block of space or time.

- Space: How long? How high? How deep?

    Gladius <u>duōs pedēs</u> longus est. (*Chap. XII, l.49*)

    vāllum castrōrum…prope <u>decem pedēs</u> altum est, et <u>duo mīlia passuum</u> longum. (*Chap. XII, ll.101-103*)

- Time: How long?

    November <u>trīgintā diēs</u> longus est. (*ll.25-26*)

    Mārtius <u>ūnum et trīgintā diēs</u> longus est. (*ll.30-31*)

In both cases the **accusative** expresses movement through space/time from point A to point B, unlike the **ablative**, which expresses a point in space/time.

Vocābula Disposita/Ordināta

Nōmina

   1st

fōrma, -ae	form, shape, figure
hōra, -ae	hour
kalendae, -ārum (*pl.*)	the 1st of the month
lūna, -ae	moon
nōnae, -ārum (*pl.*)	5th/7th of the month
stēlla, -ae	star

   2nd

aequinoctium, -ī	equinox
annus, -ī	year
autumnus, -ī	autumn
initium, -ī	beginning
saeculum, -ī	century
superlātīvus, -ī (gradus)	superlative
vesper, vesperī	evening

   3rd

aestās, aestātis (*f.*)	summer
hiems, hiemis (*f.*)	winter
imber, imbris (*m.*)	rain, shower
lūx, lūcis (*f.*)	light, daylight
mēnsis, mēnsis (*m.*)	month
nix, nivis (*f.*)	snow
nox, noctis (*f.*)	night
tempus, temporis (*n.*)	time
urbs, urbis (*f.*)	city
vēr, vēris (*n.*)	spring

   4th

īdūs, īduum (*f. pl.*)	13th/15th of the month
lacus, -ūs	lake

   5th

diēs, -ēī, (*m.*)	day, date
faciēs, -ēī	face
glaciēs, -ēī	ice
merīdiēs, -ēī (*m.*)	midday, noon, south

   Indeclinable

māne	morning

Verba

   -āre (1)

illūstrat, illūstrāre	illustrate, make clear
nōminat, nōmināre	name, call

   -ere (3)

   i-stem

incipit, incipere	begin

-īre (4)
operit, operīre   cover
Irregular
erat, erant   was, were
vult, velle   want, be willing

Adiectīva
    1st-2nd (us/er, -a, -um)
    aequus, -a, -um   equal, calm
    calidus, -a, -um   warm, hot, *f.* hot water
    clārus, -a, -um   bright, clear, loud
    decimus, -a, -um   tenth
    dīmidius, -a, -um   half
    duodecimus, -a, -um   twelfth
    exiguus, -a, -um   small, scanty
    frīgidus, -a, -um   cold, chilly, cool
    nōnus, -a, -um   ninth
    obscūrus, -a, -um   dark
    octāvus, -a, -um   eighth
    postrēmus, -a, -um   last
    quīntus, -a, -um   fifth
    septimus, -a, -um   seventh
    sextus, -a, -um   sixth
    tōtus, -a, -um   the whole of, all
    ūndecimus, -a, -um   eleventh
    3rd
    indēclīnābilis, -e   indeclinable

Numerī (indecl. unless otherwise noted)
    ducentī, -ae, -a   two hundred
    sexāgintā   sixty
    trecentī, -ae, -a   three hundred
    trīgintā   thirty
    ūndecim   eleven

Adverbia
    item   likewise, also
    māne   in the morning
    nunc   now
    quandō   when, as
    tunc   then

Coniunctiōnēs
    igitur   therefore, then, so
    vel   or

XIV. Novus Diēs

Rēs Grammaticae Novae

1. Verbs: *inquit, inquiunt*
2. Nouns: Case Uses
   a. Dative of Interest (*datīvus commodī*)
   b. Ablative of Attendant Circumstances
3. Present Participles (*participium praesēns*)
4. Adjectives
   a. *omnis -e*
   b. Numbers *duo, duae, duo* (ablative)
   c. *uter, neuter, alter, uterque*
5. Pronouns: *mihi, mē, tibi, tē* (dative/ablative)
6. Points of Style: *sē habēre*

The New Day

At dawn Marcus is roused from his morning slumbers by Davus, who also sees to it that he washes properly before putting on his *tunica* and *toga*, the clothes that were the mark of freeborn Roman men and boys.

Lectiō Prīma (Section I)

Uter, neuter, alter, uterque

Among the new words in this chapter is a group of words that are used only when **two** persons or things are concerned; they can be used as adjectives or pronouns:

uter?	which (of the two)?
neuter	neither (of the two)
alter	the other (of the two)
uterque	each (of the two)

Uter, utra, utrum is the interrogative used when there are only two alternatives ("which of the two?"), e.g.:

> *Uter puer, Mārcusne an Quīntus?*   (the conjunction *an*, not *aut*, is put between the two in question)

The answer may be:

1. *neuter, -tra, -trum* ("neither"), e.g. *neuter puer, nec Mārcus nec Quīntus*
2. *alter, -era, -erum* ("one"/"the other"), e.g. *alter puer, aut M. aut Q.*
3. *uter-, utra-, utrum- que* ("each of the two"), e.g. *uterque puer, et M. et Q*

Uterque

Where English prefers "both" followed by the plural ("both boys"), Latin has the singular *uterque*:

> *Uterque puer cubat in cubiculō parvō, neuter in cubiculō magnō.* (*ll.8-9*)
> *Uterque puer quiētus est, neuter puer sē movet.* (*ll.10-11*)

Uterque is singular and followed by a singular verb; the verb is also in the singular even if there are two subjects separated by *neque...neque, aut...aut* or *et...et*, as in:

> *et caput et pēs eī dolet* (*ll.3-4*)
> *nec caput nec pēs dolet* (*l.66*)

The general rule is that two or more subjects:

- take a verb in the plural if they denote **persons**
- if the subjects are **things**, the verb agrees with the nearest subject, as in
  pēs et caput eī dolet (*l.3-4, 64*)

Dative of Interest

In the last example (*pēs et caput eī dolet*) the dative *eī* denotes the person concerned, benefited or harmed. This use of the dative is called the **dative of interest** (*datīvus commodī*), e.g.:

> *Bracchium quoque dolet Quīntō.* (*l.4*)
> *Multīs barbarīs magna pars corporis nūda est.* (*ll.76-77*)

Duo, duae, duo

The ablative of *duo, duae, duo* is:

- masculine and neuter *duōbus*

  > *ē duōbus puerīs* (*ll.11-12*)
  > *in duōbus cubiculīs*

- feminine *duābus*

  > *ē duābus fenestrīs* (*l.16*)

Ablative of Attendant Circumstances

A noun and an adjective in the ablative can show the conditions surrounding the verb, as in:

> *Mārcus fenestrā apertā dormit.*   "with the window open" (*l.15*)
> *Is fenestrā clausā dormit.*   "with the window shut" (*l.18*)
> *Quīntus, quī oculīs apertīs iacet*   "with his eyes open" (*ll.21-22*)

Notice that the noun comes first; this is the case unless the adjective is being emphasized.

Participium Praesēns (Present Participle)

On page 104 a new form of the *verb* is introduced, the **participle** (Latin *participium*) ending in -(*ē*)*ns*:

> *puer dormiēns = puer quī dormit (ll.22-23)*
> *puer vigilāns = puer quī vigilat (l.23)*

The participle, being part verb and part adjective, was called <u>*participium*</u> (< *pars partis*). The participle:

- is a 3rd declension **adjective** with the same ending in the nōminative singular of all genders.
  > *vigilāns*, gen. -*ant|is*
  > *dormiēns*, gen. -*ent|is*

- keeps **verbal** functions, e.g.
  - ▷ it may take an object in the accusative:
    > *Dāvus cubicul<u>um</u> intrā<u>ns</u> interrogat...* (*l.25*)

- has an **ablative singular** in -*e* when it has verbal force, e.g.:
  > *Parentēs ā fīliō intrant<u>e</u> salūtantur.* (*l.91*)

- has an **ablative singular** in -*ī* only when used only as an adjective, with no verbal force:

ibi nocte silentī Ariadnam	He left Ariadne sleeping there during
dormientem reliquit.	the silent night. (*Chap. XXV, ll.99-100*)

> *Silentī* is the ablative of the present participle of *silēre*. Here it is being used only as an adjective describing the night and has no verbal force.

participle

	m./f.	n.
nom.	-*ns*	-*ns*
acc.	-*ntem*	-*ns*
gen.	-*ntis*	
dat.	-*ntī*	
abl.	-*nte/-ntī*	
pl.		
nom./acc.	-*ntēs*	-*ntia*
gen.	-*ntium*	
dat./abl.	-*ntibus*	

Lectiō Altera (Section II)

Personal Pronouns: Dative and Ablative

Mihi and *tibi* are the **datives** corresponding to the accusatives *mē* and *tē*:

> *"Affer <u>mihi</u> aquam!"* (*l.43*)
> *"<u>Mihi</u> quoque caput dolet!"* (*l.65*)
> *"<u>Tibi</u> nec caput nec pēs dolet!"* (*l.66*)

The **ablative** of these pronouns is identical with the accusative: *mē, tē*. When used as the object of the preposition *cum*, the preposition is suffixed:

> *mē-cum*
> *tē-cum*
> *sē-cum*

For example:

> *Dāvus eum <u>sēcum</u> venīre iubet: "Venī <u>mēcum</u>!"* (*ll.86-87*)
> *"Mēdus <u>tēcum</u> īre nōn potest."* (*l.117*)
> *"Alterum <u>tēcum</u> fer!"* (*l.108*)
> *"Cūr ille servus mēcum venīre nōn potest ut solet?"* (*l.120*)
> *"...stilum rēgulamque sēcum ferēns ē vīllā abit."* (*ll.127-128*)

acc.	*mē*	*tē*
dat.	*mihi*	*tibi*
abl.	*mē*	*tē*

Inquit

The verb *inquit*, "(he/she) says," is inserted after one or more words of **direct** speech:

> *"Hōra prīma est" <u>inquit</u> Dāvus, "Surge ē lectō!"* (*l.40*)
> *Servus Mārcō aquam affert et "Ecce aqua" <u>inquit.</u>* (*l.44*)

It is a **defective** verb: only *inquit inquiunt* and a few other forms of the indicative occur. Neither *inquit* nor *inquiunt* is used to begin accusative + infinitive constructions.

Lectiō Tertia (Section III)

Omnis -e

The opposite of *nūllus* is *omnis, -e* ("every," "all"), which more often appears in the plural *omnēs, -ia* (see lines 115 and 119).

Used without a noun the plural *omnēs* ("everybody") is the opposite of *nēmō* ("nobody") and the neuter plural *omnia* ("everything") is the opposite of *nihil* ("nothing").

> omnis ↔ nūllus
> omnēs ↔ nēmō
> omnia ↔ nihil

Points of Style: *sē hābēre*

Davus asks Quintus: *Quōmodo sē habet pēs tuus hodiē?* (*ll.25-26*): "How is your foot today?" Quintus answers *"Pēs male sē habet"* (*l.27*). *Sē habēre* + adverb = to be in a certain state, and is a regular way of asking how, as we say in English, "someone is doing."

Vocābula Disposita/Ordināta

Nōmina

1st

rēgula, -ae	ruler
tabula, -ae	writing tablet
toga, -ae	toga
tunica, -ae	tunic

2nd

calceus, -ī	shoe
gallus, -ī	cock, rooster
participium, -ī	participle
stilus, -ī	stylus
vestīmentum, -ī	garment, clothing

3rd

parentēs, -um (*m. pl.*)	parents

5th

rēs, reī (*f.*)	thing, matter, affair

Verba

-āre (1)

cubat, cubāre	lie (in bed)
vigilat, vigilāre	be awake
excitat, excitāre	wake up, arouse
lavat, lavāre	wash, bathe

-ēre (2)

valet, valēre	be strong, be well
solet, solēre	be accustomed
frīget, frīgēre	be cold

-ere (3)

Consonant-stem

surgit, surgere	rise, get up
affert, afferre	bring (to, forward)
mergit, mergere	dip, plunge, sink
poscit, poscere	demand, call for
induit, induere	put on (clothes)
gerit, gerere	carry, wear, carry on, do

-īre (4)

vestit, vestīre	dress

Irregular

inquit, inquiunt	(he/she) says/said

Adiectīva

1st-2nd (us/er, -a, -um)

apertus, -a, -um	open
clausus, -a, -um	closed, shut
sordidus, -a, -um	dirty, mean, base
pūrus, -a, -um	clean, pure

nūdus, -a, -um	naked
togātus, -a, -um	wearing the toga
dexter, -tra, -trum	right, *f.* the right (hand)
sinister, -tra, -trum	left, *f.* the left (hand)
neuter, -tra, -trum	neither
alter, -era, -erum	one, the other, second
uter, -tra, -trum	which (of the two)
uterque, utraque, utrumque	each of the two
3rd	
omnis, -e	all, every

Pronōmina

mihi	I, me, myself
tibi	you, yourself
mēcum	with me
tēcum	with you
sēcum	with himself/herself

Adverbia

prīmum	first
nihil/nil	nothing
quōmodo	how
hodiē	today
adhūc	so far, till now, still
deinde/dein	afterward, then

Praepositiōnēs

praeter (*prp.* + *acc.*)	past, besides, except

Coniunctiōnēs

an	or

Alia

valē, valēte	farewell, goodbye

XV. Magister et Discipulī

Rēs Grammaticae Novae

1. Verbs
   a. Personal Endings: 1st and 2nd Person
   b. *esse*
   c. *posse*
   d. Impersonal Verbs
      i. *convenit*
      ii. *licet*
2. Nouns: Case Uses
   a. Accusative of Exclamation
3. Pronouns
   a. Personal Pronouns
   b. Pronouns vs. Possessive Adjectives
   c. Reflexives in Indirect Statement

Going to School in Ancient Rome

Rome had no public school system. Parents who could afford it sent their young children to an elementary school, *lūdus*. It was run as a private enterprise by a *lūdī magister*, who taught the children reading, writing and arithmetic. We now follow Marcus to school. His teacher tries his best to maintain discipline, but he has some difficulty in keeping these boys in hand.

Lectiō Prīma (Section I)
Personal Endings: 1st and 2nd Person Singular

From the conversation between the teacher and his pupils you learn that the verbs have different endings as one speaks about oneself (**1st person**), addresses another person (**2nd person**), or speaks about someone else (**3rd person**).

The dialogue in lines 35-40 illustrates the 1st, 2nd, and 3rd singular endings:

Titus, quī librum nōn habet, "<u>Ego</u> librum nōn habe<u>ō</u>."

Magister: *"Quid? Sext<u>us</u> librum suum habe<u>t</u>, <u>tū</u> librum tuum nōn habē<u>s</u>? Cūr librum nōn habē<u>s</u>?"*

Titus: *"Librum nōn habe<u>ō</u>, quod Mārc<u>us</u> meum librum habe<u>t</u>."*

It appears from this that in the singular:

- the 1st person of the verb ends in *-ō* (*habe|ō*)
- the 2nd in *-s* (*habē|s*)
- the 3rd, as you know, in *-t* (*habe|t*)

Personal Pronouns

The verbs in the above examples are preceded by **personal pronouns** in the nominative:

ego	1st pers. sing.	*nōs*	1st pers. pl.
tū	2nd pers. sing.	*vōs*	2nd pers. pl.

But these pronouns are only used when the subject is emphasized, for example (*ll.24-26*):

Sextus: *"Num <u>ego</u> discipulus improbus sum?"*

Magister: *"Immō <u>tū</u> probus es discipulus, Sexte, at Mārcus et Quīntus et Titus improbī sunt!"*

Normally the personal ending is sufficient to show which person is meant, as in these examples (*ll.38-39*):

Magister: *"Cūr librum nōn habē<u>s</u>?"*

Titus: *"Librum nōn habe<u>ō</u>."*

Accusative of Exclamation

Diodorus expresses his frustration with the students in two different ways:

"Ō, discipul<u>ōs</u> improb<u>ōs</u>...!" (*l.23*)

"Ō improb<u>ī</u> discipul<u>ī</u>!" (*ll.101-102*, voc. pl. = nom. pl.)

The first example (*Ō, discipul<u>ōs</u> improb<u>ōs</u>*) is in the accusative, the second (*Ō improbī discipulī!*) in the vocative. What's the difference? The vocative is used to address those present, while the accusative (called the **accusative of exclamation**) exclaims **about** more than **to** the students.

Esse

The verb *esse* is irregular; in the singular it runs:

sum
es
est

Example:

"Cūr tū sōlus <u>es</u>, Sexte?" "Ego sōlus <u>sum</u>." (*ll.20-21*)

Lectiō Altera (Section II)

Personal Endings: 1st and 2nd Person Plural

The dialogue in lines 51-57 illustrates the 1st and 2nd plural endings:

> *Mārcus (ad Sextum et Titum): "Vōs iānuam nōn pulsātis cum ad lūdum venītis, nec magistrum salūtātis cum eum vidētis. Audītisne id quod dīcō?"*

> *Tum Sextus et Titus "Id quod dīcis" inquiunt "vērum nōn est: nōs iānuam pulsāmus cum ad lūdum venīmus, et magistrum salūtāmus cum eum vidēmus. Nōnne vērum dīcimus, magister?"*

It appears from this that in the plural:

- the 1st person ends in *-mus* (*pulsā|mus, vidē|mus, venī|mus*)
- the 2nd in *-tis* (*pulsā|tis, vidē|tis, dīc|itis venī|tis*)
- the 3rd, as you know, in *-nt*.

The examples in the section GRAMMATICA LATINA in LINGUA LATINA show how these **personal endings** are added to the various stems in the **present tense**.

Personal Pronouns (continued)

The plural of the **personal pronouns** in the nominative:

nōs   1st. pers. pl.
vōs   2nd pers. pl.

The accusative of *ego* and *tū* is *mē* and *tē*, but *nōs* and *vōs* are the same in the accusative (*ll.119-120*):

> *"Quid nōs verberās, magister?"*
> *"Vōs verberō."*

	sing.	pl.	sing.	pl.
nom.	ego	nōs	tū	vōs
acc.	mē	nōs	tē	vōs

Overview of Present Active Endings

1st   *-ō, -mus*
2nd   *-s, -tis*
3rd   *-t, -nt*

Notā Bene:

- before *-ō*
  - ▷ *ā* is dropped: *puls|ō* (stem *pulsā*)
  - ▷ *ē* and *ī* shortened: *habe|ō, veni|ō* (stems *habe-, veni-*)
- in 3rd conjugation consonant-stems, a short *i* is inserted before:
  - ▷ *-s: dīc|is* (stem *dīc-*)
  - ▷ *-mus: dīc|imus*
  - ▷ *-tis: dīc|itis*
  - ▷ *-t: dīc|it*

- in 3rd conjugation *i*-stems, a short *i* appears before the endings:

  ▷ *-ō* : *faci|ō* (stem *faci-*)

  ▷ *-unt*: *faci|unt*

  ▷ Other verbs of this kind which you have met are *accipere, aspicere, capere, fugere, iacere, incipere, parere.*

	1st	2nd	3rd cons.	3rd i-stem	4th
sing. 1	*puls|ō*	*habe|ō*	*dīc|ō*	*faci|ō*	*veni|ō*
2	*pulsā|s*	*habē|s*	*dīc|is*	*faci|s*	*venī|s*
3	*pulsa|t*	*habe|t*	*dīc|it*	*faci|t*	*veni|t*
pl. 1	*pulsā|mus*	*habē|mus*	*dīc|imus*	*faci|mus*	*venī|mus*
2	*pulsā|tis*	*habē|tis*	*dīc|itis*	*faci|tis*	*venī|tis*
3	*pulsa|nt*	*habe|nt*	*dīc|unt*	*faci|unt*	*veni|unt*

The Reflexive in Indirect Speech

Much of the time, changing direct to indirect speech is pretty straightforward. When reporting in acc. inf. (indirect speech) what a person says in the 1st person, however, the subject accusative is the reflexive *sē*. This is best learned by studying several examples. We have already read an example in Chapter XIV:

> *Dāvus...eum sēcum venīre iubet*: "*Venī mēcum!*": Davus orders him (Marcus) to come with him (Davus): Come with me! (*Chap. XIV, l.87*)

> *Quīntus*: "*(Ego) aeger sum*" is reported by Marcus: *Quīntus dīcit "sē aegrum esse.*" Quintus says that he is sick. (*l.82*)

> *Mārcus*: "*Ego eius librum habeō.*" becomes *Mārcus dīcit "sē eius librum habēre.*"

> *Mārcus*: "*Ego*" *inquit* "*nōn dormiō*" becomes *Mārcus dīcit "sē nōn dormīre.*"

> *Sextus et Titus*: "*Neque nōs dormīmus*" *inquiunt*, "*Vigilāmus et omnia verba tua audīmus* becomes *Sextus et Titus dīcunt "sē nōn dormīre; sē vigilāre et omnia verba eius audīre.*"

Esse (continued)

The verb *esse* is irregular; in the plural it runs:

> *sumus*
> *estis*
> *sunt*

Example:

> "*Ubi estis, puerī?*" "*In lūdō sumus.*" (*ll.113-114*)

Convenit

We first met *convenit* in Chapter VIII (see Points of Style in that chapter). *Convenit* is an **impersonal** verb from *convenīre*, i.e. only found in the 3rd person singular. It is often combined the dative case and an infinitive:

> *Tergum dolet Mārcō, neque ille lacrimat, nam lacrimāre puerō Rōmānō nōn convenit.* (*ll.62-64*)

Posse

Compounds of *esse* show the same irregular forms. As you learned in Chapter X, the "*pot*" of the verb:

- remains before the vowel "*e*" in *potes, potest*
- becomes "*pos*" before "*s*" in *possum*

In the singular *posse* runs:

> pos-<u>sum</u>
> pot-<u>es</u>
> pot-<u>est</u>

Examples (*ll.72-73*):

> *Mārcus: "Non cōnsīdō, quod sedere nōn possum."*
> *Diodōrus: "Cūr sedēre nōn potes?"*

Lectiō Tertia (Section III)

Posse (continued)

In the plural *posse* runs:

> pos-<u>sumus</u>
> pot-<u>estis</u>
> pos-<u>sunt</u>

Examples (*ll.124-127*):

> *Magister: "Quid nōn cōnsīditis?" Discipulī: "Nōn cōnsīdimus, quod sedēre nōn possumus."*
> *Diodōrus: "Quid? Sedēre nōn potestis?... Nec enim stantēs dormīre potestis!"*

Licet

The verb *licet* ("it is allowed," "one may") is also (like *convenit*) **impersonal**, i.e. only found in the 3rd person singular. It is often, like *convenit*, combined with a dative: <u>mihi</u> *licet* ("It is permitted to me," therefore "I may").

- *In lectulō dormīre licet, hīc in lūdō nōn licet dormīre!*
- cf. *necesse est* (Chapter X: it is necessary), which also takes the dative and an infinitive, e.g.:
  - ▷ *Necesse est tē pūnīre.* (*l.59-60*)

Recensiō: Pronouns vs. Possessive Adjectives

In this chapter, you learned more forms of the personal pronoun. In Chapters II, IV, V and XI, you learned the possessive adjective. Review the following forms:

	personal pronouns	possessive adjectives	personal pronouns	possessive adjectives
nom.	*ego*	*meus, mea, meum*	*nōs*	*noster, nostra, nostrum*
acc.	*mē*		*nōs*	
dat.	*mihi*			
abl.	*mē*			
nom	*tū*	*tuus, tua, tuum*	*vōs*	*vester, vestra, vestrum*
acc.	*tē*		*vōs*	
dat.	*tibi*			
abl.	*tē*			

Vocābula Disposita/Ordināta

Nōmina
  1st
  iānua, -ae   door
  sella, -ae   stool, chair
  virga, -ae   rod
  2nd
  discipulus, -ī   pupil, disciple
  lūdus, -ī   play, game, school
  magister, magistrī   schoolmaster, teacher
  tersum, -ī   back
  lectulus, -ī   bed

Verba
  -āre (1)
  exclāmō, exclāmāre   cry out, exclaim
  recitō, recitāre   read aloud
  -ēre (2)
  licet, licēre   it is allowed, one may (+ *dat.*)
  -ere (3)[1]
  cōnsīdō, cōnsīdere   sit down
  dēsinō, dēsinere   finish, stop, end
  reddō, reddere   give back, give
  -īre (4)
  pūniō, pūnīre   punish
  redeō, redīre   go back, return
  Irregular
  sum, esse   be

---

1   The first principal part will show you whether a 3rd conjugation verb is a consonant or *i*-stem; they will, therefore, no longer be separated out.

Adiectīva
 1st-2nd (us/er, -a, -um)
 malus, -a, -um   bad, wicked, evil
 sevērus, -a, -um   stern, severe
 tacitus, -a, -um   silent
 vērus, -a, -um   true, *n.* truth

Adiectīva Comparātiva (3rd)
 īnferior, -ius   lower, inferior
 posterior, -ius   back, hind, later
 prior, -ius   first, former, front

Pronōmina
 ego   I, me, myself
 tū   you, yourself
 nōs   we, us, ourselves
 vōs   you, yourselves

Adverbia
 nōndum   not yet
 statim   at once
 tum   then

Coniunctiōnēs
 antequam   before
 at   but
 sī   if
 nisi   if not, except, but
 vērum   but

Vocābula Interrogātīva
 quid?   why

Alia
 domī   at home (*locative*)

XVI. Tempestās

Rēs Grammaticae Novae

1. Verbs
   a. Deponent Verbs (*verba dēpōnentia*)
   b. Irregular Verbs
      i. *īre*
      ii. *fierī*
2. Nouns
   a. Pure *i*-Stems
   b. 1st Declension Masculine Nouns
   c. Case Uses
      i. Partitive Genitive
      ii. Ablative of Degree of Difference
      iii. Ablative with the Word *locus*
3. Participles: Ablative Absolute (*ablātīvus absolūtus*)
4. Points of Style: Word Order

Ancient Navigation

When sailing on the high seas the Roman sailor had to set his course by the sun in the daytime and by the stars at night. So east and west are named in Latin after the rising and the setting sun, *oriēns* and *occidēns,* and the word for "midday," *merīdiēs,* also means "south," while the word for "north" is the name of the constellation *septentriōnēs* (*septem triōnēs*), "the seven plow-oxen," i.e. "the Great Bear."

Lectiō Prīma (Section I)

Pure *i*-stems

There is a small group of 3rd declension nouns that are called **pure *i*-stems** because they have -*i* throughout, for example, the noun *puppis, -is* (f.), which has:
- -*im* in the accusative (instead of -*em*)
- -*ī* in the ablative singular (instead of -*e*)

Very few *i*-stems are declined in this way, e.g. the river name *Tiberis, -is* (m.):

> *Urbs Rōma nōn ad mare, sed ad Tiber<u>im</u> flūmen sita est.* (*ll.7-8*)

1st Declension Masculine Nouns

1st declension nouns (in *-a, -ae*) are feminine, except for a few which denote male persons and are therefore masculine, e.g. *nauta: nauta Rōmān<u>us</u>.*

Locus

· The ablative of *locus* may be used

- without *in* to denote location ("where"):

  ▷ *Ōstia sita est eō locō quō Tiberis in mare Īnferum īnfluit.* (*ll.15-16*)
  e<u>ō</u> loc<u>ō</u> = in eō locō. (location)

- without a preposition to denote motion "from":

  ▷ *Mēdus surgere cōnātur, nec vērō sē locō movēre potest.* (*ll.140-141*)
  loc<u>ō</u> movēre (ablative of separation)

Lectiō Altera (Section II)

Deponent Verbs (*verba dēpōnentia*)

In Section I we met *opperīrī* (= *exspectāre*) a passive form with active meaning:

> *necesse est ventum opperīrī* (*l.29*)

Many of the new words in this chapter are **deponent verbs** (*verba dēpōnentia*). These verbs have no active forms[1] hence, *verba dēpōnentia*: verbs which "lay down" the active form (Latin *dēpōnere*, "lay down").

The infinitive ends in *-rī, -ī*

-ārī:

cōnārī	attempt, try
cōnsōlārī	comfort
laetārī	be happy

-ērī:

intuērī	look at
verērī	fear

-ī:

complectī	embrace
ēgredī	go out
lābī	slip
loquī	speak
proficīscī	set out
sequī	follow

-īrī:

opperīrī	wait for
orīrī	rise

---

1   except for the participle in *-ns*, and one other form you will learn later Chapter XXIV

From the following examples you can see verbs that have **passive** forms but
active meanings

laetārī = gaudēre
verērī =timēre
egredī = exīre
nauta Neptūnum verētur = nauta Neptūnum timet
ventō secundō nāvēs ē portū ēgrediuntur = exeunt

Participles: Ablative Absolute (*ablātīvus absolūtus*)

In Chapter XIV we learned about the ablative of attendant circumstances,
which was illustrated in that chapter by

fenestrā apertā
fenestrā clausā

In this chapter we learn more about this construction. In the *marginalia* of
Section I you read that:

marī turbidō = dum mare turbidum est (l.36)
ventō secundō = dum ventus secundus est (l.38)

These are more examples of the ablative used as an adverbial phrase. Such an
adverbial phrase, grammatically independent of the rest of the sentence, is called
an **ablative absolute** (Latin *ablātīvus absolūtus*, "set free," therefore independent).
It represents the circumstances occuring around an action. In each of the following
the ablative gives further information about the verb. We find the ablative absolute
with adjectives:

Ventō secundō nāvēs ē portū ēgrediuntur. (ll.38-39)
 the ablative *ventō secundō* tells us under what circumstances the
 ships put out ("with a fair wind," "when the wind is favorable").

Nautae nec marī turbidō nec marī tranquillō nāvigāre volunt. (ll.36-37)
 They sail "when the sea is rough," "when the sea is calm"

plēnīs vēlīs...vehuntur. (ll.39-40)
 They travel "with full sails."

pedibus nūdīs (Chap. XIV, l.85)
 stands "with bare feet"

The ablative absolute is common with a participle, either present or past:

Present participle:
 Sōle oriente nāvis ē portū ēgreditur multīs hominibus spectantibus.
 (ll.64-65); "when the sun is rising," "at sunrise"... "while many people
 are looking on"

Past participle:
 fenestrā apertā dormīre (Chap. XIV, l.15): sleep "with the window
 open" (cf. *fenestrā clausā, Chap. XIV, l.15*)

Even two nouns can form an ablative absolute:

Sōle duce nāvem gubernō (l.94); "the sun being my guide," "with the sun as
a guide"

The ablative absolute may often be translated with an English temporal clause (when, while), as in the sentences above. It can also show cause (why the verb happens) and even concession (although the verb happens). If you need to translate an ablative absolute into English, it helps to start with "with" and then think about what the relationship is of the ablative absolute to the rest of the sentence.

īre

In the verb īre (and its compounds) the 1st person *eō* and 3rd person *eunt* are irregular, e.g.:

> *in patriam nostram īmus* (*l.89*)
>
> *"Nōnne gaudēs" inquit, "mea Lȳdia, quod nōs simul in patriam nostram redīmus?"* (*ll.79-81*)

eō	*īmus*
īs	*ītis*
it	*eunt*

Partitive Genitive

Since Chapter II you have been seeing the noun *numerus* followed by the genitive; in Chapter XII you learned about the genitive with *mīlia*:

> *In flūminibus et in maribus magnus numerus piscium est.* (*Chap. X, 11.41-42*)
> *Ergō mīlle passūs sunt quīnque mīlia pedum.* (*Chap. XII, ll.96-97*)
> *In castrīs Aemiliī sex mīlia mīlitum habitant.* (*Chap. XII, ll.97-98*)

These genitives give the **whole** of which the noun is a **part**; they are called **partitive genitives** (or genitives of the whole). This chapter begins with the **partitive genitive** of the relative pronoun:

> *Italia inter duo maria interest, quōrum alterum "mare Superum" appellātur; quōrum* (= *ex quibus*): "of which one…the other"
>
> cf. *nēmō eōrum* (= *ex iīs, Chap. XVII, l.12*).

Quantity terms like *multum* and *paulum* are often followed by a partitive genitive to express "that **of which**" there is a large or small quantity, e.g.:

> *paulum/multum aquae* (*ll.9, 117*)
> *paulum cibī nec multum pecūniae* (*ll.61-62*)
> *paulum temporis* (*l.108* margin)

Ablative of Degree of Difference

The ablative of *multum* and *paulum* serves to strengthen or weaken a comparative; this is called the **ablative of difference**:

> *Nāvis paulō levior fit, simul vērō flūctūs multō altiōrēs fīunt* (*ll.123-124*): "a little," "a lot"

The same forms are used with *ante* and *post* (as adverbs) to state the time difference:

> *paulō ante* (*l.148*)
> *paulō post* (*l.91*)
> cf. the ablative in *annō post* (*Chap.XIX, l.83*)
> *decem annīs ante* (*Chap. XIX, l.123*)

Lectiō Tertia (Section III)

Fierī

The infinitive *fi|erī* (3rd person *fi|t fi|unt*) is also irregular. This verb functions as the passive of *facere* (see Chapter XVIII); in connection with an adjective it comes to mean "become":

> *Mare tranquillum fit.* (*ll.97-98*)
> *Flūctūs multō altiōrēs fiunt.* (*l.124*)

Points of Style: Word Order

In Chapter XIII we met the demonstrative *is, ea, id* being used as an adjective with a dependent genitive:

> *Is mēnsis annī brevissimus est.* (*l.30*)
> *Is diēs annī prīmus est atque initium annī novī.* (*ll.58-59*)

In both of these examples we see that the demonstrative generally precedes the noun. In this chapter we see a similar example:

> *Ea pars caelī unde sōl oritur dīcitur oriēns.* (*l.45*)

In all these examples the genitive follows the noun. Another very common word order is for the genitive to come between the qualifier and its noun, as in the following example:

> *Merīdiēs dīcitur ea caelī pars ubi sōl merīdiē vidētur.* (*l.48*)

Vocābula Disposita/Ordināta

Nōmina

1st

nauta, -ae (*m.*)	sailor
ōra, -ae	border, coast

2nd

altum, -ī	the open sea
locus, -ī	place
vēlum, -ī	sail
ventus, -ī	wind

3rd

fulgur, fulguris (*n.*)	flash of lightning
gubernātor, gubernātoris (*m.*)	steersman
merx, mercis (*f.*)	commodity, *pl.* goods
nāvis, nāvis (*f.*)	ship
occidēns, occidentis (*m.*)	west
oriēns, orientis (*m.*)	east
puppis, puppis (*f.*)	stern, poop
septentriōnēs, septentriōnum, (*m. pl.*)	north
tempestās, tempestātis (*f.*)	storm

4th
flūctus, -ūs (*m.*)   wave
portus, -ūs (*m.*)   harbor
tonitrus, -ūs (*m.*)   thunder

Verba
-āre (1)
appellō, appellāre   call, address
cōnātur, cōnārī   attempt, try
cōnsōlātur, cōnsōlārī   comfort, console
flō, flāre   blow
gubernō, gubernāre   steer, govern
iactō, iactāre   throw, toss about
invocō, invocāre   call upon, invoke
laetātur, laetārī   rejoice, be glad
nāvigō, nāvigāre   sail
servō, servāre   preserve, save
turbō, turbāre   stir up, agitate
-ēre (2)
impleō, implēre   fill, complete
intuētur, intuērī   look at, watch
verētur, verērī   fear
-ere (3)
cernō, cernere   discern, perceive
cōnscendō, cōnscendere   mount, board
īnfluō, īnfluere   flow into
occidō, occidere   fall, sink, set
complectitur, complectī   embrace
ēgreditur, ēgredī   go out
lābitur, lābī   slip, drop, fall
loquitur, loquī   speak, talk
proficīscitur, proficīscī   set out, depart
sequitur, sequī   follow
-īre (4)
hauriō, haurīre   draw (water), bail
opperītur, opperīrī   wait (for), await
orītur, orīrī   rise, appear
Irregular
interest, interesse   be between
fit, fierī   be done, become, happen

Adiectīva
1st-2nd (us/er, -a, -um)
āter, -tra, -trum   black, dark
contrārius, -a, -um   opposite, contrary
īnferus, -a, -um   lower
maritimus, -a, -um   seaside, coastal

serēnus, -a, -um	clear, cloudless
situs, -a, -um	situated
superus, -a, -um	upper
tranquillus, -a, -um	calm, still
turbidus, -a, -um	agitated, stormy
dēpōnēns (*gen.* **dēpōnentis**)	deponent

Coniunctiōnēs

sīve	or, or if

Praepositiōnēs

propter (*prp.* + *acc.*)	because of

Adverbia

iterum	again, a second time
paulum	a little, little
praetereā	besides
semper	always
simul	at the same time
vix	hardly
vērō	really, however, but

XVII. Numerī Difficiles

Rēs Grammaticae Novae

1. Verbs
   a. Passive Voice
   b. *oportēre* (impersonal)
   c. *dare*
2. Nouns: Case Uses
   a. Double Accusative
3. Adjectives: Numbers
   a. Cardinals
   b. Inflection
   c. Ordinals
4. Pronouns: *quisque*
5. Adverbs

Lectiō Prīma (Section I)

Roman Coins

To teach his pupils arithmetic the teacher has recourse to coins. The current Roman coins were:

> *as* (*assis* m.) copper
> *sēstertius* (HS) = four *assēs*: brass[1]
> *dēnārius* = four *sēstertiī*: silver
> *aureus* = twenty-five *dēnāriī*: gold (*Chap. XXII, l.108*)

Quisque, quaeque, quodque

Only the first part (*quis*) of the pronoun *quisque* (each) declines; you will meet the feminine (*quaeque*) and neuter (*quodque*) in Chapter XVIII. Compare:

> *uterque*   each (of two)
> *quisque*   each

---

1   Until 217 B.C. the *sēstertius* was a small silver coin worth 2½ *assēs,* hence the abbreviation IIS (s = *sēmis* ½, so *sēmis -issis* m. (*sēs-*) = ½ *as*), which became HS; the change to 4 *assēs* was due to a fall in the copper value of the *as* (originally 1 "pound," 327 g, of copper).

Double Accusative

Note the **two accusatives** with *docēre,* one for the **person**(s) (*puerōs*), the other for the **thing** (*numerōs*) taught:

> *Magister puerōs numerōs docet.* (*ll.1-2*)

Cardinal Numbers

In Chapter IV you learned to count to ten:

ūnus, a, um	*sex*
duo, duae, duo	*septem*
trēs, tria	*octō*
quattuor	*novem*
quīnque	*decem*

To be able to count up to a hundred you must learn the multiples of ten. With the exception of 10 *decem,* 20 *vīgintī,* and 100 *centum,* they all end in *-gintā*:

10 *decem*	60 *sexāgintā*
20 *vīgintī*	70 *septuāgintā*
30 *trīgintā*	80 *octōgintā*
40 *quadrāgintā*	90 *nōnāgintā*
50 *quīnquāgintā*	100 *centum*

The numbers in between are formed by combining multiples of ten and smaller numbers with or without *et,* e.g.:

> 21 *vīgintī ūnus* or *ūnus et vīgintī*
> 22 *vīgintī duo* or *duo et vīgintī*

The cardinals 11-17 end in *-decim,* a weakened form of *decem*:

11 *ūn-decim*	15 *quīn-decim*
12 *duo-decim*	16 *sē-decim*
13 *trē-decim*	17 *septen-decim*
14 *quattuor-decim*	

but 18 and 19 show the pattern numbers will follow:

> 18 is *duo-dē-vīgintī* ("two-from-twenty")
> 19 *ūn-dē-vīgintī* ("one-from-twenty")

In the same way, 28 is *duo-dē-trīgintā* and 29 *ūn-dē-trīgintā.* Thus the last two numbers before each multiple of ten are expressed by subtracting two and one respectively from the multiple of ten in question.

Inflection of Numbers

Like *quot,* the interrogative which asks the number ("how many?"), and *tot,* the demonstrative which refers to the number ("so many"), most Latin cardinals are **indeclinable.**

Of the cardinals 1-100 only *ūn|us, -a, -um, du|o, -ae, -o* and *tr|ēs, tr|ia* are declined. You have met most forms of these numbers (the genitive, *ūn|īus, du|ōrum, -ārum, -ōrum* and *tr|ium,* is introduced in Chapter XIX).

	masc.	fem.	neut.	masc.	fem.	neut.	m./f.	neut.
nom.	ūn|us	ūn|a	ūn|um	du|o	du|ae	du|o	tr|ēs	tr|ia
acc.	ūn|um	ūn|am	ūn|um	du|ōs	du|ās	du|o	tr|ēs	tr|ia
gen.				du|ōrum	du|ārum	du|ōrum		
dat.	ūn|ī	ūn|ī	ūn|ī	du|ōbus	du|ābus	du|ōbus	tr|ibus	tr|ibus
abl.	ūn|ō	ūn|ā	ūn|ō	du|ōbus	du|ābus	du|ōbus	tr|ibus	tr|ibus

Multiples of 100 *centum* end in *-centī* (200, 300, 600) or *-gentī* (400, 500, 700, 800, 900) and are declined like adjectives of the 1st/2nd declension:

200 *du-cent\|ī, -ae, -a*   600 *ses-cent\|ī, -ae, -a*
300 *tre-cent\|ī, -ae, -a*   700 *septin-gent\|ī, -ae, -a*
400 *quadrin-gent\|ī, -ae, -a*   800 *octin-gent\|ī, -ae, -a*
500 *quīn -gent\|ī, -ae, -a*   900 *nōn-gent\|ī, -ae, -a*

Ordinal Numbers

In Chapter XIII, you learned the ordinal numbers first through twelfth:

prīm\|us, -a, -um   *septim\|us, -a, -um*
secund\|us, -a, -um   *octāv\|us, -a, -um*
terti\|us, -a, -um   *nōn\|us, -a, -um*
quārt\|us, -a, -um   *decim\|us, -a, -um*
quīnt\|us, -a, -um   *ūndecim\|us, -a, -um*
sext\|us, -a, -um   *duodecim\|us, -a, -um*

The ordinals are adjectives of the 1st/2nd declension; from the multiples of ten, 20-90, and of one hundred, 100-1000, they are formed with the suffix *-ēsim\|us, -a, -um*:

20th *vīcēsimus, -a, -um*   100th *centēsimus, -a, -um*
30th *trīcēsimus, -a, -um*   200th *ducentēsimus, -a, -um*
40th *quadrāgēsimus, -a, -um*   300th *trecentēsimus*
50th *quīnquāgēsimus*, etc.   1000th *mīllēsimus*

Notā Bene: Cardinals end in:

30-90 *-gintā*   38/39: *duo-/ūn-dē-*XL etc.
11-17 *-decim*   200, 300, 600: *-cent\|ī*
18/19: *duo-/ūn-dē-*XX   400, 500, 700, 800, 900: *-gent\|ī*
28/29: *duo-/ūn-dē-*XXX

Ordinals end in:

20th-90th, 100th-1000th: *-ēsim\|us*

A summary is given on page 308 in *Lingva Latina*.

Adverbs

The forms *rēctē, prāvē, stultē, aequē* are formed from the adjectives *rēctus, prāvus, stultus, aequus*; this formation will be dealt with in the next chapter.

Lectiō Altera (Section II)

The Passive Voice

You have been using the passive voice, in the 3rd person singular and plural, since Chapter VI. Now we see the remaining endings, the 1st and 2nd persons, singular and plural. The following sentences show examples of the passive voice (*ll.63-81*):

- 1st person:

    singular: *Cūr ego semper ā tē reprehendor, numquam laudor?*

    plural: *Nōs quoque saepe interrogāmur, nec vērō prāvē respondēmus. Itaque nōs ā magistrō laudāmur, nōn reprehendimur.*

- 2nd person:

    singular: *Tū ā mē nōn laudāris, quia numquam rēctē respondēs. Semper prāvē respondēs, ergō reprehenderis!*

    plural: *Et cūr vōs semper laudāminī? Quia id quod vōs interrogāminī facile est — ego quoque ad id rēctē respondēre possum. Vōs numquam reprehendiminī!*

- 3rd person:

    singular: *Mārcus semper ā magistrō reprehenditur, numquam laudātur.*

    plural: *Sextus et Titus ā magistrō semper laudantur, numquam reprehenduntur.*

Forming the Passive Voice

- personal endings

	sing.	pl.
1.	-r	-mur
2.	-ris	-minī
3.	-tur	-ntur

- The 1st, 2nd, and 4th conjugations: add the endings to the stem, with the same vowels as in the active.

- The third conjugation (including third *i*-stems): the vowels are the same as in the active, **except** in the 2nd person singular, where the short *i* becomes *e* before *r* (e.g. *reprehenderis*: you are being censured; *caperis*: you are being taken).

	-āre	-ēre	-ere	-īre
1st:	*laud|or*	*vere|or*	*reprehend|or.*	*largi|or*
2nd:	*laudā|ris*	*verē|ris*	*reprehend|eris*	*largī|ris*
3rd:	*laudā|tur*	*verē|tur*	*reprehend|itur*	*largī|tur*
1st:	*laudā|mur*	*verē |mur*	*reprehend|imur*	*largī|mur*
2nd:	*laudā| minī*	*verē |mini*	*reprehend|iminī*	*largī|mini*
3rd:	*laudā|ntur*	*vere|ntur*	*reprehend|untur*	*largi|untur*

Lectiō Tertia (Section III)

Oportēre (Impersonal)

The verb oportēre occurs only in the 3rd person singular, like *licet* and *convenit* (Chapter XV):

> *Prīmum cōgitāre oportet. (ll.110-111)*
> *Nōn oportet respondēre antequam interrogāris. (ll.115-116)*

Dare

The stem of the verb *da\|re* ends in a short *a*: *da\|mus, da\|tis, da\|tur, da\|te!* etc., except in *dā! dā\|s* and *dā\|ns* (before *ns* all vowels are lengthened).

Vocabula Disposita/Ordinata

Nōmina
    2nd

dēnārius, -ī	denarius (silver coin)
respōnsum, -ī	answer

    3rd

as, assis (*m.*)	as (copper coin)

Verba
    -āre (1)

cōgitō, cōgitāre	think
computō, computāre	calculate, reckon
dēmōnstrō, dēmōnstrāre	point out, show
interpellō, interpellāre	interrupt
laudō, laudāre	praise

    -ēre (2)

doceō, docēre	teach, instruct
oportet, oportēre	it is right, you should

    -ere (3)

discō, discere	learn
prōmō, prōmere	take out
repōnō, repōnere	put back

reprehendō, reprehendere	blame, censure
tollō, tollere	raise, lift, pick up, remove, take away
-īre (4)	
largior, largīrī	give generously
nesciō, nescīre	not know
partior, partīrī	share, divide
sciō, scīre	know

Adiectīva

1st-2nd (us/er, -a, -um)

centēsimus, -a, -um	hundredth
certus, -a, -um	certain, sure
doctus, -a, -um	learned, skilled
incertus, -a, -um	uncertain
indoctus, -a, -um	ignorant
industrius, -a, -um	industrious
largus, -a, -um	generous
piger, pigra, pigrum	lazy
prāvus, -a, -um	faulty, wrong
rēctus, -a, -um	straight, correct

3rd

absēns (*gen.* absentis)	absent
difficilis, e (*sup.* difficillimus)	difficult, hard
facilis, e (*sup.* facillimus)	easy
prūdēns, prūdentis	prudent, clever

Numerī

trēdecim	thirteen
quattuordecim	fourteen
quīndecim	fifteen
sēdecim	sixteen
septendecim	seventeen
duodēvīgintī	eighteen
ūndēvīgintī	nineteen
quadrāgintā	forty
quīnquāgintā	fifty
septuāgintā	seventy
quadringentī, -ae, -a	four hundred
quīngentī, -ae, -a	five hundred
sescentī, -ae, -a	six hundred
septingentī, -ae, -a	seven hundred
octingentī, -ae, -a	eight hundred
nōngentī, -ae, -a	nine hundred

Prōnōmina

quisque, quaeque, quodque	each

Adverbia

aequē	equally
numquam	never
postrēmō	finally
prāvē	wrongly
quārē	why
rēctē	correctly
saepe	often
tot	so many
ūsque	up (to), all the time

Coniunctiōnēs

quamquam	although

XVIII. Litterae Latīnae

Rēs Grammaticae Novae

1. Verbs: *facere/fierī*
2. Adjectives
    a. Superlatives (continued)
    b. *frequēns*
    c. *facilis*
3. Pronouns
    a. *īdem, eadem, idem*
    b. *quisque, quaeque, quodque*
4. Adverbs
    a. Positive, Comparative, Superlative Degrees
    b. Numerical Adverbs
5. Conjunction: *cum*
6. Points of Style: idiom *suum cuique*

Pronunciation

In the Classical period, Latin spelling gave a fairly reliable representation of the pronunciation. In some cases, however, letters continued to be written where they were no longer pronounced in colloquial Latin, e.g. *h-, -m* in the unstressed endings *-am, -em, -um* and *n* before *s*. An indication of this is the occurrence of "misspellings" in ancient inscriptions written by people without literary education, e.g. ORA for HORAM, SEPTE for SEPTEM and MESES for MENSES. In his short exercise Marcus makes several errors of this kind.

Lectiō Prīma (Section I)
Īdem, eadem, idem

The demonstrative pronoun *īdem, eadem, idem* ("the same," cf. "identical") is a compound, the first element of which is the pronoun *is, ea, id*; the addition of the suffix *-dem* causes the following changes:

• *is-dem* to *īdem*

- *eum-dem, eam-dem* to *eundem, eandem*[1].

	sing.			pl.		
	masc.	fem.	neut.	masc.	fem.	neut.
nom.	*īdem*	*eadem*	*idem*	*iīdem*	*eaedem*	*eadem*
acc.	*eundem*	*eandem*	*idem*	*eōsdem*	*eāsdem*	*eadem*
gen.	*eiusdem*	*eiusdem*	*eiusdem*	*eōrundem*	*eārundem*	*eōrundem*
dat.	*eīdem*	*eīdem*	*eīdem*	*iīsdem*	*iīsdem*	*iīsdem*
abl.	*eōdem*	*eādem*	*eōdem*	*iīsdem*	*iīsdem*	*iīsdem*

Examples:

Numerus syllabārum et vōcālium īdem est. (l.21)

in eādem syllabā (l.26)

Vocābulum prīmum utrīusque sententiae idem est, sed hoc idem vocābulum duās rēs variās significat. (ll.32-33)

Item varia vocābula eandem rem vel eundem hominem significāre possunt. (ll.33-35)

Discipulī eandem sententiam nōn eōdem modō, sed variīs modīs scrībunt. (ll.56-58)

Quisque, quaeque, quodque

The pronoun *quis-que, quae-que, quod-que* ("each") is declined like the interrogative pronoun with the addition of *-que*.

	sing.			pl.		
	masc.	fem.	neut.	masc.	fem.	neut.
nom.	*quīque*	*quaeque*	*quodque*	*quīque*	*quaeque*	*quaeque*
acc.	*quemque*	*quamque*	*quodque*	*quōsque*	*quāsque*	*quaeque*
gen.	*cuiusque*	*cuiusque*	*cuiusque*	*quōrumque*	*quārumque*	*quōrumque*
dat.	*cuique*	*cuique*	*cuique*	*quibusque*	*quibusque*	*quibusque*
abl.	*quōque*	*quāque*	*quōque*	*quibusque*	*quibusque*	*quibusque*

Examples:

Quisque discipulus in tabulā suā scrībit eās sententiās quās magister eī dictat. (ll.49-50)

Quisque puer stilum et rēgulam prōmit et dūcit līneam rēctam in tabulā suā. (ll.55-56)

Discipulus quamque litteram cuiusque vocābulī sīc legit. (ll.41-2)

Ita quodque vocābulum cuiusque sententiae ā discipulō legitur. (ll.43-44)

Quaeque syllaba vōcālem habet. (l.20)

---

1   The *m* changes to *n* by assimilation—see Chapter X—*n* being a dental consonant like *d,* cf. *septendecim* and *septentriōnēs.*

Facere/ fierī

The verb *facere* has no passive form. Instead, *fierī* functions as the passive of *facere*:

> *Vōcālis syllabam facit; sine vōcālī syllaba fierī nōn potest. (l.25)*
> *Cum syllabae iunguntur, vocābula fiunt. (l.29)*
> *Cum vocābula coniunguntur, sententiae fiunt. (ll.29-30)*

active   *facere facit, faciunt*

passive   *fierī fit, fiunt*

Notā Bene: Compounds of *facere* ending in *-ficere*, e.g. *ef-ficere*, can be used in the passive:

> *stilus ex ferrō efficitur (= fit)*

Conjunction *Cum*

The conjunction *cum* may serve to introduce a sudden occurrence, as in this example (*l.128*):

> *Titus sīc incipit: "Magister! Mārcus bis..." — cum Mārcus stilum in partem corporis eius mollissimam premit!* (English "when...," "and then...")

Frequēns

The adjective *frequēns* follows the pattern of present participles (Chapter XIV), that is, it has the same nominative in all three genders:

> *κ littera, quae frequēns est in linguā Graecā, littera Latīna rārissima est. (ll.14-15)*

> *Id vocābulum est frequentissimum. (l.101)*

> *Υ et z igitur litterae rārae sunt in linguā Latīnā, in linguā Graecā frequentēs. (ll.13-14)*

Lectiō Altera (Section II)

Points of Style: Idiom *suum cuique*

Suus, -a, -um cuique is an idiom:

Magister suam cuique discipulō tabulam reddit.	The teacher gives each student back his own tablet. (*ll.67-68*)
suum cuique	to each his (her) own: proverbial

Superlatives of Adjectives in *-er*

Adjectives in *-er*, e.g. *pulcher* and *piger*, form superlatives in *-errim|us, -a, -um* (instead of *-issim|us*). In this chapter you find *pulcherrim|us* and *pigerrim|us*, in the next *miserrim|us* and *pauperrim|us* from *miser* and *pauper*.

adj *-er*, sup. *-errim|us*

Facilis, -e

The superlative of *facilis* is *facillim|us* (l.102). Only a very few adjectives form their superlatives like *facilis*:

> *facilis, -e*: *facillimus, a, um*
> *difficilis, -e*: *difficillimus, a, um* (*Chap. XVII*)
> *gracilis, -e*: *gracillimus, a, um* slender (*Chap. XIX*)
> *humilis, -e*: *humillimus, a, um* low (*Chap. XXV*)
> *similis, -e*: *simillimus, a, um* similar (*Chap. XXXV*)
> *dissimilis, -e*: *dissimillimus, a, um* dissimilar, different

Adverbs

Remember:

- Adjectives qualify nouns.
  - ▷ The adjective answers the question: *quālis?*
    - In the sentence *puer stultus est, stultus* is an adjective qualifying the noun *puer* (*quālis est puer?*).
- Adverbs (Latin *adverbium*, from *ad verbum*) qualify verbs, adjectives and other adverbs.
  - ▷ The adverb answers the question: *quōmodo?*
    - In the sentence *puer stultē agit* the word *stultē* belongs to the verb *agit* which it modifies (*quōmodo agit puer?*).

In Chapter XVII we saw the adverbs *rēctē, prāvē, stultē, aequē* from the adjectives *rēctus, prāvus, stultus, aequus*. Similarly, in the sentence *mīles fortis est quī fortiter pugnat, fortis* is an adjective (qualifying *mīles*) and *fortiter* an adverb (modifying *pugnat*).

Positive Degree

Just as there are three degrees of adjectives, there are three of adverbs: **positive** (e.g. fast), **comparative** (e.g. faster), and **superlative** (e.g. fastest). Positive degree:

Certē pulcherrimae sunt litterae Sextī.	Sextus's letters are certainly very beautiful. (*l.73*)
"Litterae vestrae aequē foedae sunt."	Your letters are equally ugly. (*l.78*)

Adjectives of the 1st/2nd declension form adverbs ending in -ē. e.g.:

> *stult|us -a -um* → *stultē*
> *rēct|us -a -um* → *rēctē*
> *pulcher -chr|a -chr|um* → *pulchrē*

3rd declension adjectives form adverbs in *-iter* [2], e.g.:

> *fort|is -e* → *fortiter*
> *brev|is -e* → *breviter*
> *turp|is -e* → *turpiter*

---

2   If the base of an adjectives ends in *nt*, its adverb ends in *nter*, e.g. *frequens, frequenter*.

Notā Bene: Bene and *male* are irregular formations from *bonus* and *malus*, whose forms you will learn in Chapter XIX.

Comparative Degree

The **comparative of the adverb** ends in *-ius*. Note that the form of the comparative adverb is the same as the neuter of the comparative of the adjective:

    pulchrius   *fortius*   *rēctius*

Comparative Degree:

    "Tū, Tite, neque pulchrius neque foedius scrībis quam Mārcus.":
    "neither more beautifully nor more unattractively" (*ll.79-80*)

    "At certē rēctius scrībō quam Mārcus.": "more correctly" (*l.81*)

Superlative Degree

The **superlative of the adverb** ending in *-issimē* (*-errimē*) is formed regularly from the superlative of the adjective:

    pulcherrimē   *fortissimē*   *rēctissimē*

Superlative Degree:

    "Comparā tē cum Sextō, quī rēctissimē et pulcherrimē scrībit.":
    "most correctly," "most beautifully" (*ll.85-86*)

When the superlative occurs without the idea of comparison, it can be translated "very":

    Latīnē pulcherrimē recitās!   You read Latin aloud very beautifully!

Recensiō: Comparison of Adjectives and Adverbs

Adjectives

Positive Degree	Comparative Degree	Superlative Degree
rārus, rāra, rārum	*rārior, rārius*	*rārissimus, -a, -um*
mollis, molle	*mollior, mollius*	*mollissimus, -a, -um*
pulcher, pulchra, pulchrum	*pulchior, pulchrius*	*pulcherrimus, -a, -um*
facilis, facile	*facilior, facilius*	*facillimus, -a, -um*
frequēns	*frequentior, frequentius*	*frequentissimus, -a, -um*

Adverbs

Positive Degree	Comparative Degree	Superlative Degree
rārē	*rārius*	*rārissimē*
molliter	*mollius*	*mollissimē*
pulchrē	*pulchrius*	*pulcherrimē*
facile*	*facilius*	*facillimē*
frequenter	*frequentius*	*frequentissimē*

    *more rare: *faciliter*

Lectiō Tertia (Section III)
Numerical Adverbs

Numeral adverbs are formed with the suffix *-iēs* (or *-iēns*) and denote how many times an action occurs:

> *quīnqui__ēs__* 5×
> *sexi__ēs__* 6×
> *septi__ēs__* 7×, etc.

Only the first four have special forms:

> *semel*: once   *ter*: three times
> *bis*: twice   *quater*: four times

From *quot* and *tot* are formed *quoti__ēs__* and *toti__ēs__*:

> *Mārcus deciēs H scribit: H H H H H H H H H H (l.119)*
> *Quotiēs Mārcus V scribit? Quater tantum V scrībit. (ll.122-123)*
> *Quotiēs? Semel. (ll.133-134)*
> *Mārcus ter rēctē et bis prāvē scrībit. (ll.125-126)*

Vocābula Disposita/Ordināta
Nōmina
1st
cēra, -ae	wax
charta, -ae	paper
epistula, -ae	letter
māteria, -ae	material
sententia, -ae	opinion, sentence

2nd
adverbium, -ī	adverb
calamus, -ī	reed, reed pen
erus, -ī	master
ferrum, -ī	iron, sword
mendum, -ī	mistake
papȳrus, -ī	papyrus (paper)
zephȳrus, -ī	west wind

3rd
apis, apis (*f.*)	bee
cōnsonāns, cōnsonantis (*f.*)	consonant
mercēs, mercēdis (*f.*)	hire pay wages
vōcālis, vōcālis (*f.*)	vowel

Verba
-āre (1)
comparō, comparāre	liken, compare; prepare, get ready
dictō, dictāre	dictate
signō, signāre	mark, inscribe, indicate, notice, seal
significō, significāre	indcate, show, mean

-ēre (2)
dēleō, dēlēre — blot out, efface, destroy
-ere (3)
addō, addere — add, join
animadvertō, animadvertere — notice
coniungō, coniungere — connect, unite
corrigō, corrigere — correct
efficiō, efficere — bring about
imprimō, imprimere — seal, emboss
intellegō, intellegere — understand
iungō, iungere — join
legō, legere — pick, read
premō, premere — press
scrībo, scrībere — write
-īre (4)
exaudiō, exaudīre — hear plainly or favorably
Irregular
desum, deese — fall short, be lacking
supersum, superesse — be over and above, remain, survive

Adiectīva
1st-2nd
durus, -a, -um — hard
impiger, impigra, impigrum — active, energetic
rārus, -a, -um — rare
varius, -a, -um — manifold, various
3rd
frequēns (*gen.* frequentis) — crowded, numerous, frequent
mollis, molle — soft
quālis, quāle — (interrogative and relative) of what sort?
tālis, tāle — of such a sort
turpis, turpe — ugly, foul

Pronōmina
īdem, eadem, idem — the same (*adj./pronoun*)
quaeque, quodque — each

Adverbia
sīc — so, thus
ita — so, in such a way
quotiēs — as many times
totiēs — so many times
semel — once
bis — twice
ter — three times
quater — four times
quīnquiēs — five times
sextiēs — six times
deciēs — ten times

XIX. Marītus et Uxor

Rēs Grammaticae Novae

1. Verbs
   a. Imperfect of all Conjugations: Active and Passive
   b. Imperfect of *esse*
2. Nouns
   a. *domus*
   b. Case Uses
      i. Genitive of Quality/Description
      ii. Vocatives for Nouns in *-ius*
      iii. Archaic Genitive
3. Adjectives
   a. Irregular Adjectives
   b. Superlative Adjectives
   c. *nūllus/ūllus/tōtus/sōlus*
   d. Numerals: Genitive of *ūnus, duo, trēs*
   e. 3rd Declension Adjectives of One Termination
4. Points of Style: Idioms

Julius and Aemilia

Undisturbed by their noisy children, Julius and Aemilia are walking up and down in the beautiful peristyle, which is adorned with statues of gods and goddesses.

Among the names of the gods, notice the name of the supreme god *Iuppiter Iov|is*; the stem is *Iov-* (meaning "sky"), and the long nominative form is due to the addition of *pater* weakened to *-piter*. The Roman gods were identified with the Greek, e.g. *Iuppiter* with *Zeus*, his wife *Iūnō -ōnis* with *Hēra*, *Venus -eris*, the goddess of love, with *Aphrodītē*, and her son *Cupīdō -inis* ("desire") with *Eros*.

Lectiō Prīma (Section I)

Irregular Adjectives

Iuppiter has the honorific title *Optimus Māximus,* which are the superlatives of *bonus* and *magnus.* The comparison of these adjectives and their opposites *malus* and *parvus* is quite irregular. So is the comparison of *multī*: comp. *plūrēs,* sup. *plūrimī.* Look at these examples:

malus (ll.13-16):

> Nēmō deōrum <u>pēior</u> marītus est quam Iuppiter, neque ūlla dea <u>pēior</u> uxor est quam Venus.

> Inter omnēs deōs deāsque Iuppiter <u>pessimus</u> marītus est ac Venus <u>pessima</u> uxor.

bonus (ll.25-30):

> Certē Iūlius marītus <u>melior</u> quam Iuppiter est!
> Certē Aemilia uxor <u>melior</u> est quam Venus!
> Aemila Iūlium "virum <u>optimum</u>" appellat.
> Item Iūlius uxōrem suam "<u>optimam</u> omnium fēminārum" vocat.

parvus (ll.35-37):

> Quīntus <u>māior</u> est quam Iūlia et <u>minor</u> quam Mārcus.
> <u>Māximus</u> liberōrum est Mārcus, <u>minima</u> est Iūlia.

multi (ll.52, 54):

> Rōmae <u>plūrēs</u> hominēs habitant quam in ūllā aliā urbe imperiī Rōmānī.
> Urbs Rōma <u>plūrimōs</u> hominēs et <u>plūrimās</u> domōs habet.

bonus, -a, -um	melior, melius	optimus, -a,-um
malus, -a, -um	pēior, pēius	pessimus, -a, -um
magnus, -a, -um	māior, māius	māximus, -a, -um
parvus, -a, -um	minor, minus	minimus, -a, -um
multī, -ae, -a	plūres	plūrimī, -ae, -a

Superlative + Partitive Genitive; Superlative Absolute

The superlative is often linked with a partitive genitive:

> optimam om<u>nium</u> fēmin<u>ārum</u> (l.30)
> pulcherrima om<u>nium</u> de<u>ārum</u> (l.21)

Without such a genitive the superlative often denotes a **very** high degree (**absolute superlative**):

> "mea optima uxor" (l.90)
> vir pessimus (l.110)
> "mī optime vir" (l.94)
> Tunc miserrima eram. (l.107)
> virgō pauperrima (l.128)

Lines 57-58 illustrate both uses in the same sentence: *Rōma urbs māxima atque pulcherrima est tōtīus imperiī Rōmānī*:

> Absolute: *Rōma urbs māxima.* (very big)

> Partitive Genitive: *pulcherrima tōtīus imperiī Rōmānī*
> (the most beautiful of the whole of the Roman empire)

Archaic Genitive

The ending *-ās* in *māter familiās* and *pater familiās* (*ll.17, 38*) is an old genitive ending of the 1st declension (= *-ae*).

Numerals: *ūnus, duo, trēs*

You have met the other forms of the first three numbers before; in this chapter, you meet the genitive:

> *Iūlius et Aemilia sunt parentēs trium līberōrum: duōrum fīliōrum et ūnīus fīliae.* (*ll.31-32*)

The complete paradigms for these three are:

	masc.	fem.	neut.	masc.	fem.	neut.	m./f.	neut.
nom.	ūn|us	ūn|a	ūn|um	du|o	du|ae	du|o	tr|ēs	tr|ia
acc.	ūn|um	ūn|am	ūn|um	du|ōs	du|ās	du|o	tr|ēs	tr|ia
gen.	ūn|īus	ūn| īus	ūn| īus	du|ōrum	du|ārum	du|ōrum	tr|ium	tr|ium
dat.	ūn|ī	ūn|ī	ūn|ī	du|ōbus	du|ābus	du|ōbus	tr|ibus	tr|ibus
abl.	ūn|ō	ūn|ā	ūn|ō	du|ōbus	du|ābus	du|ōbus	tr|ibus	tr|ibus

You have met the variation of declension shown in *ūnus* before, in *ille* (genitive *illius*, dative *illi*), *hic* (genitive *huius*, dative *huic*, from *hui-ce*).

Nūllus/ūllus/tōtus/sōlus

Ūnus, a, um is one of a small group of pronouns and adjectives whose genitive singulars end in *-īus* and dative singulars in *ī*. You meet some more of these in this chapter:

> *nūllus, -a, -um*   none, not any
> *ūllus, -a, -um*   any (always with a negative)
> *tōtus, -a, -um*   the whole of, all
> *sōlus, -a, -um*   alone, only

All of these adjectives have a genitive *-īus* and dative *-ī* in the singular.

As you know (Chap. III), *et* is not placed before *nōn*; nor is it placed before *nūllus*: instead of "*et nūllus*" we find *neque ūllus*:

- *neque ūlla dea pēior uxor est quam Venus.* (*l.14*)
- *Iūlius ... uxōrem suam neque ūllam aliam fēminam amat.* (*ll.24-25*)
- *Aemilia ... marītum suum neque ūllum alium virum amat.* (*ll.26-27*)

So, we find *ūllus* only with a negative.

Genitive of Quality/Description

A noun + adjective in the genitive can be used to describe a quality (*genetīvus quālitātis* or **genitive of description**). For example:

> *Mārcus octō annōs habet; Quīntus est puer septem annōrum.* (*ll.33-34*)
> *Adulēscēns vīgintī duōrum annōrum erat.* (*ll.39-40*)

Imperfect of all Conjugations: Active and Passive

The last example (*Adulēscēns vīgintī duōrum annōrum erat*) has *erat,* not *est,* because this was ten years ago (he is no longer *adulēscēns*). *Est* describes the present, *erat* the past. Compare the two sentences:

> *Nunc Iūlius Aemiliam amat.*   (loves, is loving, does love)
> *Tunc Iūlius Aemiliam amābat.*   (loved, was loving, used to love)

The form *amā|bat* is the **past tense** or **preterite** (Latin *tempus praeteritum*) of the verb *amā|re,* as distinct from *ama|t,* which is the **present tense** (Latin *tempus praesēns*). The preterite or past tense occurring in this chapter is called the **imperfect** (Latin *praeteritum imperfectum,* 'uncompleted past'). The **imperfect** denotes a past state of things or an action going on (not completed) or repeated. In each of the following examples, the action goes on over a period of time:

> *Iūlius et Aemilia Rōmae habitābant*: used to live; were living
> *Iūlius cotīdiē epistulās ad Aemiliam scrībēbat*: used to write (*l.76*)
> *Iūlius male dormiēbat*: was sleeping (*l.69*)
> *Tunc ego tē amābam, tū mē nōn amābās.* (*l.98*)
> *Neque epistulās, quās cotīdiē tibi scrībēbam, legēbās.* (*ll.101-102*)

The imperfect is formed by inserting *-bā-* (1st and 2nd conjugations) or *-ēbā-* (3rd and 4th conjugations) between the stem and the person endings: in the active *-m, -mus* (1st pers.), *-s, -tis* (2nd pers.) and *-t, -nt* (3rd pers.).

In Section II of your reading you will find that the passive is formed the same way, with the passive endings: *-r, -mur* (1st pers.), *-ris, -minī* (2nd pers.) and *-tur, -ntur* (3rd pers.).

Notā bene: the 1st person ends in *-m* and *-r* (not *-ō* and *-or*) and that *ā* is shortened before *-m, -r, -t, -nt* and *-ntur* (*amā|ba|m, amā|ba|r,* etc.).

1st Conjugation (*āre*): stem + *bā*+ endings:

> *Iūlius ambulat* → *Iūlius ambulābat*
> *Signa stant* → *Signa stābant*

2nd Conjugation (*ēre*): stem + *bā* + endings:

> *tectum columnīs altīs sustinētur* → *tēctum columnīs altīs sustinēbātur*
> *Habēsne librum tuum?* → *Habēbāsne librum tuum?*

3rd and 4th Conjugation (*ere*): stem + *ēbā*+ endings

Consonant-stem:

> *Iūlius flōrēs ad Aemiliam mittit* → *Iūlius flōrēs ad Aemiliam mittēbat*
> *Cotīdiē epistulās scrībimus* → *Cotīdiē epistluās scrībēbāmus.*

Vowel-stem:

> *Aemilia flōrēs ā Iūliō accipit* → *Aemilia flōrēs ā Iūliō accipiēbat.*
> *Nihil faciō* → *Nihil faciēbam.*

4th Conjugation:

> *Dormītisne?* → *Dormiēbātisne?*
> *Saepe Rōmānī conveniunt* → *Saepe Rōmānī conveniēbant.*

Imperfect

		active		passive
sing.	1.	-(ē)ba|m	1.	-(ē)ba|r
	2.	-(ē)bā|s	2.	-(ē)bā|ris
	3.	-(ē)ba|t	3.	-(ē)bā|tur
pl.	1.	-(ē)bā|mus	1.	-(ē)bā|mur
	2.	-(ē)bā|tis	2.	-(ē)bā|minī
	3.	-(ē)ba|nt	3.	-(ē)ba|ntur

Imperfect of *esse*

You have already met the 3rd person of the imperfect of the irregular verb *esse*: *era|t, era|nt* (Chap. XIII). Now you learn the 1st and 2nd persons:

1st	*era|m, erā|mus*
2nd	*erā|s, erā|tis*
3rd	*era|t, era|nt*

Compounds of *esse*, e.g. *ab-esse*, including *posse*, show the same forms:

> *ab-era|m, ab-erā|s*, etc.
> *pot-era|m, pot-erā|s*, etc.

Domus

The noun *domus, -ūs* is a 4th declension <u>feminine</u>, but it has some 2nd declension endings:

nom.	*domus*	*domūs*
acc.	*domum*	*dom<u>ōs</u>*
gen.	*domūs*	*dom<u>ōrum</u>* (or *dom<u>uum</u>*)
dat.	*domuī*	*domibus*
abl.	*dom<u>ō</u>*	*domibus*

The form *domī* (*Chap. XV, l.81*) is locative; for this form and acc. *domum* and abl. *domō* used as adverbs without a preposition, see the next chapter.

Lectiō Altera (Section II)

3rd Declension Adjectives of One Termination

You have already learned 3rd declension adjectives that end in *-is, -e* in the nominative, where *-is* is the masculine and feminine ending and *-e* is the neuter ending, e.g.:

> *brevis, breve*
> *fortis, forte*

And in the last chapter you learned *frequēns*, an adjective with the same ending in the nominative masculine, feminine and neuter. Other 3rd declension adjectives as well have the same ending in the nominative singular masculine, feminine, and neuter. Such adjectives vary from *bevis, breve* in the nominative *only*. Two such adjectives are:

> *Dīves* (*dīvitior, dīvitissimus*: rich)
> *pauper* (*pauperior, pauperrimus*: poor)

Examples:

> *Iūlius dīves erat, nōn pauper.*
> *Aemilia pauper erat, nōn dīves.*

Lectiō Tertia (Section III)

Vocative for Nouns in *-īus*

In Chapter IV you learned that 2nd declension words in *-us* have a special form used when addressing a person, the **vocative**, ending in *-e*, e.g. *domine*. When Aemilia addresses her husband by name she uses the vocative *Iūlī*: "*Ō Iūlī!*" and she adds "*mī optime vir!*" (*ll.93-94*). The vocative of personal names in *-ius* ends in *-ī* (a contraction of *-ie*):

> *Iūlius* → *Iūlī*
> *Cornēlius* → *Cornēlī*
> *Lūcius* → *Lūcī*

The vocative of *meus* is *mī* and of *fīlius* is *fīlī*:

> "*Ō mī fīlī!*" (*Chap. XXI, l.30*)
> *mī optime vir* (*l.94*)

Ablative of Respect

In Chapter XI you encountered the **ablative of respect** (*l.55 pede aeger*). *Dignus, a, um* also takes an ablative of respect:

- *Ille vir pessimus tē dignus nōn erat!*: worthy of you (*l.110*)
- *Tu sōlus amōre meō dignus erās*: worthy of my love (*ll.111-112*)

Points of Style: Idioms

Compare:

I. Apposition

> *in urbe Rōma*: in the city of Rome (*Roma* in apposition to *urbs*)
> *Rōmae*: at/ in Rome (locative)

II. *Ante/Post*

> *ante decem annōs*: ante the preposition + the accusative
> *decem annīs ante*: ante as adverb + ablative of degree of difference
>   similarly: *paulo* ante, etc.

III. *Ita...ut/ut...ita*

> <u>Ut</u> *tunc tē amābam, <u>ita</u>*   <u>As</u> I loved you then, <u>so</u> even
> *etiam nunc tē amō.*   now I love you.
>
> <u>Ita</u> *est <u>ut</u> dīcis.*   It is just as you say.

IV. *Quam*

> relative pronoun: feminine accusative singular (*Chap. III*)
> interrogative adjective: feminine accusative singular (*Chap. III*)
> correlative: *tam....quam*: as...as (*Chap. VI*)
> adverb: how (*Chap. VIII*)
> in comparisons: than (*Chap. XII*)

V. *Opus est*

> = *necesse est*; *oportet*
> *nōn opus est mē plūs dīcere* = *nōn necesse est mē plūs dīcere*

Vocābula Disposita/Ordināta

Nōmina
   1st

columna, -ae	column
dea, -ae	goddess
mātrōna, -ae	married woman

   2nd

dōnum, -ī	gift
forum, -ī	forum
marītus, -ī	husband
praeteritum, -ī (tempus)	past tense
signum, -ī	statue, sign
tēctum, -ī	roof
templum, -ī	temple

   3rd

adulēscēns, adulēscentis (*m.*)	young person
amor, amōris (*m.*)	love
coniūnx, coniugis (*m./f.*)	spouse
flōs, flōris (*m.*)	flower
praesēns, entis (tempus)	present tense

pulchritūdō, pulchritūdinis (*f.*)   beauty
uxor, uxōris (*f.*)   wife
virgō, virginis (*f.*)   unmarried girl
4th
domus -ūs (*f.*)   house

Verba

-āre (1)
ōsculor, ōsculārī   kiss
-ēre (2)
augeō, augēre   increase
possideō, possidēre   possess
-ere (3)
minuō, minuere   diminish
mittō, mittere   send
remittō, remittere   send again, send back
-īre (4)
conveniō, convenīre   come together, fit together; fit
Irregular
opus esse   to need (+*inf. or abl.*)

Adiectīva

1st-2nd (us/er, -a, -um)
beātus, -a, -um   blessed, fortunate
dignus, -a, -um (+ *abl.*)   worthy of
magnificus, -a, -um   magnificent
miser, misera, miserum   wretched
3rd
dīves (dīvitis)   rich
gracilis, -e   slender
pauper (*gen.* pauperis)   poor
Irregular
melior, melius   better
pēior, pēius   worse
māior, māius   larger, greater
minor, minus   smaller
plūres, plura   more
optimus, -a, -um   best
pessimus, -a, -um   worst
māximus, -a, -um   largest, greatest
minimus, -a, -um   smallest
plūrimī, -ae, -a   most, a great many

Pronōmina

mī   = mihi
ūllus, -a, -um   any

Adverbia

cotīdiē   daily

minus	less
plūs (*adv. + neuter noun*)	more
tamen (*adv. + conj.*)	nevertheless

Praepositiōnēs

ergā + *acc.*	towards

XX. Parentēs

Rēs Grammaticae Novae

1. Verbs
   a. Future Tense: All Conjugations Active and Passive
   b. *velle/nōlle*
2. Nouns
   a. *domus*
   b. *carēre* + Ablative of Separation
3. Pronouns: Personal Pronouns
4. Adverbs: *minus/magis*

Julius and Aemilia Look to the Future

A happy event is in store for our Roman family. This gives the parents occasion for thoughts about the future, which in turn gives you a chance to get acquainted with the **future tense** (Latin *tempus futūrum*) of Latin verbs.

Lectiō Prīma (Section I)

Future Tense

The future is formed by the insertion between the stem and personal ending of:

(1) -b- in the 1st and 2nd conjugations, with the following vowel variations:
   a. 1st person singular in *ō*: e.g. *amā|b|ō, habē|b|ō*
   b. 3rd plural in *u*: e.g. *amā|bu|nt, amā|bu|ntur*
   c. 2nd singular **passive** in *e*: e.g. *amā|be|ris*
   d. Otherwise in *i*: e.g. *amā|bi|s, amā|bi|t, amā|bi|mus*

Notā Bene: Remember the sequence *-bō, -bi, -bu* (plus the change of *i* to *e* before *r*).

(2) In the 3rd and 4th conjugations, the sign of the future is:
   a. 1st pers. sing. *-a-* + active ending *m* as in the imperfect, e.g.:

   dīc|a|m, capi|a|m, audi|a|m
   dīc|a|r, capi|a|r, audi|a|r

b. Otherwise -ē-

   dīc|ē|s, capi|ē|s, audi|ē|s
   dīc|ē|ris, capi|ē|ris, audi|ē|ris

c. But -ē- is **shortened** to -e- before -t, -nt, -ntur:

   dīc|e|t
   dīc|e|nt
   dīc|e|ntur

future

1st & 2nd conjugation					
active	passive	active	passive	active	passive
1. *-b|ō*	*-b|or*	1. *cūrābō*	*cūrābor*	1. *dēbēbō*	*dēbēbor*
2. *-b|is*	*-b|eris*	2. *cūrābis*	*cūrāberis*	2. *dēbēbis*	*dēbēberis*
3. *-b|it*	*-b|itur*	3. *cūrābit*	*cūrābitur*	3. *dēbēbit*	*dēbēbitur*
1.pl. *-b|imus*	*-b|imur*	1. *cūrābimus*	*cūrābimur*	1. *dēbēbimus*	*dēbēbimur*
2. *-b|it is*	*-b|iminī*	2. *cūrābitis*	*cūrābiminī*	2. *dēbēbitis*	*dēbēbiminī*
3. *-b|unt*	*-b|untur*	3. *cūrābunt*	*cūrābuntur*	3. *dēbēbunt*	*dēbēbuntur*

3rd & 4th conjugation					
active	passive	active	passive	active	passive
1. *-a|m*	*-a|r*	1. *alam*	*alar*	1. *exaudiam*	*exaudiar*
2. *-ē|s*	*-ē|ris*	2. *alēs*	*alēris*	2. *exaudiēs*	*exaudiēris*
3. *-e|t*	*-ē|tur*	3. *alēt*	*alētur*	3. *exaudiet*	*exaudiētur*
1. *-ē|mus*	*-ē|mur*	1. *alēmus*	*alēmur*	1. *exaudiēmus*	*exaudiēmur*
2. *-ē|tis*	*-ē|minī*	2. *alētis*	*alēminī*	2. *exaudiētis*	*exaudiēminī*
3. *-e|nt*	*-e|ntur*	3. *alent*	*alentur*	3. *exaudient*	*exaudiēntur*

Esse: future

	sing.	pl.
1.	*erō*	*erimus*
2.	*eris*	*eritis*
3.	*erit*	*erunt*

Lectiō Altera (Section II)

Minus/magis

Note irregular adverbs *minus* (less) and *magis* (more), often paired with *quam* (than):

   Num parvulam fīliam <u>minus</u> amābis <u>quam</u> fīlium. (ll.57-58)
   Nēminem <u>magis</u> amābō <u>quam</u> parvulam fīliam. (l.59)
   Iam fīliōs tuōs <u>magis</u> amās <u>quam</u> tuam Iūliam fīliolam. (l.61-62)

Velle/nōlle

You already know the 3rd person present of the irregular verb *velle*: *vult, volunt*. The 1st and 2nd persons are: *volō, volumus* and *vīs, vultis* respectively. The negation *nōn* is not placed before *volō, volumus, volunt* and *velle*; instead we find the forms *nōlō, nōlumus, nōlunt* and *nōlle*, which are contracted from *nē + volō*, etc.:

> *Ego alteram fīliam habēre <u>volō</u>, plūrēs quam duōs fīliōs <u>nōlō</u>!* :
> want...do not want (*ll.54-55*)

> *Cūr tū fīlium habēre vīs, Iūlī?* (*l.56*)

> *Vōs virī fīliōs modo habēre vultis.* (*ll.63-64*)

> *Nōs virī etiam fīliās habēre volumus.* (*ll.72-73*)

> *Iūlia dīcit "sē patre suō carēre nōlle."* (*ll.140-141*)

present of	*velle*		*nōlle*	
	sing.	pl.	sing.	pl.
1.	*volō*	*volumus*	*nōlō*	*nōlumus*
2.	*vīs*	*vultis*	*nōn vīs*	*nōn vultis*
3.	*vult*	*volunt*	*nōn vult*	*nōlunt*

The **imperative** *nōlī, nōlīte* is used with an infinitive to express a prohibition ("don't...!"), e.g.:

> *nōlī abīre!* (*l.69*)
> *Nōlī dīcere "tatam" et "mammam."* (*l.157*)
> *Nōlīte mē "Iūliolam" vocāre! Id nōmen mē nōn decet.* (*ll.160-161*)

Lectiō Tertia (Section III)

Domus (continued)

In Chapter VI you learned that names of cities and towns express place with the accusative (to which), ablative (from which) and locative (at which). *Domus* follows the same rule: the accusative and ablative of *domus, domum* and *domo*, are used without a preposition to express motion to or from one's home, e.g.:

> *dom<u>um</u> revertentur* (*ll.123-124*)
> *dom<u>ō</u> abīre* (*l.137*)

The form *dom<u>ī</u>* is locative ("at home") e.g.:

> *domī manēre* (*l.127*)

Notā Bene:

> *domum* acc.: "to home"
> *domō* abl.: "from home"
> *domī* loc.: "at home"

Ablative of Separation

The ablative expressing "place from which" in *domō* and *Tūsculō* is the **ablative of separation**; The verb *carēre* ("be without," "lack") is completed by an ablative of separation (and not an accusative), e.g.:

> *Īnfans neque <u>somnō</u> neque <u>cibō carēre</u> potest.*: *cibō carēre = sine* + abl.: *sine cibō esse* (*ll.5-6*)

> *Iūlia dīcit "sē <u>patre suō carēre</u> nōlle."* (*l.141*)

Personal Pronouns *nōs/vōs* (continued)

The personal pronouns *nōs* and *vōs* become *nōbīs* and *vōbīs* in the ablative and dative: *ā vōbīs, ā nōbīs*

> *Necesse est mihi crās rūrsus ā vōbīs discēdere.* (*ll.129-30*)
> *Nōlī ā nōbīs discēdere!* (*l.136*)

You will see the dative in the reading in the next chapter:

> *Prīmum magister nōbīs aliquid recitāvit.* (*Chap. XXI, l.91*)
> *Tabellam vōbīs ostendam.* (*Chap. XXI, l.109*)

Recensio: personal pronouns[1]

	1st sing.	1st pl.	2nd sing.	2nd pl.
nom.	*ego*	*nōs*	*tū*	*vōs*
acc.	*mē*	*nōs*	*tē*	*vōs*
dat.	*mihi*	*nōbīs*	*tibi*	*vōbīs*
abl.	*mē*	*nōbīs*	*tē*	*vōbīs*

Recensiō

1. Expressions of comparison

....*nōn minus....quam*	no less than
nec plūs nec minus quam opus est	no more or less than is necessary
magis quam	more than

2. *nōn tantum....sed etiam = nōn solum...sed etiam*

3. "Emotion" adverbs: *minimē, profectō*

4. Expressions of time:

Eō ipsō tempore	at that very time
Eō tempore	at that time
Tempore praeteritō	in the past; at a past time
Tempore futurō	in the future; at a future time
Totam noctem	for the whole night
Tertiō quoque diē	every third day
Cotīdiē	daily
Herī	yesterday
Hodiē	today
Crās	tomorrow

---

1   For the genitive of the personal pronouns, see the Chapter XXIX.

Decem annīs post	afterwards by ten years; ten years later = *post decem annos*: after ten years (the first is an ablative of degree of difference and post is an adverb, the second a preposition + the accusative

Summary of *esse*

Present	Future	Imperfect
sum	*erō*	*eram*
es	*eris*	*erās*
est	*erit*	*erat*
sumus	*erimus*	*erāmus*
estis	*eritis*	*erātis*
sunt	*erunt*	*erant*

Vocābula Disposita/Ordināta

Nōmina

1st

cūnae, -ārum	crib
fīliola, -ae	diminuitive of *fīlia*

2nd

colloquium, -ī	conversation
fīliolus, -ī	diminuitive of *fīlius*
officium, -ī	duty
silentium, -ī	silence
somnus, -ī	sleep

3rd

īnfāns, īnfantis (*m./f.*)	baby
lac, lactis (*n.*)	milk
mulier, mulieris (*f.*)	woman, wife
nūtrīx, nūtrīcis (*f.*)	(wet) nurse
sermō, sermōnis (*m.*)	conversation

4th

gradus, -ūs (*m.*)	step

Verba

-āre (1)

cūrō, cūrāre	care for
fōr, fārī	speak
postulō, postulāre	demand

-ēre (2)

careō, carēre	lack (+*abl.*)
dēbeō, dēbēre	owe, ought
decet, decēre (*impersonal*)	be fitting, proper
maneō, manēre	remain
sileō, silēre	be silent

-ere (3)

advehō, advehere	carry to
alō, alere	nourish, raise
colloquōr, colloquī	converse
dīligō, dīligere	love, cherish
occurrō, occurrere	run up
pergō, pergere	continue
revertōr, revertī	turn back

-īre (4)

vāgiō, vāgīre	wail (of babies)

Irregular

nōlō, nōlle	be unwilling, not want
volō, velle	wish, want

Adiectīva

1st-2nd (us/er, -a, -um)

aliēnus, -a, -um	belonging to another
futūrus, -a, -um	future
necessārius, -a, -um	necessary
parvulus, -a, -um	small
ūmidus, -a, -um	humid, wet

Adverbia

crās	tomorrow
magis	more
minimē	not at all; very little
mox	soon, next
profectō	surely; for a fact
rārō	rarely

Praepositiōnēs

ad... versus (+*acc.*)	toward
ūnā cum (+ *abl.*)	together with
adversus (+*acc.*)	toward

Coniunctiōnēs

sīve... sīve	whether....or

XXI. Pugna Discipulōrum

Rēs Grammaticae Novae

1. Verbs
   a. Perfect System
      i. Indicative, Active and Passive
      ii. Infinitive
   b. Perfect Passive Participle
   c. Varieties of the Perfect stem
   d. *crēdere*
2. Nouns: Neuters of the 4th Declension
3. Pronouns: *aliquis, aliquid*

Marcus Gets into a Fight

The chapter opens with Marcus coming home from school. He seems to be in a bad way: he is wet and dirty, and his nose is bleeding. Whatever can have happened on his way home? This is what you find out reading the chapter. You are reading Marcus's version of the story, and whether it is true or not, you can use it to learn the verb forms that are used when you talk about an event that **has** taken place.

Lectiō Prīma (Section I)

Perfect System

First of all, you find the form *ambulāvit* of the verb *ambulāre* in the explanation given for the wet clothes:

> *Mārcus per imbrem ambulā<u>vit</u>.*   Marcus walked/has walked through the rain. (*ll.*7-8)

This tense is called the **perfect**, in Latin *tempus praeteritum <u>perfectum</u>*, "past completed," as distinct from the **imperfect** tense or *praeteritum <u>imperfectum</u>*, "past not completed" (Chapters XIII, XIX).

The difference is that the imperfect, as we know, describes a state of affairs or an ongoing or repeated (habitual) action in the past, while the perfect tense tells about what once happened and is now finished. Compare the two preterites in the sentences:

> *Iūlia cantā<u>bat</u>. Tum Mārcus*   Julia <u>was singing</u>. Then Marcus
> *eam pulsā<u>vit</u>!*   <u>hit</u> her!

The perfect can also denote the the present result of a past action ("the present perfect"), e.g:

> *Iam Iūlia plōra<u>t</u>, quia Mārcus*   Julia <u>is crying</u>, because Marcus <u>has hit</u>
> *eam pulsā<u>vit</u>.* (English "<u>has</u> hit")   her.

Context will tell you which sense of the perfect is more appropriate.

The tenses you have thus far learned (present, imperfect, future) have been formed from the **present stem**. The perfect is formed by adding endings (often called "secondary" endings) to the **perfect stem**. In the first section we find the secondary endings for the 3rd person: *-it* and *-ērunt*.

Examples:

> *Puerī per imbrem ambulāv<u>ērunt</u>.* (*ll.7-8*)
> *Mārcus et Titus Sextum pulsāv<u>ērunt</u>.* (*ll.13-14*)
> *Sordidus est quod humī iacu<u>it</u>.* (*ll.19-20*)
> *Et Mārcus et Sextus humī iacu<u>ērunt</u>.* (*ll.21-22*)
> *Titus vērō Mārcum vocāre audīv<u>it</u>.* (*ll.22-23*)
> *Nec vērō parentēs eum audīv<u>ērunt</u>.* (*ll.25-26*)

Perfect Passive

In the **present, future** and **imperfect tenses**, active and passive are formed from the same stem (the **present stem**), e.g.:

> *Sextus Mārcum pulsat/pulsabit/pulsabat.*
> *Mārcus ā Sextō pulsātur/pulsabitur/pulsabatur.*

In the **perfect tense**, however, the active and passive are formed:

> Active: <u>perfect stem</u> (as above): *Sextus Mārcum pulsāvit.*
> Passive: <u>perfect participle</u> + *esse*: *Mārcus ā Sextō <u>pulsātus est</u>.* ("<u>has been</u> hit") (*l.11*)
> Cf: *Vōx Sextī ā nūllō praeter puerōs <u>audīta est</u>.* (*l.26*)

The form *pulsātus -a -um* in <u>*pulsātus est*</u> is an adjective of the 1st/2nd declension, called the **perfect participle** (Latin *participium perfectī*). This participle is regularly formed by adding *t* to the present stem, followed by the various adjective endings *-us, -a, -um* etc., e.g.:

> *laudāt|us, -a, -um*
> *audīt|us, -a, -um*
> *scrīpt|us, -a, -um* (here, too, as in the perfect stem, change from *b* to *p*).

In combination with the present of *esse* (*sum, es, est,* etc.) the perfect participle is used to form the **passive of the perfect**, as in the above example; the ending of the participle then agrees with the subject, e.g.:

Iūlia ā Mārcō pulsāta est.
Puerī laudātī sunt.
Litterae ā Sextō scrīptae sunt.

The Perfect Stem

The personal endings of the perfect are added to the **perfect stem**, which is the familiar **present stem** expanded or changed. Compare the following examples:

	Present Stem	Perfect Stem
1st	*pulsā-*	*pulsāv-*
2nd	*iacē-*	*iacu-*
4th	*audī-*	*audīv-*
3rd	*dīc-*	*dīx-*
3rd	*scrīb-*	*scrīps-*

As you can see, consonant-stems undergo even greater changes in the perfect tense. The varieties of the perfect stem may seem confusing at first, but the stem in fact can undergo a limited number of changes. For example:

- 1st and 4th conjugation (present stems ending in *ā* or *ī*) regularly formed the perfect stem by the addition of *v*, e.g.:

    pulsā-: pulsāv-
    audī-: audīv-

- 2nd conjugation (stems in *-ē*) frequently drop the *ē* from the stem and add *v* (which becomes *u* when not following a vowel):

    iacē-: iacu-

- 3rd conjugation verbs (with present stems ending in a consonant) show a variety of perfect stem changes, e.g.:

    ▷ by adding *s* to the present stem, which can change the way the stem looks:

    In *scrīb-: scrīps-* voiced *b* changes to voiceless *p*
    In *dīc-: dīx-* only the spelling changes (*x* = *cs*)

scrīps- < scrībs- dīx- < dīcs-

Lectiō Altera (Section II)

Perfect System (continued)

The perfect active endings for the
- 1st person are *-ī* (s.) and *-imus* (pl.)
- 2nd person are *-istī* (s.) and *-istis* (pl.)

Examples:

Ego illum pulsāvī! (l.40)
Tūne sōlus sextum pulsāvistī? (l.41)
Ego et Titus eum pulsāvimus. (l.42)
Vōs duo ūnum pulsāvistis? (l.43)

Summary of Endings for the Perfect Active:

	sing.	pl.
1.	*-ī*	*-imus*
2.	*-istī*	*-istis*
3.	*-it*	*-ērunt*

Neuters of the 4th Declension

The two nouns *cornū, -ūs* and *genū, -ūs* are among the rare **4th declension neuters**:

	sing.	pl.	sing.	pl.
nom.	*cornū*	*cornua*	*genū*	*genua*
acc.	*cornū*	*cornua*	*genū*	*genua*
gen.	*cornūs*	*cornuum*	*genūs*	*genuum*
dat.	*cornū*	*cornibus*	*genū*	*genibus*
abl.	*cornū*	*cornibus*	*genū*	*genibus*

Aliquis, aliquid

Ali -quis, -quid is an **indefinite pronoun,** which refers to an undetermined person or thing (English "someone," "something"). It declines just like *quis quid* with *ali-* added.

> <u>*Aliquis*</u> *pedibus sordidīs in solō mundō ambulāvit.* (*ll.65-66*)
> *Prīmum magister nōbīs* <u>*aliquid*</u> *recitāvit.* (*ll.91-92*)

Lectiō Tertia (Section III)

Esse (continued)

The verb *esse* has a separate perfect stem *fu-*:

fu|ī   fu|imus
fu|istī   fu|istis
fu|it   fu|ērunt

Notā Bene: in the perfect, *esse* is completely regular.

Examples:

> *In lūdōne quoque bonus puer* <u>*fuistī*</u>? (*ll.82-83*)
> *Profectō bonus puer* <u>*fuī*</u>. (*l.84*)
> *Mārcus dīcit, sē bonum puerum* <u>*fuisse*</u>. (*l.85*)
> *Malī discipulī* <u>*fuistis*</u>! (*ll.104-105*)
> *Certē malī discipulī* <u>*fuimus*</u>. (*l.106*)

Perfect Infinitive Active

In Chapter XI you learned the accusative and infinitive construction using the present infinitive, e.g.:

> *Medicus "puerum dormīre" dīcit = Medicus inquit, "Puer dormit."*

Dormī|re is called the **present infinitive** (Latin *īnfīnītīvus praesentis*) and corresponds to the present tense *dormi|t*. Compare lines 96-97 in this chapter:

Iūlius: "Mārcus dormīvit!"
*Iūlius "Mārcum dormīv**isse**" dīcit.*

Dormīv|it is the perfect tense and the corresponding infinitive *dormīv|isse* is called the **perfect infinitive** (Latin *īnfīnītīvus perfectī*); it represents completed action and is formed by the addition of *-isse* to the perfect stem, e.g.:

- *intrāv|isse: Iūlius "Mārcum intrāv**isse**." dīcit (l.73)*
- *iacu|isse: nōn dīcit "eum humī iacu**isse**." (ll.73-74)*
- *fu|isse: Mārcus dīcit "sē bonum puerum fu**isse**." (l.85)*

The **present infinitive** represents an action happening **at the same time** as the main verb, while the **perfect infinitive** represents an action **happening after** the main verb.

present infinitive: *-re*   **perfect infinitive**: *-isse*

pulsāre	*pulsāvisse*
iacēre	*iacuisse*
scrībere	*scrīpsisse*
audīre	*audīvisse*
esse	*fuisse*

Perfect Infinitive Passive

When combined with the infinitive *esse* the perfect participle forms the **perfect infinitive passive**:

laudātum esse	to have been praised
scrīptum esse	to have been written
audītum esse	to have been heard

In the accusative + infinitive construction the participle agrees with the subject accusative e.g:

*Mārcus "sē ā magistrō laudā**tum esse**" dīcit.*
*Aemilia litter**ās** ā Mārcō scrīpt**ās** **esse** crēdit. (ll.121-122)*
Intellegēbam tē nōn cornibus, sed pugnīs pulsātum esse.

Nota Bene:

- Perfect Infinitive Passive: neuter of the perfect passive participle + *esse*
    laudāt|um esse

- Accusative + Infinitive Construction: participle agrees with the subject
    Iūliam laudātam esse
    Mārcum et Quīntum laudātōs esse

Perfect Passive Participle as an Adjective

The perfect participle is also used as an attributive adjective; it is **passive** in meaning, as opposed to the **present participle** in *-ns*, which is active:

puer laudātus = puer quī laudātus est
puer laudāns = puer quī laudat.

Adjectives as Substantives

The neuter plural of adjectives and pronouns is often used as a noun (substantively) in a general sense, e.g.:

multa	"a great deal," "many things" (*l.90*)
omnia	"everything," "all things" (*l.95*)
haec	"these things" (*l.123*)
et cētera	and all the rest

Crēdere

With the verb *crēdere* the person whom you trust or whose words you believe is put in the dative:

Mihi crēde! (*l.119*)
Mārcō nōn crēdit. (*l.140*)
Cūr nōn crēdis fīliō tuō? (*l.146*)

Summary of Perfect

Perfect Active

personal endings		
	sing.	pl.
1.	-t|us, a sum	-t|i, ae sumus
2.	-t|us, a es	-t|i, ae estis
3.	-t|us, a, um est	-t|i, ae, a sunt

personal endings		1st: *pulsā-*	*pulsāv-*
sing.	pl.	sing.	pl.
1. -ī	-imus	1. *pulsāv-ī*	*pulsāv -imus*
2. -istī	-istis	2. *pulsāv -istī*	*pulsāv -istis*
3. -it	-ērunt	3. *pulsāv -it*	*pulsāv -ērunt*

2nd: *iacē-*	*iacu-*	3rd: *scrīb-*	*scrīps*
sing.	pl.	sing.	pl.
1. *iacu -ī*	*iacu -imus*	1. *scrīps -ī*	*scrīps-imus*
2. *iacu -istī*	*iacu -istis*	2. *scrīps -istī*	*scrīps -istis*
3. *iacu -it*	*iacu -ērunt*	3. *scrīps -it*	*scrīps -ērunt*

4th: *audī-*	*audīv-*	Esse: *fu-*	
sing.	pl.	sing.	pl.
1. *audīv -ī*	*audīv -imus*	1. *fu-ī*	*fu -imus*
2. *audīv -istī*	*audīv -istis*	2. *fu -istī*	*fu -istis*
3. *audīv -it*	*audīv -ērunt*	3. *fu -it*	*fu -ērunt*

Perfect Passive

1st:			2nd:		
1.	*pulsāt|us -a*	*sum*	1.	*tent|us -a*	*sum*
2.	*pulsāt|us -a*	*es*	2.	*tent|us -a*	*es*
3.	*pulsāt|us -a -um*	*est*	3.	*tent|us -a -um*	*est*
1.	*pulsāt |ī -ae*	*sumus*	1.	*tent|ī -ae*	*sumus*
2.	*pulsāt |ī -ae*	*estis*	2.	*tent|ī -ae*	*estis*
3.	*pulsāt |ī -ae -a*	*sunt*	3.	*tent|ī -ae -a*	*sunt*
3rd: *scrīb-*		*scrīps*	**4th:** *audī-*		*audīv-*
1.	*scrīpt|us -a*	*sum*	1.	*audīt|us -a*	*sum*
2.	*scrīpt|us -a*	*es*	2.	*audīt|us -a*	*es*
3.	*scrīpt|us -a -um*	*est*	3.	*audīt|us -a -um*	*est*
1.	*scrīpt||ī -ae*	*sumus*	1.	*audīt|ī -ae*	*sumus*
2.	*scrīpt||ī -ae*	*estis*	2.	*audīt|ī -ae*	*estis*
3.	*scrīpt||ī -ae -a*	*sunt*	3.	*audīt|ī -ae -a*	*sunt*

Varieties of the Perfect Stem

- suffix *v/u* added to verb stem (*ama-v-*) or to the root (*hab-u-*)
- suffix *s* added to the root (*duc-s- = dux-*); *s* often changes the stem
- root perfect (see also Chapter XXIII):
  - ▷ the vowel of the root is lengthened; sometimes the vowel changes (*fac* → *fēc*)
  - ▷ the root is "reduplicated" by repeating the initial consonant of the verb, followed by a vowel (see also Chapter XXIII)
    - ○ usually *e*: *fallere* → *fefellisse*
    - ○ sometimes the root vowel: e.g. *mordēre, momordisse* (Chapter XXII)
    - ○ Sometimes, perfect and present stem appear identical: *ostendere* → *ostendisse*
- Some verbs have a perfect stem that cannot be easily understood just by the rules above
  - ▷ verbs formed from a lost or imaginary stem (*petere* → *petīvi*, as if from *petīre*)
  - ▷ verbs that have features peculiar to the present stem
    - ○ e.g. *scindere* → *scidisse* has a "nasal infix"[1] only in the present system
    - ○ inchoative verbs[2] with *-scō* lose the *-scō* in the perfect system (*cognōscere* → *cognōvisse*)

---

1 The consonants *m* and *n* are sounds formed partially through the nose, and are therefore called nasals. *Tangere* (Chapter XI) shows both the nasal infix and reduplication: *tangere* → *tetigisse*. Note that the "*n*" disappears in the perfect and the reduplication *te* is added to the stem, whose vowel has shortened.

2 An inchoative verb is one that suggests that action of the verb is beginning or undergoing change.

- Note on *emere* and compounds (Chapter XVIII):
  - ▷ *emere* and its compounds have a euphonic *p* before the perfect participle (try saying *emtum* and you'll find that the *p* is a very natural development from that combination)
  - ▷ *sūmere* is a compound of *emere*

The Supine Stem[3]

- Add *t* (or *s* when phonetics dictate)
  - ▷ to the present stem: *amātum, audītum*
  - ▷ to the root (with or without *i*): *habitum, ductum*
- phonetic changes
  - ▷ *dt/tt* → *s* (usually ss after a short vowel and s after a long vowel)
    claudere → *clausum*
  - ▷ *gt* → *ct*
    augēre → *auctum*

Vocābula Disposita/Ordināta

Nōmina
　1st
　causa, -ae | cause, reason
　pugna, -ae | fight
　tabella, -ae | writing-tablet
　2nd
　humus, -ī (*f.*) | ground
　imperfectum, -ī | imperfect (tense)
　perfectum, -ī (tempus) | perfect (tense)
　porcus, -ī | pig
　solum, -ī | soil, ground, floor
　3rd
　bōs, bōvis (*m./f.*) | ox
　cruor, cruōris (*m.*) | gore, blood
　sordēs, sordis (*f.*) | dirt
　　often pl. sordēs -ium
　vestis, vestis (*f.*) | clothes, cloth
　4th
　cornū, cornūs (*n.*) | horn
　genū, genūs (*n.*) | knee

3　These are not the only stem changes, but they are the most common. You will also find:
　　- sometimes a feature of the present stem appears in the supine
　　- sometimes the supine can come from a lost or imaginary stem
　　- sometimes the supine is formed by analogy from other verbs and ends in *s*
　　　instead of *t*

Verba

-āre (1)

(dubitō) dubitāre, dubitāvisse, dubitātum	doubt
(excūsō) excūsāre, excūsāvisse, excūsātum	excuse
(mūtō) mūtāre, mūtāvisse, mūtātum	change, exchange
(nārrō) nārrāre, nārrāvisse, nārrātum	relate, tell

-ere (3)

(cognōscō) cognōscere, -ōvisse, -itum	get to know, recognize
(cōnspiciō) cōnspicere	catch sight of, see
(crēdō) crēdere, -didisse: *intr. + dat.*	believe, trust, entrust
(fallō) fallere, fefellisse, falsum	deceive
(vincō) vincere, vīcisse, victum	defeat, overcome, win

-īre (4)

(mentior) mentīrī	lie

Irregular

(sum) esse fuisse, futūrum esse	be
(āiō) ais, ait, āiunt	say

Adiectīva

1st-2nd (us/er, -a, -um)

angustus, -a, -um	narrow
candidus, -a, -um	white, bright
falsus, -a, -um	false
indignus, -a, -um	unworthy, shameful
mundus, -a, -um	clean, neat
validus, -a, -um	strong

Pronōmina

aliquis, aliquid	someone, something

Adverbia

interim	meanwhile

Coniunctiōnēs

postquam	after, since

Alia

humī	on the ground (*locative*)
ain' = ais ne?	you don't say? really?

XXII. Cavē Canem

Rēs Grammaticae Novae

1. Verbs
   a. Supine: Accusative and Ablative
   b. The Three Verbal Stems, or Principal Parts
   c. Relative Time of Infinitives
   d. *ferre*
2. Participles: Ablative Absolute
   a. Relative Time of Participles
3. Pronouns
   a. *quis quid* (from *aliquis, aliquid*)
   b. *iste, ista, istud*
4. Adverbs: *forās, forīs*

Cavē Canem

The picture over the chapter represents an ancient mosaic found inside the front door of a house in Pompēiī. The picture and the warning inscription *Cavē canem!* are evidence of the way the Romans tried to safeguard their houses against intruders. Every house was guarded by a doorkeeper (*ōstiārius* or *iānitor*), who often had a watchdog to help him. So it is not easy for a stranger to be admitted to Julius's villa. First he must wake the doorkeeper, and then he has to convince him that his intentions are not hostile.

Lectiō Prīma (Section I)

The Three Verbal Stems, or Principal Parts

From the three verbal stems are derived all forms of the verb:

the **present stem**
the **perfect stem**
the **supine stem**

Consequently, to be able to **conjugate** (i.e. inflect) a Latin verb it is sufficient to know three forms, or **principal parts**, in which these stems are contained. Most useful are the three infinitives:

1. The present infinitive active, e.g. *scrīb|ere*
2. The perfect infinitive active, e.g. *scrīps|isse*
3. The perfect infinitive passive, e.g. *scrīpt|um esse*

The Supine Stem

The so-called **supine stem** provides the supine (below) and is also used to form the perfect participle—and the future participle, as you learn in the next chapter (Chap. XXIII).

The supine stem is formed:

- regularly by the addition of *t* to the present stem, e.g.:
    salūtā-: salūtāt-
    audī-: audīt-
    dīc-: dict-

- In *ē*-stems *ē* is changed to *i,* e.g.:
    terrē-: territ-

- There are several other irregularities, especially in 3rd conjugation verbs, where the addition of *t* may cause changes by assimilation, e.g.:
    scrīb-: scrīpt- (*p* is voiceless like *t*)
    claud-: claus- (*dt > tt > ss >s*)

Supine

The supine is a verb form used only in the accusative (in *-um*) and the ablative (in *-ū*).

Accusative

In this chapter the letter-carrier (*tabellārius*) tries to assure the *ōstiārius* with the words:

Ego nōn veniō vīllam oppugnā*tum* sīcut hostis, nec pecūniam postulā*tum* veniō (ll. 33-34).

Oppugnātum and *postulātum* are examples of a verb form called **supine** (Latin *supīnum*). The supine:
- ends in *-tum*
- is found with verbs of motion, e.g. *īre* and *venīre*
- expresses purpose

Other examples in this chapter are:

salūtātum venīre	to come to greet (in order to greet, with the purpose of greeting) (*l.49*)
dormītum īre	to go to sleep (in order to sleep, with the purpose of sleeping) (*l.50*)
ambulātum exīre	to go out to walk (in order to walk, with the purpose of walking) (*l.51*)
lavātum īre	to go to bathe (in order to bathe, with the purpose of bathing) (*l.52*)

Ablative

In addition the accusative expressing purpose with verbs of motion, the supine is found in the ablative. The **ablative supine** is a rare form used to modify certain adjectives, particularly *facilis* and *difficilis*. The ablative shows the respect in which the adjectives apply (cf. the ablative of respect in Chapters XI and XIX).

The following forms *dictū* and *audītū* are examples of the **ablative supine**:

> *Nōmen meum nōn est facile dīctū* (l.43) = *Nōn est facile meum nōmen dīcere.*
> *Vōx tua difficilis est audītū* (l.46) = *Difficile est vōcem tuam audīre.*
> *Id facilius est dīctū quam factū* (l.81) = *Facilius est dīcere quam facere*

The Supine Versus the Perfect Passive Particple

The **supine**:

- exists in two unchanging forms: the accusative and the ablative
- it will always end in *-um* (accusative) or *-ū* (ablative)

The **perfect passive participle** can be used just as an adjective or, combined with a verb, creates the past system in the passive. Combined with *esse*, it creates the perfect infinitive passive:

- As an **adjective**, the participle exhibits all the forms of a 1st/2nd declension adjective (like *bonus, bona, bonum*). It will agree with the word it modifies in gender, number and case.

Discipulī, ā magistrō monitī, silent.	The students, warned by the teacher, are being quiet.

- The perfect passive participle combined with the present tense of *esse* (*sum, es*, etc.) forms the perfect passive tense; the participle will agree with its subject.

Discipulī ā magistrō monitī sunt et silent.	The students were warned by the teacher and are being quiet.

- The simple perfect infinitive passive (to have been "*x*'d") consists of the neuter singular of the perfect passive participle + the present infinitive of *esse*.

monitum esse	to have been warned

- In indirect statement, the perfect infinitive passive must agree with its subject.

Puerī sciēbant sē monitōs esse.	The boys knew they had been warned.

The Three Verbal Stems in the Vocabulary

Notā Bene:

1. These are the forms that will be given in the margins of *Familia Rōmāna* whenever necessary, and the forms that appear in the vocabulary booklet that accompanies the series. In this book, however, four principal parts will be listed in the vocabulary:

   o first person singular present indicative active

   o present infinitive active

   o perfect infinitive active

   o perfect infinitive active

2. The perfect infinitive passive will be listed without *esse*

3. The perfect infinitive passive will be missing if the verb has no passive, e.g.: *posse potuisse*

4. The deponent verbs show the passive present and perfect infinitives, e.g.: *loquī locūtum esse*

The forms show various stem mutations, e.g.:

- vowel lengthening, e.g.:

  emere ēmisse ēmptum
  venīre vēnisse

- loss of *n* and *m*, e.g.:

  scindere scidisse scissum
  rumpere rūpisse ruptum

- reduplication (doubling) of syllables in the perfect, e.g.:

  pellere pepulisse pulsum

- occasionally an unchanged perfect stem, e.g.:

  solvere solvisse solūtum

To learn such stem varieties, a new exercise is now introduced in PENSVM A in LINGUA LATINA, where the missing perfect and supine stems are to be inserted in the verbs listed. Symbols used: [~] for perfect stem and [≈] for supine stem.

The principal parts (from the margins) to be learned in this chapter follow (the 1st person singular present active indicative is given in parentheses):

(aperiō), aperīre, aperuisse, apertum
(claudō), claudere, clausisse, clausum
(dīcō), dīcere, dīxisse, dictum
(emō), emere, ēmisse, ēmptum
(pellō), pellere, pepulisse, pulsum
(possum), posse, potuisse
(scindō), scindere, scidisse, scissum
(solvō), solvere, solvisse, solūtum
(sūmō), sūmere, sumpsisse, sumptum
(terreō), terrēre, terruisse, territum

(veniō), venīre, vēnisse
(vincō), vincīre, vinxisse, vinctum

Quis, Quid from *Aliquis, aliquid* (after *sī, num, nisī, ne*)

After *sī, nisī* (Chap. XV) *num*, and *ne*, the indefinite pronoun *aliquis aliquid* (someone, something) is shortened to *quis quid*. In the following examples, the pronouns *quis, quid* are not interrogative, but **indefinite** (= *aliquis*):

Sī quis vīllam intrāre vult (l.7)	"if anyone"
Num quis hīc est? (ll.27-28)	i.e. not "who," but whether "anyone" is there
Num quid tēcum fers? (ll.104-105)	i.e. not "what" but "anything" or "something."

If you find mnemonics useful, a good one for this rule is: "after *sī, nisī, num*, and *ne*, all the *alis* go away." Compare these examples:

Aliquis intrāre vult.	Someone wants to enter.
Sī quis intrāre vult.	If someone wants to enter.
Num quis intrāre vult?	Surely no one wants to enter?

Recensiō: Declension of *Quis, Quid*

quis	quid	quī	quae	quae
quem	quid	quōs	quās	quae
cuius	cuius	quōrum	quārum	quōrum
cui	cui	quibus	quibus	quibus
quō	quō	quibus	quibus	quibus

Lectiō Altera (Section II)

Iste, ista, istud

The demonstrative pronoun *iste, -a, -ud* (declined like *ille, -a, -ud*) refers to something connected with the person addressed (2nd person): Tlepolemus says *iste canis* about the doorkeeper's dog (*l.86*, "that dog of yours") and talking about Tlepolemus's cloak the doorkeeper says *istud pallium* (*l.103*).

iste	ista	istud	istī	istae	ista
istum	istam	istud	istōs	istās	ista
istīus	istīus	istīus	istōrum	istārum	istōrum
istī	istī	istī	istīs	istīs	istīs
istō	istā	istō	istīs	istīs	istīs

Recensiō

Review the following pronouns/demonstrative adjectives

hic, haec, hoc	this one (over here by me)
iste, ista, istud	that one (over there by you)
ille, illa, illud	that one (over there by him)
is, ea, id	he, she, it/this/that
ipse, ipsa, ipsum	himself, herself, itself

Ablative Absolute (continued from Chapter XVII)

Compare the following sentences:

Iānitōre dormiente, canis vigilāns iānuam cūstōdit. (l.23)
Cane vīnctō, tabellārius intrat. (l.119)

Iānitōre dormiente is the ablative absolute with the **present participle**, which expresses what is happening now, i.e. at the same time (= *dum iānitor dormit...*, "while...").

Cane vīnctō is the ablative absolute with the **perfect participle**, which expresses what has been done (= *postquam canis vīnctus est...*, "after...").

Relative Time of Participles and Infinitives

The tense of the participle is relative to the main verb:

- **present** participle is happening **at the same time** as the main verb
- **perfect** participle happened **before** the main verb

The English rendering in the sentences below demonstrates the time relationship of the main verb and the participle:

Iānitōre dormiente, canis vigilāns iānuam cūstōdit.	While the doorkeeper sleeps/is sleeping, the watchful dog guards the door.
Iānitōre dormiente, canis vigilāns iānuam cūstōdiebat.	While the doorkeeper slept/was sleeping, the watchful dog was guarding the door.
Cane vīnctō, tabellārius intrat.	When the dog was tied up, the mail carrier enters.
Cane vīnctō, tabellārius intravit.	When the dog had been tied up, the mail carrier entered.

The same time relation holds between main verbs and infinitives:

- present infinitive/participle means "same time as main verb"
- perfect infinitive/participle means "time before the main verb"

Adverbs *forās, forīs*

In this section we meet two new adverbs which both mean "outside":

- *forīs*: place where (cf. *ibi, hīc, illīc*)

   Tandem iānitor forēs aperit et Tlēpolemum forīs in imbre stantem videt (ll.56-57)

   "Manē forīs!" inquit iānitor. (l.68)

- *forās*: place to which (cf. *hūc, illūc*)

   Prius vincī canem et sine mē intrāre! Nōlī iterum mē forās in imbrem pellere! (l.115)

   "Non ego" inquit, "sed hic canis tē forās pepulit." (ll.116-117)

Recensiō: Ferre

In this chapter we meet the full conjugation of the irregular verb *ferre* (*ll.105ff.*). As you can see from the paradigm below, only the present tense of *ferre* is irregular; in the other tenses, it is completely regular:

Present	Imperfect	Future
ferō	*ferēbam*	*feram*
fers	*ferēbās*	*ferēs*
fert	*ferēbat*	*feret*
ferimus	*ferēbamus*	*ferēmus*
fertis	*ferēbatis*	*ferētis*
ferunt	*ferēbant*	*ferent*

Vocābula Disposita/Ordināta

Nōmina

1st
catēna, -ae	chain

2nd
aurum, -ī	gold
faber, fabrī	craftsman
lignum, -ī	wood
pallium, -ī	cloak
tabellārius, -ī	letter carrier
supīnum, -ī	supine (grammar)

3rd
cardō, cardinis (*m.*)	hinge
foris, foris (*f.*)	folding door
iānitor, iānitōris (*m.*)	door keeper = ōstiārius
imāgō, imāginis (*f.*)	picture, image
līmen, līminis (*n.*)	threshold

Verba

-āre (1)
(arbitrōr) arbitrārī, arbitrātum	think, judge
(rogitō) rogitāre, rogitāvisse, rogitātum	keep asking

-ēre (2)
(caveō) cavēre, cāvisse, cautum	beware
(dērīdeō) dērīdēre, dērīsisse, dērīssum	laugh at
(moneō) monēre, monuisse, monitum	advise, warn
(mordeō) mordēre, momordisse, morsum	bite
(retineō) retinēre, retinuisse, retentum	hold onto

(removeō) removēre, remōvisse,   remove
   remōtum
(terreō) terrēre, terruisse, territum   frighten
-ere (3)
(accēdō) accēdere, accessisse   approach
(admittō) admittere, admississe,   let in
   admissum
(cēdō) cēdere, cēdisse   yield (*intr.* + *dat.*)
(fremō) fremere, fremuisse   growl
(pellō) pellere, pepulisse, pulsum   strike, drive out
(prendō) prehendere, prendisse,   grab hold of
   prēnsum
(prōcēdō) prōcēdere, prōcessisse   move forward
(recēdō) recēdere, recessise   withdraw
(resistō) resistere, restitisse   resist (*intr.* + *dat.*)
(rumpō) rumpere, rūpisse, ruptum   break
(scindō) scindere, scidisse, scissum   rip, tear
(sinō) sinere, sīvisse, situm   allow
(solvō) solvere, solvisse, solūtum   loose (also pay)
(tremō) tremere, tremuisse   tremble
-īre (4)
(cūstōdiō) cūstōdīre, cūstōdīvisse,   guard
   cūstōdītum
(saliō) salīre, saluisse   leap
(vinciō) vincīre, vinxisse, vinctum   bind
Irregular
(ferō) ferre, tulisse, lātum   carry, bear

Adjectiva
1st-2nd (us/er, -a, -um)
aureus, -a , -um   golden
ferreus, -a, -um   iron
ligneus, -a, -um   wooden
3rd
ferōx, (ferōcis)   fierce, ferocious

Pronōmina
iste   that one (of yours)
quis, quid   shortened from *aliquis, aliquid*

Adverbia
anteā   before
forās   outside (toward)
forīs   outside (place where)
nuper   recently
posteā   after
prius   before
quīn   why not? in fact

scīlicet	naturally, of course
sīcut	just as
tandem	finally

Praepositiōnēs

extrā + *acc.*	outside
intrā + *acc.*	inside, within

XXIII. Epistula Magistrī

Rēs Grammaticae Novae

1. Verbs
   a. Participles
      i. Future Participle
      ii. *Eō, īre*: Present Participle and Summary
   b. Infinitives
      i. Future Active Infinitive
      ii. Future Passive Infinitive
   c. *pudēre* (impersonal)
   d. Perfect Stem, Continued (*ferre*, root perfects, reduplicated)
   e. Principal Parts

Julius Responds to Diodorus's Letter

At the end of Chapter XVIII an angry Diodorus (the schoolmaster) wrote a letter to Marcus's father. In this chapter you find out what is in that letter. The reproduction heading the chapter shows the kind of handwriting the ancient Romans used. Compare this with the text on page 180 of LINGUA LATINA, and you will have no difficulty in deciphering the script.

Lectiō Prīma (Section I)

Recensio: Participles (Sections I and II)

The first two readings in this chapter offer a good review of the participles and infinitives you have learned thus far:

- Perfect participle in an ablative absolute: <u>*Signō integrō*</u>, *nēmō scit.* (*ll.*19-20)
- Present participle in an ablative absolute: *Tacente Mārcō...* (*l.*55)
- Present participle: *Interim Mārcus pallidus et* <u>*tremēns*</u> *patrem* <u>*legentem*</u> *spectat.* (*ll.*34-36)
- Perfect participle: *vidēsne* <u>*nōmen*</u> *"Sextī" litterīs plānīs in parte superiōre* <u>*īnscrīptum*</u>? (*ll.*63-64)
- Present infinitive active: *Nōlō hās litterās* <u>*legere*</u>. (*l.*15)

- Present infinitive passive: *Tūne putās tē hīs litterīs laudārī, Mārce?* (*ll.49-50*)
- Perfect infinitive active: *Magister plānīs verbīs scrībit "tē discipulum improbissimum fuisse ac foedē et prāvē scrīpsisse!"* (*ll.60-61*)
- Perfect infinitive passive: *Tantum sciō epistulam Tūsculō missam et ā tabellāriō ad tē lātam esse.* (*ll.8-9*)

Ferre

The principal parts of the irregular verb *ferre tulisse lātum* come from different stems and must be memorized. Examples:

> *Ecce epistula quam illinc ad tē tulit.* (*ll.3-4*)
> *Tantum sciō epistulam Tūsculō missam et ā tabellāriō ad tē lātam esse.* (*ll.8-9*)

Lectiō Altera (Section II)
Pudēre (Impersonal)

When Marcus has been caught cheating, his father says, *"Nōnne tē pudet hoc fēcisse?"* (*l.79*)

The **impersonal** verb *pudet*:

- tells that a feeling of shame affects one
- the person affected is in the accusative, e.g.:
  > *mē pudet* (= *mihi pudor est,* "I feel ashamed").
- the cause of the feeling of shame can be expressed by an infinitive, as above, or by a genitive, e.g.:
  > *Puerum pudet factī suī.* (*l.82*)

Pudēre (it causes shame) is one of a few impersonal verbs[1] that follow this pattern:

- verb + accusative of person concerned (or "subject") and either
  - ▷ genitive of person/thing affected (or "object")
  - ▷ infinitive that completes the thought
- examples:
  > *Pudet mē pigritiae meae.*   I'm embarrassed about my laziness.
  > *Pudet mē hoc dīcere.*   I'm ashamed to say this.

Lectiō Tertia (Section III)
The Future Participle

Julius has to answer the letter. So after putting Marcus in his place, he says, *"Iam epistulam scrīptūrus sum"* (*l.125*). He could have said, *"Iam epistulam scrībam"* using the ordinary future tense *scrībam,* for *scrīptūrus sum* is merely an extended form of the future which serves to express what someone intends to do or is on the point of doing; it is composed of the present of *esse* and *scrīptūrus,* which is the **future participle** (Latin *participium futūrī*) of *scrībere.*

---

1   The other verbs are *piget* (it causes revulsion or displeasure), *paenitet* (it causes regret), *miseret* (it causes pity) and *taedet* (it causes boredom).

The **difference** between the simple future and the periphrasis of the future participle with a form of *esse* is one of inflection. The simple future means the speaker intends to do something at some point in the future (which point can be made more by use of an adverb or time expression), while the future participle plus *esse* suggests that the subject is on the point of acting.

The future participle:

- is formed by adding ≈*ūr|us, -a, -um* to the participle/supine stem, e.g.:

    pugnāt|ūr|us from *pugnāre*
    pārit|ūr|us from *pārēre*
    dormīt|ūr|us from *dormīre.*

- as an adjective means "about to X" "intending to X"
- agrees in gender, number and case with its noun
- as a verb (combined with *esse*) points to the immediate future
- examples:

pugnātūrus est	he is about to fight, intending to fight, he will fight
pāritūrus est	he about to obey, intending to obey, he will obey
dormītūrus est	he is about to sleep, intending to sleep, he will sleep

The future participle of *esse* is *futūr|us,* a form you know already from the expression *tempus futūrum.* All of these forms can be seen in context in Marcus's plea to his parents (*ll.84-87*):

> *Certē malus puer fuī, sed posthāc bonus puer <u>futūrus sum</u>: semper vōbīs <u>pāritūrus sum</u>, numquam <u>pugnātūrus sum</u> in viā nec umquam in lūdō <u>dormītūrus sum</u>.*

Future Active Infinitive

The **future infinitive** (*īnfīnītīvus futūrī*) is composed of the future participle and *esse.* In the following sentence, *scrīptūrum esse* is a future infinitive. Compare Julius's direct remark that he is about to write a letter with the reported statement:

> *"Epistulam scrīptūrus sum." (l.125)*
> *Iūlius dīcit "sē epistulam scrī<u>ptūrum esse</u>." (ll.125-126)*

Other examples are:

futūrum esse	*pugnātūrum esse*
pāritūrum esse	*dormītūrum esse*

These infinitives are all used in the report of Marcus's promises (*ll.89-93*)

> *Mārcus "sē malum puerum fuisse" fatētur ac simul prōmittit "sē posthāc bonum puerum <u>futūrum esse</u>, semper sē parentibus <u>pāritūrum esse</u> nec umquam in viā <u>pugnātūrum</u> nec in lūdō <u>dormītūrum esse</u>" — id quod saepe antehāc prōmīsit!*

The future active infinitive (summary):

- is comprised of the future active participle and the infinitive of the verb to be (*esse*)

- when used as a simple infinitive, the participle is neuter and singular:

    dormītūrum esse   to be about to sleep
    ductūrum esse   to be about to lead

- when used in indirect statement, the participle agrees with its subject:

    Puerī dīcunt sē dormītūrōs esse.   The boys say that they are
                                                about to go to sleep.

    Puellae dīcunt sē dormītūrās esse   The girls say that they are
                                                about to go to sleep.

Future Passive Infinitive

The future passive infinitive is comprised of the supine and the present passive infinitive to the verb to go (*īrī*). This form never changes: it is always the supine + *īrī*. For example:

    Aemilia Mārcum ā Iūliō verberātum   Aemilia thinks Marcus will be
    īrī putat.   beaten by his father. (*ll.114-115*)

    Ego eum nec mūtātum esse nec posthāc mūtātum īrī crēdō. (will be changed)
    (*ll.118-119*)

The supine, you will remember from the previous chapter (XXII), expresses purpose. When Julius gets up to go, Aemilia suspects mischief and (using the supine with *īre* to express purpose) asks, *"Mārcumne verberātum īs?"* (*ll.113-114*). Her misgivings could be expressed in the acc. + inf.: *Aemilia Iūlium Mārcum verberātum īre putat,* but to avoid the ambiguity of two accusatives the passive form is preferred, hence: *Aemilia Mārcum ā patre verberātum īrī putat.* (*ll.114-115*)

Notā bene: The supine does not change, regardless of the subject:

    Dīc eī "respōnsum meum crās ā Mārcō trāditum īrī." (ll.132-133)
    Dīc eī "epistulam meam crās ā Mārcō trāditum īrī."

Summary: Future Participles and Infinitives

The **future active participle** can be used just as an adjective or, combined with a verb, creates a periphrasis of the future. Combined with *esse*, it creates the future infinitive active:

- as an adjective, it:
    ▷ exhibits all the forms of a 1st/2nd declension adjective (like *bonus, bona, bonum*)
    ▷ agrees with the word it modifies in gender, number and case
- as a verb (combined with *esse*), it:
    ▷ can be used instead of the future tense
    ▷ the participle will agree with its subject

The **future infinitive active** consists of the neuter singular of the future active participle + the present infinitive of *esse*:

- in indirect statement, the participle must agree with its subject

Recensiō: Summary of Infinitives and Participles

Now you have all the infinitives:

- present active and passive
- perfect active and passive
- future active and passive

You also have almost all the participles:

- present active (there is no present passive)
- perfect passive
- perfect active (deponent verbs only: passive forms but active meaning)
- future active
- the gerundive (Chap. XXXIII) is sometimes called the future passive participle

Again, the tense, or time, of infinitives and participles is purely relative: it does not show absolute time. It is relative to the tense of the main verb:

- The present infinitive/participle shows time **simultaneous** with the main verb.
- The perfect infinitive/participle shows time **prior** to the main verb.
- The future infinitive/participle shows time **subsequent** to the main verb.

Summary: Infinitives

	Active	Passive
Present	*-āre*	*-ārī*
	-ēre	*-ērī*
	-ere	*-ī*
	-īre	*-īrī*
Past	Perfect stem + *isse*	Perfect passive participle + *esse*
Future	Supine stem + *ūrum esse*	Supine + *īrī*

Summary: Participles

For contrast, here is a summary of participles.

	Active	Passive
Present	*-āns*	
	-ēns	
	-ēns / iēns	
	-iēns	
Past	(deponents)	*-tus, ta, tum* (*t* can undergo changes: *claudere, clausus*)
Future	Supine stem + *ūrus, ūra, ūrum*	*-tus, ta, tum* (*t* can undergo changes: *claudere, clausus*)

Eō, īre

The present participle of *īre* looks regular enough: *i|ēns,* but the declension is irregular: acc. *eunt|em,* gen. *eunt|is,* etc. So also compounds, e.g. *red-īre,* part. *red-iēns -eunt|is.* Examples in *ll.106-107.*

Present Participle

sing.	masc./fem.	neut.
nom.	*iens*	*iens*
acc.	*euntem*	*iens*
gen.	*euntis*	*euntis*
dat.	*euntī*	*euntī*
abl.	*eunte/ī*	*eunte/ī*

pl.	masc./fem.	neut.
nom.	*euntēs*	*euntia*
acc.	*euntēs*	*euntia*
gen.	*euntium*	*euntium*
dat.	*euntibus*	*euntibus*
abl.	*euntibus*	*euntibus*

Recensiō: Forms of the Perfect Stem

In Chapter XXI you learned that in addition to adding *u/v* to the stem (with or without the stem vowel: *amāvisse/habuisse*), or *s* (e.g. *dīcere, dīxisse < dīcsisse*), perfects are fomed from the root of the verb or from the reduplicated root.

Root Perfects: A "root perfect" is a verb that forms the perfect tense by adding the endings directly to the root of the verb without the addition of any intevening tense sign (e.g. *v* or *s*). Root perfects can show:

- vowel lengthening

  legere lēgisse lēctum
  fugere fūgisse

- vowel change

  facere fēcisse

Reduplicated Perfects: A perfect stem is called reduplicated when it repeats the initial consonant of the verb, as in the verb *dare. Dare* is an unusual looking verb because the stem is basically *d.* In the perfect tense, the stem repeats the *d,* separated from the original *d* of the root by another vowel (*d + e + d*) and adds the endings: *dare dedisse. Trā-dere* (= *trāns + dare*) and *per-dere* (= *per + dare*) are compounds of *dare,* which explains the perfect *trā-didisse* and *per-didisse.*

  perdere, perdidī, perditum
  trādere, trādidī, trāditum

Principal Parts

The principal parts (from the margins) to be learned in this chapter are (the 1st person singular present active indicative is given in parentheses):

(afferō < ad + ferō) afferre, attulisse, allātum esse
(dēbeō) dēbere, dēbuisse, dēbitum esse
(dūcō) dūcere, dūxisse, dūctum esse
(faciō) facere, fēcisse, factum esse
(ferō) ferre, tulisse, lātum esse
(fugiō) fugere, fūgisse
(inclūdō < in + claudō) inclūdere, inclusisse, inclusum esse
(legō) legere, lēgisse, lēctum esse
(mereō) merēre, meruisse, meritum esse
(mittō) mittere, mīsisse, missum esse
(ostendō) ostendere, ostendisse
(perdō) perdere, perdidisse, perditum esse
(trādō) trādere, trādidisse, trāditum esse

Recensiō: Impersonal Verbs

decet	it is fitting
licet	it is permitted
necesse est	it is necessary
oportet	it is right (morally right)
opus est	it is needed

Vocābula Disposita/Ordināta

Nōmina
1st

litterae, -ārum	a letter = *epistula*
verbera, -ae	a lashing

2nd

factum, -ī	deed
prōmissum, -ī	promise
signum, -ī	sign, statue

3rd

clāvis, clāvis (*f.*)	key
comes, comitis (*m./f.*)	companion
laus, laudis (*f.*)	praise
pudor, pudōris (*m.*)	(good) shame

4th

vultus, vultūs	face, facial expression

Verba
-āre (1)

(comitor) comitārī, comitātum	accompany
(negō) negāre, negāvisse, negātum	deny, say…not

-ēre (2)

(contineō) continēre, continuisse, contentum	contain
(dēbeō) dēbēre, dēbuisse, dēbitum	owe, ought
(fateor) fatērī, fassum	acknowledge
(mereō) merēre, meritum	earn, deserve
(palleō) pallēre	be pale
(pudet) pudēre, puduit	feel shame (impersonal)
(rubeō) rubēre	be red

-ere (3)

(āvertō) āvertere	turn aside or away
(dīmittō) dīmittere, dīmīsisse, dīmissum	send in different directions
(inclūdō) inclūdere, inclūsisse, inclūsum	shut in
(īnscrībō) īnscrībere, īnscrīpsisse, īnscrīptum	inscribe
(perdō) perdere, perdidisse, perditum	lose
(prōmittō) prōmittere, prōmīsisse, prōmissum	promise
salūtem dīcere	say hi
(solvō) solvere, solvisse, solūtum	loose, pay
(trādō) trādere, trādidisse, trāditum	hand over or down

Adiectīva

1st-2nd (us/er, -a, -um)

integer, -ra, -rum	whole, undamaged
pallidus, -a, -um	pale
plānus, -a, -um	level
superior, superius	higher

Pronōmina

quidnam?	what in the world?
quisnam?	who in the world?

Adverbia

antehāc	before this
fortasse	perhaps
herī	yesterday
hinc	from here
illinc	from there
posthāc	after this
umquam	ever (always in neg. context)

Praepositiōnēs

ob + *acc.*	on account of

XXIV. Puer Aegrōtus

Rēs Grammaticae Novae

1. Verbs
   a. Pluperfect Tense: Active and Passive
   b. Deponent Verbs: Perfect Tense
   c. *nōscere*
   d. Principal Parts
2. Adjectives
   a. Comparisons
      i. Conjunction *quam*
      ii. Ablative of Comparison
3. Pronouns: Reflexive Pronoun
4. Adverbs: Adverbs in ō
5. Points of Style
   a. *quid agis?*
   b. *posse*
   c. Hyperbaton

Quintus Hears about his Brother's Troubles

From his sickbed Quintus calls Syra and asks her to tell him what has been going on while he has been lying alone and feeling left out of things. Syra readily gives him all the details of Marcus's return home and what had gone before.

Lectiō Prīma (Section I)
Adverbs

In Chapter XVIII you learned about adverbs ending in *-ter* (e.g. *fortiter*) and in *-ē* (e.g. *stultē*). Note the **adverbs** ending in *-ō*:

> *subitō* (*l.12*)   *rārō*
> *certō* (*l.59*)   *prīmō* (*l.100*, "at first")[1]
> *postrēmō* (*l.78*)

---

1   Cf. *prīmum*, l.68, adv. "first"

Reflexive Pronoun

Of the **reflexive pronoun** the form *sē* is accusative and ablative, the **dative** is *sibi* (cf. *tibi, mihi*):

- Syra: *"Doletne tibi pēs adhūc?"*
- Puer *"pedem sibi dolēre" ait: "Valdē mihi dolet pēs."* (*ll.23-24*)

acc.	*sē*
gen.	*See Chap. XXIX*
dat.	*sibi*
abl.	*sē*

Comparisons

There are two ways of expressing comparison between two things:

1. The conjunction *quam* ("than") is used in comparisons after the comparative. Comparisons in any case can be made with quam, "than;" the second member of the comparison will go into the same case as the first, e.g.:

   Mārcus pigrior est quam Quīntus.
   Pēs dexter multō māior est quam pēs laevus! (*l.6*)
   Pulchrius scrīpserātis et recitāverātis quam Mārcus. (*ll.113-114*)

2. Instead of using *quam* it is possible to put the second term in the **ablative**. This construction, the **ablative of comparison**, is used only when the first member of the comparison is in the nominative or the accusative case, e.g.:

   Mārcus pigrior est Quīntō
   Nunc pēs dexter māior est pede laevō. (*l.30*)
   Cēterum in hāc rē is nōn pēior fuerat cēterīs. (*l.77*)
   Is canis lupō ferōcior est! (*l.90*)
   Melior sum frātre meō! (*l.108*)
   Ego Mārcum bene nōvī, nec putō eum vōbīs stultiōrem esse. (*ll.115-116*)
   At certē pigrior est nōbīs! (*l.117*)

Deponent Verbs (continued from Chapter XVI)

You learned the present tense of deponents in Chapter XVI. Deponent verbs like *cōnārī* and *mentīrī* are always **passive in form**, *except* for the **present** and **future** participles:

cōnāns, mentiēns	trying, lying
cōnātūrus, mentītūrus	about to try, about to lie

Just as the present tense has the form of the present passive, the **perfect tense** has the form of the perfect passive. It is formed by the perfect participle and *esse*. Some examples of perfect participles:

patī: passus: tergī dolōrēs passus est. (*l.47*)
loquī: locūtus: saepe dē eā locūtus est. (*l.60*)
verērī: veritus: Tabellārius canem veritus est. (*l.88*)
fatērī: fassus: Mārcus "sē mentītum esse" fassus est. (*l.101*, note the perfect infinitive: *mentītum esse*)

Compare the present and the perfect tense:

Quīntus surgere cōnātur	Quintus tries to rise
Quīntus surgere cōnātus est	Quintus has tried to rise.
Mārcus mentītur	Marcus is lying.
Mārcus mentītus est	Marcus has lied.

The **imperative** of deponent verbs ending in -*re* is treated in the next chapter, but note:

> *Cōnsōlāre mē, Syra!* (*l.40*)
> *loquere mēcum!* (*l.41*)
> *immō laetāre* (*l.44*)

Lectiō Altera (Section II)

The Pluperfect Tense

Through Syra's report to Quintus you learn the tense called **pluperfect** (Latin *tempus plūsquamperfectum*). It is used to express that an action comes before some point in the past, i.e. that something <u>had</u> taken place (*ll.65-67*):

> *Mārcus nōn modo ūmidus erat quod per imbrem ambulāverat, sed etiam sordidus atque cruentus, quod humī iacuerat et ā Sextō pulsātus erat. Puerī enim in viā pugnāverant.*

The pluperfects explain why Marcus **was** (*erat*) wet and dirty: he **had** (previously) walked, had lain, had been hit, had fought (*ambulāv|erat iacu|erat, pulsāt|us erat* and *pugnāv|erant*).

In the **active** the pluperfect is formed by the insertion of -*erā*- (shortened -*era*-) between the perfect stem and the personal endings:

1st person	~*era|m*, ~*erā|mus*
2nd	~*erā|s*, ~*erā|tis*
3rd	~*era|t* ~*era|nt*

ambulā +v+era+m: I had walked (etc.)	*iac+u+era+m*: I had lain (etc.)
ambulā +v+erā+s	*iac+u+ erā +s*
ambulā +v+era+t	*iac+u+era+t*
ambulā +v+erā+mus	*iac+u+erā+mus*
ambulā +v+erā+tis	*iac+u+erā+tis*
ambulā +v+era+nt	*iac+u+era+nt*

In the **passive** the pluperfect is composed of the perfect participle and the imperfect of *esse* (*eram, erās, erat*, etc.), e.g.:

> *Mārcus ā Sextō pulsātus erat* = *Sextus Mārcum pulsāverat.*

> *pulsātus, -a, -eram*: I had been hit (etc.)
> *pulsātus, -a, -erās*
> *pulsātus, -a, -erat*
> *pulsātī, -ae, -erāmus*
> *pulsātī, -ae, -erātis*
> *pulsātī, -ae, -erant*

→ In the GRAMMATICA LATINA — both of LINGUA LATINA and beginning on page 257 of this book — you find examples of all the forms of the four conjugations and of *esse* (*fu|era|m, fu|erā|s, fu|era|t*, etc.).

Nōscere

The perfect *nōvisse* of *nōscere* ("get to know") has present force: "be acquainted with," "know," e.g.:

> *Quōmodo Mēdus puellam Rōmānam nōscere potuit?"* (*ll.57-58*)
> *Nesciō quōmodo, sed certō sciō eum aliquam fēminam nōvisse."* (*ll.59-60*)
> *Canis tē nōvit, ignōrat illum.* (*l.94*)

Principal Parts

The principal parts (from the margins) to be learned in this chapter are (the 1st person singular present active indicative is given in brackets):

> (*cadō*) *cadere, cecidisse*
> (*cognōscō*) *cognōscere, cognōvisse, cognitum*
> (*cōnor*) *cōnārī, cōnātus sum*
> (*dō*) *dare, dedisse, datum*
> (*eō*) *īre, īvisse/ iisse, ītum*
> (*fateor*) *fatērī, fassus sum*
> (*frangō*) *frangere, frēgisse, frāctum*
> (*lavō*) *lavāre, lavisse, lautum* (*lavātum*)
> (*loquor*) *loquī, locūtus sum*
> (*lūdō*) *lūdere, lūdisse*
> (*mentior*) *mentīrī, mentītum*
> (*mordeō*) *mordēre, momordisse, morsum*
> (*nōscō*) *nōscere, nōvisse*
> (*percutiō*) *percutere*
> (*reprehendō*) *reprehendere, reprehendisse, reprehensum*
> (*vereor*) *verērī, veritum*
> (*videō*) *vidēre, vīdisse, visum*
> (*volō*) *velle, voluisse*

Points of Style

Quid agis

> *Quid agis = quō modo te habēs?*

> *Syra Quīntō loquitur: "Sed tū quid agis? Doletne tibi pēs adhūc?"*　　　How are you? Does your foot still hurt? (*ll.22-23*)

Posse

Syra's remonstration to Quintus illustrates the idiomatic use of *posse*:

> *Mīror tē crūs nōn frēgisse. Facile ōs frangere potuistī.* (*ll.32-33*)

English would have used the perfect of "break" in both clauses: "I'm amazed that you **did not break** your leg. You could easily **have broken** a bone." *Posse*, however, works differently. To express what could have happened in the past, but didn't, Latin uses a past tense of the verb *posse* with a present infinitive.

Hyperbaton

When Quintus hears Syra's narration of what Marcus had done, the word order of his question reflects what is uppermost in his mind: his mother's reaction:

Māter quid dīxit? (*l.71*)

Marcus throws emphasis on the word *mater* by putting it first. Making the word order reflect the emphasis of thought is called **hyperbaton**.

Recensiō: The Verbal System (thus far)

Verbs have:

person	first, second, third
number	singular, plural
tense	present, future, imperfect, perfect, pluperfect
voice	active (subject acts); passive (subject acted upon)
finite mood	indicative (*Fact*: asks question; makes statements), imperative (*Order*: gives an order; commands)

Outside the finite[2] verbal system you have thus far learned the following verbal forms:

infinitive
supine
participle

Tense

Tense shows two things:

duration in time (going on or completed)
position in time (past, present, future)

Present tense: what is in progress right now

Future: what will be in progress in the future

Imperfect: what was in progress in the past

Perfect: shows completion in the present (i.e. in relation to present time, the action is completed.

Pluperfect: shows completion in the past (i.e. the action was completed in relation to another completed action)

Examples:

Indicative

I.	*Iūlius signum frangit.*	Julius is breaking the seal.
	Ā Iūliō signum frangitur.	The seal is being broken by Julius.
	Iūlius signum franget.	Julius will break the seal.
	Ā Iūliō signum frangētur.	The seal will be broken by Julius.
	Iūlius signum frangēbat.	Julius was breaking the seal.
	Ā Iūliō signum frangēbatur.	The seal was being broken by Julius.
	Iūlius signum frēgit.	Julius broke/has broken the seal.

---

2   Finite: that is, verbs which have a personal ending limiting their meaning.

Ā Iūliō signum frāctum est.	The seal has been broken by Julius.
Iūlius signum frēgerat.	Julius had broken the seal.
Ā Iūliō signum frāctum erat.	The seal had been broken by Julius.

II.	*Latīnē discere cōnor.*	I am trying to learn Latin, I do try, I try
	Latīnē discere cōnābar.	I was trying to learn Latin, I used to try, I tried
	Latīnē discere cōnābor.	I will try to learn Latin.
	Latīnē discere cōnātus/a sum.	I have tried to learn Latin; I tried to learn Latin, I did try
	Latīnē discere cōnātus/a eram, sed nōn potuī.	I had tried to learn Latin, but I could not.

Participle

I.	*frangēns, frangentis*	breaking
	frāctūrus, a, um	about to break
	frāctus, a, um	having been broken
II.	*cōnāns, cōnantis*	trying
	cōnātūrus, a, um	about to try
	cōnātus, a, um	having tried (notice active meaning!)

Infinitive

I.	*frangere*	to break
	frangī	to be broken
	frāctūrum esse	to be about to break
	frāctum īrī	to be about to be broken
	frēgisse	to have broken
	frāctum esse	to have been broken
II.	*cōnārī*	to try
	cōnātūrum esse	to be about to try
	cōnātum esse	to have tried

Infinitive in indirect statement

I.	Present	
	Videō puerōs signum frangere.	I see that the boys are breaking the seal.
	Videō signum ā puerīs frangī.	I see that the seal is being broken by the boys.
	Videō puerōs signum frāctūros esse.	I see that the boys will break the seal.
	Videō signum ā puerīs frāctum īrī.	I see that the seal will be broken by the boys.
	Videō puerōs signum frēgisse.	I see that the boys broke/have broken the seal.

Videō signum ā puerīs frāctum esse.	I see that the seal has been broken by the boys.

II. Past

Vīdī puerōs signum frangere.	I saw that the boys were breaking the seal.
Vīdī signum ā puerīs frangī.	I saw that the seal was being broken by the boys.
Vīdī puerōs signum frāctūrōs esse.	I saw that the boys would break the seal.
Vīdī signum ā puerīs frāctum īrī.	I saw that the seal would be broken by the boys.
Vīdī puerōs signum frēgisse.	I saw that the boys had broken the seal.
Vīdī signum ā puerīs frāctum esse.	I saw that the seal had been broken by the boys.

Vocābula Disposita/Ordināta

Nōmina

2nd

plūsquam perfectum, -ī, (*n.*)	pluperfect (tense)

3rd

dolor, dolōris, (*m.*)	pain, grief
latus, lateris, (*n.*)	side
os, ossis, (*n.*)	bone

4th

sonus, -ūs, (*m.*)	sound
strepitus, -ūs, (*m.*)	noise, din
tumultus, -ūs, (*m.*)	uproar

Verba

-āre (1)

(ignōrō) ignōrāre, ignōrāvisse, ignōrātum	not to know, be ignorant of
(mīror) mīrārī, mīrātum esse	wonder at

-ēre (2)

(fleō) flēre, flēvisse, flētum	weep

-ere (3)

(convertō) convertere, convertisse, convertum	turn
(cupiō) cupere, cupīvisse	want, desire
(frangō) frangere, frēgisse, frāctum	break
(nōscō) nōscere, nōvisse, nōtum	get to know; *pf*: know
(patior) patī, passum	suffer, permit, allow
(percutiō) percutere, percussisse, percussum	strike, hit
(recumbō) recumbere, recubuisse	lie down, lie back

Adiectīva
  1st-2nd (us/er, -a, -um)
  aegrōtus, -a, -um   sick
  cruentus, -a, -um   bloody, gory
  laevus, -a, -um   left
  subitus, -a, -um   sudden
  3rd
  impār (*gen.* imparis)   unequal
  pār (*gen.* paris)   equal

Coniunctiōnēs
  etsī   even if, although

Adverbia
  aliter   otherwise
  certō[3]   for certain
  cēterum   besides, however
  continuō   immediately
  dēnuō   anew, again
  intus   within
  prīmō   at first
  subitō   suddenly
  valdē   strongly, very (much)

Praepositiōnēs
  iūxtā + *acc.*   next to, beside

---

3   Cf: *certē*: certainly, at any rate

XXV. Thēseus et Mīnōtaurus

Rēs Grammaticae Novae

1. Verbs
   a. Imperative of Deponent Verbs
   b. Accusative and Infinitive
      i. *velle*
      ii. *iubēre* (continued)
2. Participle Perfect (deponents)
3. Nouns: Case Use
   a. Locative
   b. Ablative of Respect
   c. Ablative of Manner
   d. Objective Genitive
   e. *oblīvīscī* with Genitive/Accusative
4. Adverbs: Adverbs of Place
5. Points of Style
   a. *quī = et is*
   b. *bene/male velle*

Greek Mythology: Theseus and the Minotaur

In this and the next chapter we will leave the family and read some well-known Greek myths. These thrilling stories have fascinated readers through the ages, and innumerable poets and artists have drawn inspiration from the narrative art of the Greeks.

Lectiō Prīma (Section I)

Adverbs of Place

In this chapter we add to your store of adverbs signalling place:

Answering "*ubi?*":

hīc (Chap. III)	ibi: <u>Ibi</u> nāvis mea parāta est. (l.93-94)
illīc (Chap. VII)[1]	

---

1   *Notā Bene*: The accent on *illīc* is on the ultima (*illíc*): see Chapter VII.

Answering *unde?*

> *hinc (Chap. XXIII)*
>
> *illinc (Chap. XXIII): Nēmō quī tāle aedificium semel intrāvit rūrsus <u>illinc</u> exīre potest. (ll.30-31)*

In this chapter we see adverbs answering *quō?*

> *hūc: Auxiliō huius fīlī <u>hūc</u> ad mē redībis (ll.73-74)*
> *illūc: <u>hūc</u> et <u>illūc</u> currēns (l.110)*

Velle + Accusative and Infinitive

Like *iubēre,* the verb *velle* can take the accusative + infinitive construction:

> *Tē hīc manēre <u>volō</u>*   I want you to... *(ll.2-3)*
> *Quam fābulam <u>mē</u> tibi nārrāre <u>vīs?</u>*   Do you want me to... *(ll.2-4)*

Ablative of Respect (continued from Chapter XI)

In Chapters XI, XIX, and XXII you learned that the ablative case is used to show the respect in which something is true:

> *Nec modo <u>pede</u>, sed etiam <u>capite aeger</u> est. (Chap. XI, l.55)*
> *Tū sōlus <u>amōre meō</u> dignus erās. (Chap. XIX, l.111)*
> *Vōx tua difficilis est <u>audītū</u>. (Chap. XXII, ll.45-46)*

Similarly, a new name can be presented with *nōmine* ("by name," abl. of respect), e.g.:

> *mōnstrum terribile, <u>nōmine</u> Mīnōtaurus (ll.25-26)*
> *parva īnsula <u>nōmine</u> Naxus*

Lectiō Altera (Section II)

Locative (continued)

In Chapter VI you learned about constructions of place with the names of cities and towns. The place-names mentioned in the story can be found on the map of Greece. Among the names of towns note the <u>plural</u> forms *Athēnae* and *Delphī*:

nom.	*Athēn<u>ae</u>, Delphī*
acc.	*Athēn<u>ās</u>, Delph<u>ōs</u>*
abl.	*Athēn<u>īs</u>, Delph<u>īs</u>*

The accusative and ablative, as you know, serve to express motion to and from the town. Theseus goes:

> *Athēn<u>īs</u> in Crētam (l.34)*
> *ē Crētā Athēn<u>ās</u>*

But the **locative** of plural town names has the same form as the ablative, so that *Athēnīs* can also mean *in urbe Athēnīs:*

> *Thēseus Athēn<u>īs</u> vīvēbat. (ll.51-52)*

The rule about the use of the accusative, ablative and locative of names of cities and towns (i.e. no prepositions) also applies to the names of small islands, e.g. *Naxus*:

acc.   *Nax<u>um</u> = ad īnsulam Naxum* (*l.99*)
abl.   *Nax<u>ō</u> = ab/ex īnsulā Naxō* (*l.100*)
loc.   *Nāx<u>ī</u> = in īnsulā Naxō* (*l.132*)

Ablative of Manner (*Ablātīvus Modī*)

The ablative can express the way or manner in which an action is done, as you see in lines 142-43:

Quī multōs annōs Athēnās <u>magnā</u> <u>cum</u> <u>gloriā</u> rēxit. ("with great glory")

We saw this construction much earlier, but without a preposition:
Vocābulum "īnsula" dēclinātur <u>hōc</u> <u>modō</u>. ("in this way") (*Chap. IX, l.90*)

Mārcus perterritus ad vīllam currit et <u>magnā</u> <u>vōce</u> clāmat. ("with a great voice," "loudly") (*Chap X, ll.111-112*)

Notā Bene: The preposition *cum* in the *ablātīvus modī* is optional if the noun is modified by an adjective (*magnā cum gloriā, magnā vōce, hōc modō*). If there is no adjective (e.g. *cum gloriā*), *cum* must be used.

Objective/Subjective Genitive

Transitive verbs like *timēre* and *amāre* are generally used with an object in the accusative, e.g.:

mort<u>em</u> timēre
patri<u>am</u> amāre

Nouns and adjectives (including participles used as adjectives) that are derived from verbs, e.g. *timor* and *amor*, can be combined with a **genitive** to denote what is the object of that verb (e.g. fear or love of something/someone).

timor mort<u>is</u>   fear of death (*l.77*)
amor patri<u>ae</u>   love of country (*l.86*)

Such a genitive is called an **objective genitive**. Other examples are:

timor mōnstr<u>ōrum</u> (*ll.21-22*): *timor < timēre*
expugnātiō urb<u>is</u> (*ll.45-46*): *expugnātiō < expugnāre*
nex Mīnōtaur<u>ī</u> (*l.88*): *nex < necāre*
cupiditās pecūni<u>ae</u> (*ll.122-123*): *cupiditās < cupere*
cupidus aurī atque sanguinis (*ll.44-47*) = *quī cupit aurum atque sanguinem*
patri<u>ae</u> amāns (*l.51*) = *quī patri<u>am</u> amat*

Iubēre + Accusative and Infinitive (continued)

You have seen several examples of the accusative and infinitive with the verb *iubēre*.

An active infinitive expresses what a person is to do:
Medicus Quīntum linguam ostend<u>ere</u> iubet. (*Chap.XI, ll.69-70*)

A passive infinitive expresses what is to be done to a person, like *dūcī* in:
[Rēx] eum (ā mīlitibus) in labyrinthum dūcī iussit. ("ordered him <u>to be taken</u> into the labyrinth") (*l.59*)

Perfect Participle of Deponents

You know (Chapter XIV) that present participles can have an object:

Dāvus cubiculum intrāns (l.25)
Mārcus oculōs aperiēns (ll.37-38)

In the same way, perfect participle of deponent verbs (being active in meaning) can be used with the subject of the sentence to express what a person has/had done or did:

haec <u>locūta</u> Ariadna... ("having said/after saying this...") (l.74)
Thēseus fīlum Ariadnae <u>secūtus</u>... ("following...") (ll.84-85)
Aegeus <u>arbitrātus</u>... ("who believed...") (ll.137-138)

Compare

An ablative absolute with a perfect passive participle:

hīs dictīs, Ariadna   (*literally*) these things having been said, Ariadna...

A nominative feminine singular perfect participle of a deponent verb, which is active in meaning:

haec locūta, Ariadna   Ariadna, having spoken these things...

Points of Style

Quī = et is

A relative pronoun after a period functions as a demonstrative pronoun referring to a word in the preceding sentence. That is, the relative can be a transitional, connecting word, e.g. :

Thēseus Athēnīs vīvēbat. <u>Quī</u> (="and he") *nūper Athēnās vēnerat.* (ll.51-52)

Ā Daedalō, virō Athēniēnsī, aedificātus erat. <u>Quī</u> iam antequam ex urbe Athēnīs in Crētam vēnit, complūrēs rēs mīrābilēs fēcerat. (l.34)

Mīnōs autem fīliam virginem habēbat, cui nōmen erat Ariadna. <u>Quae</u> (="and she") *cum prīmum Thēseum cōnspexit, eum amāre coepit cōnstituitque eum servāre.* (ll.60-62)

Thēseus rēx Athēniēnsium factus est. <u>Quī</u> multōs annōs Athēnās magnā cum glōriā rēxit. (ll.141-143)

Bene/male velle

The idiomatic expressions *bene velle* (to wish someone well) and *male velle* (to wish someone ill) take a dative of person; from the participle (*bene volens* and *male volens*) come the English words benevolent and malevolent. Example:

Rēx enim Athēniēnsibus male volēbat. (ll.48-49)

Lectiō Tertia (Section III)

Imperative of Deponent Verbs

The **imperative of deponent verbs** ends in:
- *-re* in the singular (cons.-stems *-ere*)
- *-minī* in the plural (cons.-stems *-iminī*)

Notā bene:

- the plural imperative of deponents looks identical to the 2nd plural indicative
- the singular imperative of deponents *looks like* a present active infinitive

You have already seen examples of *-re* in Chapter XXIV, e.g.:

Intuēre pedēs meōs, Syra! (*ll.28-29*)
loquere mēcum! (*l.41*)
immō laetāre (*l.44*)

In this chapter Theseus says to Ariadne (<u>singular</u> <u>imperative</u>):

"Opperīre mē!" (*l.75*)
"Et tū sequere mē! Proficīscere mēcum Athēnās!" (*ll.95-96*)

To his countrymen, Theseus uses the <u>plural</u> <u>imperative</u> (*ll.92-93*):

Laetāminī, cīvēs meī!
Intuēminī gladium meum cruentum!
Sequiminī mē ad portum!

Oblīvīscī with Genitive/Accusative

The verb *oblīvīscī* can be completed both by an accusative direct object as well as by the genitive. *Oblīvīscī* can take an accusative when the object is a thing:

oblīvīscere illīus virī! (*l.126*)

Nōn facile est amōris antīquī oblīvīscī. (*l.128*)

Quis tam facile prōmissum oblīvīscitur quam vir quī fēminam amāvit? (*ll.119-120*)

Redeō ad nārrātiōnem fābulae, quam prope oblīta sum. (*ll.129-130*)

Nāvigandum, fugiendum

The forms *nāvigandum* and *fugiendum* (*ll.94, 97*) will be taken up in Chapter XXVI.

Recensiō: Adverbs of Place

ubi?	in what place?	*quō*?	to what place?
ibi	in that place, there	(*eō*: to that place: Chap. XXVIII)
illīc	in that place	*illūc*	to that place[2]
hīc	in this place	*hūc*	to this place

unde? from what place?
(*inde*: from that place: Chap. XXIX)

illinc from that place
hinc from this place

hūc atque illūc here and there (to this place and to that)
hīc atque illīc here and there (on this side and that)

---

2 Like *illīc*, *illūc* is accented on the ultima (i.e. originally *illūce*).

More adverbs

   brevī (*brevī tempore*)   in a short time
   quotannīs   every year
   ūnā cum + abl   together with

Vocābula Disposita/Ordināta

Nōmina

1st

fābula, -ae	story
glōria, -ae	glory
mora, -ae	delay

2nd

aedificium, -ī	building
agnus, -ī	lamb
auxilium, -ī	help, aid
fīlum, -ī	thread
labyrinthus, -ī	labyrinth
mōnstrum, -ī	monster
saxum, -ī	rock
taurus, -ī	bull

3rd

cīvis, cīvis (*m./f.*)	citizen
cupiditās, cupiditātis (*f.*)	desire
expugnātiō, expugātiōnis (*f.*)	conquest
lītus, lītoris (*n.*)	shore
moenia moenium (*n. pl.*)	walls
mors, mortis (*f.*)	death
nārrātiō, nārrātiōnis (*f.*)	story
nex, necis (*f.*)	death
rēx, rēgis (*m.*)	king

4th

cōnspectus, -ūs (*m.*)	sight, view
currus, -ūs (*m.*)	chariot
exitus, -ūs (*m.*)	way out, end

Verba

Notā Bene: Not all verbs have all principal parts (e.g. *maerēre* and *patēre* exist only in the present system).

-āre (1)

(aedificō) aedificāre, aedificāvisse, aedificātum esse   build
(necō) necāre, necāvisse, necātum esse   kill
(vorō) vorāre, vorāvisse, vorātum esse   devour

-ēre (2)

(maereō) maerēre	grieve
(pateō) patēre	lie open (*intr.*)
(polliceor) pollicērī, pollicitum esse	promise

-ere (3)

(cōnstituō) cōnstituere, cōnstituisse, cōnstitutum esse	decide, fix
(dēscendō) dēscendere, dēscendisse, dēscensum esse	descend
(dēserō) dēserere, dēseruisse, dēsertum esse	leave, desert
(incipiō) incipere, coepisse, coeptum esse	begin
(interficiō) interficere, interfēcisse, interfectum esse	kill
(oblīviscor) oblīvīscī, oblītum esse	forget
(occidō) occīdere, occīdisse, occīsum esse	kill
(prōspiciō) prōspicere, prōspexisse, prōspectum esse	look out, look ahead
(regō) regere, rēxisse, rēctum esse	rule
(trahō) trahere, trāxisse, tractum esse	drag

Adiectīva

1st-2nd (us/er, -a, -um)

cupidus, -a, -um	desirous
parātus, -a, -um	ready
saevus, -a, -um	savage
timidus, -a, -um	timid

3rd

complūrēs, -e	very many
humilis, -e	low
mīrābilis, -e	wonderful, marvellous
terribilis, -e	terrible

Adverbia

brevī	in a short time
forte	by chance
hūc	to this place
ibi	there, in that place
illūc	to that place
ōlim	once, long ago
quotannīs	every year

XXVI. Daedalus et Īcarus

Rēs Grammaticae Novae

1. Verbs
    a. Future Imperative
    b. *vidērī*
2. Verbal Noun: Gerund (*gerundium*)
3. Adjectives
    a. Adjectives in -*er*
    b. Irregular Superlatives *summus* and *īnfimus*
4. Pronoun
    a. *quisquam*
    b. Summary of Negative Expressions
5. Points of Style: Participles

Daedalus and Icarus

The story of the boy Icarus, who soared up to the scorching sun only to be plunged into the sea as the sun melted the wax that fastened his wings, has always been admired as a beautiful poetic picture of the penalty for arrogance and rashness. Syra, too, uses the story to warn Quintus to be careful.

Lectiō Prīma (Section I)

Gerund

In Chapter XXV, you read:

> *Ibi nāvis mea parāta est ad nāvigandum.* (ll.93-94)
> *Parāta sum ad fugiendum.* (l.97)

The words *nāvigandum* and *fugiendum* are verbal nouns, called gerunds. The **gerund**:

- is characterized by -*nd*- added to the present stem
    ▷ before consonant- and *ī*-stems (3rd and 4th conjugations) a short *e* is inserted before -*nd*-:

> *ad vīv|end|um*
> *ad audi|end|um*

- corresponds to English verbal nouns in "-ing"
- is a 2nd declension neuter noun:
  ▷ accusative ends in -nd*um* (*pugna|nd|um*)
  ▷ the genitive in -nd*ī* (*pugna|nd|ī*)
  ▷ the dative and ablative in -nd*ō* (*pugna|nd|ō*)
- does not exist in the nominative (use infinitive instead)

Uses of the Gerund

In this chapter you find several examples of the gerund in the different cases (except the dative, which is rarely used). The first occurrence of uses not introduced in the first reading are indicated in parentheses.

- The **accusative** is only found after *ad* and expresses **purpose**, e.g.:

Hodiē plūs temporis ad nārrandum nōn habeō.	I do not have more time today for recounting (stories). (*ll.10-11*)
Haud longum tempus nōbīs reliquum est ad vīvendum.	There is not much time left to us for living. (*l.28*)
ūna via nōbīs patet ad fugiendum	one road lies open to us for fleeing. (*l.36*)

- The **genitive** occurs:
  ▷ with nouns, e.g.:

fīnem nārrandī facere (= *fīnem nārrātiōnis f.*)	to make an end of telling (*l.13*)
cōnsilium fugiendī (= *cōnsilium fugae*)	a plan for escaping (*ll.55-56*)
Haud difficilis est ars volandī.	The art of flying is hardly difficult. (*l.72*)
Tempus dormiendī est. (= *tempus est dormīre*)	It is time for sleeping. (*ll.122-123*)

  ▷ or as an objective genitive with the adjectives *cupidus* and *studiōsus*:

cupidus audiendī	desirous of hearing (*ll.17-18, cf. l.108*)
studiōsus volandī	eager for flying (*l.43*)

  ▷ *causā* + the genitive of the gerund denotes cause or purpose:

Nōn sōlum dēlectandī causā, vērum etiam monendī causā nārrātur fābula	Not only for the sake of delighting but even for the sake of warning is the story being told (*ll.134-135*)

  ▷ The **ablative** of the gerund is found after *in* and *dē*:

in volandō	in flying (*l.80*)
dē amandō	about loving (*l.154*)

  ▷ or alone as the ablative of means or cause:

Puerī scrībere discunt scrībendō.	Boys learn to write by writing.
Fessus sum ambulandō.	I am tired out by walking. (*l.24; cf. ll.129-130*)

Adjectives in -*er*

Adjectives that have -*er* in the masc. nom. sing. are found both among 1st/2nd declension adjectives (as you learned in Chapter V):

> *niger, gr|a, gr|um*
> *miser, er|a, er |um*
> *līber, er|a, er|um*

And among third declension adjectives (as you learned in Chapter XIII):

> *September, (gen.) Septembris*
> *Octōber, (gen.) Octōbris*
> *November, (gen.) Novembris*
> *December, (gen.) Decembris*

The following are examples of third declension adjectives in -*er* that have three endings in the nominative (-*er*, (*e*)*ris*, (*e*)*re*):

> *celer, celer|is, celer|e*
> *ācer, ācr|is, ācr|e*

Notā Bene:

- Look to the feminine and neuter nominative singulars to see whether an adjective in -*er* has the *e* (like *celer, celeris*) or lacks it (like *ācer, ācris*).
- Adjectives in -*er* have -*errimus* in the superlative, e.g. *celerrimus, ācerrimus*.

Summary of 3rd Declension Adjective forms

Third declension adjectives exhibit three different nominative groups:

a. One nominative form: Adjectives ending in -*ns* and -*x*, like *prūdēns* and *audāx* (gen. *prūdent|is, audāc|is*) have the same form in the nominative masculine, feminine, and neuter:

> *vir/fēmina/cōnsilium prūdēns*
> *vir/fēmina/cōnsilium audāx*

b. Two nominative forms: Adjectives ending in -*is*, -*e*, like *brevis, breve; gravis, grave*, have one form for the masculine and feminine, and one for the neuter:

> *vir/fēmina gravis; cōnsilium grave*
> *hōra/mensis brevis; tempus breve*

c. Three nominative forms: Adjectives ending in -*er* (see above) have a different nominative ending for masculine, feminine, and neuter:

> *Vir acer; fēmina acris; cōnsilium acre*

Negative Expressions

In Chapter III you learned that Latin uses the conjunction *neque* to express "and not, but not" (instead of *et nōn* and *sed nōn*). Similarly, in Chapter XIX we found *neque ūllus* for "and no one," **not** "*et nūllus.*" This chapter adds two more such negations:

- The pronoun *quis-quam, quid-quam* ("anyone," "anything") is likewise used in a negative context. Latin does not express "and no one" and "and nothing" by *et nēmō, et nihil*, but by *neque quisquam* (*l.26*, "and no one"), *nec quidquam* (*Chap. XXVII, l.106*, "and nothing");

  ▷ *Quidquam* is changed by assimilation to *quicquam*

- Similarly, *et* is avoided before *numquam* by using *neque umquam* (*Chap. XXIII, l.26*, "and never").

Summary

and not/but not	*neque/ nec*
and no one	*neque/nec ūllus*
and no one	*neque/nec quisquam*
and nothing	*neque/nec quicquam*
and never	*neque umquam*

āēr

The 3rd declension masculine noun *āēr* is borrowed from the Greek and keeps its Greek ending *-a* in the acc. sing. *āer|a̱* (*l.22*, = *āer|em*).

nom.	*āer*
acc.	*āer|a̱*
gen.	*āer|is*

Lectiō Altera (Section II)

Irregular Superlatives *summus* and *īnfimus*

- *summus* (*l.79*) comes from *super(us), -era, -erum* (comparative *superior*)
- *īnfimus* (*l.77*) comes from *īnfer(us), -era, -erum* (comparative *īnferior*)

Future Imperative

Instead of the short imperative *es! es|te!* of *esse* the longer form in *-tō -tōte* is often preferred: *es|tō! es|tōte!*

> *Cautus estō, mī fīlī!* (*l.81; cf. l.138*)

In other verbs this so-called **future imperative** is not very common (it will be treated in Chapter XXXIII).

Lectiō Tertia (Section III)

Vidērī

Vidērī, the passive of vidēre, is used (with nom. + inf.) in the sense of "seem (to be)", e.g.:

> Īnsulae haud parvae sunt, quamquam parvae esse <u>videntur</u>. (ll.92-94)

In this function a dative is often added, e.g.:

> Mēlos īnsula nōn tam parva est quam <u>tibi</u> <u>vidētur</u>.
> (ll.94-95, = quam tū putās; cf. ll.96-97, 125);

> puer <u>sibi</u> vidētur volāre (ll.143-145, = sē volāre putat).

Points of Style: Participles

This chapter offers many examples of how participles contribute to the strongly verbal nature of Latin:

> <u>Daedalus</u> in labyrinthō <u>inclūsus</u> errābat. (l.19)

> Nēmō <u>nōs</u> <u>volantēs</u> persequī poterit. (l.42)

> Tum puerum <u>ōsculātus</u> "Parātī sumus ad volandum" inquit. (ll.75-76)

> Haec verba <u>locūtus</u> Daedalus cum fīliō sūrsum ē labyrinthō ēvolāvit. (ll.83-84)

> Aliquī pāstor, quī forte <u>suspiciēns</u> eōs tamquam magnās <u>avēs</u> <u>volantēs</u> vīdit. (ll.85-86)

> novā lībertāte <u>dēlectātī</u> (l.89)

> Īcarus dēspiciēns multitūdinem īnsulārum mīrātus est. (ll.90-91)

> dēspiciēbat <u>mīrāns</u> (l.106)

> <u>Sōlem</u> in caelō serēnō <u>lūcentem</u> suspexit. (ll.107-108)

> <u>Puer</u> <u>territus,</u> lacertōs nūdōs <u>quatiēns,</u> in mare cecidit. (ll.115-116)

> lībertātem <u>quaerēns</u> mortem invēnit (l.122)

> quī currum patris regere <u>cōnātus</u> item dē summō caelō cecidit (ll.127-128)

> Hīs verbīs <u>puerō</u> <u>monitō</u> (l.141)

> Neque Quīntus <u>eam abeuntem</u> revocat. (l.142)

Vocābula Disposita/Ordināta

Nōmina
  1st
  fuga, -ae   flight
  nātūra, -ae   nature
  paenīnsula, -ae   peninsula
  penna, -ae   feather, wing
  2nd
  cōnsilium, -ī   plan
  gerundium, -ī   gerund
  lacertus, -ī   arm
  3rd
  ars, artis (f.)   art, skill
  carcer, carceris (m.)   prison
  ignis, ignis (m.)   fire
  lībertās, lībertātis (f.)   freedom
  multitūdō, multitūdinis (f.)   large number, multitude
  opus, operis (n.)   work
  orbis, orbis (f.)   circle, orbit
  4th
  cāsus, -us   fall, case

Verba
  -āre (1)
  (aberrō) aberrāre, aberrāvisse,   wander away, stray
    aberrātum
  (ēvolō) ēvolāre, ēvolāvisse, ēvolātum   fly away
  (excōgitō) excōgitāre, excōgitāvisse,   think out, devise
    excōgitātum
  (imitor) imitārī, imitātum   imitate
  (iuvō) iuvāre, iūvisse, iūtum   help, delight
  (levō) levāre, levāvisse, levātum   lift, raise
  (revocō) revocāre, revocāvisse,   call back
    revocātum
  -ēre (2)
  (videor) vidērī, vīsum   be seen, seem
  -ere (3)
  (accidō) accidere, accidisse   happen, occur
  (cōnsūmō) cōnsūmere, cōnsumpsisse,   consume, spend
    cōnsumptum
  (cōnsequor) cōnsequī, cōnsecutum   follow, overtake
  (cōnficiō) cōnficere, cōnfēcisse,   make, accomplish
    confectum
  (dēspiciō) dēspicere, dēspexi,   look down (at)
    dēspectum
  (effugiō) effugere, effūgisse   escape

(fīgō) fīgere, fīxisse, fīxum	fix, fasten
(perficiō) perficere, perfēcisse, perfectum	complete, accomplish
(persequor) persequī, persecutum	follow, pursue
(quatiō) quatere	shake
(suspiciō) suspicere, suspexisse, suspectum	look up (at)
(ūrō) ūrere, ussisse, ustum	burn

-ire (4)

(inveniō) invenīre, invēnisse, inventum	find
(molliō) mollīre, mollīvisse, mollītum	make soft, soften

Adjectiva
1st-2nd (us/er, -a, -um)

cautus, -a, -um	cautious
īnfimus, -a, -um	lowest
līber, libera, liberum	free
propinquus, -a, -um	near, close
reliquus, -a, -um	remaining, left
studiōsus, -a, -um	interested in + *gen.*
summus, -a, -um	highest
temerārius, -a, -um	reckless

3rd

audāx (*gen.* audācis)	bold
celer, celeris, celere	swift
ingēns (*gen.* ingentis)	huge, vast

Pronōmina

quisquam, quidquam	anyone, anything

Adverbia

deorsum	down
haud	not, scarcely
paene	nearly, almost
quidem	indeed
quoniam	since
sūrsum	up
tamquam	although
vērum	but

Coniunctiōnēs

sīn	but if

Praepositiōnēs

trāns + *acc.*	across

XXVII. Rēs Rūsticae

Rēs Grammaticae Novae

1. Verbs
   a. Moods in Latin
   b. Subjunctive Mood
      i. Present Subjunctive: Active/Passive
      ii. Verbs of Demanding and Effecting: *verba postulandī et curandī*
      iii. Present Subjunctive of Irregular *esse*
   c. Translating the Subjunctive
2. Nouns: Case Uses
   a. Ablative
      i. Ablative of Instrument
      ii. Ablative of Separation
      iii. Prepositions with Ablative
         1. *prae*
         2. *prō*
         3. *abs*
   b. Accusative: *Preposition circā*
3. Adverb: *parum*
4. Conjunctions
   a. *ut*
   b. *quam* + the Superlative
5. *Alia*
   a. *nē...quidem*: not ...even
   b. *locus, locī/loca*

Julius's Estate

Julius is the owner of a large estate in the Alban Hills, *mōns Albānus,* near Tusculum and the Alban Lake, *lacus Albānus.* The running of the farm is left to tenant-farmers, *colōnī.* Julius follows their work with great interest when he is in residence in his Alban villa. Here we meet him walking in his fields and vineyards, questioning his men about the quality of the crops.

Lectiō Prīma (Section I)

Ablative of Instrument (*Ablātīvus Instrūmentī*) (continued)

The **ablative of instrument** (Chapters VI and VIII) appears in the discussion of the use of the farmers' tools (*īnstrūmentum*) (*ll.18-20*):

> Frūmentum falce metitur.
> Quō īnstrūmentō serit agricola?

The verb *ūtī* ("use") takes the ablative of instrument, not the accusative (*ll.20-22*):

> Quī serit nūllō īnstrūmentō ūtitur praeter manum.
> Quī arat arātrō ūtitur.
> Quī metit falce ūtitur.
> Quī serit manū suā ūtitur.

In addition to "use" *ūtī* also means "enjoy," "treat," etc.:

> Amicīs meīs bene ūtor.   I treat my friends well.
> Vinō numquam ūtor.   I never use (drink, enjoy) wine.

Locus, plural: *locī/loca*

Instead of the regular plural *locī* of *locus* you often find the neuter form *loca,* *-ōrum* (*l.30*) which is usual in the concrete sense (places, localities); *locī* is used for passages in books, topics, points of argument.

> Italia est terra fertilis, sed multa *loca* Italiae nōn arantur. (*ll.30-31*)
>
> Theophrastus cum tractat *locōs* ab Aristotele ante tractātos.
> When Theophrastus treats subjects previously treated by Aristotle.[1]

Lectiō Altera (Section II)

Subjunctive Mood

In addition to many new words, you learn important new verb forms in this chapter. Compare the sentences:

> Servus tacet et audit.
> Dominus imperat ut servus tace*at* et audi*at*.

The first sentence uses the **indicative mood** (Latin *modus indicātīvus*)—*tace|t* and *audi|t*—to tell us what the slave actually does. The second sentence uses the **subjunctive mood** (Latin *modus coniūnctīvus*)—*tace|at* and *audi|at*—to expess what

---

1   Cicero, *de Finibus* 1.2.6.

the master wants his slave to do. *Taceat* and *audiat* are the **present subjunctive** (in Latin *coniūnctīvus praesentis*) of *tacēre* and *audīre*.

Moods (*Modī*) in Latin

Remember, language is an attempt to express thought. So the mood used in a sentence reflects the way the speaker sees that thought.

- The **indicative** (*indicātīvus*) makes a statement or asks a question.[2] The attitude of the speaker is simple "fact" or "question."
- The **imperative** (*imperātīvus*) gives a direct command.
- The **subjunctive** (*coniūnctīvus*) expresses an abstract idea, such as the will (volitive), or wish (optative) of the speaker. The subjunctive is used in dependent (subordinate) and independent clauses.

  ▷ Common subjunctive uses in **dependent** clauses:

    indirect commands (*Chap. XXVII*)
    noun clauses (substantive clauses) (*Chap. XXVII*)
    final (purpose) clauses (*Chap. XXVIII*)
    consecutive (result) clauses (*Chap. XXVIII*)
    cum temporal, *cum* causal, *cum* concessive (*Chap. XXIX*)

  ▷ Common subjunctive uses in **independent** clauses:

    deliberative questions (*Chap. XXIX*)
    wishes (*Chap. XXXII*)

Present Subjunctive

Forms of present subjunctive:

- 2nd, 3rd and 4th conjugations insert -*ā/a*— between the present stem and the personal endings:

active	passive
-a|m	-a|r
-ā|s	-ā|ris
-a|t	-ā|tur
-ā|mus	-ā|mur
-ā|tis	-ā|minī
-a|nt	-a|ntur

- 1st conjugation, the *ā*-stems, which have -*ā*- in the present indicative, have -*ē/e*- before the personal endings in the present subjunctive:

-e|m	-e|r
-ē|s	-ē|ris
-e|t	-ē|tur
-ē|mus	-ē|mur
-ē|tis	-ē|minī
-e|nt	-e|ntur

---

2   In Chapter XXIX you will learn about questions in the subjunctive (deliberative questions).

→ In the section GRAMMATICA LATINA of LINGUA LATINA and starting on page 270 of this book, you will find examples of verbs with all these endings.

Breviter: The present subjunctive is formed with an *e* in 1st conjugation verbs, and an *a* in the other conjugations.

Translating the Subjunctive: The best way to read Latin is not to translate, but to understand in Latin. That requires knowing how your own language works as well as Latin! Then you can say to yourself: how does this work in my language? That may mean there are several ways to translate any given construction. The English translations below aim at showing the variety of interpretations possible. Some may seem rather literal and strained, others too free.

Verba postulandī

While the indicative is used to express that something does actually happen, the subjunctive expresses a desire or effort that something shall happen. Such an **indirect command** can be introduced by verbs that order (*verba postulandī*):

> imperāre   ōrāre
> postulāre   monēre

These *verba postulandī*—verbs that order, ask, warn, etc.—are often followed by object clauses introduced by *ut*, or, if they are negative (see Section III) by *nē* (or *ut nē*) and the subjunctive. Examples will be found in the account of Julius's dealings with his men, e.g.:

Iūlius colōnō <u>imperat</u> ut <u>mercēdem solv</u>at.	Julius orders the farmer to pay his fee/ gives an order to the farmer that he pay/ commands the farmer in order that he pay. (*ll.81-82*)

> *Vōs <u>moneō</u> <u>ut</u> industriē in vīneīs labō<u>rētis</u>. (l.126)*

Complements in *Verba Postulandī*

Notice that the person commanded in each of the three sentences is expressed in a different case:

> *Iūlius <u>colōnō</u> imperat ut mercēdem solvat. (ll.81-82)*
> *Colōnus <u>eum</u> ōrat ut patientiam habeat. (ll.92-93)*
> *Num uxor <u>abs tē</u> postulat ut tū prō mātre īnfantēs cūrēs? (ll.100-101)*

The case depends on the verb used.

Dative (intransitive verbs):

> *imperāre eī ut*
> *persuādēre eī ut*

Āb + ablative (the following verbs suggest "seek from"):

> *quaerere ab eō ut*
> *petere ab eō ut*
> *postulāre ab eō ut*

Accusative:

> *rogāre eum ut*
> *ōrāre eum ut*
> *monēre eum ut*

Notā bene: **iubēre** (order) does not regularly take an indirect command, but the accusative and infinitive construction. Compare:

> *Vōs* <u>*moneō*</u> *ut industriē in vīneīs labōr<u>ētis</u>.* (*ll.125-126*)
>
> *Iubeō vōs industriē in vīneīs labōr<u>āre</u>.*
>
> *Medicus Quīntum ōs aperīre atque linguam ostendere iubet.* (*Chap. XI, ll.69-70*)
>
> *Medicus Quīntō imperat ut ōs aperiat atque linguam ostendat.*

Ut

Most Latin *ut*-clauses with the subjunctive correspond to English "that" -clauses.

Remember: *ut* is also a comparative conjunction, meaning "like" or "as," and is followed:

- by the indicative:

  > <u>*ut*</u> *tempestās mare tranquillum turbā<u>vit</u>, <u>ita</u>* (as...thus)... (*ll.8-9*)
  >
  > *ut spēr<u>ō</u>* (*l 149*)
  >
  > *Cūr ille servus mēcum venīre nōn potest <u>ut</u> solet?* (*Chap. XIV, l.120*)

- by a noun adjective:

  > *Oculī lupī in umbrā lūcent <u>ut</u> gemmae et dentēs <u>ut</u> magarītae.* (*Chap. IX, ll.72-73*)
  >
  > *Puer quiētus super lectum iacet <u>ut</u> mortuus.* (*Chap. XI, ll.103-104*)
  >
  > *Gallia autem prōvincia Rōmāna est, <u>ut</u> Hispānia, Syria, Aegyptus.* (*Chap. XII, ll.63-64*)
  >
  > <u>*ut*</u> *saxa...vorāginēs...praedōnēs* (*Chap. XXVIII, ll.131-132*)

Nē...quidem

The negation *nē* is also used in *nē...quidem* ("not even"):

> *Nē in Campāniā quidem plūrēs vīllae sunt.* (*l.55*)
> *Nē assem quidem habeō.* (*l.86*)
> *Nē verbum quidem dīc!*

Prae, prō, abs

The prepositions *prae* and *prō* take the ablative; the basic meaning of both is "before," from which other meanings are derived (*prae ll.63, 83, prō ll.71, 72*):

> *Arātor duōs validōs bovēs quī arātrum trahunt <u>prae sē</u> agit.* (*ll.13-14*)
>
> *Quamquam nūllō modō labōrem agricolārum sordidum indignumve esse exīstimat, tamen sē <u>prae agricolīs</u> beātum esse cēnset.* (*ll.61-63*)
>
> *Colōnus pallidus <u>prae metū</u> loquī nōn potest.* (*l.83*)

>Colōnus est agricola quī nōn suōs, sed aliēnōs agrōs <u>prō dominō absentī</u> colit. (ll.71-72)

>Mercēdem dominō solvit <u>prō frūgibus</u> agrōrum. (l.72)

Abs for ab is found only before *tē*: abs *tē*:

>Cūr nōndum solvistī mercēdem quam ter quaterve iam abs tē poposcī. (ll.79-80, = ā tē).

Ablative of Separation

Note the **ablative of separation** (without *ab*) with:

>*<u>Pellere</u>*: ut tē <u>agrīs meīs</u> pellant. (l.89)

>*<u>prohibēre</u>* Nōlī mē <u>officiō meō</u> prohibēre! (ll.173-174)

Parum

The adverb *parum* often means not "a little" but "too little," as in the following examples:

>*<u>Parum</u>* temporis habeō ad opus rūsticum. (ll.98-99)

>Imber brevis quem hodiē habuimus frūmentō prōfuit quidem, sed <u>parum</u> fuit. (ll.130-131)

Lectiō Tertia (Section III)

Verba curandī

Verba curandī (verbs that show an effort to get something done) can be used to give commands as well:

cūrāre:	*cūrā ut*	*facere:*	*fac ut*
labōrāre:	*labōrā ut*	*cavēre:*	*cavē nē*
efficere:	*effice ut*		

Verba curandī are not always in the imperative, however, but are often followed by object clauses,[3] e.g.:

Calor sōlis nōn ipse per sē efficit ut vīnum bonum sit.	The heat of the sun does not itself through its own agency bring it about that/effect that/accomplish that the wine is good/does not make the wine good. (ll.124-125)
Faciam ut tergum eī doleat.	I will make his back hurt (*literally*: I will bring it about that the back to him hurts). (l.153)

---

3   An "object clause" is a dependent clause that functions as the object of the verb.

Like *verba postulandī, verba cūrandī* are often followed by object clauses introduced by *ut,* or, if they are negative, by *nē* (or *ut nē*) and the subjunctive.

Prīmum cūrā ut uxor et līberī valeant, tum vērō labōrā ut pecūniam solvās.	First of all take care that/make sure that (your) wife and children be well/are well, then surely work to pay the money/work so that you can pay the money. (*ll.111-113*)

Fac ut ovēs ex agrīs agantur! (*ll.175-76*)

Officium tuum est cūrāre nē ovēs aberrent nēve ā lupō rapiantur. (*ll.161-162*)

As appears from the last example, the second of two negative clauses is introduced by *nē-ve,* i.e. *nē* with the attached conjunction *-ve,* which has the same value as *vel.*

Summary:

ut + subjunctive	command, ask that something happen
nē / ut nē + subjunctive	command, ask that something not happen

Subjunctive of *esse*

In lines 151-152 we find an example of the irregular present subjunctive of *esse*: *Ego vērō cūrābō nē ille pāstor neglegēns sit nēve dormiat!* Here are the other forms:

sim	sīmus
sīs	sītis
sit	sint

Quam + the superlative

Quam + superlative (with or without *posse*) denotes the highest possible degree:

Pāstor quam celerrimē potest ad ovēs suās currit. "as quickly as possible" (*ll.177-178*)

Vocābula Disposita/Ordināta

Nōmina
1st

agricola, -ae (*m.*)	farmer
cōpia, -ae	abundance
cūra, -ae	care, concern
lāna, -ae	wool
patientia, -ae	patience
ūva, -ae	grape
vīnea, -ae	vineyard

2nd

ager, agrī	field
arātrum, -ī	plough
colōnus, -ī	(tenant) farmer
coniunctīvus	subjunctive
frūmentum, -ī	grain

īnstrūmentum, -ī	tool, instrument
negōtium, -ī	business
ōtium, -ī	leisure
pābulum, -ī	fodder
praedium, -ī	estate
vīnum, -ī	wine
3rd	
calor, calōris (*m.*)	heat
falx, falcis (*f.*)	sickle
frīgus, frīgoris (*n.*)	chill, cold
frūgēs, frūgum (*f. pl.*)	crops
grex, gregis (*m.*)	herd
labor, labōris (*m.*)	labor, toil
pecus, pecoris, (*n.*)	livestock, cattle
precēs, precum (*f. pl.*)	prayers
regiō, regiōnis (*f.*)	region
rūs, rūris (*n.*)	countryside
sēmen. sēminis (*n.*)	seed
vītis, vītis (*f.*)	vine

Verba

-āre (1)	
(arō) arāre, arāvisse, arātum	plough
(rigō) rigāre, rigāvisse, rigātum	water
(labōrō) labōrāre, labōrāvisse, labōrātum	work, toil
(exīstimō) exīstimāre, exīstimāvisse, exīstimātum	think
(ōrō) ōrāre, ōrāvisse, ōrātum	beg, pray
-ēre (2)	
(cēnseō) cēnsēre, cēnsuisse, cēnsum	think
(noceō) nocēre, nocuisse	harm (*intr.* + *dat.*)
(prohibeō) prohibēre, prohibuisse	keep off, prevent
-ere (3)	
(cingō) cingere, cinxisse, cinctum	bind round; surround
(colō) colere, coluisse, cultum	cultivate
(crēscō) crēscere, crēvisse	grow
(invehō) invehere, invēxisse, invectum	import
(metō) metere	reap, harvest
(neglegō) neglegere, neglēxisse, neglēctum	neglect
(pāscō) pāscere, pāvisse, pāstum	to pasture

(prōiciō) prōicere, prōiecisse, prōiectum	throw forward
(quiescō) quiēscere, quiēvisse	rest
(rapiō) rapere, rapuisse, raptum	tear away, carry off
(serō) serere, sēvisse, satum	sow
(spargō) spargere, sparsisse, sparsum	sprinkle
(ūtor) ūtī, ūsus sum	use (+*abl.*)

Irregular

(prōsum) prōdesse, prōfuisse	to be profitable, of advantage (+*dat.*)

Adjectīva

1st-2nd (us/er, -a, -um)

amoenus, -a, -um	pleasant (of places)
gravidus, -a , -um	heavy, weighty, pregnant
immātūrus, -a, -um	not ripe
inhūmānus, -a, -um	inhumane
mātūrus, -a, -um	ripe, early
rūsticus, -a, -um	of the country; rustic
siccus, -a, -um	dry
suburbānus, -a, -um	near the city
trīcēsimus, -a, -um	30th
urbānus, -a, -um	of the city, sophisticated

3rd

fertilis, -e	fertile
neglegēns (*gen.* neglegentis)	careless
patiēns (*gen.* patientis)	enduring, patient
rudis, -e	rough

Adiectīva

nēquam/ nēquior, nēquius/ nēquissimus, -a, -um	worthless

Pronōmina

quīdam, quaedam, quoddam	a certain

Adverbia

circā	around
dēnique	finally
parum	little; too little; *also indec. noun*
prae	before
tantum	only; so much; *also indec. noun*

Coniunctiōnēs

nē	*negative conjunction*
-ve	or

Praepositiōnēs

abs = ā, ab (*before* te)	
circā + *acc.*	around
prae + *abl.*	before, in front of, in comparison with
prō + *abl.*	before, in front of, on behalf of

XXVIII. Perīcula Maris

Rēs Grammaticae Novae

1. Verbs
   a. Imperfect Subjunctive: Active and Passive
   b. Tense in the Subjunctive
   c. Uses of the Subjunctive
      i.   Purpose (Final) Clauses
      ii. Result (Consecutive) Clauses
   d. Indirect Statement vs. *verba postulandī*
   e. *velle, nōlle, mālle*
   f. *īre* (Present Subjunctive)
2. Pronoun: Reflexive (continued)

Medus and Lydia at Sea

In this chapter and the next you hear more about Medus and Lydia. When the violent storm dies down, their ship sails on over the open sea. Lydia shows Medus the little book that she has brought with her and reads aloud from it, and in this way you become acquainted with the oldest Latin translation of the New Testament, used by St. Jerome in the 4th century in his Latin version of the Bible (the so-called Vulgate, *Vulgāta*, the "popular" version).

Lectiō Prīma (Section I)
Imperfect Subjunctive

When Lydia explains the power of Jesus Christ to Medus, she uses *verba curandī*:

> *Quī medicus verbīs sōlīs potest facere ut hominēs caecī videant, surdī audiant, mūtī loquantur, claudī ambulent?* (*ll.30-32*)

Compare what happens to the verb in the subjunctive clause when the main verb is in the past:

> In Iūdaeā Iēsūs nōn sōlum _faciēbat ut_ caecī _vidērent_, surdī _audīrent_, mūtī _loquerentur_, vērum etiam verbīs _efficiēbat_ ut mortuī _surgerent_ et _ambulārent_. (ll.34-37)

When the main verb refers to the past, the tense of the subjunctive changes as well. Just as the present subjunctive tells us the verb is incomplete in present time, the imperfect subjunctive tells us the verb is incomplete in past time (see below, Sequence of Tense).

Forming the Imperfect Subjunctive

The imperfect subjunctive is formed by inserting between the present stem and the personal endings:

_-rē-_

in consonant-stems _-erē_

1st, 2nd and 4th conjugations insert _-rē-/-re_ between the present stem and the personal endings, e.g.:[1]

ambulā|re|m	vidē|re|m	audī|re|m
ambulā|rē|s	vidē|rē|s	audī|rē|s
ambulā|re|t	vidē|re|t	audī|re|t
ambulā|rē|mus	vidē|rē|mus	audī|rē|mus
ambulā|rē|tis	vidē|rē|tis	audī|rē|tis
ambulā|re|nt	vidē|re|nt	audī|re|nt

3rd conjugation inserts _-erē-/-ere_ between the present stem and the personal endings:

surg|ere|m	fac|ere|m
surg|erē|s	fac|erē|s
surg|ere|t	fac|ere|t
surg|erē|mus	fac|erē|mus
surg|erē|tis	fac|erē|tis
surg|ere|nt	fac|ere|nt

Summary of Imperfect Subjunctive Endings

active

sing. 1. -(ā, ē, e, ī) re|m
2. -(ā, ē, e, ī) rē|s
3. -(ā, ē, e, ī) re|t

pl. 1. -(ā, ē, e, ī) rē|mus
2. -(ā, ē, e, ī) rē|tis
3. -(ā, ē, e, ī) re|nt

---

[1] Remember: short e before _-m, -t, -nt, -r, -ntur_

passive
sing.   1.   *-(ā, ē, e, ī) re|r*
           2.   *-(ā, ē, e, ī) rē|ris*
           3.   *-(ā, ē, e, ī) rē|tur*
pl.   1.   *-(ā, ē, e, ī) rē|mur*
           2.   *-(ā, ē, e, ī) rē|minī*
           3.   *-(ā, ē, e, ī) re|ntur*

esse

	sing.	pl.
1.	*esse|m*	*essē|mus*
2.	*essē|s*	*essē|tis*
3.	*esse|t*	*esse|nt*

→ Examples of all the forms of the four conjugations, active and passive, and of *esse* are found in the section GRAMMATICA LATINA, of LINGUA LATINA and at the back of this book.

Tense in the Subjunctive

Just like with infinitives and participles, time (tense) in the subjunctive is not about absolute time as much as relation. The present and imperfect subjunctives in dependent clauses represent **incompleted action** relative to the main verb.

If the main verb:
- is present or future, use the present subjunctive to indicate incomplete action
- refers to the past (perfect, imperfect or pluperfect), the imperfect subjunctive indicates incomplete action[2]

Compare the sentences:

Magister mē monet ut taceam et audiam.
Magister mē monēbat (/monuit/monuerat) ut tacērem et audīrem.

Sequence of Tense

Main Verb	Subordinate Verb	
	incompleted action	completed action
present future	present subjunctive	(Chap. XXXII)
past tense	imperfect subjunctive	(Chap. XXXIII)

Lectiō Altera (Section II)
Uses of the Subjunctive: Result

The subjunctive, introduced by *ut*, is used in clauses that tell the consequence of the main clause. These are called **result clauses**. The main clause that introduces

---

2   A perfect tense main verb can be followed by the present subjunctive if the perfect tense represents a present state (e.g. I have arrived=I am here), e.g. Chapter XXXIV, l.31-32: *nisi tam fortiter pugnāvit ut spectātōrēs eum vīvere velint.*

the result clause usually contains a word (note below *tam, ita*) that signals the result. Result clauses are also called consecutive clauses (*consecūtīvus, -a, -um < cōnsequī*) as they show what naturally follows from the idea in the main clause.

Result clauses (show tendency or effect, *ut* translated "that"):

Num quis <u>tam</u> stultus est <u>ut</u> ista vēra esse crē<u>dat</u>?	*ut…crēdat* tells the consequence of anyone being so stupid: For who is <u>so</u> stupid <u>that</u> he would believe these things are true? (*ll.90-91*)
Nam trēs diī, Neptūnus, Iuppiter, Plūtō, mundum ūniversum <u>ita</u> inter sē dīvīsērunt <u>ut</u> Iuppiter rēx caelī <u>esset</u>.	For three gods, Neptune, Juppiter, Pluto, divided the whole world among themselves <u>in such a way that</u> Jupiter was king of the sky. (*ll.85-87*)

There are more examples in Chapter XXIX.

Sē (continued)

In *ut/nē*-clauses expressing an indirect command the reflexive pronouns *sē, sibi, suus* refer to the subject of the main verb, i.e. the person ordering, requesting, etc. Compare:

Dāvus eum <u>sēcum</u> venīre iubet.: i.e. *eī imperat ut <u>sēcum</u> veniat* (*Chap. XIV, l.86-87*)

Pāstor dominum ōrat nē <u>sē</u> verberet.: i.e. *nē pastōrem* (*Chap. XXVII, ll.158-159*)

Mēdus eam rogat ut aliquid <u>sibi</u> legat.: i.e. *ut Mēdō* (*ll.56-57*)

[Iaīrus] Iēsum rogāvit ut fīliam <u>suam</u> mortuam suscitāret. (*l.65-66*)

Lectiō Tertia (Section III)

Uses of the Subjunctive: Purpose (Final)

The subjunctive, introduced by *ut*, is used in clauses that tell the end or goal of the main clause. These are called purpose, or final, clauses.

Purpose clauses (show intention, *ut* translated "to" or "in order to":

Praedōnēs nāvēs persequuntur, <u>ut</u> mercēs et pecūniam rapi<u>ant</u> nautāsque occī<u>dant</u>.	Pirates follow the ships <u>in order to</u> (or just "<u>to</u>") seize and kill. (*ll.132-134*)

Petrus ambulābat super aquam, <u>ut</u> venī<u>ret</u> ad Iēsum. (*ll.102-103*)

Ē vīllā fūgī, <u>ut</u> verbera vītā<u>rem</u> atque <u>ut</u> amīcam meam vidē<u>rem</u> ac semper cum eā <u>essem</u>. (*ll.162-163*)

Indirect Statement versus *Verba Postulandī* (Indirect Commands)

Note the difference between:

- *verba dīcendī et sentiendī*, which are combined with the acc. + inf.
- *verba postulandī*, which take an *ut*-clause in the subjunctive.

Some verbs can have both functions, e.g. *persuādēre* in these two examples:

> *Mihi nēmō persuādēbit hominem super mare ambulāre posse.*: no one will persuade/ convince me that... (*ll.110-111*)

> *Mēdus mihi persuāsit ut sēcum venīrem.*: Medus persuaded me to... (*ll.174-175*)

In both senses *persuādēre* takes the dative (like *oboedīre, impendēre, servīre, prōdesse,* and *nocēre*).

Īre: Present Subjunctive

The present subjunctive of *īre* (*cūrābō ut salvī in Graeciam eāmus, ll.145-146*):

indicative	subjunctive
eō	*eam*
īs	*eās*
it	*eat*
īmus	*eāmus*
ītis	*eātis*
eunt	*eant*

Velle, nōlle, mālle

In addition to *velle, nōlle* (= *nōn velle*), this chapter presents *mālle* (*magis velle*), to "want more," or "prefer." *Mālle* is often followed by *quam*:

> *Ego Rōmae vīvere mālō quam in Graeciā.* (*ll.150-151*)
> *Nōs cīvēs Rōmānī morī mālumus quam servīre!* (*ll.154-155*)

Volō, velle, voluisse to be willing, want		*Nōlō, nōlle, nōluisse* to be unwilling, not want		*Mālō, mālle, māluisse* to prefer	
volō	*volumus*	*nōlō*	*nōlumus*	*mālō*	*mālumus*
vīs	*vultis*	*nōn vīs*	*nōn vultis*	*māvīs*	*māvultis*
vult	*volunt*	*nōn vult*	*nōlunt*	*māvult*	*mālunt*

Recensiō: Subordinate Subjunctive Clauses

Comparative clause: *ut* + indicative:

> *Ut tempestās mare tranquillum turbāvit, ita verba Lydiae animum Mēdī turbāvērunt* ("as...thus"). (*ll.8-10*)

Verba postulandī et cūrandī + *ut/nē* subjunctive:

> *Quī medicus verbīs sōlīs potest facere ut hominēs caecī videant, surdī audiant, mūtī loquantur, claudī ambulent?* (*ll.30-32*)

> *In Iūdaeā Iēsūs nōn sōlum faciēbat ut caecī vidērent, surdī audīrent, mūtī loquerentur, vērum etiam verbīs efficiēbat ut mortuī surgerent et ambulārent.* (*ll.34-37*)

> *Ille cūrāvit ut nōs ē tempestāte servārēmur nēve mergerēmur—vel potius nōs ipsī quī mercēs ēiēcimus.* (*ll.127-129*)

> *Cūrābō ut omnia perīcula vītēmus ac salvī in Graeciam eāmus.* (*ll.145-146*)

"Legam tibi" inquit "dē virō claudō cui Iēsūs imperāvit ut surgeret et tolleret lectum suum et domum ambulāret." (ll.58-60)

Modo dīxistī "Chrīstum etiam mortuīs imperāvisse ut surgerent et ambulārent." (ll.61-62)

In Italiā dominō sevērō serviēbam quī ā mē postulābat ut opus sordidum facerem nec mihi pecūlium dabat. (ll.158-160)

Sī quid prāvē fēceram, dominus imperābat ut ego ab aliīs servīs tenērer et verberārer. (ll.160-161)

Multīs prōmissīs eī persuāsī ut mēcum ex Italiā proficīscerētur, Lȳdia enim Rōmae vīvere māvult quam in Graeciā. (ll.163-165)

Certē nōn laetō animō Rōmā profecta sum, et difficile fuit mihi persuādēre ut amīcās meās Rōmānās dēsererem. (ll.172-174)

Num dominus ille sevērus, quī tibi imperābat ut opus sordidum facerēs, tantum pecūlium tibi dabat prō opere sordidō? (ll.181-183)

Reflexive *sē, sibi, suus* in indirect command:

Mēdus, quī legere nōn didicit, Lȳdiae librum reddit eamque rogat ut aliquid sibi legat. (ll.56-57)

"Audī igitur quod scrīptum est dē Iaīrō, prīncipe quōdam Iūdaeōrum, quī Iēsum rogāvit ut fīliam suam mortuam suscitāret. (ll.64-66)

Nec prōmissīs sōlīs Mēdus mihi persuāsit ut sēcum venīrem, sed etiam dōnō pulcherrimō. (ll.174-175)

Purpose/final clause: *ut/nē* + subjunctive (*fīnālis -e < fīnis,* "end," "purpose"):

Praedōnēs maritimī quī nāvēs persequuntur, ut mercēs et pecūniam rapiant nautāsque occīdant. (ll.132-134)

Ōstiā igitur hanc nāvem cōnscendimus, ut in Graeciam nāvigārēmus. (ll.165-167)

Sed herī ē vīllā fūgī, ut verbera vītārem, atque ut amīcam meam vidērem ac semper cum eā essem. (ll.161-163)

Result/consecutive clause: *ut* + subjunctive:

Tanta ūnīus deī potestās nōn est. Nam trēs diī, Neptūnus, Iuppiter, Plūtō, mundum ūniversum ita inter sē dīvīsērunt, ut Iuppiter rēx caelī esset, rēx maris esset Neptūnus, Plūtō autem rēgnāret apud Īnferōs, ubi animae mortuōrum velut umbrae versārī dīcuntur. (ll.85-89)

Num quis tam stultus est ut ista vēra esse crēdat? (ll.90-91)

Num tū tam stultus es ut haec crēdās? (ll.109-110)

Compare

Indirect statement: *verba dīcendī et sentiendī* → accusative + infinitive:

Mihi nēmō persuādēbit hominem super mare ambulāre posse! (ll.110-111)

Nōnne id tibi persuāsit eum habēre potestātem maris et ventōrum? (ll.115-116)

Vocābula Disposita/Ordināta

Nōmina

1st

fāma, -ae	report, reputation
nāvicula, -ae	small boat
turba, -ae	crowd
vigilia, -ae	night watch

2nd

animus, -ī	mind, emotion, courage
dictum, -ī	saying
fretum, -ī	strait
libellus, -ī	small book
mundus, -ī	world
pecūlium, -ī	money (given to slaves); "slave stipend"
perīculum, -ī	risk; danger

3rd

phantasma, phantasmatis (n.)	ghost, apparition
potestās, potestātis (f.)	power, ability
praedō, praedōnis (m.)	robber, pirate
prīnceps, prīncipis (m.)	chief, leader, head man
tībīcen, tībicinis (m.)	flute player
tranquillitās , tranquillitātis (f.)	tranquility
vōrāgō, vōrāginis (f.)	abyss, whirlpool

Verba

-āre (1)

(adōrō) adōrāre, adōrāvisse, adōrātum	adore, worship
(admiror) admirārī, admiratus sum	wonder at
(cessō) cessāre, cessāvisse, cessātum	cease, stop
(memorō) memorāre, memorāvisse, memorātum	relate, recall
(rēgnō) rēgnāre, rēgnāvisse, rēgnātum	rule
(rogō) rogāre, rogāvisse, rogātum	ask
(salvō) salvāre, salvāvisse, salvātum	make safe
(spērō) spērāre, spērāvī, spērātum	hope for
(suscitō) suscitāre, suscitāvisse, suscitātum	wake up, rouse
(tumultuor) tumultuārī, tumultuātum	make an uproar
(versor) versārī, versātum	move about, be present
(vītō) vītāre, vītāvī, vītātum	avoid

-ēre (2)

(habeor) habērī, habitus sum	be held, be considered
(impendeō) impendēre, impendisse	threaten (*intr.* + *dat.*)
(persuādeō) persuādēre, persuāsisse	persuade, convince (*intr.* + *dat.*)

-ere (3)

(apprehendō) apprehendere, apprehendisse, apprehensum	seize
(disiungō) disiungere, disiunxisse, disiunctum	unyoke, separate
(ēiciō) ēicere, ēiecisse, ēiectum	throw out, eject
(ēvolvō) ēvolvere, ēvolvisse, ēvolutum	unroll
(extendō) extendere, extendisse, extentum	extend
(morior) morī, mortuus sum	die
(nāscor) nāscī, nātus sum	be born

-īre (4)

(oboediō) oboedīre, -īvisse/īisse	obey (+ *dat.*)
(pereō) perīre, perīisse	perish
(perveniō) pervenīre, pervēnisse	arrive
(serviō) servīre, -īvisse/īisse, -ītum	be a slave to, serve (+ *dat.*)

Irregular

(mālō) mālle, mālui	prefer

Adiectīva

1st- 2nd (us/er, -a, -um)

attentus, -a, -um	attentive
caecus, -a, -um	blind
claudus, -a, -um	lame
mūtus, -a, -um	mute
perīculōsus, -a, -um	dangerous
quadrāgēsimus, -a, -um	fortieth
salvus, -a, -um	safe
surdus, -a, -um	deaf
tūtus, -a, -um	safe
ūniversus, -a, -um	the whole of, entire

3rd

cōnstāns (*gen.* cōnstantis)	steady, firm
immortālis, -e	immortal
mortālis, -e	mortal

Adverbia

potius	rather
utrum	whether

Coniunctiōnēs

velut	as, as if

XXIX. Nāvigāre Necesse Est

Rēs Grammaticae Novae

1. Verbs
   a. Uses of the Subjunctive
      i.   Deliberative Questions
      ii. Indirect Questions
   b. *Cum* Clauses
      i.   *Cum* Temporal (Indicative)
      ii. *Cum* Temporal and Causal (Subjunctive)
   c. Compound Verbs
2. Nouns: Case Uses
   a. Genitive of Value
   b. Genitive of the Charge
   c. Partitive Genitive
3. Pronouns: Personal

"What Shall I Do?"

The Roman merchant, who is ruined because his goods had to be thrown overboard during the storm to keep the ship afloat, cannot fully share the joy of the others at being saved.

Lectiō Prīma (Section I)

Deliberative Questions

In his distress, the merchant exclaims *"Heu, mē miserum!"* (acc. in exclamation) and asks in despair (*ll.22-23*):

> *Quid faciam?*   What am I to do? What can I do?
> *Quid spērem?*   What am I to hope for? What can I hope for?

In this kind of **deliberative** question, when you ask irresolutely what to do, the verb is in the subjunctive. Deliberative questions expect either to get a directive as an answer, either in the form of the imperative or the subjunctive, or no answer at all (that is, they are asked in desperation with no hope of an answer).

Further Examples:

> *Quōmodo uxōrem et līberōs al__am__? (l.23)*
>
> *Gubernātor perterritus exclāmat: "Ō dī bonī! Quid __faciāmus__?" (ll.198-199)*
>
> *Sed quōmodo __vīvāmus__ sine pecūniā? Quōmodo cibum et vestem __emam__ īnfantibus meīs? (ll.51-52)*
>
> *Quid ergō __faciam__? Ipse dē nāve __saliam__, an in eādem nāve __maneam__ vōbīscum? (ll.56-57)*

Genitive of Value

In order to indicate how much you value something, genitives like *magnī, parvī, plūris, minōris* can be added to *aestimāre* (or *facere* in the same sense). Examples:

> *Mercātōrēs mercēs suās __magnī__ aestimant, vītam nautārum __parvī__ aestimant! (ll.6-7)*
>
> *Nōnne līberōs __plūris__ aestimās quam mercēs istās? (ll.26-27)*

Lectiō Altera (Section II)
Clauses with the Subordinate Conjunction *cum*

You first learned the conjunction *cum* in Chapter X. After the conjunction *cum* the verb can be in the indicative or the subjunctive, depending on the force of *cum*.

After *cum* the verb is in the **indicative:**[1]

- in temporal clauses, meaning "when." We met this use of *cum* in Chapter X:

  > *Cum avis volat, ālae moventur. (Chap. X, l.15)*
  > *Cum syllabae iunguntur, vocābula fīunt. (Chap. XVIII, l.29)*
  > *Cum vocābula coniunguntur, sententiae fīunt. (Chap. XVIII, ll.29-30)*

- in clauses describing something that happens usually or repeatedly,[2] e.g.:

  > *Semper gaudeō __cum__ dē līberīs meīs cōgitō. (l.47)*
  > *Tū numquam mē salūtābās, __cum__ mē vidēbās. (Chap. XIX, ll.99-100)*

After *cum* the verb is in the **subjunctive:**

- when *cum* means "since," "because" or "as," the subjunctive can be present (with a present main verb) or imperfect (with a past tense main verb):

  > *Gubernātor, cum omnēs attentōs __videat__, hanc fābulam nārrat. (ll.76-77)*
  >
  > *__Cum__ iam vītam dēspērā__ret__, id ūnum ōrāvit. (ll.88-89)*
  >
  > *Ānulum abiēcit, __cum__ sēsē nimis fēlīcem esse cēns__ēret__. (ll.156-157)*
  >
  > *Polycratēs, cum ānulum suum recognōsceret, māximā laetitiā affectus est (ll.171-172)*

---

1   When the *cum* clause follows the main clause and provides the main focus of the sentence, the indicative is used. This construction is called *cum inversum*. Compare the force of the two English sentences: When I was reading, the phone rang; I was reading when the phone rang. In both sentences, the focus of the sentence is on the phone ringing.

2   *Cum* in this function is called "*cum*" *iterātīvum* (from *iterāre*, "repeat").

- When the *cum* refers to the past and means "when," its verb is mostly in the imperfect subjunctive, e.g.:

  Cum Ariōn ex Italiā in Graeciam nāvigāret magnāsque dīvitiās sēcum habēret. (*ll.78-80*)

  Cum haec falsa nārrārent, Ariōn repente appāruit. (*ll.110-111*)

Indirect Questions

When questions are reported, that is, indirect, the verb goes into the subjunctive. Compare Lydia's (direct) question with her reminder (indirect) of that question in this chapter:

"Nōnne tua erat ista pecūnia?"	"Wasn't that your money?" (*Chap. XXVIII, l.187*)
"Modo tē interrogāvī tuane esset pecūnia."	"I just asked you if that was your money." (*ll.127-128*)

As the the object of the verb *interrogāre*, the verb in **indirect question** goes into the subjunctive.

Similarly, *Num haec fābula vēra est?* after *dubitāre* becomes:

  dubitō num haec fābula vēra sit. (*ll.116-117*)

Consider the implied levels of questions in (*ll.105-106*):

  "Ubi est Ariōn et quid facit? (direct question)

  Scītisne ubi sit Ariōn et quid faciat? (indirect question)

  Rēx eōs interrogat "num sciant ubi sit Ariōn et quid faciat?" (indirect, present main verb)

  Rēx eōs interrogāvit "num scīrent ubi esset Ariōn et quid faceret?" (indirect, past main verb)

Notā bene: Sometimes the reported question is deliberative (see above); context will make this clear:

  Vir ita perturbātus est ut sē interroget, utrum in mare saliat an in nāve remaneat. (*ll.57-59*) = a result clause introducing an indirect deliberative question; what he originally asked himself was "Should I leap into the sea or remain on the boat," and this becomes: "The man is so distressed that he asks himself whether he should leap into the sea or remain on the boat."

  Mēdus rubēns nescit quid respondeat. (*Chap. XXVIII, l.184*): "Medus, blushing, does not know what he should respond;" Medus originally asks himself "what should I respond?"

More Result Clauses

We met consecutive clauses (clauses of result) in the last chapter. Here are further examples from this chapter:

  Vir ita perturbātus est ut sē interroget. (*ll.57-58*)

  Ariōn tam pulchrē fidibus canēbat ut alter Orpheus appellārētur. (*ll.66-67*)

  An tam ignārus es ut etiam Orpheus tibi ignōtus sit? (*ll.67-68*)

Is fidicen nōbilissimus fuit quī <u>tam</u> pulchrē <u>canēbat</u> <u>ut</u> bēstiae ferae, nātūram suam oblītae, <u>accēderent</u>. (ll.70-72)

Nautae precibus eius <u>ita</u> <u>permōtī sunt</u> <u>ut</u> manūs quidem ab eō <u>abstinērent</u>. (ll.86-87)

<u>Tanta</u> erat potestās eius, tanta glōria tantaeque dīvitiae, ut nōn sōlum aliī tyrannī, sed etiam dī immortālēs eī <u>invidērent</u>. (ll.158-160)

Piscem cēpit quī <u>tam</u> fōrmōsus erat ut piscātor eum nōn <u>vēnderet</u>. (ll.167-168)

Words that signal result clauses

tantus, -a, -um	so great	adjective of magnitude, quantity
talis, tale	of such a sort	adjective of quality
eius modī	of such a sort	descriptive genitive
tot	so many	adjective of quantity
sīc	in this way	adverb
ita	so, in such a way	adverb
adeō	for far, to such an extent	adverb
tam	so	adverb: only with adjs. & other advs.

Under GRAMMATICA LATINA examples are shown of typical *ut*- and *nē*-clauses.

Summary: Purpose and Result

- **Purpose** clauses show the goal of the main verb (in order to); **result** the consquence of the modified (*tam, tantus, ita*) word.
- **Purpose** clauses are negated by *ne*; **result** clauses are negated by *ut* plus a negative.

	Negative Purpose	Negative Result
that...not	*nē*	*ut...nōn*
that...no one	*nē quis*	*ut...nēmō*
that...nothing	*nē quid*	*ut...nihil*
that...never	*nē umquam*	*ut...numquam*

Lectiō Tertia (Section III)

Genitive of the Charge

With *accūsāre* the charge is in the genitive:

Lȳdia pergit eum fūrtī accūsāre.: accuses him <u>of theft</u> (l.137)

Partitive Genitive (continued)

A partitive genitive may qualify a pronoun, e.g.:

aliquid pecūliī (l.135)
nihil malī (l.157)
quid novī? (Chap. XXXI, ll.2-3)

The partitive genitive of *nōs, vōs* is *nostrum, vestrum*:

nēmō <u>nostrum</u>/<u>vestrum</u> (ll.39, 42-43)

Personal Pronouns (continued from Chap. XX)

There are two forms for the genitive plural of the personal pronouns. The forms *meī, tuī, nostrī, vestrī,* and *suī* (used for singular and plural) are generally used as **objective genitives**, e.g.:

amor meī　love of me (as opposed to *amor meus*: my love)
timor vestrī　fear of you (as opposed to *timor vester*: your fear)

The forms *nostrum* and *vestrum*, as you learned in the previous section, are partitive. It is helpful to distinguish the two by memorizing a phrase. A good one is the partitive phrase Cicero often uses when addressing his audience: *quis vestrum?* (who of you?)

Recensiō: Personal Pronouns

	1st sing.	1st pl.	2nd sing.	2nd pl.	Reflexive
nom.	*ego*	*nōs*	*tū*	*vōs*	
acc.	*mē*	*nōs*	*tē*	*vōs*	*sē*
gen.	*meī*	*nostrī/ nostrum*	*tuī*	*vestrī/ vestrum*	*suī*
dat.	*mihi*	*nōbīs*	*tibi*	*vōbīs*	*sibi*
abl.	*mē*	*nōbīs*	*tē*	*vōbīs*	*sē*

Compound Verbs

Many verbs are formed with **prefixes**, mostly prepositions. Examples in this chapter:

dē-terrēre　　　　*per-movēre*
ā-mittere　　　　*sub-īre*
in-vidēre　　　　*expōnere*
per-mittere　　　*re-dūcere* (*re-* means "back" or "again")

Prefixes cause a short *a* or *e* in the verbal stem to be changed to *i*. Thus from:

facere is formed　*af-, cōn-, ef-, per-ficere*
capere　　　　　*ac-, in-, re-cipere*
rapere　　　　　*ē-, sur-ripere*
salīre　　　　　*dē-silīre*
fatērī　　　　　*cōn-fitērī*
tenēre　　　　　*abs-, con-, re-tinēre*
premere　　　　*im-primere*

Similarly, in compounds *iacere* becomes *-iicere*, but the spelling *ii* is avoided by writing *-icere*, e.g.:

ab-, ad-, ē-, prō-icere (pronounce [-*yíkere*])

Recensiō: Indicative/ Subjunctive
Indicative

Ut Orpheus cantū suō ferās ad sē alliciēbat, ita tunc Ariōn canendō piscēs allēxit ad nāvem. (ll.93-95)

Subitō mercātor ē dīvitissimō pauperrimus factus est. (ll.17-18)

Ita spērābat sē magnum lucrum factūrum esse. (l.15)

Laetitia vestra mē nōn afficit. (l.45)

Nec quisquam nostrum trīstitiā tuā afficitur. (ll.46-47)

Quisnam est Ariōn? Nē nōmen quidem mihi nōtum est. (ll.63-64)

Mercātōrēs mercēs suās magnī aestimant, vītam nautārum parvī aestimant! (ll.6-7)

Nōnne līberōs plūris aestimās quam mercēs istās? (ll.26-27)

Sī fūrtum fēcī, tuā causā id fēcī. (l.139)

Nāvis autem vēlīs sōlīs nōn tam vēlōciter vehitur quam ante tempestātem, nam vēla ventō rapidō scissa sunt. (ll.191-193)

"Per deōs immortālēs!" inquit gubernātor, cum prīmum nāvem appropinquantem prōspexit, "Illa nāvis vēlōx nōs persequitur." (ll.187-189)

Purpose

Is laetus Ōstiā profectus est cum mercibus pretiōsīs quās omnī pecūniā suā in Italiā ēmerat eō cōnsiliō ut eās māiōre pretiō in Graeciā vēnderet. (ll.12-15)

Eō enim cōnsiliō nummōs surripuī ut dōnum pretiōsum tibi emerem. (ll.139-141)

Rēctē dīcis: meae mercēs ēiectae sunt, ut nāvis tua salva esset! (ll.34-35)

Mercēs iēcimus ut nōs omnēs salvī essēmus. (ll.36-37)

Orpheus etiam ad Īnferōs dēscendit ut uxōrem suam mortuam inde redūceret... Sed perge nārrāre dē Ariōne. (ll.73-75)

Verba Postulandi

Nōlī tū mē cōnsōlārī quī ipse imperāvistī ut mercēs meae iacerentur! (ll.30-32)

Quid iuvat deōs precārī ut rēs āmissae tibi reddantur? Frūstrā hoc precāris. (ll.54-55)

Sed tamen imperāvērunt ut statim in mare dēsilīret! (ll.87-88)

At nōlīte mē monēre ut laetus sim, postquam omnia mihi ēripuistis! (ll.43-45)

Hāc fābulā monēmur ut semper bonō animō sīmus nēve umquam dē salūte dēspērēmus. Dum anima est, spēs est. (ll.122-124)

Ille vērō, cōnsiliō eōrum cognitō, pecūniam cēteraque sua nautīs dedit, hoc sōlum ōrāns ut sibi ipsī parcerent. (ll.81-83)

Itaque gubernātor imperat ut nāvis rēmīs agātur. (l.193)

Vocābula Disposita/Ordināta

Nōmina

1st

dīvitiae, -ārum	riches
fortūna, -ae	fortune
iactūra, -ae	throwing away, loss
invidia, -ae	envy, ill-will
laetitia, -ae	happiness
trīstitia, -ae	sadness
vīta, -ae	life

2nd

beneficium, -ī	good deed
delphīnus, -ī	dolphin
dorsum, -ī	back
fundus, -ī	bottom
fūrtum, -ī	theft
lucrum, -ī	profit
maleficium, -ī	evil deed
rēmus, -ī	oar
tyrannus, -ī	tyrant

3rd

carmen, carminis (*n.*)	song, poem
fēlīcitās, fēlīcitātis (*f.*)	happiness
fidicen, fidicinis (*f.*)	flute-player
fūr, fūris (*m.*)	thief
nāvigātiō, nāvigātiōnis (*f.*)	sailing
piscātor, piscātōris (*m.*)	fisherman
salūs, salūtis (*f.*)	safety

4th

cantus, -ūs	song

5th

fidēs, -ēī	loyalty, faith
spēs, -ēī	hope

Verba

-āre (1)

(aestimō) aestimāre, -āvisse, -ātum	value, estimate
(appropinquō) appropinquāre, -āvisse	approach (*intr. + dat.*)
(dēspērō) dēspērāre, -āvisse, -ātum	lose hope
(dōnō) dōnāre, -āvisse, -ātum	give, present with
(perturbō) perturbāre, -āvisse, -ātum	disturb
(precor) precārī, precātum	pray, beg
(secō) secāre, secuisse, sectum	cut

-ēre (2)

(abstineō) abstinēre, abstinuisse, abstentum	keep off
(appāreō) appārēre, appāruisse	appear (*intr. + dat.*)
(cōnfiteor) cōnfitērī, cōnfesssus sum	confess
(dēterreō) dēterrēre, dēterruisse, dēterritum	deter
(invideō) invidēre, invīdisse	envy, grudge (*intr. + dat.*)
(permoveō) permovēre, permōvisse, permōtum	move deeply
(remaneō) remanēre, remansisse, remansum	remain
(stupeō) stupēre, stupuisse	be agast
(suādeō) suādēre, suāsisse	advise (*intr. + dat.*)

-ere (3)

(abiciō) abicere, abiēcisse, abiectum	throw away
(adiciō) adicere, adiēcisse, adiectus	add
(afficiō) afficere, affēcisse, affectum	affect, stir
(alliciō) allicere, allēxisse, allectum	attract
(āmittō) āmittere, āmīsisse, āmissum	lose
(dētrahō) dētrahere, detrāxisse, detractum	pull off
(ēripiō) ēripere, ēripuisse, ēreputum	snatch away, deprive
(expōnō) expōnere, exposuisse, expositum	put out, expose
(parcō) parcere, pepercisse	spare (*intr. + dat.*)
(permittō) permittere, permīsisse	allow, permit (*intr. + dat.*)
(queor) querī, questus sum	complain
(recognōscō) recognōscere, recognōvisse	recognize
(redūcō) redūcere, redūxisse, reductum	lead back
(surripiō) surripere, surripuisse, surreptum	steal

-īre (4)

(dēsiliō) dēsilīre, dīsiluisse	jump down
(fīniō) fīnīre, fīnīvisse, finītum	finish

Irregular

(subeō) subīre, subīisse	undergo

Adiectīva
    1st -2nd (us/er, -a, -um)

celsus, -a, -um	tall, high
ignārus, -a, -um	ignorant, unaware
ignōtus, -a, -um	unknown
maestus, -a, -um	sad
mīrus, -a, -um	surprising, strange
nōtus, -a, -um	known
pretiōsus, -a, -um	precious
rapidus, -a, -um	rapid

    3rd

fallāx (*gen.* fallācis)	false, deceitful
fēlīx (*gen.* fēlicis)	lucky, fortunate
nōbilis, -e	well-known, famous
vēlōx (*gen.* vēlōcis)	swift

Pronōmina

nōnnūllī, -ae, -a	several
sēsē	*intensive form of* **se**

Adverbia

frūstrā	in vain
inde	from there
nōnnumquam	often
prōtinus	immediately, at once
repente	suddenly

Coniunctiōnēs

quasi	as if

XXX. Convīvium

Rēs Grammaticae Novae

1. Verbs
   a. Uses of the Subjunctive
      i. Horatatory Subjunctive
   b. Future Perfect Indicative Tense
   c. *miscēre/aspergere*
   d. *fruī*
2. Nouns
   a. *sitis* (Pure *i*-Stem)
   b. *vās*
3. Adjectives
   a. Distributive Numbers
4. Adverbs from 3rd Declension Adjectives

Convīvium (Dinner Party)

In this and the following chapter you read about a dinner party in the home of Julius and Aemilia. The guests are good friends of the family. The dinner begins at the early hour of four o'clock in the afternoon (*hōra decima*), the normal time of the principal meal of the Romans. We hear about the arrangement of a typical Roman dining-room, the *trīclīnium*, where the guests reclined on couches. Such a dining-room was not designed for large parties, for not more than three guests could lie on each of the three couches grouped around the little table.

Lectiō Prīma (Section I)

Fruor, fruī

Like *ūtī ūsum esse* (see *l.38*) the deponent verb *fruī* ("delight in," "enjoy") takes the ablative:

> *ōtiō fruor* (*l.23*)
> *Orontēs vītā rūsticā nōn fruitur.* (*l.35*)
> *cotīdiē bonō vīnō fruor* (*l.59*)

Adverbs from 3rd Declension Adjectives (continued)

3rd declension adjectives in *-ns* form adverbs in *-nter*, e.g.:

> *cōnstāns -ant|is*, (contraction of *cōnstantiter*) → *cōnsta<u>nter</u>*
> *prūdēns -ent|is* → *prūde<u>nter</u>*
> *dīligēns -ent|is* → *dīlige<u>nter</u>*
> *patiēns -entis* → *patie<u>nter</u>*

Examples:

> *dīlige<u>nter</u> cūrō ut colōnī agrōs meōs bene colant* (*ll.33-34*)
> *Prūde<u>nter</u> facis* (*l.35*)
> *Patie<u>nter</u> exspectā, dum servī lectōs sternunt.* (*l.82; cf. Chap. XXXIII, l.120*)

Lectiō Altera (Section II)

Distributive Numbers

When using repetitive numbers, to say how many guests are reclining on each couch, for example, we might say in English "three to a couch," or "three each/apiece," or "in threes." Latin does not use the usual numerals *ūnus, duo, trēs*, but the numbers *singulī, bīnī, ternī*:

In <u>singulīs</u> lectīs aut <u>singulī</u> aut <u>bīnī</u> aut <u>ternī</u> convīvae accubāre solent.	Dinner guests usually recline on individual couches in ones or twos or threes. (*ll.74-75*)

These **distributive numerals**:

- are adjectives of the 1st/2nd declension
- all end in *-<u>n</u>|ī -ae -a*, except *singul|ī -ae -a*
- are used when the same number is used repetitively, that is, applies to more than one person or thing, e.g.:

> *bis <u>bīna</u>* (2×2) *sunt quattuor*
> *bis <u>terna</u>* (2×3) *sunt sex*
> *In vocābulīs "mea" et "tua" sunt <u>ternae</u> litterae et <u>bīnae</u> syllabae*

Future Perfect Indicative

To indicate that an action will not be completed until some point in the future, the **future perfect** is used (Latin *futūrum perfectum*), e.g.:

> *Cēnābimus cum prīmum cocus cēnam parā<u>verit</u> et servī trīclīnium ōrnā<u>verint</u>.* (*ll.83-84*)

To form the future perfect:

- Active: the perfect stem with the following endings:

1st	*~er|ō*	*~eri|mus*
2nd	*~eri|s*	*~eri|tis*
3rd	*~eri|t*	*~eri|nt*

- Passive: the perfect participle and the future of *esse* (*erō, eris, erit*, etc.), e.g:

> *Brevī cēna parā<u>ta</u> et trīclīnium ōrnā<u>tum erit</u>.* (*ll.84-85; cf. l.14*)

This tense is especially common in **conditional** clauses (beginning with *sī*) in cases where some future action must be completed before something else can take place, e.g.:

> *Discipulus laudābitur, sī magistrō pār<u>uerit</u>.*

Further examples of this use will be found in the section GRAMMATICA LATINA.

Lectiō Tertia (Section III)

Independent Subjunctive: Hortatory

When at last the servant announces that dinner is ready, Julius says:

> *Trīclīnium intr<u>ēmus</u>!*   Let us enter the dining room! (*ll.86-87*)

At table he raises his glass with the words:

> *Ergō bib<u>āmus</u>!*   Therefore, let us drink! (*l.120*)

The forms *intrēmus* and *bibāmus* are the present subjunctive (1st pers. pl.) of *intrāre* and *bibere*; accordingly they denote an action that is intended or encouraged, in this case an exhortation ("let's..."). In the next chapter you will find further examples of this **hortatory** subjunctive (Latin *hortārī*, "exhort").

Sitis/vās

Sitis, -is f. is a pure *i*-stem (*see Chap. XVI*):

acc.	*-im*	(*sit<u>im</u> patī, l.55*)
abl.	*-ī*	(*sit<u>ī</u> perīre, l.57*)

Vās, vās|is n. follows the 3rd declension in the singular, but the 2nd declension in the plural: *vās|a, -ōrum* (*l.93: ex vās<u>īs</u> aureīs*).

Miscēre/aspergere

Wine was not often drunk undiluted (*merum*); it was customary to mix (*miscēre*) one's wine with water. The verbs *miscēre* (to mix) can be completed by an accusative and ablative or dative and accusative. The Latin expression is either:

> accusative and ablative
> *vīnum aquā (cum aquā) miscēre*   mix wine with water (*l.115*)

> dative and accusative
> *mel vīnō miscēre*   mix honey (in)to wine (*l.132*)

Aspergere (to sprinkle) follows the same pattern:

> *cibum sāle aspergere*   sprinkle food with salt (*l.111*)
> *sālem carnī aspergere*   sprinkle salt (on)to meat (*l.109-110*)

Recensiō: Cum

Cum referring to the future: Indicative

> *Cēnābimus cum prīmum cocus cēnam parāverit et servī trīclīnium ōrnāverint.* (*ll.82-84*)

> *Tum dēmum hoc vīnum cum illō comparāre poterimus, cum utrumque gustāverimus.* (*ll.143-144*)

Cum iterative: Indicative

Nec vērō omnēs mercātōrēs domī remanent, cum mercēs eōrum nāvibus vehuntur. (Chap. XXIX, ll.8-9)

Cum igitur paucissimī sunt convīvae, nōn pauciōrēs sunt quam trēs, cum plūrimī, nōn plūrēs quam novem — nam ter ternī sunt novem. (ll.75-78)

Cum strict temporal: Indicative

"Per deōs immortālēs!" inquit gubernātor, cum prīmum nāvem appropinquantem prōspexit. (Chap. XXIX, ll.187-188)

Sex hōrae iam sunt cum cibum nōn sūmpsī. Venter mihi contrahitur propter famem. (ll.40-42)

"Haec carō valdē mihi placet" inquit Fabia cum prīmum carnem gustāvit. (ll.106-107)

Cum prīmum meum vīnum pōtāveritis, Falernum pōtābitis! (ll.145-146)

Sex hōrae iam sunt cum cibum nōn sumpsī. (ll.40-41)

Octō diēs iam sunt cum Rōmae nōn fuī.

Cum circumstantial: Subjunctive

Cum Arīōn, nōbilissimus suī temporis fidicen, ex Italiā in Graeciam nāvigāret magnāsque dīvitiās sēcum habēret, nautae pauperēs, quī hominī dīvitī invidēbant, eum necāre cōnstituērunt. (Chap. XXIX, ll.78-81)

Respondērunt "hominem, cum inde abīrent, in terrā Italiā fuisse eumque illīc bene vīvere, aurēs animōsque hominum cantū suō dēlectāre atque magnum lucrum facere." (Chap. XXIX, ll.106-109)

Cum causal: Subjunctive

Gubernātor, cum omnēs attentōs videat, hanc fabulam nārrat. (Chap. XXIX, ll.76-77)

Ibi homō territus, cum iam vītam dēspērāret, id ūnum ōrāvit ut sibi licēret vestem ōrnātam induere et fidēs capere et ante mortem carmen canere. (Chap. XXIX, ll.187-188)

Ānulum abiēcit, cum sēsē nimis fēlīcem esse cēnsēret. (Chap. XXIX, ll.156-157)

Polycratēs, cum ānulum suum recognōsceret, māximā laetitiā affectus est. (Chap. XXIX, ll.171-172)

Midās enim, quamquam terram, lignum, ferrum manū tangendō in aurum mūtāre poterat, fame et sitī moriēbātur, cum cibus quoque et pōtiō, simul atque ā rēge tācta erat, aurum fieret. (Chap. XXXI, ll.38-42)

Opus nōn est vetus exemplum Graecum afferre, cum complūrēs fābulae nārrentur dē Rōmānīs puerīs quī ita servātī sunt. (Chap. XXXI, ll.154-156)

Vocābula Disposita/Ordināta

Nōmina
    1st

cēna, -ae	dinner
convīva, -ae (*m./f.*)	dinner guest
culīna, -ae	kitchen

    2nd

argentum, -ī	silver
balneum, -ī	bath
bonum, -ī	blessing, good
cocus, -ī	cook
convīvium, -ī	dinner party
merum, -ī	unmixed wine
minister, -rī	attendant (*cf.* **magister**)
trīclīnium, -ī	dining room

    3rd

carō, carnis (*f.*)	meat
famēs, famis (*f.*)	hunger
genus, generis (*n.*)	kind, sort
holus, holeris (*n.*)	vegetable
hospes, hospitis (*m./f.*)	guest, stranger
iter, itineris (*n.*)	journey, trip
mel, melis (*n.*)	honey
nux, nucis (*f.*)	nut
sāl, sālis (*n.*)	salt
sitis, is (*f.*)	thirst (*acc.* **sitim**)
vās, vāsis (*n.*)	container (**plura vasa, orum**)

Verba
    -āre (1)

(accubō) accubāre, accubuisse	recline at the table
(apportō) apportāre, -āvisse, -ātum	carry to
(cēnō) cēnāre, -āvisse, -ātum	dine
(exōrnō) exōrnāre, -āvisse, -ātum	decorate
(gustō) gustāre, -āvisse, -ātum	taste
(līberō) līberāre, -āvisse, -ātum	set free
(nūntiō) nūntiāre, -āvisse, -ātum	announce
(parō) parāre, -āvisse, -ātum	get, prepare
(pōtō) pōtāre, -āvisse, -ātum (or **pōtum**)	drink

    -ēre (2)

(compleō) complēre, -plēvisse, -plētum	fill up
(misceō) miscēre, miscuisse, mixtum	mix
(placeō) placēre, placuisse	please (*intr.*+ *dat.*)
(salvēre iubeō) salvēre, iubēre	greet

-ere (3)

(accumbō) accumbere, accubuisse	recline at the table
(aspergō) aspergere, aspersisse, aspersus	sprinkle/strew on
(contrahō) contrahere, -trāxisse, -tractum	contract
(coquō) coquere, coxisse, coctus	cook
(ēligō) ēligere, ēlēgisse, ēlectus	pick out, choose
(fruor) fruī, frūctus sum	enjoy + *abl.*
(fundō) fundere, fūdisse, fūsus	pour
(recipiō) recipere, recēpisse, receptum	receive
(requiēscō) requiēscere	rest
(sternō) sternere, strāvisse, strātus	spread, strew
(vīsō) vīsere	go to see, visit

-īre (4)

(exhauriō) exhaurīre, eshausisse, exhaustus	drain, drink up

Irregular

(praesum) praeesse, praefuisse	be in charge over (*intr.* + *dat.*)
(perferō) perferre, pertulisse, perlātum	carry through
(prōferō) prōferre, prōtulisse, prōlātum	bring forward

Adiectīva

1st-2nd (us/er -a, -um)

acerbus, -a, -um	bitter
acūtus, -a, -um	sharp
argenteus, -a, -um	made of silver
bīnī, -ae, -a	two at a time
calidus, -a, -um	hot
glōriōsus, -a, -um	full of glory
īmus, -a, -um	bottom of
inexspectātus, -a, -um	unexpected
iūcundus, -a, -um	pleasant, agreeable
lībertīnus, -a, -um	freed
medius, -a, -um	middle of
merus, -a, -um	unmixed pure
molestus, -a, -um	annoying
singulī, -ae, -a	one at a time
tardus, -a, -um	late, tardy
ternī, -ae, -a	three at a time

3rd

dīligēns (*gen.* dīligentis)	careful, accurate
dulcis, -e	sweet

Adverbia
    dēmum   finally
    diū   for a long time
    equidem   indeed
    paulisper   for a short time
    prīdem   some time ago, previously
    sānē   certainly, truly

Praepositiōnēs
    circiter *prep. + acc.*   around, near (*adv.* approximately)

XXXI. Inter Pōcula

Rēs Grammaticae Novae

1. Verbs
   a. Uses of the Subjunctive
      i. Optative Subjunctive
      ii. Jussive Subjunctive
   b. *ōdisse*
   c. Semi-deponents
2. Nouns: Case uses
   a. Dative of Agent
   b. Preposition *cōram*
   c. Preposition *super*
3. Adjectives
   a. Verbal Adjective: Gerundive (*gerundīvum*)
   b. Passive Periphrastic
4. Pronouns: Indefinite Relative Pronouns

An Enthusiastic Dinner Conversation

As the wine flows the conversation among the guests proceeds more freely. The room echoes with discussions, stories and the latest gossip.

Lectiō Prīma (Section I)
Indefinite Relative Pronouns

We have seen relative pronouns without an antecedent express the idea of "whoever" and "whatever" (where one might have expected *is quī...*, *id quod*), e.g.:

Quī spīrat vīvus est.	Whoever breathes is alive. (*Chap. X, ll.48-49*)
Quod Mārcus dīcit vērum nōn est.	What (or whatever) Marcus says is not true. (*Chap. XV, l.58-59*)

The same idea is expressed by the **indefinite relative pronouns** *quis-quis* and *quid-quid* ("whoever" and "whatever"), e.g.:

Quisquis amat valeat! (*l.196*)

Quidquid is often changed to *quicquid* by assimilation:

> *Dabō tibi quidquid optāveris. (l.29)*

Future Perfect Tense (continued)

This chapter offers many more examples of the future perfect tense, used to express an action that must be completed *before* another future action:

> *Nēmō tibi quidquam scrībet dē rēbus urbānīs, nisi prius ipse epistulam scrīpseris (ll.7-8)*

> *"Dabō tibi" inquit "quidquid optāveris." Statim Midās "Ergō dā mihi" inquit "potestātem quidquid tetigerō in aurum mūtandī.¹ (ll.29-31)*

> *Profectō eum verberābō atque omnibus modīs cruciābō, sī eum invēnerō priusquam Italiam relīquerit. Nisi pecūniam mihi reddiderit, in cruce fīgētur!" (ll.63-66)*

Lectiō Altera (Section II)

Ōdisse

The defective verb *ōdisse* ("to hate") has no present stem, but the perfect has present force: *ōdī* ("I hate"). is the opposite of *amō*; *ōdisse* and its opposite, *amāre* are contrasted in *Servī dominum clēmentem amant, sevērum ōdērunt (ll.93-94)*.

Cf. (Chapter XXIV) *nōvisse*, perfect of *nōscere* ("get to know"), meaning "know": *nōvī*, "I know."

Cōram/Super

The preposition *cōram* ("in the presence of," "before") takes the ablative:

> *cōram exercitū (l.122)*

Super, which usually takes the accusative ("above"), when used instead of *dē* in the sense "about," "concerning," also takes the ablative:

> *super Chrīstiānīs (l.147)*
> *super fēminā falsā et īnfidā (l.200)*

Lectiō Tertia (Section III)

Gerundive

In Chapter XXVI, you learned about the **gerund** (Latin *gerundium*), a **verbal noun** with forms in the accusative, genitive, dative and ablative of the neuter singular; it is active in meaning. The **gerundive** (Latin *gerundīvum*) is a **verbal adjective**. Orontes's *"Vīvant omnēs fēminae amandae!" (ll.172-173)* offers an example of the gerundive, which:

- is formed like the gerund by adding *-nd-* or *-end-* to the present stem
- is an **adjective** of the 1st/2nd declension (*ama|nd|us, -a, -um < amāre*)
- is passive in meaning
- expresses what is to be done to a person or thing

---

1   The future perfect is here used with a present tense main verb as *potestātem mūtandī = poterō mūtāre*.

The gerundive can be used as an adjective or with the verb *esse* to express obligation.

- As an **adjective**:

fēmina amanda	(worthy of being loved): a lovely, charming, or lovable woman
discipulus laudandus	(< *laudāre* worthy of praise): a praise-worthy or hardworking pupil
liber legendus	(< *legere* worthy of being read): a good book, a must-read

- Most frequently the gerundive is used with some form of the verb *esse* and is called a **passive periphrastic**; it expresses what must happen, as in these examples:

   Pater quī īnfantem exposuit ipse necandus est! (*ll.132-133*): "should/must be killed"

   Ille servus nōn pūniendus, sed potius laudandus fuit. (*ll.161-162*): "should not have been punished, but rather praised"

   Nunc merum bibendum est!" (*l.177*): "must be drunk"

The gerundive is a passive form; **agent** (the person by whom the action is to be performed) is expressed by the **dative** (not *ab* + ablative):

   Quidquid dominus imperāvit servō faciendum est. (*ll.159-160*): "must be done"

The passive periphrastic can be used without a subject:

Bibendum nōbīs est!	We must drink! (There must be drinking by us)
Tacendum est!	Silence! (*l.178*)
Dormiendum omnibus est!	Everyone to sleep!

Remember:
- Gerund: active noun used only in the accusative, genitive, dative and ablative of the neuter singular.
- Gerundive: passive adjective expressing what must be done and takes a dative of agent.

Optative, Hortatory, Jussive Subjunctives Compared

Orontes, who has had quite a bit to drink, illustrates three related uses of the subjunctive: optative, hortatory and jussive. All three are expressions of the will of the speaker.

- **Optative**: an expression of wish (may he/she/they) (more in Chapter XXXII)

   Vīvat fortissimus quisque! Vīvant omnēs fēminae amandae! (*ll.172-173*)

   Quisquis amat valeat! Pereat quī nescit amāre! Bis tantō pereat quisquis amāre vetat!" (*ll.196-197*, *per-eat* is the present subjunctive of *per-īre*)

- **Hortatory** (see Chapter XXX): an expression of encouragment or exhortation in the 1st person plural ("let us")

"Gaudeāmus atque amēmus!"	Let us rejoice and let us love! (*l.173*)
Vīvāmus omnēs et bibāmus. (*ll.183-184*)	
Pōcula funditus exhauriāmus. (*l.184*)	
Redeāmus ad meum Mēdum servum.	Let's get back to my slave Medus.

- **Jussive**: a command expressed in the third person ("let him, her, let them")

"Quisquis fēminās amat, pōculum tollat et bibat mēcum!"	Whoever loves women, let him lift up his cup and drink with me! (*ll.176-177*)

The optative subjunctive expresses a wish; hortatory an exhortation; jussive a command. For all three the negative is *nē*:

Nē pereat!	May he not perish!
Nē pōcula funditus exhauriāmus!	Let us not drain our glasses dry!
Nē bibat!	Let him not drink!

Quisque + Superlative

When *quisque* and the superlative are used together, the phrase means "all the X." Cicero spoke of *optimus quisque*, "all the best men." Orontes cries:

Vīvat fortissimus quisque!	May all the bravest men live! (*l.172*: i.e. "everyone according as he is the bravest," "all the bravest men")

Semi-Deponents

There are a very few verbs in Latin that are called semi-deponent. The semi-deponent verb *audēre*, for example, is active in the present but passive in the perfect: *audēre* (to dare) *ausum esse* (to have dared):

Ille iuvenis fēminam illam pulcherrimam abdūcere ausus est. (*ll.168-169*)

Perterritus Quīntus cultrum medicī sentit in bracchiō, nec oculōs aperīre audet. (*Chap. XI, ll.97-98*)

Conversely, *revertī* is deponent in the present tense, but not in the perfect: *revertisse*; thus *revertitur* (she returns) but *revertit* (she returned).[2]

Graffiti

The inscription on page 259 is a **graffito** ("scratching" in Italian) which a lovesick youth has scratched on a wall in Pompeii. It will help you to decipher the characters when you know that the inscription contains the two verses quoted by Orontes (*ll.196-197*; only the first syllable is missing).

---

2   *Revertere* exists in both active and deponent forms (*reverto, revertere, revertī* and *revertor, revertī, reversus sum*); in present the deponent forms are more common, in the perfect, the active forms.

Vocābula Disposita/Ordināta

Nōmina
    1st

iniūria, -ae	injury, injustice
memoria, -ae	memory
nūgae, -ārum	trifles
parricīda, -ae (*m./f.*)	murderer of a near relative or head of state
poena, -ae	punishment

    2nd

praemium, -ī	reward
supplicium, -ī	punishment

    3rd

crux, crucis (*f.*)	cross
iūs, iūris (*n.*)	law, right; *also* gravy, soup
iuvenis, iuvenis (*m./f.*)	young person (*not an i-stem*)
lēx, lēgis (*f.*)	law, motion, bill
mōs, mōris (*m.*)	custom, habit; *pl.* behavior, morals
mūnus, mūneris (*n.*)	service, duty, gift
pōtiō, pōtōnis (*f.*)	drink
rūmor, rūmōris (*m.*)	rumor
scelus, sceleris (*n.*)	crime, wickedness
senex, senis (*m.*)	old man (*not an i-stem*)

    5th

fidēs, -ēī	loyalty, good faith

Verba
    -āre (1)

(cruciō) cruciāre, cruciāvisse, cruciātum	torture
(ēducō) ēducāre, ēducāvisse, ēducātum	train; educate; rear
(fābulor) fābulārī, fābulātum	chat; tell a story
(interpellō) interpellāre, interpellāvisse, interpellātum	interrupt, break in
(optō) optāre, optāvisse, optātum	choose, wish for
(vetō) vetāre, vetuisse, vetitus	forbid

    -ēre (2)

(lateō) latēre, latuisse	lie hidden, lurk

    -ere (3)

(abdūcō) abdūcere, abdūxisse, abductum	lead away, carry off
(aufugiō) aufugere, aufūgisse	run away, escape
(cōnfīdō) cōnfīdere, cōnfīsum	trust (+ *dat.*)
(fīdō) fīdere, fīsum	trust, rely on (+ *dat.*)

(ignōscō) ignōscere, ignōvisse,
    ignōtum — forgive (+ *dat.*)
(odī) ōdisse, -ōsus — hate
(retrahō) retrahere, retrāxisse,
    retractum — draw back, withdraw
(statuō) statuere, statuisse, statutum — fix, determine
Irregular
(auferō) auferre, abstulisse, ablātum — carry off

Adiectīva
1st-2nd (us/er, -a, -um)

asinīnus, -a, -um — asinine
avārus, -a, -um — greedy
ēbrius, -a, -um — drunk
fīdus, -a, -um — loyal, faithful
fugitīvus, -a, -um — fugitive
īnfīdus, -a, -um — treacherous
iniūstus, -a, -um — unjust
invalidus, -a, -um — weak
iūstus, -a, -um — just
nimius, -a, -um — too big
nōnāgēsimus, -a, -um — ninetieth
scelestus, -a, -um — wicked
vetus (*gen.* veteris) — old

3rd

clēmēns (*gen.* clementis) — merciful
crūdēlis, -e — cruel
dēbilis, -e — weak
impatiēns (*gen.* impatientis) — impatient
īnfēlīx (*gen.* īnfēlīcis) — unlucky
praesēns (*gen.* praesentis) — present
sapiēns (*gen.* sapientis) — wise

Pronōmina
quisquis, quidquid — whoever, whatever, each, all

Adverbia
aliquantum (*adv.*) — to some extent
funditus — utterly (*from the root*)
ideō — for that reason
namque — for in fact (*strong* **nam**)
nimium/nimis (*adv.*) — too much
priusquam — before, sooner, rather
quantum (*as adv.*) — so much as, as much as
quamobrem — why? therefore

Praepositiōnēs
cōram + *abl.* — in the presence of (*also adv.*)
super + *abl.* — over (*also adv.*)

XXXII. Classis Rōmāna

Rēs Grammaticae Novae

1. Verbs
   a. Perfect Subjunctive: Active and Passive
   b. Uses of the Subjunctive
      i. Optative Subjunctive (Continued)
      ii. Fear Clauses
      iii. *fit/accidit ut* + Subjunctive
   c. Verbs of Remembering and Forgetting
   d. *velle*: Present Subjunctive
2. Nouns: Cases Uses
   a. Ablative of Description
   b. Ablative of Separation
   c. *vīs/vīrēs*
3. Pronouns: *aliquis/aliquid*

Medus and Lydia at Sea

The fear of pirates gives rise to a long discussion on board the ship. Medus tells the story of the circumstances in which he was sent to prison and sold as a slave. This story mollifies Lydia, so when finally the danger is over, the two are once more on the best of terms.

Lectiō Prīma (Section I)
Subjunctive with Noun Clauses

You have seen clauses acting as the objects of verbs (Chapter XXVIII). A clause can also act as the subject of a verb. The impersonal expressions *fit* and *accidit* may be followed by an *ut*-clause with the subjunctive telling what happens; the *ut*-clause is the subject of *fit*:

> *Rārō fit ut nāvis praedōnum in marī internō appāreat.* (ll.42-43)

Ablative

of Description

A noun + adjective in the ablative can be used to describe a quality (*ablātīvus quālitātis* or **ablative of description**):

> *tantā audāciā sunt* (*l.49*)
> *bonō animō esse* (*Chap. XXIX, ll.122-123*)

(Cf. genitive of description, Chapter XIX)

of Separation

We saw the ablative of separation with *carēre* in Chapter XX and with *pellere* and *prohibēre* in Chapter XXVII. With *līberāre* and with *opus esse* as well we find the ablative of separation without a preposition:

> *servitūte līberābantur* (*l.6*)
> *Quid opus est armīs?* (*l.78*)
> *seu pecūniā seu aliā rē mihi opus erit* (*l.118*)
> *Quid verbīs opus est?* (*l.195*)

Vīs

The noun *vīs* ("strength," "force," "violence") has only three forms in the singular:

nom.	*vīs*
acc.	*vim* (l.13)
abl.	*vī* (*l.77*)

The plural *vīrēs, vīrium* means physical strength:

> *Nautae omnibus vīribus rēmigant.* (*l.53, ll.65-66*)

Lectiō Altera (Section II)

Verbs of Remembering and Forgetting

In Chapter XXV you learned *oblīvīscī* can take a genitive as object:

> *Nōn facile est amōris antīquī oblīvīscī.* (*Chap. XXV, l.128*)
> *Numquam beneficiī oblītus sum.* (*l.26*)

Its opposites, *reminīscī* and *meminisse*, meaning "to remember," also can take a genitive as an object:

> *Nec vērō quidquam difficilius esse vidētur quam beneficiōrum meminisse.* (*ll.125-126*)
> *Eius temporis reminīscor.* (*ll.155-156*)

Like *oblīvīscī*, both *reminīscī* and *meminisse* can also take accusative objects:

> *Duōs versūs reminīscor ē carmine* (*ll.101-102*)
> *Tune nōmen eius meministī?* (*ll.106-107*)

Note: *meminisse* a defective verb which, like *ōdisse* (Chapter XXXI), has no present stem: the perfect form *meminī* ("I remember") is the opposite of *oblītus sum* ("I have forgotten").

Velle

The present subjunctive of *velle*:

Indicative		Subjunctive	
volō	*volumus*	*velim*	*velīmus*
vīs	*vultis*	*velīs*	*velītis*
vult	*volunt*	*velit*	*velint*

Perfect Subjunctive

During the discussion, the merchant quotes two verses without giving the poet's name. The helmsman does not ask a direct question: *"Quī poēta ista scrīpsit?"* with the verb in the indicative, but uses an indirect question with the subjunctive:[1] *"Nesciō quī poēta ista scrīp<u>serit</u>"* (l.106). *Scrīps|erit* is the **perfect subjunctive** (Latin *coniūnctīvus perfectī*) of *scrībere*.

This tense is formed in the **active** by inserting *-eri-* between the perfect stem and the personal endings:

1st singular	~*eri|m*
2nd	~*eri|s*
3rd	~*eri|t*
1st plural	~*eri|mus*
2nd	~*eri|tis*
3rd	~*eri|nt*

Notā Bene: The perfect subjunctive looks like the future perfect indicative **except** for the 1st person singular ~*erim* (where the future perfect has ~*erō*).

In the **passive** the perfect subjunctive is composed of the perfect participle and the present subjunctive of *esse* (*sim, sīs, sit*, etc.):

> *Iūlius dubitat num Mārcus ā magistrō laudā<u>tus sit</u>* (= *num magister Mārcum laudāverit*).

Perfect Subjunctive

active   perfect stem + *eri* + endings

passive   participle stem + present subjunctive of *esse*

Recensiō: *Ferre*

For review, compare the present, imperfect, and perfect subjunctives of *fero, ferre, tulisse, lātum*:

---

1   First seen in Chapter XXIX: *Modo tē interrogāvī tuane <u>esset</u> pecūnia"* (*ll.127-128*) and *dubitō num haec fābula vēra <u>sit</u>* (*ll.116-117*).

Tense	Active	Passive
Present	*feram* *ferās* *ferat* *ferāmus* *ferātis* *ferant*	*ferar* *ferāris* *ferātur* *ferāmur* *ferāmini* *ferantur*
Imperfect	*ferrem* *ferrēs* *ferret* *ferrēmus* *ferrētis* *ferrent*	*ferrer* *ferrēris* *ferrētur* *ferrēmur* *ferrēmini* *ferrentur*
Perfect	*tulerim* *tuleris* *tulerit* *tulerimus* *tuleritis* *tulerint*	*lātus, a sim* *lātus, a sīs* *lātus, a est* *lātī, ae sīmus* *lātī, ae sītis* *lātī, ae sint*

Perfect Subjunctive in Subordinate Clauses

You have learned (Chapter XXVIII) that the present and imperfect subjunctives represent incompleted action in subjunctive subordinate clauses. The present subjunctive is used with a present or future tense main verb and the imperfect with a past tense main verb.

The perfect subjunctive represents completed action in a subjunctive subordinate clause when the main verb is present or future.

Sequence of Tense

Main Verb	Subordinate Verb	
	incompleted action	completed action
present future	present subjunctive	perfect subjunctive
past tense	imperfect subjunctive	(Chapter XXXIII)

Perfect Subjunctive in Indirect Questions

The perfect subjunctive is used in indirect questions concerning completed actions, when the main verb is in the present, present perfect, or future tense, as in the above examples (*scrīpserit, laudātus sit, laudāverit*) and the following:

Haud sciō an ego ita dīxerim.   I might say that.[2] (*l.84*)

Nesciō quī poēta ita scrīpserit. (*l.106*)

Mīror unde pecūniam sūmpseris ut aliōs redimerēs. (*ll.132-133*)

Ego mīror cūr id mihi nōn nārrāveris. (*l.134*)

---

2   *Haud sciō an* is an idiom meaning "I think x is probably the case" (the same is true of *nesciō an* and *dubitō an*).

Sed nesciō cūr hoc vōbīs nārrāverim (*ll.154-155*)

Scīsne quantum pīrātae ā Iūliō Caesare captō postulāverint? (*ll.168-169*)

Mīlitēs ignōrant quī homō sīs et quid anteā fēceris. (*ll.215-216*)

Iamne oblītus es quid modo dīxeris? (Note the (present) perfect) (*l.82*)

Nārrābō vōbīs breviter quōmodo amīcum ē servitūte redēmerim atque ipse ob eam grātiam servus factus sim. (*l.137*)

Sēstertius

After *mīlia* the partitive genitive plural of *sēstertius* has the older short ending *-um* in instead of *-ōrum: decem mīlia sēstertium* (*ll.91, cf. l.170*).

Lectiō Tertia (Section III)

Perfect Subjunctive in Prohibitions (Negative Command)

With *nē* the 2nd person of this tense expresses a prohibition:

Nē timueris! Nē timueritis! (*ll.215, 199 = nōlī/nōlīte timēre!*)
Nē dēspērāveris! (*l.162*)
Nē eum abiēceris! (*l.182*)
Nē oblīta sīs mē servum fugitīvum esse. (*ll.211-212*)

Remember: Prohibitions can also be expressed with *nōlī/nōlīte* and the infinitive.

Optative Subjunctive (continued)

In Chapter XXXII we saw the subjunctive can express a wish (optative subjunctive). Wishes are often introduced by the adverb *utinam*, e.g.:

Utinam aliquandō līber patriam videam!	May I sometime see my country as a free man! (*l.157*)
Utinam ille ānulus vītam tuam servet!	May that ring save your life! (*ll.182-182*)
Utinam salvī in Graeciam perveniant! (*l.223*)	

Utinam can be left untranslated in English ("may I see my country") or be translated by "I wish that" or similar. The negation *nē* is also used with an optative subjunctive, e.g.:

- *Utinam nē pīrātae mē occīdant!* (*ll.179-180*)

Clauses Expressing Fear

An expression of fear that something may happen implies a wish that it may **not** happen; this is why verbs expressing fear, *timēre, metuere* and *verērī*, are followed by:

- *nē* + subjunctive (fear that x <u>will</u> happen) e.g.:

Timeō nē pīrātae mē occīdant.	I fear the pirates may kill me; the *nē*-clause corresponds to an English "that"-clause).

- *ut* + subjunctive (fear that x <u>will not</u> happen) e.g.:

Timeō ut ille veniat.	I fear he may not come.

If you separate the two clauses, you can see how the sentences work:

> *Timeō* (I am afraid) *nē pīrātae mē occīdant* (may the pirates not kill me!) becomes: I fear that the pirates may kill me.

> *Timeō* (I am afraid) *ut ille veniat* (may he come!) becomes: I fear he may not come.

The Prefix *ali-*

The prefix *ali-* serves to make interrogative words indefinite:

quot?	how many?	*ali-quot*: some, several	
quandō?	when?	*ali-quandō*: at sometime or other, once	
quantum?	how much?	*ali-quantum*: a certain amount	
quis? quid?	who? what?	*ali-quis, ali-quid.*: someone, something	

Recall, however, from Chapter XXII that *quis quid* is used (without *ali-*) as an indefinite pronoun after *sī, nisī, num* and after *nē*:

> *Nihil cuiquam nārrāvī dē eā rē, nē quis mē glōriōsum exīstimāret.* (ll.135-136)

> *Vērum hōc ānulō sī quis servārī potest, nōn ego, sed amīca mea servanda est.* (ll.180-181)

Recensiō: "Qu" words

aliquī, qua, quod	some
aliquis, quid	someone, something
quī, quae, quod	who, which, he who
quī, quae, quod (...?)	what, which (...?)
quia	because
quid (*n.*) (*v.* **quis**)	what, anything
quid *adv.*	why
quīdam, quadam, quoddam	a certain, some
quidem	indeed, certainly
nē quidem	not even
quidnī	why not
quisquid, quidquid	whatever, anything that
quis, quae, quid	who, what
quis, quid (si/num/ne...)	anyone, anything
quisnam, quidnam	who/what ever?
quisquam, quidquam	anyone, anything
quisque, quaeque, quodque	each
quisquis	whoever, anyone who
quō *adv.*	where (to)
quod (= quia)	because, that
quod (*n.*) (*v.* **qui**)	what, which, that which
quōmodo	how
quoniam	as, since
quoque	also, too
quot	how many

Vocābula Disposita/Ordināta

Nōmina

1st

amīcitia, -ae	friendship
audācia, -ae	boldnesss
grātia, -ae	favor; gratitude, thanks (*pl.*)
incola, -ae (*m./f.*)	inhabitant
inopia, -ae	lack
pīrāta, -ae (*m.*)	pirate
poēta, -ae (*m.*)	poet
victōria, -ae	victory

2nd

amphitheātrum, -ī	amphitheatre
populus, -ī	the people (*not* a person)
talentum, -ī	a talent (sum of money)

3rd

classis, classis (*f.*)	fleet
condiciō, condicōnis (*f.*)	agreement, contract; condition
gēns, gentis (*f.*)	tribe, nation
servitūs, servitūtis (*f.*)	slavery
victor, victōris (*m.*)	victor
vīrēs, vīrium (*f. pl.*)	strength
vīs (*f.*)	force, power
voluntās, voluntātis (*f.*)	will, desire, good will

4th

cursus, -ūs	running, forward movement; course

Verba

-āre (1)

(adiūvō) adiūvāre, adiūvisse, adiūtum	help
(armō) armāre, armāvisse, armātum	arm
(minor) minārī, minātum	threaten
(rēmigō) rēmigāre, rēmigāvisse, rēmigatum	move back, return
(repugnō) repugnāre, repugnāvisse	fight back (*mostly intr.*)

-ēre (2)

(dissuādeō) dissuādēre, dissuādisse	dissuade
(tueor) tuērī, tuitum & tūtum	see, watch, protect

-ere (3)

(contemnō) contemnere, contempsisse, contemptum	think little of, scorn
(dēsistō) dēsistere, dēstitisse	leave off, cease
(ēducō) ēdūcere, ēdūxisse, ēductum	lead out
(flectō) flectere, flexisse, flectum	bend
(meminī) meminisse	keep in mind, remember (+ *gen.* or *acc.*)

(praepōnō) praepōnere, praeposuisse, praepositum	put (*acc.*) before (*dat.*); in charge of
(percurrō) percurrere, percucurrisse	run through
(redimō) redimere, redēmisse, redemptum	buy back
(reminīscor) reminīscī	call to mind, recollect (+ *gen.* or *acc.*)
(submergō) submergere, -mersisse, -mersum	sink, submerge

Irregular

(offerō) offerre, obtulisse, oblātum	offer, present
(praeferō) praeferre, praetulisse, praelātum	prefer
(referō) referre, rettulisse, relātum	bring back, return

Adiectīva
1st-2nd (us/er, -a, -um)

adversus, -a, -um	opposed, adverse
cārus, -a, -um	dear
cūnctus, -a, -um	all
ēgregius, -a, -um	outstanding
grātus, -a, -um	grateful, pleasing
īnfēstus, -a, -um	dangerous
internus, -a, -um	internal, domestic
mercātōrius, -a, -um	mercantile
mūtuus, -a, -um	on loan
nūbilus, -a, -um	cloudy
proximus, -a, -um	closest
superbus, -a, -um	lofty, arrogant

3rd

commūnis, -e	shared, common
inermis, -e	(in + arm) unarmed
vīlis, -e	cheap

Adverbia

aliquandō	sometime or other, finally
aliquot	some, several
dōnec	until
etiamnunc	even now
intereā	meanwhile
ubīque	anywhere, everywhere

Coniunctiōnēs

neu	or not; and not (nēve...nēve)
seu	or if, or (sive...sive)
utinam	if that, only that, would that

XXXIII. Exercitus Rōmānus

Rēs Grammaticae Novae

1. Verbs
   a. Pluperfect Subjunctive
   b. Uses of the Subjunctive
      i.   Pluperfect Subjunctive in Subordinate Clauses
      ii. Optative Subjunctive: Unfulfilled Wishes
      iii. Contrafactual Conditions
   c. Passive of Intransitive Verbs
   d. Future Imperative
   e. *velle*: Imperfect Subjunctive
2. Nouns: Case Uses
   a. Ablative of Respect (continued)
3. Adjectives
   a. Gerundive Attraction
   b. Distributive Numerals (continued)

Aemilia Writes to her Brother

The chapter consists mainly of a letter to Aemilia from her brother, who is in Germania on military service. From this letter you learn more military terms.

Lectiō Prīma (Section I)
Distributive Numerals (continued)

In Chapter XXX you learned that distributive numbers are those used repetitively. Here are more distributive numerals:

    10   *dēnī, ae, a (l.2)*
    4   *quaternī, ae, a (l.3)*
    5   *quīnī, ae, a (l.3)*
    6   *sēnī, ae, a (l.3)*

The distributive numerals are used with nouns that occur only in the plural, i.e. *pluralia tantum*. e.g.:

> *bīna castra*   two camps
> *bīnae litterae*   (= *duae epistulae*)

When distributive numbers are used with nouns that are *pluralia tantum ūnī, -ae, -a* and *trīnī, -ae, -a* are used instead of *singuli, -ae, -a* and *terni, -ae, -a*, e.g.:

> *ūnae litterae*   (= *ūna epistula*)
> *trīnae litterae*   (= *trēs epistulae*)

> *Quaeris ā mē cūr tibi ūnās tantum litterās scrīpserim, cum interim trīnās quaternāsve litterās ā tē accēperim.* (*ll.*90-92)

Velle, nōlle, mālle (continued)

The imperfect subjunctive of *mālle* and *nōlle* follows the (perfectly regular) pattern of *velle* (margin, page 274). Review the forms of the present indicative and present and imperfect subjunctive:

Indicative		Subjunctive Present		Imperfect	
volō	*volumus*	*velim*	*velīmus*	*vellem*	*vellēmus*
vīs	*vultis*	*velīs*	*velītis*	*vellēs*	*vellētis*
vult	*volunt*	*velit*	*velint*	*vellet*	*vellent*
nōlō	*nōlumus*	*nōlim*	*nōlīmus*	*nōllem*	*nōllēmus*
nōn vīs	*nōn vultis*	*nōlīs*	*nōlītis*	*nōllēs*	*nōllētis*
nōn vult	*nōlunt*	*nōlit*	*nōlint*	*nōllet*	*nōllent*
mālō	*mālumus*	*mālim*	*mālīmus*	*māllem*	*māllēmus*
māvīs	*māvultis*	*mālīs*	*mālītis*	*māllēs*	*māllētis*
māvult	*mālunt*	*mālit*	*mālint*	*māllet*	*māllent*

Lectiō Altera (Section II)

Optative Subjunctive: Wishes Unfulfilled in the Present

In Chapter XXXI you learned that the present subjunctive (with or without *utinam*) expresses a wish for the future. When we express a wish for the present, it **has** to be one that isn't true for the present (e.g. "I wish I weren't in class right now!"). There are various names for such wishes (which are optative subjunctive): unfulfilled, unrealistic, and contrafactual (contrary to fact). The verb is in the imperfect subjunctive, e.g. Aemilius' unrealistic wishes:

> *Utinam ego Rōmae essem!* (*l.*67)
> *Utinam hic amnis Tiberis esset et haec castra essent Rōma!* (*ll.*70-71)

Aemilius is not, in fact, in Rome; the river is not the Tiber and the camp is not Rome. The verb is not in the present, but in the imperfect subjunctive.

Conditions in the Subjunctive: Present Unreal (Contrafactual)

Just as wishes can be unfulfilled (contrafactual), so too can conditions. The following sentences express a **condition** that can never be realized; here, too, the imperfect subjunctive is used to express unreality:

Sī Mercurius essem ālāsque habērem, in Italiam volārem!	If I were Mercury and had wings, I would fly into Italy (but I'm not Mercury and I don't have wings). (*ll.73-75*)

Nisi nōs hīc essēmus fīnēsque imperiī dēfenderēmus, hostēs celeriter Dānuvium et Alpēs trānsīrent atque ūsque in Italiam pervenīrent, nec vōs in Latiō tūtī essētis. (*ll.82-85*)

Sī mihi tantum esset ōtiī quantum est tibi, in epistulīs scrībendīs nōn minus dīligēns essem quam tū. (*ll.93-95*)

Gerundive Attraction

The gerund can take a direct object, e.g. *fīnem nārrandī* (Chapter XXVI). Latin writers often preferred an alternate construction: substituting a noun/gerundive phrase for the gerund and the accusative; the meaning is the same in each case. Some examples:

fīnem nārrandī (*Chap. XXVI, l.149*)	*fīnem fabulae nārrandae*
cupidus patriam videndī	*cupidus patriae videndae* (*l.80*)
fessus longās fābulās audiendō (*Chap. XXVI, l.123*)	*fessus longīs fabulīs audiendīs*
studiōsus legendī	*studiōsus librōrum legendōrum*

When adding an object to a gerund prepositional phrase, Latin writers consistently use a gerundive/noun combination (not the gerund plus object), e.g.:

Gerund prepositional phrase	Gerundive/noun phrase
ad scrībendum: "for writing"	*ad epistulam scrībendam*: "for writing a letter" (*ll.97-98*)
in scrībendō: "in writing"	*in epistulīs scrībendīs*: "in writing letters" (*ll.94-95*)
ad dēfendendum	*ad castra dēfendenda* (*l.116*)
ad persequendum	*ad eōs persequendōs = ut eōs persequerentur*) (*l.132*)

Lectiō Tertia (Section III)

Passive of Intransitive Verbs

Intransitive verbs, you have learned, do not take an accusative direct object. Intransitive verbs can be used in the passive, however, if they are used impersonally (that is, in the third person with no subject: "it") *Pugnāre* is impersonal in this example:

ā Rōmānīs fortissimē pugnātum est = Rōmānī fortissimē pugnāvērunt.

Mediā nocte in castra nūntiātum est... (*l.105*)

> *Cum complūrēs hōrās ita fortissimē ā nostrīs, ab hostibus cōnstanter ac nōn timidē* <u>*pugnātum esset*</u>.

literally: "when there had been fighting by our men…by the enemy," but more idiomatically "when our men and the enemy had fought…" (*ll.119-121*)

Pluperfect Subjunctive

The last remaining Latin tense is the **pluperfect subjunctive** (Latin *coniūnctīvus plūsquamperfectī*). It is formed in the **active** by inserting *-issē-* (shortened *-isse-*) between the perfect stem and the personal endings:

1st singular	~isse|m
2nd	~issē|s
3rd	~isse|t
1st plural	~issē|mus
2nd	~issē|tis
3rd	~isse|nt

The **passive** is composed of the perfect participle and the imperfect subjunctive of *esse* (*essem, essēs, esset*, etc.).

Pluperfect Subjunctive in Subordinate Clauses

Just as the perfect signifies completed action in a subordinate clause after a present or future tense verb, the pluperfect is used to show completed action after a past tense main verb.

Sequence of Tense

Main Verb	Subordinate Verb	
	incompleted action	completed action
present future	present subjunctive	perfect subjunctive
past tense	imperfect subjunctive	pluperfect subjunctive

The pluperfect subjunctive occurs in subordinate clauses such as:

- *cum*-clauses (where *cum* + pluperf. subj. = *postquam* + perf. ind.)

  Quī cum arma cēp<u>issent</u> et vāllum ascend<u>issent</u> (=postquam… cēpērunt/ascendērunt), prīmō mīrābantur quamobrem mediā nocte ē somnō excitātī essent…(*ll.109-111*)

  Cum complūrēs hōrās ita fortissimē ā nostrīs…pugnā<u>tum esset</u>. (*ll.119-121*)

- indirect questions concerning completed action in the past, i.e. with the main verb in the preterite (imperfect, perfect or pluperfect).

  Ego quoque dubitāre coeperam num nūntius vērum dīx<u>isset</u>. (*ll.112-113*)

Optative Subjunctive: Wishes Unfulfilled in the Past

Just as the imperfect subjunctive expresses a wish that is not coming true in the present, the **pluperfect subjunctive** expresses a wish that didn't come true in the past, as in Aemilius's final remarks:

Utinam patrem audīvissem!	If only I had listened to my father (but I didn't)! (*l.166*)

Conditions in the Subjunctive: Past Unreal (Contrafactual)

The imperfect subjunctive expresses a condition unfulfilled in the present, while the pluperfect subjunctive expresses a condition unfulfilled in the past, e.g.:

Sī iam tum hoc intellēxissem, certē patrem audīvissem nec ad bellum profectus essem.	If I had understood…I would have listened and I would not have set out. (*ll.181-182*)
Malus amīcus fuissem, nisi lacrimās effūdissem super corpus amīcī mortuī, cum ille sanguinem suum prō mē effūdisset.	I would have been a bad friend, had I not shed tears, since he would have shed…. (*ll.163-165*)

More examples can be found in GRAMMATICA LATINA.

Thus, the **imperfect subjunctive** expresses a wish/condition which is **not** true in the present. The **pluperfect subjunctive** expresses a wish/condition that was not true in the past:

utinam veniat	may he come (in the future)
utinam venīret	would that he were coming (but he is not)
utinam vēnisset	would that he had come (but he did not)

Ablative of Respect (continued)

The **ablative of respect** (which answers the question "in what respect?") was introduced in Chapter XI (*pede aeger, l.55*), Chapter XIX (*amōre dignus, ll.111-112*) and again in Chapter XXV (*nōmine Mīnōtaurus, l.26*). In the expression *hostēs numerō superiōrēs* (*l.144*), *numerō* shows in what way the enemy are superior: "in number," "numerically."

Future Imperative

Aemilius ends his letter with some requests (ll.187-189). Here he uses the so-called **future imperative**.

The future imperative adds to the present stem:

- Vowel Stems
  - ▷ *-tō* (sing.), *-tōte* (pl.)

    nārrā|tō -tōte

- Consonant Stems
  - ▷ *itō -itōte*

    scrīb|itō -itōte

- Irregular
  - ▷ *es|tō, es|tōte* from *esse*
  - ▷ *fer|tō, fer|tōte* from *ferre*

Recensiō

I. Summary of Conditions

With the indicative

- Present Indicative:

Sī iam hoc intellegis, certē patrem audīs.	If you already understand this, you are certainly listening to your father. (*cf. ll.181-182*)

  Sī aeger est, in lūdum īre nōn potest. (*cf. Chap. XV, l.83*)

- Future Indicative:

Sī hoc intellēxeris, certē patrem audiēs.	If you will have understood this this, you will certainly listen to your father.

  Nōnne laetus eris, sī fīliolam habēbis? (*cf. Chap. XX, ll.153-154*)

  Profectō eum verberābō atque omnibus modīs cruciābō, sī eum invēnerō priusquam Italiam relīquerit. (*Chap. XXXI, ll.63-65*)

- Past Indicative:

Sī iam tum hoc intellēxistī, certē patrem audīvistī.	If you already at that time understood this, you certainly listened to your father.

  Sī quid prāvē feceram, dominus imperābat ut ego ab aliīs servīs tenērer et verberārer. (*cf. Chap. XXVIII, ll.160-161*)

With the subjunctive

- Present Subjunctive (ideal: "should ...would"):[1]

Sī hoc intellegās, certē patrem audias.	If you should understand this, you would certainly listen to your father.
Sī quid prāvē faciam, dominus imperet ut ego ab aliīs servīs tenear et verberer.	If I should do something wrong, my master would order....

- Imperfect Subjunctive (present unreal: "were...would"):

Sī iam hoc intellegerēs, certē patrem audīvissēs.	If you already understood this (but you clearly don't), you certainly would be listening to your father (but you aren't).

- Pluperfect Subjunctive (past unreal):

Sī iam tum hoc intellēxissēs, certē patrem audīvissēs.	If you had already then understood this (but you clearly didn't), you certainly would have listened to your father (but you didn't).

---

1   N.B.: There are no examples of this type of condition in your text.

II. Some Subjunctive Signals

Ut

- Purpose
  - ▷ incompleted action: present or imperfect subjunctive
- Result
  - ▷ incompleted action: present or imperfect subjunctive
- Optative
  - ▷ present subjunctive for a future wish
  - ▷ imperfect subjunctive for a wish unfulfilled in the present
  - ▷ pluperfect subjunctive for a wish unfulfilled in the past
- Indirect command
  - ▷ incompleted action: present or imperfect subjunctive
- Indirect question (= how)
  - ▷ main verb refers to present or future:
    - o present subjunctive if subordinate verb expresses incompleted action
    - o perfect subjunctive if subordinate verb expresses completed action
  - ▷ main verb refers to past:
    - o imperfect subjunctive if subordinate verb expresses incompleted action
    - o pluperfect subjunctive if subordinate verb expresses completed action
- Negative fear (i.e. fear that something will not happen/has not happened)
  - ▷ main verb refers to present or future:
    - o present subjunctive if subordinate verb expresses incompleted action
    - o perfect subjunctive if subordinate verb expresses completed action
  - ▷ main verb refers to past:
    - o imperfect subjunctive if subordinate verb expresses incompleted action
    - o pluperfect subjunctive if subordinate verb expresses completed action

Utinam

- Wish (see optative subjunctive)

Nē

- Purpose
  - ▷ incompleted action: present or imperfect subjunctive
- Optative
  - ▷ present subjunctive for a future wish
  - ▷ imperfect subjunctive for a wish unfulfilled in the present
  - ▷ pluperfect subjunctive for a wish unfulfilled in the past

- Hortatory
  ▷ present subjunctive
- Indirect command
  ▷ incompleted action: present or imperfect subjunctive
- Prohibition
  ▷ perfect subjunctive
- Affirmative fear (*nē* or *nē nōn*)
  ▷ main verb refers to present or future:
    ○ present subjunctive if subordinate verb expresses incompleted action
    ○ perfect subjunctive if subordinate verb expresses completed action
  ▷ main verb refers to past:
    ○ imperfect subjunctive if subordinate verb expresses incompleted action
    ○ pluperfect subjunctive if subordinate verb expresses completed action

Nē...nōn
- Fear

Ut...nōn
- Result
  ▷ incompleted action: present or imperfect subjunctive

Cum
- Circumstances: subjunctive
- Causal: subjunctive
- (+ ablative: preposition)
- (Pinpointing the time: indicative)
- (Repeated action: "whenever": indicative (usually))

Vocābula Disposita/Ordināta

Nōmina

1st

rīpa, -ae	riverbank

2nd

gaudium, -ī	joy
lēgātus, -ī	envoy, delegate
legiōnārius, -ī	legionary
proelium, -ī	battle
stipendium, -ī	salary
studium, -ī	interest, study

3rd

aetās, aetatis (*f.*)	age
agmen, agminis (*n.*)	army on the march, file
amnis, amnis (*m.*)	river

cohors, cohortis (*f.*)	cohort
ēnsis, ēnsis (*m.*)	sword
imperātor, imperātōris	general, emperor
legiō, -ōnis (*f.*)	legion
ōrdō, ōrdinis (*f.*)	order
pāx, pācis (*f.*)	peace
ratis, ratis (*f.*)	raft
valētūdō, valētūdinis	health
virtūs, virtūtis (*f.*)	virtue
vulnus, vulneris (*n.*)	wound
5th	
aciēs, -ēī	line of battle
caedēs, -ēī	slaughter

Verba

-āre (1)

(circumdō) circumdare, circumdedisse, circumdatum	surround
(commemorō) commemorāre, -āvisse,-ātum	mention
(convocō) convocāre, -āvisse, -ātum	call together
(cōpulō) cōpulāre, -āvisse, -ātum	join, connect
(dēsīderō) dēsīderāre, -āvisse, -ātum	long for, miss
(fatīgō) fatīgāre, -āvisse, -ātum	tire out, weary
(hortor) hortārī, hortātum	encourage, urge
(praestō) praestāre, praestitisse	furnish, fulfill
(properō) properāre, -āvisse, -ātum	hasten, hurry
(vulnerō) vulnerāre, -āvisse, -ātum	wound

-ēre (2)

(studeō) studēre, studuisse	devote oneself to (+ *dat.*)

-ere (3)

(adiungō) adiungere, adiunxisse, adiunctum	add to, join
(caedō) caedere, cecīdisse, caesum	beat, fell, kill
(cogō) cōgere, cōegisse, coactum	compel, force
(effundō) effundere, effūdisse, effusum	pour out
(ērumpō) ērumpere, ērūpisse, ēruptum	break out
(excurrō) excurrere, excucurrisse, excursum	run out, rush out
(īnstruō) īnstruere, īnstruxisse, īnstructum	draw up, arrange
(prōcurrō) prōcurrere, prōcucurrisse, prōcursum	run forward, charge
(prōgredior) prōgredī, prōgressum	go forward, advance

-īre (4)

(mūniō) mūnīre, mūnīvisse, mūnītum	fortify

Irregular

fore	= futurum esse
(trānsferō) trānsferre, trānstulisse, trānslātum	transfer, transport
(trānseō) trānsīre, trānsīvisse	cross, pass

Adiectīva

1st-2nd (us/er, -a, -um)

arduus, -a, -um	steep
dēnī, -ae, -a	ten at a time
dīrus, -a, -um	dreadful
horrendus, -a, -um	dreadful
idōneus, -a, -um	suitable
ōtiōsus, -a, -um	leisured, idle
posterus, -a, -um	next, following
prīvātus, -a, -um	private
pūblicus, -a, -um	public
quaternī, -ae, -a	four at a time
quīnī, -ae, -a	five at a time
rīdiculus, -a, -um	ridiculous
sēnī, -ae, -a	six at a time
trīnī, -ae, -a	three at a time
ūnī, -ae, -a	one at a time

3rd

citerior, citerius	nearer
incolumis, -e	unharmed, safe
mīlitāris, -e	military
ulterior, ulterius	farther, more distant

Pronōmina

plērīque, plēraeque, plēraque	most

Adverbia

diūtius	longer (*comp. of* diū)
etenim	and indeed, for
ferē	about, almost
praecipuē	especially
prīdiē	the day before
quamdiū	how long, as long as
tamdiū	so long, as long

Praepositiōnēs

citrā + *acc.*	on this side
secundum + *acc.*	along
ultrā + *acc.*	on that (the far) side

XXXIV. De Arte Poēticā

Rēs Grammaticae Novae

1. Verbs
   a. Intransitive Verbs
   b. Contraction
2. Nouns
   a. "Poetic Plural"
   b. Case use: *in* + Accusative
3. Meter
   a. Syllables
      i. Quantity
      ii. Division
   b. Metric Feet
      i. Hexameter
      ii. Pentameter
      iii. Elegaic Couplet
      iv. Hendecasyllables

Latin Poetry

By now you have advanced so far that you can begin to read Latin poetry. In this chapter you find poems by Catullus (c. 86-54 B.C.), Ovid (*Ovidius*, 43 B.C.—17 A.D.), and Martial (*Mārtiālis*, c. 40-104 A.D.). At the party Cornelius starts by quoting a line from Ovid's *Ars amātōria*, which makes Julius and Cornelius quote passages from a collection of love poems, *Amōrēs,* by the same poet. Julius goes on to read aloud some short poems by Catullus and a selection of Martial's witty and satirical epigrams (*epigrammata*). These epigrams are short poems in elegaic couplets (see below).[1]

Reading Poetry

When first reading the poems you will have to disregard the verse form and concentrate on the content. A major obstacle to understanding is the free word

---

1   Divisions between epigrams are marked in the text by a dash (—).

order, which often causes word groups to be separated. Here the inflectional endings will show you what words belong together; in some cases you will find marginal notes to help you, e.g. *ut ipsae spectentur* (*l.57*), *nōbilium equōrum* (*l.62*), *amor quem facis* (*l.65*), *meae puellae dīxī* (*l.71*). Some supplementary (implied) words are given in italics. However, the important thing is to visualize the situation and enter into the poet's ideas. The comments made on the poems will be useful for this purpose.

Meter

When you understand the meaning and content of the poems, it is time for you to study the structure of the verses, that is, the **meter**. This is explained in the GRAMMATICA LATINA section. The following is a summary of the rules:

Syllabic Quantity: The decisive factor in Latin verse structure is the length or **quantity** of the syllables. Syllables ending in a short vowel (*a, e, i, o, u, y*) are **short** and are to be pronounced twice as quickly as **long** syllables, i.e. syllables ending in a long vowel (*ā, ē, ī, ō, ū, ȳ*), a diphthong (*ae, oe, au, eu, ui*), or a consonant. In other words: **A syllable is short if it ends in a short vowel; all other syllables are long.** A long syllable is marked [—] and a short syllable [∪].

Syllabic Division: For the division into syllables, each **verse** (*versus*, "line") is treated like one long word:

- **A consonant at the end of a word is linked with a vowel (or h-) at the beginning of the next.** In a word like *satis*, therefore, the last syllable is short if the next word begins with a vowel or *h*-, e.g. in the combination *satis est*, where *-s* is linked with the following *e* in *est*: *sa-ti-s⌢est*—whereas the syllable *tis* is long in *satis nōn est*: *sa-tis-nō-n⌢est*.
- **A vowel (and -am, -em, -im, -um) at the end of a word is dropped before a vowel (or h-) beginning the next word**, e.g. *atque oculōs*: *atqu'oculōs*; *modo hūc*: *mod'hūc*; *passerem abstulistis*: *passer'abstulistis* (in *est* and *es* the *e* is dropped, e.g. *sōla est*: *sōla'st*; *vērum est*: *vērum'st*; *bella es*: *bella's*). This is called elision, the vowel is said to be **elided** (Latin *ē-līdere*, "eject," "eliminate").

Metric Feet: Each verse can be divided into a certain number of **feet** (Latin *pedēs*) composed of two or three syllables. The commonest feet are:
- the **trochee** (Latin *trochaeus*), consisting of one long and one short syllable [— ∪]
- the **iamb** (Latin *iambus*), one short and one long [∪ —]
- the **dactyl** (Latin *dactylus*), one long and two short syllables [— ∪∪]
- The two short syllables of the dactyl are often replaced by one long syllable, making a foot consisting of two long syllables [— —] which is called a **spondee** (Latin *spondēus*).

Hexameter: The favorite verse with Latin poets is the **hexameter**, which consists of six feet, the first five of which are dactyls or spondees—the fifth, however, is always a dactyl, and the sixth a spondee (or trochee):[2]

— ∪∪| — ∪∪| — ∪∪| — ∪∪| — ∪∪| — *

Pentameter: The hexameter often alternates with the slightly shorter **pentameter**, which can be divided into two halves of 2½ feet, each conforming to the beginning of the hexameter (but there are no spondees in the second half):

— ∪∪| — ∪∪| — || — ∪∪| — ∪∪| —

Elegaic Couplet: The pentameter never stands alone, but always comes after a hexameter (in the text the pentameters are indented). Such a couplet, consisting of a hexameter and a pentameter, is called an **elegiac couplet**, because it was used in **elegies**, i.e. poems expressing personal sentiments, mainly love poems.

Hendecasyllables: Catullus frequently uses the **hendecasyllable** (Latin *versus hendecasyllabus*, "eleven-syllable verse"), which consists of these eleven syllables:

— — — ∪∪ — ∪ — ∪ — *

It can be divided into a spondee, a dactyl, two trochees and a spondee (or trochee). (Occasionally the first syllable is short.)

Reading Verse Aloud

When Latin verse is read aloud, the rhythm is marked by the regular alternation of long and short syllables. Two short syllables are equivalent in length to one long. In modern European verse rhythm is marked by accent. Therefore modern readers of Latin verse are apt to put a certain accent on the first syllable of each foot. This may help you to get an idea of the verse rhythm, but do not forget that accent is of secondary importance in Latin verse, the important thing is the quantity of the syllables.

Plural for Singular

The Roman poets sometimes use the plural ('poetic plural') instead of the singular, especially forms in -*a* from neuters in -*um*, when they are in need of short syllables, e.g. *mea colla* (*l.75* for *meum collum*) and *post fāta* (*l.180* for *post fātum*). Like other authors a Roman poet may also use the 1st person plural (*nōs, nōbīs, noster*) about himself. You see this when Catullus calls his friend *venuste noster* (*l.152*) and when Martial in his epigram on the response of the public to his books calls them *libellōs nostrōs* and concludes with the words *nunc nōbīs carmina nostra placent* (*ll.163, 166*).

In + accusative—> against

Martial, who himself writes poems *in inimīcōs*, says about the poet Cinna: *Versiculōs in mē nārrātur scrībere Cinna* (*l.172*). Here *in* + accusative has "hostile" meaning (= *contrā*, cf. the phrase *impetum facere in hostēs*).

---

2   The asterisk (*) signifies a syllable that can be either long or short.

Nominative and Infinitive with Passive Verbs

The passive *nārrātur,* like *dīcitur* (*Chap. XIII, l.52*), is combined with the nom. + inf.: *Cinna scrībere nārrātur/dīcitur* = *Cinnam scrībere nārrant/dīcunt.*

Intransitive Verbs

Besides *imperāre* and *pārēre* you have met many other verbs which take the dative:

crēdere	*appropinquāre*
nocēre	*placēre*
oboedīre	*(cōn)fīdere*
impendēre	*ignōscere*
servīre	*resistere*
(per)suādēre	*minārī*
invidēre	*studēre*
parcere	

Several compounds with *-esse* also take a dative:

prōd-esse	*de-esse* ("fail")
prae-esse	*ad-esse* ("stand by," "help")

In this chapter you find further examples:

favēre (*l.40*)
nūbere (*l.126*)
plaudere (*l.217*)

The impersonal verb *libet,* which—like *licet*—is usually combined with a dative:

mihi libet (*l.35,* "it pleases me," "I feel like," "I want,"
cf. *mihi licet,* "I may," "I am allowed"

Contractions

- A double *i* (*ii, iī*) is apt to be contracted into one long *ī,* as you have seen in the form *dī* for *diī.*
- When *h* disappears in *mihi* and *nihil,* we get the contracted forms *mī* and *nīl* (e.g. *ll.118, 174*).
- You also find *sapīstī* for *sapiistī* (*l.190*)—the latter form being a contraction of *sapīvistī;* the final *v* of the perfect stem tends to disappear, so that, e.g.:

    -īvisse becomes *-iisse/-īsse*
    -āvisse becomes *-āsse*
    -āvistī becomes *-āstī:* (*Chap. XXVIII, l.106*)
    nōvisse becomes *nōsse*
    nōverat becomes *nōrat.*

This last form, the pluperfect of *nōscere,* comes to mean "knew," e.g.:

Ovidius ingenium mulierum tam bene nōverat quam ipsae mulierēs. (*ll.54-55*)

suamque nōrat ipsam (: dominam) tam bene quam puella mātrem (*ll.93-94*)

Vocābula Disposita/Ordināta

Nōmina
  1st
  arānea, -ae   spider, cobweb
  aurīga, -ae (m.)   charioteer, driver
  cōmoedia, -ae   comedy
  dēliciae, -ārum (f. pl.)   delight, pet
  lucerna, -ae   lamp
  nota, -ae   mark, sign
  opera, -ae   effort, pains
  palma, -ae   palm
  tenebrae, -ārum (f. pl.)   darkness
  2nd
  bāsium, -ī   kiss
  cachinnus, -ī   laugh, guffaw
  circus, -ī   circle, orbit, circus
  fātum, -ī   fate
  gremium, -ī   lap
  ingenium, -ī   nature, character
  lūdus, -ī   play, game, school
  ocellus, -ī   (little) eye
  odium, -ī   hatred
  prīncipium, -ī   beginning
  scalpellum, -ī   scalpel, surgical knife
  theātrum, -ī   theatre
  3rd
  certāmen, certāminis (n.)   contest fight
  gladiātor, -tōris (m.)   gladiator
  mēns, mentis (f.)   mind
  opēs, opum (f. pl.)   wealth
  passer, passeris (m.)   sparrow
  ratiō, ratiōnis (f.)   reason
  rēte, rētis (n.)   net
  spectātor, spectātōris (m.)   spectator
  testis, -is (m.)   witness
  4th
  anus, -ūs (f.)   old woman
  rīsus, -ūs   laughter, laugh
  sinus -ūs   fold (of toga)
  Indeclinable
  nīl   nothing (=nihil)
  Grammatica
  dactylus, -ī   dactyl
  dipthongus, -ī   dipthong
  epigramma, epigrammatis (n.)   epigram

hendecasyllabus, -ī	"11 syllable verse"
hexameter, hexametrī	having 6 metrical feet
iambus, -ī	iamb
pentameter, pentametrī	having 5 metrical feet
spondēus, -ī	spondee
trochaeus, -ī	trochee
versiculus, -ī	a little line of verse (*diminuitive of versus, ūs*)

Verba

-āre (1)

(affirmō) affirmāre, affirmāvisse, affirmātum	assert, affirm
(certō) certāre, certāvisse, certātum	contend, fight
(conturbō) conturbāre, conturbāvisse, conturbātum	mix up, confound
(dēvorō) dēvorāre, dēvorāvisse, dēvorātum	swallow up, devour
(excruciō) excruciāre, excruciāvisse, excruciātum	torture, torment
(implicō) implicāre, implicuisse, implicitum	enfold
(ōscitō) ōscitāre, ōscitāvisse, ōscitātum	gape, yawn
(pīpiō) pīpiāre, pīpiāvisse, pīpiātum	chirp

-ēre (2)

(faveō) favēre, fāvisse	favor, support + *dat.*
(libet) libēre	it pleases + *dat.*
(lūgeō) lūgēre, lūxisse	mourn

-ere (3)

(accendō) accendere, accendisse, accensum	light, enflame
(ēlīdō) ēlīdere, ēlīsisse, ēlīsum	omit, elide
(ērubēscō) ērubēscere, ērubuisse	blush
(laedō) laedere, laesisse, laesum	injure, hurt
(nūbō) nūbere, nūpsisse	marry + *dat.*
(plaudō) plaudere, plausisse, plausum	clap, applaud + *dat.*
(requīrō) requīrere, requīsīvisse, requīsitum	seek, ask
(sapiō) sapere, sapīvisse	be wise, have sense

-īre (4)

(circumsiliō) circumsilīre, circumsilīvisse	hop about
(prōsiliō) prōsilīre, prōsiluisse	spring forth

Adiectīva

1st-2nd (us/er, -a, -um)

bellus, -a, -um	lovely, pretty
dubius, -a, -um	undecided, doubtful
geminus, -a, -um	twin
gladiātōrius, -a, -um	gladiatorial
iocōsus, -a, -um	humorous funny
mellītus, -a, -um	sweet
misellus, -a, -um	poor, wretched
niveus, -a, -um	snow white
perpetuus, -a, -um	continuous, permanent
poēticus, -a, -um	poetical
scaenicus, -a, -um	theatrical
sērius, -a, -um	serious
tenebricōsus, -a, -um	dark
turgid(ul)us, -a, -um	swollen
ultimus, -a, -um	most distant, last
venustus, -a, -um	charming

3rd

ācer, -cris, -cre	keen, active fierce
circēnsis, -e	of the circus

Adverbia

dein	afterward, then
interdum	now and then
libenter	with pleasure, gladly
plērumque	mostly

Coniunctiōnēs

dummodo	provided that, if only

XXXV: Ars Grammatica

Now that you have worked your way through all the declensions and conjugations of the Latin language, it is time to pause and take a comprehensive look at the grammatical system. To give you an opportunity to do this we present, in a slightly abbreviated form, a Latin grammar, the *Ars grammatica minor,* written by the Roman grammarian Dōnātus, c. 350 A.D. This grammar is based on the works of earlier grammarians, rearranged in the form of question and answer, so it gives us an idea of the teaching methods used in antiquity—and much later, for the "Donat" was a favorite schoolbook in Europe throughout the Middle Ages. Now it is up to you to show that you have learned enough to answer the questions on grammar put to school-children in the Roman Empire. Apart from omissions, marked [...], the text of Donatus is unaltered (only in the examples on page 303 of *Lingua Latina* some infrequent words have been replaced by others).

The Latin grammatical terms are still in use. However, the **part of speech** (*pars ōrātiōnis*) which the Roman grammarians called *nōmina* is now divided into **nouns** (or **substantives**) and **adjectives**. The term *nōmen adiectīvum* dates from antiquity, but it was not till medieval times that the term *nōmen substantīvum* was coined (in English "noun substantive" as opposed to "noun adjective"). As a matter of fact, several of the Latin grammatical terms are adjectives which are generally used "substantively" with a noun understood, e.g. (*cāsus*) *nōminātīvus,* (*numerus*) *plūrālis,* (*modus*) *imperātīvus,* (*gradus*) *comparātīvus,* (*genus*) *fēminīnum. Genus* is "gender" in English; Donatus counts four genders, because he uses the term *genus commune* about words that may be both masculine and feminine, e.g. *sacerdōs -ōtis,* "priest/priestess" (other examples *cīvis, incola, īnfāns, testis, bōs, canis*).

The hexameter quoted by Donatus (*l.212*) to illustrate the use of *super* with the ablative, is taken from the end of the first book of the *Aeneid,* the famous poem in which Vergil (*Vergilius*) recounts the adventures of the Trojan hero Aeneas during his flight from Troy (*Trōia*). Driven by a storm to Africa he is received in Carthage (*Carthāgō*) by Queen *Dīdō,* who questions him about the fate of the other Trojans, King Priam (*Priamus*) and his son Hector.

Vocābula Disposita/Ordināta

Nōmina

  1st

īra, -ae	anger
mūsa, -ae	a muse (one of the 9 daughters of memory)

  2nd

scamnum, -ī	stool

  3rd

admīrātiō, admīrātiōnis (*f.*)	wonder, admiration
ōrātiō, ōrātiōnis (*f.*)	speech
sacerdōs, sacerdōtis (*m.*)	priest

  4th

affectus, -ūs	mood, feeling

  Grammatica

appellātīvum, -ī (*nōmen*)	common noun
cāsus, -ūs (*m.*)	fall, case
causālis (*coniūnctiō*) (*f.*)	causal conjunction
comparātiō, comparātiōnis (*f.*)	a comparison
coniugātiō, coniugātiōnis (*f.*)	conjugation
coniūnctiō, coniūnctiōnis (*f.*)	conjunction
cōpulātīva (*coniūnctiō*) (*f.*)	copulative conjunction
disiūnctīva (*coniūnctiō*) (*f.*)	disjunctive conjunction
explētīva (*coniūnctiō*) (*f.*)	exclamatory conjunction
interiectiō, interiectiōnis (*f.*)	interjection
optātīvus (*modus*)	optative (wishing) mood
positīvus (*gradus*)	positive degree1
proprium, ī (*nōmen*)	proper noun
quālitās, quālitātis (*f.*)	quality
quantitās, quantitātis (*f.*)	quantity
ratiōnālis (*coniūnctiō*) (*f.*)	conjunction showing the train of thought
significātiō, significātiōnis (*f.*)	meaning, sense
speciēs, -ēī	appearance, aspect, sort
synōnymum, -ī	synonym

Verba

  -āre (1)

(explānō) explānāre, -āvisse, -ātum	explain
(luctor) luctārī, luctātum	wrestle
(ōrdinō) ōrdināre, -āvisse, -ātum	put in order

  -ere (3)

(adnectō) adnectere	bind, tie
(dēmō) dēmere, dēmpsisse, dēmptum	take away

---

1   of an adjective or adverb

| (īnflectō) īnflectere | inflect[2] |
| mentiōnem facere | mention |

Adiectīva
1st-2nd (us/er, -a, -um)

| inconditus, -a, -um | unpolished, rough |

3rd

| similis, -e | similar |

Adverbia

dumtaxat	only, just
forsitan	maybe, perhaps
proptereā	therefore
quāpropter	why
quidnī	why not
sīquidem	seeing that, since
tantundem	just as much

Praepositiōnēs

| adversus/-um (*prp. +acc.*) | toward, against |
| cis (*prp. +acc.*) | on this side of |

Interiectiōnēs

attat	exclamation of joy, pain, wonder, fright
eia	exclamation of joy, pleased surprise; also "come on," "hurry up"
ēn	presents something important and/or unexpected
euax	exclamation of joy
papae	exclamation of wonder and joy

---

2   Inflect to form the pattern of a word, decline a noun or conjugate a verb

Morphology

The Parts of Speech

The **parts of speech**, or word classes, are:
- **Noun** (or **substantive**), e.g. *Mārcus, Rōma, puer, oppidum leō, aqua, color, pugna, mors,* etc.
- **Adjective**, e.g. *Rōmānus, bonus, pulcher, brevis,* etc.
- **Pronoun**, e.g. *tū, nōs, is, hic, ille, quis, quī, nēmō,* etc.
- **Verb**, e.g. *amāre, habēre, venīre, emere, īre, esse,* etc.
- **Adverb**, e.g. *bene, rēctē, fortiter, ita, nōn, hīc,* etc.
- **Conjunction**, e.g. *et, neque, sed, aut, quia, dum, sī, ut,* etc.
- **Preposition**, e.g. *in, ab, ad, post, inter, sine, dē,* etc.
- **Interjection**, e.g. *ō, ei, heu, heus, ecce,* etc.
- **Numerals** are nouns and adjectives which denote numbers, e.g. *trēs, tertius, ternī.*
- Adverbs, conjunctions, prepositions and interjections are **indeclinable** words, so-called **particles**.

Nouns

Gender, number, case

There are three **genders**: masculine, e.g. *servus*, **feminine**, e.g. *ancilla*, and **neuter**, e.g. *oppidum*.

There are two **numbers**: singular, e.g. *servus*, and **plural**, e.g. *servī*. Nouns which have no singular are called **pluralia tantum**.

There are six **cases**: nominative, e.g. *servus*, **accusative**, e.g. *servum*, **genitive**, e.g. *servī*, **dative**, e.g. *servō*, **ablative**, e.g. *(ā) servō*, and **vocative**, e.g. *serve*.

genders: masc., m.
          fem. , f.
          neut., n.

numbers: sing. pl.
cases: nom.
          acc.
          gen.
          dat.
          abl.
          voc.

Stem and ending

The **stem** is the main part of a word, e.g. *serv-, ancill-, oppid-, magn-, brev-*, to which various inflectional **endings** are added, e.g. *-um, -ī, -am, -ae, -ō, -ēs, -ibus*.

In the examples in this book the stem is separated from the ending with a thin vertical stroke [|], e.g. *serv|us, serv|ī*.

stems: *serv-, ancill-, oppid-,* etc.

endings: *-ī, -am, -ae,* etc.

257

Declensions

There are five **declensions**:

1st declension: gen. sing. -*ae*, e.g. *īnsul|a -ae*.

2nd declension: gen. sing. -*ī*, e.g. *serv|us -ī, oppid|um -ī*.

3rd declension: gen. sing. -*is*, e.g. *sōl sōl|is, urb|s -is*.

4th declension: gen. sing. -*ūs*, e.g. *man|us -ūs*.

5th declension: gen. sing. -*ēī/-eī*, e.g. *di|ēs -ēī, r|ēs -eī*.

First Declension

Genitive: sing. -*ae*, pl. -*ārum*.

Example: *īnsul|a -ae* f.

	sing.	pl.
nom.	*īnsul|a*	*īnsul|ae*
acc.	*īnsul|am*	*īnsul|ās*
gen.	*īnsul|ae*	*īnsul|ārum*
dat.	*īnsul|ae*	*īnsul|īs*
abl.	*īnsul|ā*	*īnsul|īs*

Masculine (male persons): *nauta, agricola, aurīga, pīrāta, poēta,* etc.

Second Declension

Genitive: sing. -*ī*, pl. -*ōrum*.

1. Masculine.

Examples: ***equ|us -ī, liber libr|ī, puer puer|ī***.

	sing.	pl.	sing.	pl.	sing.	pl.
nom.	*equ|us*	*equ|ī*	*liber*	*libr|ī*	*puer*	*puer|ī*
acc.	*equ|um*	*equ|ōs*	*libr|um*	*libr|ōs*	*puer|um*	*puer|ōs*
gen.	*equ|ī*	*equ|ōrum*	*libr|ī*	*libr|ōrum*	*puer|ī*	*puer|ōrum*
dat.	*equ|ō*	*equ|īs*	*libr|ō*	*libr|īs*	*puer|ō*	*puer|īs*
abl.	*equ|ō*	*equ|īs*	*libr|ō*	*libr|īs*	*puer|ō*	*puer|īs*
voc.	*equ|e*					

A few are feminine, e.g. *hum|us -ī, papÿr|us -ī, Aegypt|us -ī. Rhod|us -ī*.

Nom. sing. -*ius*, voc. -*ī*: *Iūlius, Iūlī! fīlius, fīlī!*

2. Neuter.

Example: ***verb|um -ī***.

	sing.	pl.
nom.	*verb|um*	*verb|a*
acc.	*verb|um*	*verb|a*
gen.	*verb|ī*	*verb|ōrum*
dat.	*verb|ō*	*verb|īs*
abl.	*verb|ō*	*verb|īs*

Margin notes:

declension (decl.)
1st decl.: gen. -*ae*
2nd decl.: gen. -*ī*
3rd decl.: gen. -*is*
4th decl.: gen. -*ūs*
5th decl.: gen. -*ēī/-eī*

-*a*	-*ae*
-*am*	-*ās*
-*ae*	-*ārum*
-*ae*	-*īs*
-*ā*	-*īs*

-*us*/-	-*ī*
-*um*	-*ōs*
-*ī*	-*ōrum*
-*ō*	-*īs*
-*ō*	-*īs*
-*e*	

-*um*	-*a*
-*um*	-*a*
-*ī*	-*ōrum*
-*ō*	-*īs*
-*ō*	-*īs*

Third Declension

Genitive: sing. *-is*, pl. *-um/-ium*.

[A] Genitive plural: *-um*.

1. Masculine and feminine.

Examples: *sōl sōl|is* m., *leō leōn|is* m., *vōx vōc|is* f.

	sing.	pl.	sing.	pl.	sing.	pl.		
nom.	*sōl*	*sōl|ēs*	*leō*	*leōn|ēs*	*vōx*	*vōc|ēs*	*-/-s*	*-ēs*
acc.	*sōl|em*	*sōl|ēs*	*leōn|em*	*leōn|ēs*	*vōc|em*	*vōc|ēs*	*-em*	*-ēs*
gen.	*sōl|is*	*sōl|um*	*leōn|is*	*leōn|um*	*vōc|is*	*vōc|um*	*-is*	*-um*
dat.	*sōl|ī*	*sōl|ibus*	*leōn|ī*	*leōn|ibus*	*vōc|ī*	*vōc|ibus*	*-ī*	*-ibus*
abl.	*sōl|e*	*sōl|ibus*	*leōn|e*	*leōn|ibus*	*vōc|e*	*vōc|ibus*	*-e*	*-ibus*

[1] Nom. *-er*, gen. *-r|is: pater patr|is* m., *māter mātr|is* f.   *-er -r|is*

[2] Nom. *-or*, gen. *-ōr|is: pāstor -ōr|is* m.   *-or -ōr|is*

[3] Nom. *-ōs*, gen. *-ōr|is: flōs flōr|is* m.   *-ōs -ōr|is*

[4] Nom. *-ō*, gen. *-in|is: virgō -in|is* f., *homō -in|is* m.   *-ō -in|is*

[5] Nom. *-x*, gen. *-g|is: lēx lēg|is* f., *rēx rēg|is* m.   *-x -g|is*

[6] Nom. *-ex*, gen. *-ic|is: index -ic|is* m.   *-ex -ic|is-s -t|is*

[7] Nom. *-s*, gen. *-t|is: aetās -āt|is* f., *mīles -it|is* m.   *-s -d|is*

[8] Nom. *-s*, gen. *-d|is: laus laud|is* f., *pēs ped|is* m.

[9] Irregular nouns: *sanguis -in|is* m.; *coniūnx -iug|is* m./f.; *senex sen|is* m.; *bōs bov|is* m./f., pl. *bov|ēs boum*, dat./abl. *bōbus/būbus*.

2. Neuter

Examples: *ōs ōr|is*, **corpus** *corpor|is*, **opus** *-er|is*, **nōmen** *nōmin|is*.

	sing.	pl.	sing.	pl.		
nom.	*ōs*	*ōr|a*	*corpus*	*corpor|a*	*-*	*-a*
acc.	*ōs*	*ōr|a*	*corpus*	*corpor|a*	*-*	*-a*
gen.	*ōr|is*	*ōr|um*	*corpor|is*	*corpor|um*	*-is*	*-um*
dat.	*ōr|ī*	*ōr|ibus*	*corpor|ī*	*corpor|ibus*	*-ī*	*-ibus*
abl.	*ōr|e*	*ōr|ibus*	*corpor|e*	*corpor|ibus*	*-e*	*-ibus*
nom.	*opus*	*oper|a*	*nōmen*	*nōmin|a*		
acc.	*opus*	*oper|a*	*nōmen*	*nōmin|a*		
gen.	*oper|is*	*oper|um*	*nōmin|is*	*nōmin|um*		
dat.	*oper|ī*	*oper|ibus*	*nōmin|ī*	*nōmin|ibus*		
abl.	*oper|e*	*oper|ibus*	*nōmin|e*	*nōmin|ibus*		

Irregular nouns: *cor cord|is; caput capit|is; lac lact|is; os oss|is* (gen. pl. *-ium*); *mel mell|is; iter itiner|is; vās vās|is*, pl. *vās|a -ōrum* (2nd decl.); *thema -at|is*.   *-ma -mat|is*

[B] Genitive plural: *-ium*.

1. Masculine and feminine.

Examples: **nāv|is** *-is* f., **urb|s** *-is* f., **mōns** *mont|is* m.

	sing.	pl.	sing.	pl.	sing.	pl.
nom.	*nāv|is*	*nāv|ēs*	*urb|s*	*urb|ēs*	*mōns*	*mont|ēs*
acc.	*nāv|em*	*nāv|ēs*	*urb|em*	*urb|ēs*	*mont|em*	*mont|ēs*
gen.	*nāv|is*	*nāv|ium*	*urb|is*	*urb|ium*	*mont|is*	*mont|ium*
dat.	*nāv|ī*	*nāv|ibus*	*urb|ī*	*urb|ibus*	*mont|ī*	*mont|ibus*
abl.	*nāv|e*	*nāv|ibus*	*urb|e*	*urb|ibus*	*mont|e*	*mont|ibus*

[Margin:]
-(i)s　-ēs
-em　-ēs
-is　-ium
-ī　-ibus
-e　-ibus

[1] Nom. *-is*, acc. *-im* (pl. *-īs*), abl. *-ī*: *pupp|is -is* f., *Tiber|is -is* m.

[Margin:] -is, acc. -im, abl. -ī

[2] Nom. *-ēs*, gen. *-is*: *nūb|ēs -is* f.

[Margin:] -ēs -is

[3] Nom. *-x*, gen. *-c|is*: *falx falc|is* f.

[Margin:] -x -c|is

[4] Irregular nouns: *nox noct|is* f.; *nix niv|is* f.; *carō carn|is* f.; *as ass|is* m.; *vīs*, acc. *vim*, abl. *vī*, pl. *vīr|ēs -ium* f.

2. Neuter

Examples: **mar|e** *-is*, **animal** *-āl|is*.

	sing.	pl.	sing.	pl.
nom.	*mar|e*	*mar|ia*	*animal*	*animāl|ia*
acc.	*mar|e*	*mar|ia*	*animal*	*animāl|ia*
gen.	*mar|is*	*mar|ium*	*animāl|is*	*animāl|ium*
dat.	*mar|ī*	*mar|ibus*	*animāl|ī*	*animāl|ibus*
abl.	*mar|ī*	*mar|ibus*	*animāl|ī*	*animāl|ibus*

[Margin:]
-e/-　-ia
-e/-　-ia
-is　-ium
-ī　-ibus
-ī　-ibus

Fourth Declension

Genitive: sing. *-ūs*, pl. *-uum*.

Examples: **port|us** *-ūs* m., **corn|ū** *-ūs* n.

	sing.	pl.	sing.	pl.
nom.	*port|us*	*port|ūs*	*corn|ū*	*corn|ua*
acc.	*port|um*	*port|ūs*	*corn|ū*	*corn|ua*
gen.	*port|ūs*	*port|uum*	*corn|ūs*	*corn|uum*
dat.	*port|uī*	*port|ibus*	*corn|ū*	*corn|ibus*
abl.	*port|ū*	*port|ibus*	*corn|ū*	*corn|ibus*

[Margin:]
-us　-ūs　　-ū　-ua
-um　-ūs　　-ū　-ua
-ūs　-uum　　-ūs　-uum
-uī　-ibus　　-ū　-ibus
-ū　-ibus　　-ū　-ibus

dom|us -ūs f., abl. *-ō*, pl. *dom|ūs -ōrum* (*-uum*), acc. *-ōs*.

Fifth Declension

Genitive: sing. *-ēī/-eī*, pl. *-ērum*.

Examples: **di|ēs** *-ēī* m. (f.), **rēs** *reī* f.

nom.	*di|ēs*	*di|ēs*	*rēs*	*rēs*
acc.	*di|em*	*di|ēs*	*rem*	*rēs*
gen.	*di|ēī*	*di|ērum*	*reī*	*rērum*
dat.	*di|ēī*	*di|ēbus*	*reī*	*rēbus*
abl.	*di|ē*	*di|ēbus*	*rē*	*rēbus*

[Margin:]
-ēs　-ēs
-em　-ēs
-ēī/-eī　-ērum
-ēī/-eī　-ēbus
-ē　-ēbus

ADJECTIVES

First and Second Declensions

[A] Genitive singular -ī -ae -ī.

Example: **bon|us** -a -um.

	singular masc.	fem.	neut.	plural masc.	fem.	neut.
nom.	bon|us	bon|a	bon|um	bon|ī	bon|ae	bon|a
acc.	bon|um	bon|am	bon|um	bon|ōs	bon|ās	bon|a
gen.	bon|ī	bon|ae	bon|ī	bon|ōrum	bon|ārum	bon|ōrum
dat.	bon|ō	bon|ae	bon|ō	bon|īs	bon|īs	bon|īs
abl.	bon|ō	bon|ā	bon|ō	bon|īs	bon|īs	bon|īs
voc.	bon|e					

-us	-a	-um
-um	-am	-um
-ī	-ae	-ī
-ō	-ae	-ō
-ō	-ā	-ō
-ī	-ae	-a
-ōs	-ās	-a
-ōrum	-ārum	-ōrum
-īs	-īs	-īs
-īs	-īs	-īs
-er	-(e)r|a	-(e)r|um

Examples: **niger** -gr|a -gr|um, **līber** -er|a -er|um.

	sing. masc.	fem.	neut.	masc.	fem.	neut.
nom.	niger	nigr|a	nigr|um	līber	līber|a	līber|um
acc.	nigr|um	nigr|am	nigr|um	līber|um	līber|am	līber|um

etc. (as above, but voc. = nom. -er)

[B] Genitive singular -īus.

Example: **sōl|us** -a -um, gen. -īus, dat. -ī.

		masc.	fem.	neut.	
sing.	nom.	sōl|us	sōl|a	sōl|um	pl. (as bon|ī -ae -a)
	acc.	sōl|um	sōl|am	sōl|um	
	gen.	sōl|īus	sōl|īus	sōl|īus	
	dat.	sōl|ī	sōl|ī	sōl|ī	
	abl.	sōl|ō	sōl|ā	sōl|ō	

-us	-a	-um
-um	-am	-um
-īus	-īus	-īus
-ī	-ī	-ī
-ō	-ā	-ō

Third Declension

[A] Genitive plural -ium (abl. sing. -ī).

Example: **brev|is** -e.

	singular masc./fem.	neut.	plural masc./fem.	neut.
nom.	brev|is	brev|e	brev|ēs	brev|ia
acc.	brev|em	brev|e	brev|ēs	brev|ia
gen.	brev|is	brev|is	brev|ium	brev|ium
dat.	brev|ī	brev|ī	brev|ibus	brev|ibus
abl.	brev|ī	brev|ī	brev|ibus	brev|ibus

-is	-e	-ēs	-ia
-em	-e	-ēs	-ia
-is	-is	-ium	-ium
-ī	-ī	-ibus	-ibus
-ī	-ī	-ibus	-ibus

Examples: **ācer** ācr|is ācr|e, **celer** -er|is -er|e.

	sing. masc. fem.	neut.	masc. fem.	neut.
nom.	ācer ācr|is	ācr|e	celer celer|is	celer|e
acc.	ācr|em	ācr|e	celer|em	celer|e

-er -(e)r|is	-(e)r|e
-(e)r|em	-(e)r|e

etc. (as above) etc. (as above)

Examples: **fēlīx**, gen. -īc|is; **ingēns**, gen. -ent|is (-x < -c|s, -ns < -nt|s)

		masc./fem.	neut.	masc./fem.	neut.
sing.	nom.	fēlīx	fēlīx	ingēns	ingēns
	acc.	fēlīc|em	fēlīx	ingent|em	ingēns
	gen.	fēlīc|is	fēlīc|is	ingent|is	ingent|is

-s	-s
-em	-s
-is	-is

etc. (as above) etc. (as above)

[B] Genitive plural *-um* (abl. sing. *-e*).

Examples: ***prior*** *prius*, gen. *priōr|is*; ***vetus***, gen. *veter|is*.

		masc./fem.	neut.	masc./fem.	neut.
sing.	nom.	*prior*	*prius*	*vetus*	*vetus*
	acc.	*priōr|em*	*prius*	*veter|em*	*vetus*
	gen.	*priōr|is*	*priōr|is*	*veter|is*	*veter|is*
	dat.	*priōr|ī*	*priōr|ī*	*veter|ī*	*veter|ī*
	abl.	*priōr|e*	*priōr|e*	*veter|e*	*veter|e*
pl.	nom.	*priōr|ēs*	*priōr|a*	*veter|ēs*	*veter|a*
	acc.	*priōr|ēs*	*priōr|a*	*veter|ēs*	*veter|a*
	gen.	*priōr|um*	*priōr|um*	*veter|um*	*veter|um*
	dat.	*priōr|ibus*	*priōr|ibus*	*veter|ibus*	*veter|ibus*
	abl.	*priōr|ibus*	*priōr|ibus*	*veter|ibus*	*veter|ibus*

Margin:
- , -
-*em* -
-*is* -*is*
-*ī* -*ī*
-*e* -*e*
-*ēs* -*a*
-*ēs* -*a*
-*ium* -*ium*
-*ibus* -*ibus*
-*ibus* -*ibus*

So *pauper* (m./f.), gen. *-er|is*; *dīves*, gen. *dīvit|is*.

Comparison

There are three **degrees: positive**, e.g. *longus*, **comparative**, e.g. *longior*, and **superlative**, e.g. *longissimus*.

The comparative ends in *-ior* and is declined like *prior*. The superlative ends in *-issim|us (-im|us)* and is declined like *bon|us*.

Margin:
degrees:
positive (pos.)
comparative (comp.)
superlative (sup.)

[A] Superlative *-issim|us*.

Margin:
-*us -a -um* / -(i)s (-e)
-*ior -ius -iōr|is*
-*issim|us -a -um*

pos.	*long|us -a -um*	*brev|is -e*	*fēlīx -īc|is*
comp.	*long|ior -ius -iōr|is*	*brev|ior -ius -iōr|is*	*fēlīc|ior -ius -iōr|is*
sup.	*long|issim|us-a-um*	*brev|issim|us -a -um*	*fēlīc|issim|us -a -um*

[B] Superlative *-rim|us, -lim|us*.

Margin:
-*er* -*il|is*
-(e)*rior* -*ilior*
-*errim|us* -*illim|us*

pos.	*piger -gr|a -gr|um*	*celer -er|is -er|e*	*facil|is -e*
comp.	*pigr|ior -ius -iōr|is*	*celer|ior -ius -iōr|is*	*facil|ior -ius -iōr|is*
sup.	*piger|rim|us -a -um*	*celer|rim|us -a -um*	*facil|lim|us -a -um*

[C] Irregular comparison

positive	comparative	superlative
bon|us -a -um	*melior -ius -iōr|is*	*optim|us -a -um*
mal|us -a -um	*pēior -ius -iōr|is*	*pessim|us -a -um*
magn|us -a -um	*māior -ius -iōr|is*	*māxim|us -a -um*
parv|us -a -um	*minor minus -ōr|is*	*minim|us -a -um*
mult|um -ī	*plūs plūr|is*	*plūrim|um -ī*
mult|ī -ae -a	*plūr|ēs -a -ium*	*plūrim|ī -ae -a*
(*īnfrā*) *īnfer|us*	*īnferior -ius -iōr|is*	*īnfim|us/īm|us -a -um*
(*suprā*) *super|us*	*superior -ius -iōr|is*	*suprēm|us/summ|us -a -um*
(*intrā*)	*interior -ius -iōr|is*	*intim|us -a -um*
(*extrā*)	*exterior -ius -iōr|is*	*extrēm|us -a -um*
(*citrā*)	*citerior -ius -iōr|is*	*citim|us -a -um*
(*ultrā*)	*ulterior -ius -iōr|is*	*ultim|us -a -um*
(*prae*)	*prior -ius -iōr|is*	*prīm|us -a -um*
(*post*)	*posterior -ius -iōr|is*	*postrēm|us -a -um*
(*prope*)	*propior -ius -iōr|is*	*proxim|us -a -um*
vetus -er|is	*vetustior -ius -iōr|is*	*veterrim|us -a -um*

ADJECTIVES AND ADVERBS

Adjectīves of the 1st/2nd declension form adverbs in *-ē*, e.g. *rēct|us* > *rēct|ē̠*.

-ē

Adjectives of the 3rd declension form adverbs in *-iter,* e.g. *fort|is* > *fort|iter.*

-iter

The comparative of the adverbs ends in *-ius* (= neuter of the adjective), e.g. *rēct|ius,* the superlative ends in *-issimē* (*-imē*), e.g. *rēct|issimē.*

-ius
-issimē

Adjective declension	Adverb positive	comparative	superlative
1st/2nd *rēct|us -a -um*	*rēctē*	*rēctius*	*rēctissimē*
pulcher -chr|a -um	*pulchrē*	*pulchrius*	*pulcherrimē*
miser -er|a -er|um	*miserē*	*miserius*	*miserrimē*
3rd *fort|is -e*	*fortiter*	*fortius*	*fortissimē*
ācer ācr|is ācr|e	*ācriter*	*ācrius*	*ācerrimē*
celer -er|is -er|e	*celeriter*	*celerius*	*celerrimē*
fēlīx	*fēlīciter*	*fēlīcius*	*fēlīcissimē*

Nom. sing. *-ns,* adverb *-nter: prūdēns -ent|is,* adv. *prūdenter.*

-nter (< *-ntiter*)

Some adjectives of the 1st/2nd declension form adverbs in *-ō,* e.g. *certō, falsō, necessāriō, rārō, subitō, tūtō, prīmō, postrēmō* (adjectives: *cert|us, fals|us, necessāri|us,* etc.).

-ō

Irregular adverbs: *bene* < *bon|us, male* < *mal|us, valdē* < *valid|us, facile* < *facil|is, difficulter* < *difficil|is, audācter* < *audāx.*

NUMERALS

Roman	Arabic	Cardinal numbers	Ordinal numbers	Distributive numbers
I	1	ūn|us -a -um	prīm|us -a -um	singul|ī -ae -a (ūn|ī)
II	2	du|o -ae -o	secund|us	bīn|ī
III	3	tr|ēs -ia	terti|us	tern|ī (trīn|ī)
IV	4	quattuor	quārt|us	quatern|ī
V	5	quīnque	quīnt|us	quīn|ī
VI	6	sex	sext|us	sēn|ī
VII	7	septem	septim|us	septēn|ī
VIII	8	octō	octāv|us	octōn|ī
IX	9	novem	nōn|us	novēn|ī
X	10	decem	decim|us	dēn|ī
XI	11	ūn-decim	ūn-decim|us	ūn-dēn|ī
XII	12	duo-decim	duo-decim|us	duo-dēn|ī
XIII	13	trē-decim	terti|us decim|us	tern|ī dēn|ī
XIV	14	quattuor-decim	quārt|us decim|us	quatern|ī dēn|ī
XV	15	quīn-decim	quīnt|us decim|us	quīn|ī dēn|ī
XVI	16	sē-decim	sext|us decim|us	sēn|ī dēn|ī
XVII	17	septen-decim	septim|us decim|us	septēn|ī dēn|ī
XVIII	18	duo-dē-vīgintī	duo-dē-vīcēsim|us	duo-dē-vīcēn|ī
XIX	19	ūn-dē-vīgintī	ūn-dē-vīcēsim|us	ūn-dē-vīcēn|ī
XX	20	vīgintī	vīcēsim|us	vīcēn|ī
XXI	21	vīgintī ūn|us /ūn|us et vīgintī	vīcēsim|us prīm|us /ūn|us et vīcēsim|us	vīcēn|ī singul|ī /singul|ī et vīcēn|ī
XXX	30	trīgintā	trīcēsim|us	trīcēn|ī
XL	40	quadrāgintā	quadrāgēsim|us	quadrāgēn|ī
L	50	quīnquāgintā	quīnquāgēsim|us	quīnquāgēn|ī
LX	60	sexāgintā	sexāgēsim|us	sexāgēn|ī
LXX	70	septuāgintā	septuāgēsim|us	septuāgēn|ī
LXXX	80	octōgintā	octōgēsim|us	octōgēn|ī
XC	90	nōnāgintā	nōnāgēsim|us	nōnāgēn|ī
C	100	centum	centēsim|us	centēn|ī
CC	200	ducent|ī -ae -a	ducentēsim|us	ducēn|ī
CCC	300	trecent|ī	trecentēsim|us	trecēn|ī
CCCC	400	quadringent|ī	quadringentēsim|us	quadringēn|ī
D	500	quīngent|ī	quīngentēsim|us	quīngēn|ī
DC	600	sescent|ī	sescentēsim|us	sescēn|ī
DCC	700	septingent|ī	septingentēsim|us	septingēn|ī
DCCC	800	octingent|ī	octingentēsim|us	octingēn|ī
DCCCC	900	nōngent|ī	nōngentēsim|us	nōngēn|ī
M	1000	mīlle	mīllēsim|us	singula mīlia
MM	2000	duo mīlia	bis mīllēsim|us	bīna mīlia

[1] ūn\|us -a -um is declined like sōl\|us: gen. -īus, dat. -ī.

[2] du\|o -ae -o and tr\|ēs -ia:

	masc.	fem.	neut.	masc./fem.	neut.
nom.	du|o	du|ae	du|o	tr|ēs	tr|ia
acc.	du|ōs/o	du|ās	du|o	tr|ēs	tr|ia
gen.	du|ōrum	du|ārum	du|ōrum	tr|ium	tr|ium
dat.	du|ōbus	du|ābus	du|ōbus	tr|ibus	tr|ibus
abl.	du|ōbus	du|ābus	du|ōbus	tr|ibus	tr|ibus

[3] mīl\|ia -ium (n. pl.) is declined like mar\|ia (3rd decl.).

Numeral adverbs

1× semel	6× sexiēs	11× ūndeciēs	40× quadrāgiēs	90× nōnāgiēs
2× bis	7× septiēs	12× duodeciēs	50× quīnquāgiēs	100× centiēs
3× ter	8× octiēs	13× ter deciēs	60× sexāgiēs	200× ducentiēs
4× quater	9× noviēs	20× vīciēs	70× septuāgiēs	300× trecentiēs
5× quīnquiēs	10× deciēs	30× trīciēs	80× octōgiēs	1000× mīliēs

PRONOUNS

Personal Pronouns

	1st person		2nd person	
	sing.	pl.	sing.	pl.
nom.	*ego*	*nōs*	*tū*	*vōs*
acc.	*mē*	*nōs*	*tē*	*vōs*
dat.	*mihi*	*nōbīs*	*tibi*	*vōbīs*
abl.	*mē*	*nōbīs*	*tē*	*vōbīs*

partitive gen.:
nostrum, vestrum
mī = mihi

3rd person - and demonstrative pronoun

	singular			plural			reflexive
	masc.	fem.	neut.	masc.	fem.	neut.	pronoun
nom.	*i|s*	*e|a*	*i|d*	*i|ī*	*e|ae*	*e|a*	
acc.	*e|um*	*e|am*	*i|d*	*e|ōs*	*e|ās*	*e|a*	*sē*
gen.	*e|ius*	*e|ius*	*e|ius*	*e|ōrum*	*e|ārum*	*e|ōrum*	
dat.	*e|ī*	*e|ī*	*e|ī*	*i|īs*	*i|īs*	*i|īs*	*sibi*
abl.	*e|ō*	*e|ā*	*e|ō*	*i|īs*	*i|īs*	*i|īs*	*sē*

nom. pl. e\|ī = i\|ī
sēsē = sē

e\|īs = i\|īs

Possessive Pronouns

	singular	plural
1st pers.	*me|us -a -um*	*noster -tr|a -tr|um*
2nd pers.	*tu|us -a -um*	*vester -tr|a -tr|um*
3rd pers.	*su|us -a -um* (reflexive)	

eius, eōrum, eārum (gen. of *is ea id*)

me\|us, voc. sing. *mī.*

Demonstrative Pronouns

		singular			plural		
		masc.	fem.	neut.	masc.	fem.	neut.
[1]	nom.	*hic*	*haec*	*hoc*	*hī*	*hae*	*haec*
	acc.	*hunc*	*hanc*	*hoc*	*hōs*	*hās*	*haec*
	gen.	*huius*	*huius*	*huius*	*hōrum*	*hārum*	*hōrum*
	dat.	*huic*	*huic*	*huic*	*hīs*	*hīs*	*hīs*
	abl.	*hōc*	*hāc*	*hōc*	*hīs*	*hīs*	*hīs*
[2]	nom.	*ill|e*	*ill|a*	*ill|ud*	*ill|ī*	*ill|ae*	*ill|a*
	acc.	*ill|um*	*ill|am*	*ill|ud*	*ill|ōs*	*ill|ās*	*ill|a*
	gen.	*ill|īus*	*ill|īus*	*ill|īus*	*ill|ōrum*	*ill|ārum*	*ill|ōrum*
	dat.	*ill|ī*	*ill|ī*	*ill|ī*	*ill|īs*	*ill|īs*	*ill|īs*
	abl.	*ill|ō*	*ill|ā*	*ill|ō*	*ill|īs*	*ill|īs*	*ill|īs*

[3] *ist\|e -a -ud* is declined like *ill\|e -a -ud*.

[4] *ips\|e -a -um* is declined like *ill\|e* except neut. sing.
ips\|um.

[5] *is ea id*, demonstrative and personal: see above!

[6] *ī-dem ea-dem idem* (< *is ea id* + *-dem*):

	singular			plural		
	masc.	fem.	neut.	masc.	fem.	neut.
nom.	*īdem*	*eadem*	*idem*	*iīdem*	*eaedem*	*eadem*
acc.	*eundem*	*eandem*	*idem*	*eōsdem*	*eāsdem*	*eadem*
gen.	*eiusdem*	*eiusdem*	*eiusdem*	*eōrundem*	*eārundem*	*eōrundem*
dat.	*eīdem*	*eīdem*	*eīdem*	*iīsdem*	*iīsdem*	*iīsdem*
abl.	*eōdem*	*eādem*	*eōdem*	*iīsdem*	*iīsdem*	*iīsdem*

īdem < is-dem
-n-dem < -m-dem
nom. pl. eīdem = iīdem
eīsdem = iīsdem

Interrogative Pronouns

[1] *quis quae quid* (subst.); *quī/quis... quae... quod...* (adj.).

	singular			plural		
	masc.	fem.	neut.	masc.	fem.	neut.
nom.	*quis/quī*	*quae*	*quid/quod*	*quī*	*quae*	*quae*
acc.	*quem*	*quam*	*quid/quod*	*Quōs*	*quās*	*quae*
gen.	*cuius*	*cuius*	*cuius*	*quōrum*	*quārum*	*quōrum*
dat.	*cui*	*cui*	*cui*	*quibus*	*quibus*	*quibus*
abl.	*quō*	*quā*	*quō*	*quibus*	*quibus*	*quibus*

[2] *uter utr|a utr|um*, gen. *utr|īus*, dat. *utr|ī* (like *sōl|us*, but nom. m. sg. *ut<u>er</u>*).

Relative Pronoun

[1] *quī quae quod*

	singular			plural		
	masc.	fem.	neut.	masc.	fem.	neut.
nom.	*quī*	*quae*	*quod*	*quī*	*quae*	*quae*
acc.	*quem*	*quam*	*quod*	*quōs*	*quās*	*quae*
gen.	*cuius*	*cuius*	*cuius*	*quōrum*	*quārum*	*quōrum*
dat.	*cui*	*cui*	*cui*	*quibus*	*quibus*	*quibus*
abl.	*quō*	*quā*	*quō*	*quibus*	*quibus*	*quibus*

[2] *quī- quae- quod-cumque* (indefinite relative) = *quis-quis quid-quid/quic-quid* (indecl. subst.).

Indefinite Pronouns

nēmō < ne- + homō

[1] *nēmō*, acc. *nēmin|em*, dat. *nēmin|ī*.

nīl = nihil

[2] *nihil*, neuter (indecl.)

[3] *ūll|us -a -um* and *nūll|us -a -um* are declined like *sōl|us*.

neuter < ne- + uter

[4] *neuter -tr|a -tr|um* and *uter-que utr|a-que utr|um-que* are declined like *uter*: gen. *neutr|īus*, *utr|īus-que*.

[5] *alter -er|a -er|um*, gen. *-er|īus*, dat. *-er|ī*.

[6] *ali|us -a -ud*, dat. *ali|ī* (gen. *alter|īus*).

The following pronouns are declined like *quis/quī*:

n. pl. *(ali-)qua*

[7] *ali-quis/-quī -qua -quid/-quod* and (*sī, nisi, nē, num*) *quis/quī qua quid/quod*.

[8] *quis-quam quid-quam/quic-quam*.

-n-dam < -m-dam

[9] *quī-dam quae-dam quid-dam/quod-dam*, acc. sing. m. *quen-dam*, f. *quan-dam*, gen. pl. m./n. *quōrun-dam*, f. *quārun-dam*.

[10] *quis-que quae-que quid-que/quod-que*.

[11] *quī- quae- quid-/quod-vīs = quī- quae- quid-/quod-libet*.

VERBS

Voice and Mood

The **voice** of the verb is either **active**, e.g. *amat,* or **passive**, e.g. *amātur.* Verbs which have no active voice (except participles and gerund), e.g. *cōnārī, loquī,* are called **deponent** verbs.

The **moods** of the verb are: **infinitive**, e.g. *amāre,* **imperative**, e.g. *amā,* **indicative**, e.g. *amat,* and **subjunctive**, e.g. *amet.*

Tense, Number, Person

The **tenses** of the verb are: **present**, e.g. *amat,* **future**, e.g. *amābit,* **imperfect**, e.g. *amābat,* **perfect**, e.g. *amāvit,* **pluperfect**, e.g. *amāverat,* and **future perfect**, e.g. *amāverit.*

The **numbers** of the verb are: **singular**, e.g. *amat,* and **plural**, e.g. *amant.*

The **persons** of the verb are: **1st person**, e.g. *amō,* **2nd person**, e.g. *amās,* and **3rd person**, e.g. *amat.* Verbs which have no 1st and 2nd persons, e.g. *licēre* and *pudēre,* are called **impersonal**.

Conjugations

There are four **conjugations**:

[1] **1st conjugation**: inf. *-āre, -ārī* e.g. *amāre, cōnārī.*

[2] **2nd conjugation**: inf. *-ēre, -ērī* e.g. *monēre, verērī.*

[3] **3rd conjugation**: inf. *-ere, -ī* e.g. *legere, ūtī.*

[4] **4th conjugation**: inf. *-īre, -īrī* e.g. *audīre, partīrī.*

Stem

Verbal stems:

The **present stem**, e.g. *amā-, monē-, leg-, audī-.*

The **perfect stem**, e.g. *amāv-, monu-, lēg-, audīv-.*

The **supine stem**, e.g. *amāt-, monit-, lēct-, audīt-.*

Personal endings

[1]	Active		Passive	
	sing.	pl.	sing.	pl.
pers. 1	*-m/-ō*	*-mus*	*-r/-or*	*-mur*
pers. 2	*-s*	*-tis*	*-ris*	*-minī*
pers. 3	*-t*	*-nt*	*-tur*	*-ntur*

[2] Endings of the perfect indicative active:

	sing.	pl.
pers. 1	~ī	~imus
pers. 2	~istī	~istis
pers. 3	~it	~ērunt (~ēre)

Sidebar notes:

voice: act.
pass.

mood: inf. ind.
imp. subj.

tense: pres. perf.
imperf.
pluperf.
fut. fut. perf.

number: sing.
plur.

person: 1
2
3

conjugations:
[1] -āre/-ārī
[2] -ēre/-ērī
[3] -ere/-ī
[4] -īre/-īrī

verbal stems:
present stem [-]
perfect stem [~]
supine stem [≈]

after a consonant:

-ō	-imus	-or	-imur
-is	-itis	-eris	-iminī
-it	-unt	-itur	-untur

Conjugation

[A] Active

Infinitive

present

| | [1] *amā\|re* | [2] *monē\|re* | [3] *leg\|ere* | [4] *audī\|re* |

perfect

amāv\|isse   *monu\|isse*   *lēg\|isse*   *audīv\|isse*

future

amāt\|ūr\|um esse   *monit\|ūr\|um esse*   *lēct\|ūr\|um esse*   *audīt\|ūr\|um esse*

Indicative

present

	[1]	[2]	[3]	[4]
sing. 1	*am|ō*	*mone|ō*	*leg|ō*	*audi|ō*
2	*amā|s*	*monē|s*	*leg|is*	*audī|s*
3	*ama|t*	*mone|t*	*leg|it*	*audi|t*
pl. 1	*amā|mus*	*monē|mus*	*leg|imus*	*audī|mus*
2	*amā|tis*	*monē|tis*	*leg|itis*	*audī|itis*
3	*ama|nt*	*mone|nt*	*leg|unt*	*audi|unt*

imperfect

sing. 1	*amā|ba|m*	*monē|ba|m*	*leg|ēba|m*	*audi|ēba|m*
2	*amā|bā|s*	*monē|bā|s*	*leg|ēbā|s*	*audi|ēbā|s*
3	*amā|ba|t*	*monē|ba|t*	*leg|ēba|t*	*audi|ēba|t*
pl. 1	*amā|bā|mus*	*monē|bā|mus*	*leg|ēbā|mus*	*audi|ēbā|mus*
2	*amā|bā|tis*	*monē|bā|tis*	*leg|ēbā|tis*	*audi|ēbā|tis*
3	*amā|ba|nt*	*monē|ba|nt*	*leg|ēba|nt*	*audi|ēba|nt*

future

sing. 1	*amā|b|ō*	*monē|b|ō*	*leg|a|m*	*audi|a|m*
2	*amā|b|is*	*monē|b|is*	*leg|ē|s*	*audi|ē|s*
3	*amā|b|it*	*monē|b|it*	*leg|e|t*	*audi|e|t*
pl. 1	*amā|b|imus*	*monē|b|imus*	*leg|ē|mus*	*audi|ē|mus*
2	*amā|b|itis*	*monē|b|itis*	*leg|ē|tis*	*audi|ē|tis*
3	*amā|b|unt*	*monē|b|unt*	*leg|e|nt*	*audi|e|nt*

perfect

sing. 1	*amāv|ī*	*monu|ī*	*lēg|ī*	*audīv|ī*
2	*amāv|istī*	*monu|istī*	*lēg|istī*	*audīv|istī*
3	*amāv|it*	*monu|it*	*lēg|it*	*audīv|it*
pl. 1	*amāv|imus*	*monu|imus*	*lēg|imus*	*audīv|imus*
2	*amāv|istis*	*monu|istis*	*lēg|istis*	*audīv|istis*
3	*amāv|ērunt*	*monu|ērunt*	*lēg|ērunt*	*audīv|ērunt*

pluperfect

sing. 1	*amāv|era|m*	*monu|era|m*	*lēg|era|m*	*audīv|era|m*
2	*amāv|erā|s*	*monu|erā|s*	*lēg|erā|s*	*audīv|erā|s*
3	*amāv|era|t*	*monu|era|t*	*lēg|era|t*	*audīv|era|t*
pl. 1	*amāv|erā|mus*	*monu|erā|mus*	*lēg|erā|mus*	*audīv|erā|mus*
2	*amāv|erā|tis*	*monu|erā|tis*	*lēg|erā|tis*	*audīv|erā|tis*
3	*amāv|era|nt*	*monu|era|nt*	*lēg|era|nt*	*audīv|era|nt*

future perfect

sing. 1	*amāv|er|ō*	*monu|er|ō*	*lēg|er|ō*	*audīv|er|ō*
2	*amāv|eri|s*	*monu|eri|s*	*lēg|eri|s*	*audīv|eri|s*
3	*amāv|eri|t*	*monu|eri|t*	*lēg|eri|t*	*audīv|eri|t*
pl. 1	*amāv|eri|mus*	*monu|eri|mus*	*lēg|eri|mus*	*audīv|eri|mus*
2	*amāv|eri|tis*	*monu|eri|tis*	*lēg|eri|tis*	*audīv|eri|tis*
3	*amāv|eri|nt*	*monu|eri|nt*	*lēg|eri|nt*	*audīv|eri|nt*

Marginal endings (left column):

[1, 2, 4]   [3]
–re   –ere

~isse
≈ūr\|us -a -um esse

[1, 2, 4]   [3]
–ō   –ō
–s   –is
–t   –it
–mus   –imus
–tis   –itis
–(u)nt   –unt

[1, 2]   [3, 4]
–ba\|m   –ēba\|m
–bā\|s   –ēbā\|s
–ba\|t   –ēba\|t
–bā\|mus   –ēbā\|mus
–bā\|tis   –ēbā\|tis
–ba\|nt   –ēba\|nt

[1, 2]   [3, 4]
–b\|ō   –a\|m
–b\|is   –ē\|s
–b\|it   –e\|t
–b\|imus   –ē\|mus
–b\|itis   –ē\|tis
–b\|unt   –e\|nt

~ī
~istī
~it
~imus
~istis
~ērunt

~era\|m
~erā\|s
~era\|t
~erā\|mus
~erā\|tis
~era\|nt

~er\|ō
~eri\|s
~eri\|t
~eri\|mus
~eri\|tis
~eri\|nt

Subjunctive

present

					1]	[2, 3, 4]
sing.1	*am|e|m*	*mone|a|m*	*leg|a|m*	*audi|a|m*	*(-)e|m*	*-a|m*
2	*am|ē|s*	*mone|ā|s*	*leg|ā|s*	*audi|ā|s*	*(-)ē|s*	*-ā|s*
3	*am|e|t*	*mone|a|t*	*leg|a|t*	*audi|a|t*	*(-)e|t*	*-a|t*
pl.1	*am|ē|mus*	*mone|ā|mus*	*leg|ā|mus*	*audi|ā|mus*	*(-)ē|mus*	*-ā|mus*
2	*am|ē|tis*	*mone|ā|tis*	*leg|ā|tis*	*audi|ā|tis*	*(-)ē|tis*	*-ā|tis*
3	*am|e|nt*	*mone|a|nt*	*leg|a|nt*	*audi|a|nt*	*(-)e|nt*	*-a|nt*

imperfect

					[1, 2, 4]	[3]
sing.1	*amā|re|m*	*monē|re|m*	*leg|ere|m*	*audī|re|m*	*-re|m*	*-ere|m*
2	*amā|rē|s*	*monē|rē|s*	*leg|erē|s*	*audī|rē|s*	*-rē|s*	*-erē|s*
3	*amā|re|t*	*monē|re|t*	*leg|ere|t*	*audī|re|t*	*-re|t*	*-ere|t*
pl.1	*amā|rē|mus*	*monē|rē|mus*	*leg|erē|mus*	*audī|rē|mus*	*-rē|mus*	*-erē|mus*
2	*amā|rē|tis*	*monē|rē|tis*	*leg|erē|tis*	*audī|rē|tis*	*-rē|tis*	*-erē|tis*
3	*amā|re|nt*	*monē|re|nt*	*leg|ere|nt*	*audī|re|nt*	*-re|nt*	*-ere|nt*

perfect

sing.1	*amāv|eri|m*	*monu|eri|m*	*lēg|eri|m*	*audīv|eri|m*	≈*eri|m*
2	*amāv|eri|s*	*monu|eri|s*	*lēg|eri|s*	*audīv|eri|s*	≈*eri|s*
3	*amāv|eri|t*	*monu|eri|t*	*lēg|eri|t*	*audīv|eri|t*	≈*eri|t*
pl.1	*amāv|eri|mus*	*monu|eri|mus*	*lēg|eri|mus*	*audīv|eri|mus*	≈*eri|mus*
2	*amāv|eri|tis*	*monu|eri|tis*	*lēg|eri|tis*	*audīv|eri|tis*	≈*eri|tis*
3	*amāv|eri|nt*	*monu|eri|nt*	*lēg|eri|nt*	*audīv|eri|nt*	≈*eri|nt*

pluperfect

sing.1	*amāv|isse|m*	*monu|isse|m*	*lēg|isse|m*	*audīv|isse|m*	≈*isse|m*
2	*amāv|issē|s*	*monu|issē|s*	*lēg|issē|s*	*audīv|issē|s*	≈*issē|s*
3	*amāv|isse|t*	*monu|isse|t*	*lēg|isse|t*	*audīv|isse|t*	≈*isse|t*
pl.1	*amāv|issē|mus*	*monu|issē|mus*	*lēg|issē|mus*	*audīv|issē|mus*	≈*issē|mus*
2	*amāv|issē|tis*	*monu|issē|tis*	*lēg|issē|tis*	*audīv|issē|tis*	≈*issē|tis*
3	*amāv|isse|nt*	*monu|isse|nt*	*lēg|isse|nt*	*audīv|isse|nt*	≈*isse|nt*

Imperative

present

					[1, 2, 4]	[3]
sing.	*amā*	*monē*	*leg|e*	*audī*	–	*-e*
pl.	*amā|te*	*monē|te*	*leg|ite*	*audī|te*	*-te*	*-ite*

future

sing.	*amā|tō*	*monē|tō*	*leg|itō*	*audī|tō*	*-tō*	*-itō*
pl.	*amā|tōte*	*monē|tōte*	*leg|itōte*	*audī|tōte*	*-tōte*	*-itōte*

Participle

present

				[1, 2]	[3, 4]
amā|ns -ant|is	*monē|ns -ent|is*	*leg|ēns -ent|is*	*audi|ēns -ent|is*	*-ns* *-nt|is*	*-ēns* *-ent|is*

future

amāt|ūr|us -a -um	*monit|ūr|us -a -um*	*lēct|ūr|us -a -um*	*audīt|ūr|us -a -um*	≈*ūr|us -a -um*

Supine

I	*amāt|um*	*monit|um*	*lēct|um*	*audīt|um*	≈*um*
II	*amāt|ū*	*monit|ū*	*lēct|ū*	*audīt|ū*	≈*ū*

Gerund

					[1, 2]	[3, 4]
acc.	*ama|nd|um*	*mone|nd|um*	*leg|end|um*	*audi|end|um*	*-nd|um*	*-end|um*
gen.	*ama|nd|ī*	*mone|nd|ī*	*leg|end|ī*	*audi|end|ī*	*-nd|ī*	*-end|ī*
abl.	*ama|nd|ō*	*mone|nd|ō*	*leg|end|ō*	*audi|end|ō*	*-nd|ō*	*-end|ō*

[B] Passive

Infinitive

present

	[1] *amā|rī*	[2] *monē|rī*	[3] *leg|ī*	[4] *audī|rī*

perfect

	amāt|um esse	*monit|um esse*	*lēct|um esse*	*audīt|um esse*

future

	amāt|um īrī	*monit|um īrī*	*lēct|um īrī*	*audīt|um īrī*

Left-column endings:

[1, 2, 4]   [3]
−rī   −ī

≈us -a -um esse

≈um īrī

Indicative

present

[1, 2, 4] [3]
−or   −or
−ris   −eris
−tur   −itur
−mur   −imur
−minī   −iminī
−(u)ntur   −untur

	sing. 1	*am|or*	*mone|or*	*leg|or*	*audi|or*
	2	*amā|ris*	*monē|ris*	*leg|eris*	*audī|ris*
	3	*amā|tur*	*monē|tur*	*leg|itur*	*audī|tur*
	pl. 1	*amā|mur*	*monē|mur*	*leg|imur*	*audī|mur*
	2	*amā|minī*	*monē|minī*	*leg|iminī*	*audī|minī*
	3	*ama|ntur*	*mone|ntur*	*leg|untur*	*audi|untur*

imperfect

[1, 2]   [3, 4]
−ba\|r   −ēba\|r
−bā\|ris   −ēbā\|ris
−bā\|tur   −ēbā\|tur
−bā\|mur   −ēbā\|mur
−bā\|minī   −ēbā\|minī
−ba\|ntur   −ēba\|ntur

	sing. 1	*amā|ba|r*	*monē|ba|r*	*leg|ēba|r*	*audi|ēba|r*
	2	*amā|bā|ris*	*monē|bā|ris*	*leg|ēbā|ris*	*audi|ēbā|ris*
	3	*amā|bā|tur*	*monē|bā|tur*	*leg|ēbā|tur*	*audi|ēbā|tur*
	pl. 1	*amā|bā|mur*	*monē|bā|mur*	*leg|ēbā|mur*	*audi|ēbā|mur*
	2	*amā|bā|minī*	*monē|bā|minī*	*leg|ēbā|minī*	*audi|ēbā|minī*
	3	*amā|ba|ntur*	*monē|ba|ntur*	*leg|ēba|ntur*	*audi|ēba|ntur*

future

[1, 2]   [3, 4]
−b\|or   −a\|r
−b\|eris   −ē\|ris
−b\|itur   −ē\|tur
−b\|imur   −ē\|mur
−b\|iminī   −ē\|minī
−b\|untur   −e\|ntur

	sing. 1	*amā|b|or*	*monē|b|or*	*leg|a|r*	*audi|a|r*
	2	*amā|b|eris*	*monē|b|eris*	*leg|ē|ris*	*audi|ē|ris*
	3	*amā|b|itur*	*monē|b|itur*	*leg|ē|tur*	*audi|ē|tur*
	pl. 1	*amā|b|imur*	*monē|b|imur*	*leg|ē|mur*	*audi|ē|mur*
	2	*amā|b|iminī*	*monē|b|iminī*	*leg|ē|minī*	*audi|ē|minī*
	3	*amā|b|untur*	*monē|b|untur*	*leg|e|ntur*	*audi|e|ntur*

perfect

≈us -a (-um)
sum
es
est
≈ī -ae (-a)
sumus
estis
sunt

		amāt|us	*monit|us*	*lēct|us*	*audīt|us*
	sing. 1	*sum*	*sum*	*sum*	*sum*
	2	*es*	*es*	*es*	*es*
	3	*est*	*est*	*est*	*est*
		amāt|ī	*monit|ī*	*lēct|ī*	*audīt|ī*
	pl. 1	*sumus*	*sumus*	*sumus*	*sumus*
	2	*estis*	*estis*	*estis*	*estis*
	3	*sunt*	*sunt*	*sunt*	*sunt*

pluperfect

≈us -a (-um)
eram
erās
erat
≈ī -ae (-a)
erāmus
erātis
erant

		amāt|us	*monit|us*	*lēct|us*	*audīt|us*
	sing. 1	*eram*	*eram*	*eram*	*eram*
	2	*erās*	*erās*	*erās*	*erās*
	3	*erat*	*erat*	*erat*	*erat*
		amāt|ī	*monit|ī*	*lēct|ī*	*audīt|ī*
	pl. 1	*erāmus*	*erāmus*	*erāmus*	*erāmus*
	2	*erātis*	*erātis*	*erātis*	*erātis*
	3	*erant*	*erant*	*erant*	*erant*

future perfect

	amāt|us	monit|us	lēct|us	audīt|us	≈us -a (-um)
sing.1	erō	erō	erō	erō	erō
2	eris	eris	eris	eris	eris
3	erit	erit	erit	erit	erit
	amāt|ī	monit|ī	lēct|ī	audīt|ī	≈ī -ae (-a)
pl.1	erimus	erimus	erimus	erimus	erimus
2	eritis	eritis	eritis	eritis	eritis
3	erunt	erunt	erunt	erunt	erunt

Subjunctive
Present

					[1]	[2, 3, 4]
sing.1	am|e|r	mone|a|r	leg|a|r	audi|a|r	(–)e|r	–a|r
2	am|ē|ris	mone|ā|ris	leg|ā|ris	audi|ā|ris	(–)ē|ris	–ā|ris
3	am|ē|tur	mone|ā|tur	leg|ā|tur	audi|ā|tur	(–)ē|tur	–ā|tur
pl.1	am|ē|mur	mone|ā|mur	leg|ā|mur	audi|ā|mur	(–)ē|mur	–ā|mur
2	am|ē|minī	mone|ā|minī	leg|ā|minī	audi|ā|minī	(–)ē|minī	–ā|minī
3	am|e|ntur	mone|a|ntur	leg|a|ntur	audi|a|ntur	(–)e|ntur	–a|ntur

Imperfect

					[1, 2, 4]	[3]
sing.1	amā|re|r	monē|re|r	leg|ere|r	audī|re|r	–re|r	–ere|r
2	amā|rē|ris	monē|rē|ris	leg|erē|ris	audī|rē|ris	–rē|ris	–erē|ris
3	amā|rē|tur	monē|rē|tur	leg|erē|tur	audī|rē|tur	–rē|tur	–erē|tur
pl.1	amā|rē|mur	monē|rē|mur	leg|erē|mur	audī|rē|mur	–rē|mur	–erē|mur
2	amā|rē|minī	monē|rē|minī	leg|erē|minī	audī|rē|minī	–rē|minī	–erē|minī
3	amā|re|ntur	monē|re|ntur	leg|ere|ntur	audī|re|ntur	–re|ntur	–ere|ntur

Perfect

	amāt|us	monit|us	lēct|us	audīt|us	≈us -a (-um)
sing.1	sim	sim	sim	sim	sim
2	sīs	sīs	sīs	sīs	sīs
3	sit	sit	sit	sit	sit
	amāt|ī	monit|ī	lēct|ī	audīt|ī	≈ī -ae (-a)
pl.1	sīmus	sīmus	sīmus	sīmus	sīmus
2	sītis	sītis	sītis	sītis	sītis
3	sint	sint	sint	sint	sint

Pluperfect

	amāt|us	monit|us	lēct|us	audīt|us	≈us -a (-um)
sing.1	essem	essem	essem	essem	essem
2	essēs	essēs	essēs	essēs	essēs
3	esset	esset	esset	esset	esset
	amāt|ī	monit|ī	lēct|ī	audīt|ī	≈ī -ae (-a)
pl.1	essēmus	essēmus	essēmus	essēmus	essēmus
2	essētis	essētis	essētis	essētis	essētis
3	essent	essent	essent	essent	essent

Participle
Perfect

amāt|us	monit|us	lēct|us	audīt|us	≈us -a -um
-a -um	-a -um	-a -um	-a -um	

Gerundive

				[1, 2]	[3, 4]
ama|nd|us	mone|nd|us	leg|end|us	audi|end|us	–nd|us -a	–end|us -a
-a -um	-a -um	-a -um	-a -um	-um	-um

Deponent verbs

[1, 2, 4]   [3]
−rī   −ī
≈us -a -um esse
≈ūr|us -a -um esse

Infinitive

pres.	cōnā|rī	verē|rī	ūt|ī	partī|rī
perf.	cōnāt|um esse	verit|um esse	ūs|um esse	partīt|um esse
fut.	cōnāt|ūr|um esse	verit|ūr|um esse	ūs|ūr|um esse	partīt|ūr|um esse

3rd pers. sing.
≈(i)tur
≈(ē)bā|tur
−b|itur −ē|tur
≈us -a -um est
≈us -a -um erat
≈us -a -um erit

Indicative

pres.	cōnā|tur	verē|tur	ūt|itur	partī|tur
imperf.	cōnā|bā|tur	verē|bā|tur	ūt|ēbā|tur	parti|ēbā|tur
fut.	cōnā|b|itur	verē|b|itur	ūt|ē|tur	parti|ē|tur
perf.	cōnāt|us est	verit|us est	ūs|us est	partīt|us est
pluperf.	cōnāt|us erat	verit|us erat	ūs|us erat	partīt|us erat
fut. perf.	cōnāt|us erit	verit|us erit	ūs|us erit	partīt|us erit

(-)ē|tur −ā|tur
≈(e)rē|tur
≈us -a -um sit
≈us -a -um esset

Subjunctive

pres.	cōn|ē|tur	vere|ā|tur	ūt|ā|tur	parti|ā|tur
imperf.	cōnā|rē|tur	verē|rē|tur	ūt|erē|tur	partī|rē|tur
perf.	cōnāt|us sit	verit|us sit	ūs|us sit	partīt|us sit
pluperf.	cōnāt|us esset	verit|us esset	ūs|us esset	partīt|us esset

[1, 2, 4]   [3]
−re   −ere
−minī   −iminī

Imperative

sing.	cōnā|re	verē|re	ūt|ere	partī|re
pl.	cōnā|minī	verē|minī	ūt|iminī	partī|minī

[1, 2]   [3, 4]
−ns   −ēns
≈us -a -um
≈ūr|us -a -um
−um −ū

Participle

pres.	cōnā|ns	verē|ns	ūt|ēns	parti|ēns
perf.	cōnāt|us	verit|us	ūs|us	partīt|us
fut.	cōnāt|ūr|us	verit|ūr|us	ūs|ūr|us	partīt|ūr|us

Supine cōnāt|um -ū   verit|um -ū   ūs|um -ū   partīt|um -ū

[1, 2]   [3, 4]
−nd|um   −end|um

Gerund

cōna|nd|um   vere|nd|um   ūt|end|um   parti|end|um

−nd|us -a   −end|us -a
−um   −um

Gerundive

cōna|nd|us   vere|nd|us   ūt|end|us   parti|end|us

Third conjugation: present stem -i

Examples: *capere, patī* (present stem: *capi-, pati-*).

i > e before r

cape|re < *capi|re
capī < *capi|ī
patī < *pati|ī

cape|ris < *capi|ris
pate|ris < *pati|ris

Infinitive	act.	pass.	dep.
present	cape|re	cap|ī	pat|ī

Indicative

present

		act.	pass.	dep.
sing.	1	capi|ō	capi|or	pati|or
	2	capi|s	cape|ris	pate|ris
	3	capi|t	capi|tur	pati|tur
pl.	1	capi|mus	capi|mur	pati|mur
	2	capi|tis	capi|minī	pati|minī
	3	capi|unt	capi|untur	pati|untur

imperfect

		act.	pass.	dep.
sing.	1	capi|ēba|m	capi|ēba|r	pati|ēba|r
	2	capi|ēbā|s	capi|ēbā|ris	pati|ēbā|ris
	3	capi|ēba|t	capi|ēbā|tur	pati|ēbā|tur
pl.	1	capi|ēbā|mus	capi|ēbā|mur	pati|ēbā|mur
	2	capi|ēbā|tis	capi|ēbā|minī	pati|ēbā|minī
	3	capi|ēba|nt	capi|ēba|ntur	pati|ēba|ntur

future

sing.	1	*capi|a|m*	*capi|a|r*	*pati|a|r*
	2	*capi|ē|s*	*capi|ē|ris*	*pati|ē|ris*
	3	*capi|e|t*	*capi|ē|tur*	*pati|ē|tur*
pl.	1	*capi|ē|mus*	*capi|ē|mur*	*pati|ē|mur*
	2	*capi|ē|tis*	*capi|ē|minī*	*pati|ē|minī*
	3	*capi|e|nt*	*capi|e|ntur*	*pati|e|ntur*

Subjunctive
present

sing.	1	*capi|a|m*	*capi|a|r*	*pati|a|r*
	2	*capi|ā|s*	*capi|ā|ris*	*pati|ā|ris*
	3	*capi|a|t*	*capi|ā|tur*	*pati|ā|tur*
pl.	1	*capi|ā|mus*	*capi|ā|mur*	*pati|ā|mur*
	2	*capi|ā|tis*	*capi|ā|minī*	*pati|ā|minī*
	3	*capi|a|nt*	*capi|a|ntur*	*pati|a|ntur*

imperfect

sing.	1	*cape|re|m*	*cape|re|r*	*pate|re|r*
	2	*cape|rē|s*	*cape|rē|ris*	*pate|rē|ris*
	3	*cape|re|t*	*cape|rē|tur*	*pate|rē|tur*
pl.	1	*cape|rē|mus*	*cape|rē|mur*	*pate|rē|mur*
	2	*cape|rē|tis*	*cape|rē|minī*	*pate|rē|minī*
	3	*cape|re|nt*	*cape|re|ntur*	*pate|re|ntur*

cape\|rem < *capi\|rem

Imperative

sing.	*cape*	*pate|re*
pl.	*capi|te*	*pati|minī*

cape < *capi

Participle

present	*capi|ēns -ent|is*	*pati|ēns -ent|is*
Gerund	*capi|end|um*	*pati|end|um*
Gerundive	*capi|end|us*	*pati|end|us*

Irregular verbs I: present stem

1. Infinitive *es\|se* (stem *es-, er-, s-*).

Indicative			Subjunctive		Imperative	
pres.	imperf.	fut.	pres.	imperf.	pres.	fut.
s|um	*er|a|m*	*er|ō*	*s|i|m*	*es|se|m*	*es*	*es|tō*
es	*er|ā|s*	*er|is*	*s|ī|s*	*es|sē|s*	*es|te*	*es|tōte*
es|t	*er|a|t*	*er|it*	*s|i|t*	*es|se|t*		
s|umus	*er|ā|mus*	*er|imus*	*s|ī|mus*	*es|sē|mus*		
es|tis	*er|ā|tis*	*er|itis*	*s|ī|tis*	*es|sē|tis*		
s|unt	*er|a|nt*	*er|unt*	*s|i|nt*	*es|se|nt*		

er- ante vōcālem

so:

ab- ad- de- in- inter- prae-
prōd- super-esse

prōd-est prō-sunt
  prōd-e... prō-s...
de-est dē-sunt
in-est īn-sunt

2. Infinitive *posse*.

Indicative			Subjunctive	
pres.	imperf.	fut.	pres.	imperf.
pos-sum	*pot-eram*	*pot-erō*	*pos-sim*	*possem*
pot-es	*pot-erās*	*pot-eris*	*pos-sīs*	*possēs*
pot-est	*pot-erat*	*pot-erit*	*pos-sit*	*posset*
pos-sumus	*pot-erāmus*	*pot-erimus*	*pos-sīmus*	*possēmus*
pot-estis	*pot-erātis*	*pot-eritis*	*pos-sītis*	*possētis*
pos-sunt	*pot-erant*	*pot-erunt*	*pos-sint*	*possent*

pot-e...
pos-s...

<table>
<tr><td>

nōlle < ne- + velle

mālle < magis + velle

</td><td>

3. Infinitive *velle, nōlle, mālle.*

Indicative

pres.	vol|ō	nōl|ō	māl|ō
	vīs	nōn vīs	māvīs
	vul|t	nōn vult	māvult
	vol|umus	nōl|umus	māl|umus
	vul|tis	nōn vultis	māvultis
	vol|unt	nōl|unt	māl|unt
imperf.	vol|ēba|m	nōl|ēba|m	māl|ēba|m
	vol|ēbā|s	nōl|ēbā|s	māl|ēbā|s
fut.	vol|a|m	nōl|a|m	māl|a|m
	vol|ē|s	nōl|ē|s	māl|ē|s

Subjunctive

pres.	vel|i|m	nōl|i|m	māl|i|m
	vel|ī|s	nōl|ī|s	māl|ī|s
	vel|i|t	nōl|i|t	māl|i|t
	vel|ī|mus	nōl|ī|mus	māl|ī|mus
	vel|ī|tis	nōl|ī|tis	māl|ī|tis
	vel|i|nt	nōl|i|nt	māl|i|nt
imperf.	velle|m	nōlle|m	mālle|m
	vellē|s	nōllē|s	māllē|s
	velle|t	nōlle|t	mālle|t
	vellē|mus	nōllē|mus	māllē|mus
	vellē|tis	nōllē|tis	māllē|tis
	velle|nt	nōlle|nt	mālle|nt

Participle

pres.	vol|ēns	nōl|ēns	

</td></tr>
</table>

nōl\|ī -īte + inf.

Imperative

sing.		nōl|ī
pl.		nōl|īte

4. Infinitive *ī\|re.*

passive (impersonal)
ī\|rī
ī\|tur ī\|bā\|tur ī\|b\|itur
e\|ā\|tur ī\|rē\|tur
gerundive:
e\|und\|um (est)

Indicative			Subjunctive		Imperative	
pres.	imperf.	fut.	pres.	imperf.	pres.	fut.
e|ō	ī|ba|m	ī|b|ō	e|a|m	ī|re|m	ī	ī|tō
ī|s	ī|bā|s	ī|b|is	e|ā|s	ī|rē|s	ī|te	ī|tōte
i|t	ī|ba|t	ī|b|it	e|a|t	ī|re|t		Participium
ī|mus	ī|bā|mus	ī|b|imus	e|ā|mus	ī|rē|mus		i|ēns e|unt|is
ī|tis	ī|bā|tis	ī|b|itis	e|ā|tis	ī|rē|tis		Gerundium
e|unt	ī|ba|nt	ī|b|unt	e|a|nt	ī|re|nt		e|und|um

5. Infinitive *fi\|erī.*

Indicative				Subjunctive	
pres.	imperf.	fut.	pres.	imperf.	
fī|ō	fī|ēba|m	fī|a|m	fī|a|m	fi|ere|m	
fī|s	fī|ēbā|s	fī|ē|s	fī|ā|s	fi|erē|s	
fī|t	fī|eba|t	fī|e|t	fī|a|t	fi|ere|t	
fī|mus	fī|ēbā|mus	fī|ē|mus	fī|ā|mus	fi|erē|mus	
fī|tis	fī|ēbā|tis	fī|ē|tis	fī|ā|tis	fi|erē|tis	
fī|unt	fī|ēba|nt	fī|e|nt	fī|a|nt	fi|ere|nt	

6. Infinitive: active *fer|re*, passive *fer|rī*.

Indicative

	act.	pass.		act.	pass.
pres.	*fer|ō*	*fer|or*	imperf.	*fer|ēba|m*	*fer|ēba|r*
	fer|s	*fer|ris*		*fer|ēbā|s*	*fer|ēbā|ris*
	fer|t	*fer|tur*			
	fer|imus	*fer|imur*	fut.	*fer|a|m*	*fer|a|r*
	fer|tis	*fer|iminī*		*fer|ē|s*	*fer|ē|ris*
	fer|unt	*fer|untur*		*fer|e|t*	*fer|ē|tur*

Subjunctive

	act.	pass.		act.	pass.
pres.	*fer|a|m*	*fer|a|r*	imperf.	*fer|re|m*	*fer|re|r*
	fer|ā|s	*fer|ā|ris*		*fer|rē|s*	*fer|rē|ris*
	fer|a|t	*fer|ā|tur*		*fer|re|t*	*fer|rē|tur*
	fer|ā|mus	*fer|ā|mur*		*fer|rē|mus*	*fer|rē|mur*
	fer|ā|tis	*fer|ā|minī*		*fer|rē|tis*	*fer|rē|minī*
	fer|a|nt	*fer|a|ntur*		*fer|re|nt*	*fer|re|ntur*

	Imperative	Participle	Gerund	Gerundive
pres.	*fer fer|te*	*fer|ēns*	*fer|end|um*	*fer|end|us*
fut.	*fer|tō -tōte*			

7. Infinitive: act. *ēs|se*, pass. *ed|ī*.

Indicative			Subjunctive	
pres.	imperf.	fut.	pres.	imperf.
ed|ō	*ed|ēba|m*	*ed|a|m*	*ed|i|m (-a|m)*	*ēs|se|m*
ēs	*ed|ēbā|s*	*ed|ē|s*	*ed|ī|s (-ā|s)*	*ēs|sē|s*
ēs|t	*ed|ēba|t*	*ed|e|t*	*ed|i|t (-a|t)*	*ēs|se|t*
ed|imus	*ed|ēbā|mus*	*ed|ē|mus*	*ed|ī|mus (-ā|mus)*	*ēs|sē|mus*
ēs|tis	*ed|ēbā|tis*	*ed|ē|tis*	*ed|ī|tis (-ā|tis)*	*ēs|sē|tis*
ed|unt	*ed|ēba|nt*	*ed|e|nt*	*ed|i|nt (-a|nt)*	*ēs|se|nt*

pass. ind. pres. 3rd pers.
ēs|tur ed|untur

	Imperative	Participle	Gerund	Gerundive
pres.	*ēs ēs|te*	*ed|ēns*	*ed|end|um*	*ed|end|us*
fut.	*ēs|tō -tōte*			

8. Infinitive *da|re*.

Present stem *da-* (short *a*): *da|re*, *da|mus*, *da|ba|m*, *da|b|ō*, *da|re|m*, etc., except *dā* (imp.), *dā|s* (ind. pres. 2 sing.), *dā|ns* (pres. part.).

Defective verbs

9. *ait*

Indicative

pres.	*āi|ō*	--	imperf.	*āi|ēba|m*	*āi|ēbā|mus*
	ai|s	--		*āi|ēbā|s*	*āi|ēbā|tis*
	ai|t	*āi|unt*		*āi|ēba|t*	*āi|ēba|nt*

ain'? = ais-ne?

10. *inquit*

Indicative

pres.	*inquam*	--	fut.	--
	inquis	--		*inquiēs*
	inquit	*inquiunt*		*inquiet*

11. Verbs without present stem:

memin|isse (imperative: *memen|tō -tōte*)
ōd|isse

Irregular verbs II: perfect and supine stems
First conjugation

		pres. inf.	perf. inf.	perf. part./sup.
ac-cubāre	1.	*cubā|re*	*cubu|isse*	*cubit|um*
	2.	*vetā|re*	*vetu|isse*	*vetit|um*
ex-plicāre	3.	*im-plicā|re*	*-plicu|isse*	*-plicit|um*
	4.	*secā|re*	*secu|isse*	*sect|um*
ad-iuvāre	5.	*iuvā|re*	*iūv|isse*	*iūt|um*
	6.	*lavā|re*	*lāv|isse*	*laut|um/lavāt|um*
	7.	*stā|re*	*stet|isse*	
prae-stāre	8.	*cōn-stā|re*	*-stit|isse*	
circum-dare	9.	*da|re*	*ded|isse*	*dat|um*

Second conjugation

		pres. inf.	perf. inf.	perf. part./sup.
	10.	*docē|re*	*docu|isse*	*doct|um*
	11.	*miscē|re*	*miscu|isse*	*mixt|um*
	12.	*tenē|re*	*tenu|isse*	*tent|um*
abs- re- sus-tinēre	13.	*con-tinē|re*	*-tinu|isse*	*-tent|um*
	14.	*cēnsē|re*	*cēnsu|isse*	*cēns|um*
	15.	*dēlē|re*	*dēlēv|isse*	*dēlēt|um*
	16.	*flē|re*	*flēv|isse*	*flēt|um*
com- ex-plēre	17.	*im-plē|re*	*-plēv|isse*	*-plēt|um*
	18.	*cavē|re*	*cāv|isse*	*caut|um*
	19.	*favē|re*	*fāv|isse*	*faut|um*
per- re-movēre	20.	*movē|re*	*mōv|isse*	*mōt|um*
	21.	*sedē|re*	*sēd|isse*	*sess|um*
	22.	*possidē|re*	*possēd|isse*	*possess|um*
in-vidēre	23.	*vidē|re*	*vīd|isse*	*vīs|um*
	24.	*augē|re*	*aux|isse*	*auct|um*
	25.	*lūcē|re*	*lūx|isse*	
	26.	*lūgē|re*	*lūx|isse*	
	27.	*iubē|re*	*iuss|isse*	*iuss|um*
dē-rīdēre	28.	*rīdē|re*	*rīs|isse*	*rīs|um*
dis- per-suādēre	29.	*suādē|re*	*suās|isse*	*suās|um*
dē-tergēre	30.	*tergē|re*	*ters|isse*	*ters|um*
re-manēre	31.	*manē|re*	*māns|isse*	*māns|um*
	32.	*re-spondē|re*	*-spond|isse*	*-spōns|um*
	33.	*mordē|re*	*momord|isse*	*mors|um*
	34.	*fatē|rī*	*fass|um esse*	
	35.	*cōn-fitē|rī*	*-fess|um esse*	
	36.	*solē|re*	*solit|um esse*	
	37.	*audē|re*	*aus|um esse*	
	38.	*gaudē|re*	*gavīs|um esse*	

Third conjugation

39.	*leg|ere*	*lēg|isse*	*lēct|um*
40.	*ē-lig|ere*	*-lēg|isse*	*-lēct|um*
41.	*em|ere*	*ēm|isse*	*ēmpt|um*
42.	*red-im|ere*	*-ēm|isse*	*-ēmpt|um*
43.	*cōn-sīd|ere*	*-sēd|isse*	
44.	*ēs|se ed|ō*	*ēd|isse*	*ēs|um*
45.	*ag|ere*	*ēg|isse*	*āct|um*
46.	*cōg|ere*	*co-ēg|isse*	*co-āct|um*
47.	*cap|ere -iō*	*cēp|isse*	*capt|um*
48.	*ac-cip|ere -iō*	*-cēp|isse*	*-cept|um*	re-cipere
49.	*fac|ere -iō*	*fēc|isse*	*fact|um*	imp. fac!
50.	*af-fic|ere -iō*	*-fēc|isse*	*-fect|um*	cōn- ef- inter- per- ficere
51.	*iac|ere -iō*	*iēc|isse*	*iact|um*	
52.	*ab-ic|ere -iō*	*-iēc|isse*	*-iect|um*	ad- ē- prō-icere
53.	*fug|ere -iō*	*fūg|isse*		au- ef-fugere
54.	*vinc|ere*	*vīc|isse*	*vict|um*	
55.	*fund|ere*	*fūd|isse*	*fūs|um*	ef-fundere
56.	*re-linqu|ere*	*-līqu|isse*	*-lict|um*	
57.	*rump|ere*	*rūp|isse*	*rupt|um*	ē-rumpere
58.	*frang|ere*	*frēg|isse*	*frāct|um*	
59.	*carp|ere*	*carps|isse*	*carpt|um*	
60.	*dīc|ere*	*dīx|isse*	*dict|um*	imp. dīc! dūc!
61.	*dūc|ere*	*dūx|isse*	*duct|um*	ab- ē- re-dūcere
62.	*scrīb|ere*	*scrīps|isse*	*scrīpt|um*	īn-scrībere
63.	*nūb|ere*	*nūps|isse*	*nupt|um*	
64.	*a-spic|ere -iō*	*-spex|isse*	*-spect|um*	cōn- dē- prō- re- su- spicere
65.	*al-lic|ere -iō*	*-lēx|isse*	*-lect|um*	
66.	*reg|ere*	*rēx|isse*	*rēct|um*	
67.	*cor-rig|ere*	*-rēx|isse*	*-rēct|um*	
68.	*perg|ere*	*per-rēx|isse*		
69.	*surg|ere*	*sur-rēx|isse*		
70.	*dīlig|ere*	*dīlēx|isse*	*dīlēct|um*	
71.	*intelleg|ere*	*intellēx|isse*	*intellēct|um*	
72.	*negleg|ere*	*neglēx|isse*	*neglēct|um*	
73.	*cing|ere*	*cīnx|isse*	*cīnct|um*	
74.	*iung|ere*	*iūnx|isse*	*iūnct|um*	ad- con- dis-iungere
75.	*coqu|ere*	*cox|isse*	*coct|um*	
76.	*trah|ere*	*trāx|isse*	*tract|um*	con- dē- re-trahere
77.	*veh|ere*	*vēx|isse*	*vect|um*	ad- in-vehere
78.	*īn-stru|ere*	*-strūx|isse*	*-strūct|um*	
79.	*flu|ere*	*flūx|isse*		īn-fluere
80.	*vīv|ere*	*vīx|isse*		part. fut. vīct|ūr|us
81.	*sūm|ere*	*sūmps|isse*	*sūmpt|um*	cōn-sūmere
82.	*prōm|ere*	*prōmps|isse*	*prōmpt|um*	
83.	*dēm|ere*	*dēmps|isse*	*dēmpt|um*	

	84.	ger|ere	gess|isse	gest|um
	85.	ūr|ere	uss|isse	ust|um
	86.	fīg|ere	fīx|isse	fīx|um
īn-flectere	87.	flect|ere	flex|isse	flex|um
ac- dis- prō- re- cēdere	88.	cēd|ere	cess|isse	cess|um
	89.	claud|ere	claus|isse	claus|um
	90.	in-clūd|ere	-clūs|isse	-clūs|um
	91.	dīvid|ere	dīvīs|isse	dīvīs|um
	92.	lūd|ere	lūs|isse	lūs|um
	93.	laed|ere	laes|isse	laes|um
	94.	ē-līd|ere	-līs|isse	-līs|um
	95.	plaud|ere	plaus|isse	plaus|um
ā- ad- dī- per- prō- re- *mittere*	96.	mitt|ere	mīs|isse	miss|um
	97.	quat|ere -iō	--	quass|um
	98.	per-cut|ere -iō	-cuss|isse	-cuss|um
sub-mergere	99.	merg|ere	mers|isse	mers|um
	100.	sparg|ere	spars|isse	spars|um
	101.	a-sperg|ere	-spers|isse	-spers|um
	102.	prem|ere	press|isse	press|um
	103.	im-prim|ere	-press|isse	-press|um
	104.	contemn|ere	contemps|isse	contempt|um
	105.	stern|ere	strāv|isse	strāt|um
	106.	cern|ere	crēv|isse	crēt|um
	107.	ser|ere	sēv|isse	sat|um
	108.	arcess|ere	arcessīv|isse	arcessīt|um
	109.	cup|ere -iō	cupīv|isse	cupīt|um
	110.	sap|ere -iō	sapi|isse	
	111.	pet|ere	petīv|isse	petīt|um
	112.	quaer|ere	quaesīv|isse	quaesīt|um
	113.	re-quīr|ere	-quīsīv|isse	-quīsīt|um
	114.	sin|ere	sīv|isse	sit|um
	115.	dēsin|ere	dēsi|isse	dēsit|um
ap- dē- ex- im- prae- re- *pōnere*	116.	pōn|ere	posu|isse	posit|um
in-colere	117.	al|ere	alu|isse	alt|um
	118.	col|ere	colu|isse	cult|um
	119.	dēser|ere	dēseru|isse	dēsert|um
	120.	rap|ere -iō	rapu|isse	rapt|um
sur-ripere	121.	ē-rip|ere -iō	-ripu|isse	-rept|um
	122.	trem|ere	tremu|isse	
	123.	frem|ere	fremu|isse	
re-cumbere	124.	ac-cumb|ere	-cubu|isse	
	125.	tang|ere	tetig|isse	tāct|um
	126.	cad|ere	cecid|isse	
oc-cidere	127.	ac-cid|ere	-cid|isse	
	128.	caed|ere	cecīd|isse	caes|um
	129.	oc-cīd|ere	-cīd|isse	-cīs|um

130.	curr|ere	cucurr|isse	curs|um	
131.	ac-curr|ere	-curr|isse	-curs|um	ex- oc- per- prō-currere
132.	par|ere -iō	peper|isse	part|um	
133.	pell|ere	pepul|isse	puls|um	
134.	parc|ere	peperc|isse		
135.	can|ere	cecin|isse		
136.	fall|ere	fefell|isse		per- red- trā-dere
137.	ad-d|ere	-did|isse	-dit|um	
138.	crēd|ere	crēdid|isse	crēdit|um	
139.	vēnd|ere	vēndid|isse		dē- re-sistere
140.	cōn-sist|ere	-stit|isse		
141.	scind|ere	scid|isse	sciss|um	
142.	bib|ere	bib|isse		
143.	dēfend|ere	dēfend|isse	dēfēns|um	ap- re-prehendere
144.	prehend|ere	prehend|isse	prehēns|um	cōn- dē-scendere
145.	a-scend|ere	-scend|isse	-scēns|um	
146.	ac-cend|ere	-cend|isse	-cēns|um	
147.	ostend|ere	ostend|isse	ostent|um	ā- con-vertere
148.	vert|ere	vert|isse	vers|um	
149.	minu|ere	minu|isse	minūt|um	
150.	statu|ere	statu|isse	statūt|um	
151.	cōn-stitu|ere	-stitu|isse	-stitūt|um	
152.	indu|ere	indu|isse	indūt|um	
153.	metu|ere	metu|isse		
154.	solv|ere	solv|isse	solūt|um	ē-volvere
155.	volv|ere	volv|isse	volūt|um	re-quiēscere
156.	quiēsc|ere	quiēv|isse		
157.	crēsc|ere	crēv|isse		
158.	ērubēsc|ere	ērubu|isse		
159.	nōsc|ere	nōv|isse		
160.	ignōsc|ere	ignōv|isse	ignōt|um	
161.	cognōsc|ere	cognōv|isse		
162.	pāsc|ere	pāv|isse		
163.	posc|ere	poposc|isse		
164.	disc|ere	didic|isse		
165.	fer|re	tul|isse	lāt|um	
166.	af-fer|re	at-tul|isse	cognit|um	
167.	au-fer|re	abs-tul|isse	pāst|um	
168.	ef-fer|re	ex-tul|isse	ē-lāt|um	
169.	of-fer|re	ob-tul|isse	ob-lāt|um	
170.	re-fer|re	rettul|isse	re-lāt|um	per- prae- prō- trāns- ferre
171.	toll|ere	sustul|isse	sublāt|um	
172.	in-cip|ere -iō	coep|isse	coept|um	
173.	fīd|ere	fīs|um esse		cōn-fīdere
174.	revert|ī	revert|isse	revers|um	
175.	loqu|ī	locūt|um esse		col-loquī

cōn- per-sequī	176. *sequ|ī*	*secūt|um esse*	
	177. *quer|ī*	*quest|um esse*	
	178. *mor|ī -ior*	*mortu|um esse*	
	179. *pat|ī -ior*	*pass|um esse*	
prō-gredī	180. *ē-gred|ī -ior*	*-gress|um esse*	
	181. *ūt|ī*	*ūs|um esse*	
	182. *complect|ī*	*complex|um esse*	
	183. *lāb|ī*	*lāps|um esse*	
	184. *nāsc|ī*	*nāt|um esse*	
	185. *proficīsc|ī*	*profect|um esse*	
	186. *oblīvīsc|ī*	*oblīt|um esse*	

Fourth conjugation

	187. *aperī|re*	*aperu|isse*	*apert|um*
	188. *operī|re*	*operu|isse*	*opert|um*
	189. *salī|re*	*salu|isse*	
circum- prō-silīre	190. *dē-silī|re*	*-silu|isse*	
ex-haurīre	191. *haurī|re*	*haus|isse*	*haust|um*
	192. *vincī|re*	*vīnx|isse*	*vīnct|um*
	193. *sentī|re*	*sēns|isse*	*sēns|um*
ad- con- in- per- re- venīre	194. *venī|re*	*vēn|isse*	*vent|um*
	195. *reperī|re*	*repper|isse*	*repert|um*
ab- ad- ex- per- red-	196. *ī|re e|ō*	*i|isse*	*it|um*
sub- trāns-īre	197. *opperī|rī*	*oppert|um esse*	
pres. stem orī-/ori-	198. *orī|rī ori|tur*	*ort|um esse*	

Irregular verbs III

	pres. inf.		perf. inf.
	199. *vel|le vol|ō*		*volu|isse*
	200. *nōl|le*		*nōlu|isse*
inter- prae- super- esse	201. *māl|le*		*mālu|isse*
	202. *es|se sum*		*fu|isse*
fut. part. futūr|us	203. *posse pos-sum*		*potu|isse*
fut. inf. futūr|um esse, fore	204. *ab-esse*		*ā-fu|isse*
	205. *ad-esse ad-/as-sum*		*af-fu|isse*
	206. *de-esse dē-sum*		*dē-fu|isse*
	207. *prōd-esse prō-sum*		*prō-fu|isse*
	208. *fi|erī fī|ō*		*fact|um esse*

Alphabetical List of Irregular Verbs

(Numbers refer to the lists of irregular verbs by conjugation that begins on page 276.)

A

abdūcere 61
abesse 204
abicere 52
abīre 196
abstinēre 13
accēdere 88
accendere 146
accidere 127
accipere 48
accubāre 1
accumbere 124
accurrere 131
addere 137
adesse 205
adicere 52
adīre 196
adiungere 74
adiuvāre 5
admittere 96
advehere 77
advenīre 194
afferre 166
afficere 50
agere 45
alere 117
allicere 65
āmittere 96
aperīre 187
appōnere 116
apprehendere 144
arcessere 108
ascendere 145
aspergere 101
aspicere 64
audēre 37
auferre 167
aufugere 53
augēre 24
āvertere 148

B

bibere 142

C

cadere 126
caedere 128
canere 135

capere 47
carpere 59
cavēre 18
cēdere 88
cēnsēre 14
cernere 106
cingere 73
circumdare 9
circumsilīre 190
claudere 89
cōgere 46
cognōscere 161
colere 118
colloquī 175
complectī 182
complēre 17
cōnficere 50
cōnfīdere 173
cōnfitērī 35
coniungere 74
cōnscendere 145
cōnsequī 176
cōnsīdere 43
cōnsistere 140
cōnspicere 64
cōnstāre 8
cōnstituere 151
cōnsūmere 81
contemnere 104
continēre 13
contrahere 76
convenīre 194
convertere 148
coquere 75
corrigere 67
crēdere 138
crēscere 157
cubāre 1
cupere 109
currere 130

D

dare 9
deesse 206
dēfendere 143
dēlēre 15
dēmere 83
dēpōnere 116
dērīdēre 28

dēscendere 145
dēserere 119
dēsilīre 190
dēsinere 115
dēsistere 140
dēspicere 64
dētergēre 30
dētrahere 76
dīcere 60
dīligere 70
dīmittere 96
discēdere 88
discere 164
disiungere 74
dissuādēre 29
dīvidere 91
docēre 10
dūcere 61

E

ēdūcere 61
efferre 168
efficere 50
effugere 53
effundere 55
ēgredī 180
ēicere 52
ēlīdere 94
ēligere 40
emere 41
ēripere 121
ērubēscere 158
ērumpere 57
esse 202
ēsse 44
ēvolvere 155
excurrere 131
exhaurīre 191
exīre 196
explēre 17
expōnere 116

F

facere 49
fallere 136
fatērī 34
favēre 19
ferre 165
fīdere 173
fierī 208

fīgere 86
flectere 87
flēre 16
fluere 79
frangere 58
fremere 123
fugere 53
fundere 55

G

gaudēre 38
gerere 84

H

haurīre 191

I

iacere 51
ignōscere 160
implēre 17
implicāre 3
impōnere 116
imprimere 103
incipere 172
inclūdere 90
incolere 118
induere 152
īnflectere 87
īnfluere 79
īnscrībere 62
īnstruere 78
intellegere 71
interesse 202
interficere 50
invehere 77
invenīre 194
invidēre 23
īre 196
iubēre 27
iungere 74
iuvāre 5

L

lābī 183
laedere 93
lavāre 6
legere 39
loquī 175
lūcēre 25

Index of Nouns, Adjectives and Verbs

Nouns

1st Declension
Gen. sing. *-ae*, pl. *-ārum*

Feminine

āla	*fenestra*	*littera*	*puella*
amīca	*fera*	*lucerna*	*pugna*
amīcitia	*fīlia*	*lūna*	*rēgula*
ancilla	*fōrma*	*mamma*	*rīpa*
anima	*fortūna*	*margarīta*	*rosa*
aqua	*fossa*	*māteria*	*sagitta*
aquila	*fuga*	*mātrōna*	*scaena*
arānea	*gemma*	*memoria*	*sella*
audācia	*gena*	*mēnsa*	*sententia*
bēstia	*glōria*	*mora*	*silva*
catēna	*grammatica*	*Mūsa*	*stēlla*
cauda	*grātia*	*nātūra*	*syllaba*
causa	*hasta*	*nāvicula*	*tabella*
cēna	*herba*	*nota*	*tabula*
cēra	*hōra*	*opera*	*terra*
charta	*iactūra*	*ōra*	*toga*
columna	*iānua*	*paenīnsula*	*tunica*
cōmoedia	*iniūria*	*pāgina*	*turba*
cōpia	*inopia*	*palma*	*umbra*
culīna	*īnsula*	*patientia*	*ūva*
cūra	*invidia*	*patria*	*vēna*
dea	*īra*	*pecūnia*	*via*
domina	*lacrima*	*penna*	*victōria*
epistula	*laetitia*	*persōna*	*vigilia*
fābula	*lāna*	*pila*	*vīlla*
fāma	*lectīca*	*poena*	*vīnea*
familia	*līnea*	*porta*	*virga*
fēmina	*lingua*	*prōvincia*	*vīta*

(pl.)

cūnae	*dīvitiae*	*nōnae*	*tenebrae*
dēliciae	*kalendae*	*nūgae*	*tībiae*

Masculine (/feminine)

agricola	*convīva*	*nauta*	*poēta*
aurīga	*incola*	*parricīda*	*pīrāta*

2nd Declension
Gen. sing. *-ī*, pl. *-ōrum*
1. Nom. sing. *-us (-r)*
Masculine

agnus	*cibus*	*fluvius*	*lūdus*
amīcus	*circus*	*fundus*	*lupus*
animus	*cocus*	*gallus*	*marītus*
annus	*colōnus*	*gladius*	*medicus*
ānulus	*delphīnus*	*hortus*	*modus*
asinus	*dēnārius*	*inimīcus*	*mundus*
avunculus	*deus*	*labyrinthus*	*mūrus*
barbarus	*digitus*	*lacertus*	*nāsus*
cachinnus	*discipulus*	*lectus*	*nīdus*
calamus	*dominus*	*lēgātus*	*numerus*
calceus	*equus*	*libellus*	*nummus*
campus	*erus*	*lībertīnus*	*nūntius*
capillus	*fīlius*	*locus*	*ōceanus*
ocellus	*pullus*	*servus*	*taurus*
oculus	*Rāmus*	*Sēstertius*	*titulus*
ōstiārius	*rēmus*	*Somnus*	*tyrannus*
petasus	*rīvus*	*sonus*	*umerus*
populus	*sacculus*	*stilus*	*ventus*
pugnus	*saccus*	*tabernārius*	*zephyrus*

(nom. sing. *-er*)

ager agrī	*faber -brī*	*magister -trī*	*puer -erī*
culter -trī	*liber -brī*	*minister -trī*	*vesper -erī*

(pl.)
līberī

Feminine

humus	*papÿrus*	*Aegyptus*	*Rhodus*

2. Nom. sing. *-um*, plur *-a*
Neuter

aedificium	*example*	*mōnstrum*	*scamnum*
aequinoctium	*factum*	*negōtium*	*scūtum*
arātrum	*fātum*	*odium*	*saeculum*
argentum	*ferrum*	*officium*	*saxum*
ātrium	*fīlum*	*oppidum*	*scalpellum*
aurum	*folium*	*ōrnāmentum*	*signum*
auxilium	*forum*	*ōsculum*	*silentium*
baculum	*fretum*	*ōstium*	*solum*
balneum	*frūmentum*	*ōtium*	*speculum*
bāsium	*fūrtum*	*ōvum*	*stipendium*
bellum	*gaudium*	*pābulum*	*studium*
beneficium	*gremium*	*pallium*	*supplicium*
bonum	*imperium*	*pecūlium*	*talentum*
bracchium	*impluvium*	*pēnsum*	*tēctum*
caelum	*ingenium*	*perīculum*	*templum*
capitulum	*initium*	*peristÿlum*	*tergum*
cerebrum	*īnstrūmentum*	*pīlum*	*theātrum*
colloquium	*labrum*	*pirum*	*trīclīnium*
collum	*lignum*	*pōculum*	*vāllum*
cōnsilium	*līlium*	*praedium*	*vēlum*
convīvium	*lucrum*	*praemium*	*verbum*
cubiculum	*maleficium*	*pretium*	*vestīgium*
dictum	*malum*	*prīncipium*	*vestīmentum*
dōnum	*mālum*	*prōmissum*	*vīnum*
dorsum	*mendum*	*respōnsum*	*vocābulum*

(pl.)

arma -ōrum	*castra -ōrum*	*loca -ōrum*	*vāsa -ōrum*

3rd Declension

Gen. sing. *-is*
1. Gen. pl. *-um*

Masculine

āēr āeris	*coniūnx -iugis*	*grex -egis*
amor -ōris	*cruor -ōris*	*gubernātor -ōris*
arātor -ōris	*dolor -ōris*	*homō -inis*
bōs bovis	*dux ducis*	*hospes -itis*
calor -ōris	*eques -itis*	*iānitor -ōris*
carcer -eris	*fidicen -inis*	*imperātor -ōris*
cardō -inis	*flōs -ōris*	*iuvenis -is*
clāmor -ōris	*frāter -tris*	*labor -ōris*
color -ōris	*fūr fūris*	*leō -ōnis*
comes -itis	*gladiātor -ōris*	*mercātor -ōris*
mīles -itis	*praedō -ōnis*	*senex senis*
mōs mōris	*prīnceps -ipis*	*sermō -ōnis*
ōrdō -inis	*pudor -ōris*	*sōl sōlis*
passer -eris	*pulmō -ōnis*	*spectātor -ōris*
pāstor -ōris	*rēx rēgis*	*tībīcen -inis*
pater -tris	*rūmor -ōris*	*timor -ōris*
pedes -itis	*sacerdōs -ōtis*	*victor -ōris*
pēs pedis	*sāl salis*	
piscātor -ōris	*sanguis -inis*	

(pl.)

parentēs -um   *septentriōnēs -um*

Feminine

aestās -ātis	*māter -tris*	*quālitās -ātis*
aetās -ātis	*mentiō -ōnis*	*ratiō -ōnis*
arbor -oris	*mercēs -ēdis*	*salūs -ūtis*
condiciō -ōnis	*mulier -eris*	*servitūs -ūtis*
crux -ucis	*multitūdō -inis*	*significātiō -ōnis*
cupiditās -ātis	*nārrātiō -ōnis*	*soror -ōris*
expugnātiō -ōnis	*nāvigātiō -ōnis*	*tempestās -ātis*
fēlīcitās -ātis	*nex necis*	*tranquillitās -ātis*
hiems -mis	*nūtrīx -īcis*	*uxor -ōris*
imāgō -inis	*nux nucis*	*valētūdō -inis*
laus laudis	*ōrātiō -ōnis*	*virgō -inis*
legiō -ōnis	*pāx pācis*	*virtūs -ūtis*
lēx lēgis	*potestās -ātis*	*voluntās -ātis*
lībertās -ātis	*pōtiō -ōnis*	*vorāgō -inis*
lūx lūcis	*pulchritūdō -inis*	*vōx vōcis*

(pl.)

frūgēs -um   *opēs -um*   *precēs -um*

Neuter (pl. nom. /acc. *-a*)

agmen -inis	*holus -eris*	*pectus -oris*
caput -itis	*iecur -oris*	*pecus -oris*
carmen -inis	*iter itineris*	*phantasma -atis*
certāmen -inis	*iūs iūris*	*praenōmen -inis*
cognōmen -inis	*lac lactis*	*rūs rūris*
cor cordis	*latus -eris*	*scelus -eris*
corpus -oris	*līmen -inis*	*sēmen -inis*
crūs -ūris	*lītus -oris*	*tempus -oris*
epigramma -atis	*mel mellis*	*thema -atis*
flūmen -inis	*mūnus -eris*	*vās vāsis*
frīgus -oris	*nōmen -inis*	*vēr vēris*
fulgur -uris	*opus -eris*	*vulnus -eris*
genus -eris	*ōs ōris*	

(pl.)

verbera -um   *viscera -um*

2. Gen. pl. *-ium*
Masculine

amnis	*hostis*	*oriēns -entis*
as assis	*ignis*	*orbis*
cīvis	*imber -bris*	*pānis*
collis	*īnfāns -antis*	*piscis*
dēns dentis	*mēnsis*	*pōns pontis*
ēnsis	*mōns montis*	*testis*
fīnis	*occidēns -entis*	*venter -tris*

Fēminine

apis	*avis*	*classis*
ars artis	*caedēs -is*	*clāvis*
auris	*carō carnis*	*cohors -rtis*
cōnsonāns -antis	*mors -rtis*	*Ratis*
falx -cis	*nāvis*	*sitis*
famēs -is	*nix nivis*	*urbs -bis*
foris	*nox noctis*	*vallis*
frōns -ontis	*nūbēs -is*	*vestis*
gēns gentis	*ovis*	*vītis*
mēns mentis	*pars partis*	*vōcālis*
merx -rcis	*puppis*	

(pl.)

fidēs -ium	*sordēs -ium*	*vīrēs -ium*

Neuter

animal -ālis	*mare -is*	*rēte -is*

(pl.)

mīlia -ium	*moenia -ium*

4th Declension
Gen. sing. *-ūs*, pl. *-uum*
Masculine

affectus	*cursus*	*impetus*	*sinus*
arcus	*equitātus*	*lacus*	*strepitus*
cantus	*exercitus*	*metus*	*tonitrus*
cāsus	*exitus*	*passus*	*tumultus*
cōnspectus	*flūctus*	*portus*	*versus*
currus	*gradus*	*rīsus*	*vultus*

Feminine

anus	*domus*	*manus*

(pl.)
īdūs -uum
Neuter

cornū	*genū*

5th Declension
Gen. sing. *-ēī/-eī* (pl. *-ērum*)
Feminine

aciēs -ēī	*glaciēs -ēī*	*fidēs -eī*	*spēs -eī*
faciēs -ēī	*speciēs -ēī*	*rēs reī*	

Masculine

diēs -ēī	*merīdiēs -ēī*

Adjectives

1st/2nd Declension
Nom. sing. m. -*us*, f. -*a*, n. -*um*

acerbus	*armātus*	*centēsimus*	*doctus*
acūtus	*asinīnus*	*certus*	*dubius*
adversus	*attentus*	*cēterus*	*dūrus*
aegrōtus	*aureus*	*clārus*	*ēbrius*
aequus	*avārus*	*claudus*	*ēgregius*
albus	*barbarus*	*clausus*	*exiguus*
aliēnus	*beātus*	*contrārius*	*falsus*
altus	*bellus*	*crassus*	*ferreus*
amīcus	*bonus*	*cruentus*	*ferus*
amoenus	*caecus*	*cūnctus*	*fessus*
angustus	*calidus*	*cupidus*	*fīdus*
antīquus	*candidus*	*decimus*	*foedus*
apertus	*cārus*	*dignus*	*fōrmōsus*
arduus	*cautus*	*dīmidius*	*frīgidus*
argenteus	*celsus*	*dīrus*	*fugitīvus*
futūrus	*maestus*	*perpetuus*	*sextus*
gemmātus	*magnificus*	*perterritus*	*siccus*
gladiātōrius	*magnus*	*pessimus*	*situs*
glōriōsus	*malus*	*plānus*	*sordidus*
grātus	*maritimus*	*plēnus*	*studiōsus*
gravidus	*mātūrus*	*poēticus*	*stultus*
horrendus	*māximus*	*postrēmus*	*summus*
ignārus	*medius*	*praeteritus*	*superbus*
ignōtus	*mellītus*	*prāvus*	*superus*
immātūrus	*mercātōrius*	*pretiōsus*	*surdus*
improbus	*merus*	*prīmus*	*suus*
īmus	*meus*	*prīvātus*	*tacitus*
incertus	*minimus*	*propinquus*	*tantus*
inconditus	*mīrus*	*proprius*	*tardus*
indignus	*misellus*	*proximus*	*temerārius*
indoctus	*molestus*	*pūblicus*	*tenebricōsus*
industrius	*mortuus*	*pūrus*	*timidus*
īnferus	*mundus*	*quantus*	*tertius*
īnfēstus	*mūtus*	*quārtus*	*togātus*
īnfīdus	*mūtuus*	*quiētus*	*tranquillus*
īnfimus	*necessārius*	*quīntus*	*turbidus*
inhūmānus	*nimius*	*rapidus*	*turgidus*
inimīcus	*niveus*	*rārus*	*tūtus*
iniūstus	*nōnus*	*rēctus*	*tuus*
internus	*nōtus*	*reliquus*	*ultimus*
invalidus	*novus*	*rīdiculus*	*ūmidus*
iocōsus	*nūbilus*	*Rōmānus*	*ūniversus*
īrātus	*nūdus*	*rūsticus*	*urbānus*
iūcundus	*obscūrus*	*saevus*	*vacuus*
iūstus	*octāvus*	*salvus*	*validus*
laetus	*optimus*	*sānus*	*varius*
laevus	*ōtiōsus*	*scaenicus*	*venustus*
largus	*pallidus*	*scelestus*	*vērus*
Latīnus	*parātus*	*secundus*	*vīvus*
lātus	*parvulus*	*septimus*	-*issimus*
legiōnārius	*parvus*	*serēnus*	sup.
ligneus	*pecūniōsus*	*sērius*	-*ēsimus*
longus	*perīculōsus*	*sevērus*	num.

(pl.)

cēterī	*paucī*	*singulī*	*ducentī*
multī	*plērī-que*	*bīnī*	*trecentī*
nōnnūllī	*plūrimī*	*cēt.*	*cēt.*

Nom. sing. *-er -(e)ra -(e)rum*

aeger -gra -grum	*niger -gra -grum*	*ruber -bra -brum*
āter -tra -trum	*noster -tra -trum*	*sinister -tra -trum*
dexter -tra -trum	*piger -gra -grum*	*vester -tra -trum*
impiger -gra -grum	*pulcher -chra*	*līber -era -erum*
integer -gra -grum	*-chrum*	*miser -era -erum*

3rd Declension
Nom. sing. m./f. *-is*, n. *-e*

brevis	*fertilis*	*levis*	*rudis*
circēnsis	*fortis*	*mīlitāris*	*similis*
commūnis	*gracilis*	*mīrābilis*	*tālis*
crūdēlis	*gravis*	*mollis*	*tenuis*
dēbilis	*humilis*	*mortālis*	*terribilis*
difficilis	*immortālis*	*nōbilis*	*trīstis*
dulcis	*incolumis*	*omnis*	*turpis*
facilis	*inermis*	*quālis*	*vīlis*

Nom. sing. m./f./n. *-ns*, gen. *-ntis*

absēns	*dēpōnēns*	*ingēns*	*prūdēns*
amāns	*dīligēns*	*neglegēns*	*sapiēns*
clēmēns	*frequēns*	*patiēns*	*-ns* part.
cōnstāns	*impatiēns*	*praesēns*	pres.

Nom. sing. m./f./n. *-x*, gen. *-cis*

audāx	*fēlīx*	*īnfēlīx*
fallāx	*ferōx*	*vēlōx*

Nom. sing. m. *-er*, f. *-(e)ris*, n. *-(e)re*

ācer ācris	*celer -eris*	*September -bris*
Octōber -bris	*November -bris*	*December -bris*

Verbs

1st Conjugation

Inf. pres. act. -*āre*, pass. -*ārī*

aberrāre	*dare*	*iuvāre*	*properāre*
accubāre	*dēlectāre*	*labōrāre*	*pugnāre*
accūsāre	*dēmōnstrāre*	*lacrimāre*	*pulsāre*
adiuvāre	*dēsīderāre*	*lātrāre*	*Putāre*
adōrāre	*dēspērāre*	*laudāre*	*recitāre*
aedificāre	*dēvorāre*	*lavāre*	*rēgnāre*
aegrōtāre	*dictāre*	*levāre*	*rēmigāre*
aestimāre	*dōnāre*	*līberāre*	*repugnāre*
affīrmāre	*dubitāre*	*memorāre*	*revocāre*
amāre	*ēducāre*	*mīlitāre*	*Rigāre*
ambulāre	*errāre*	*mōnstrāre*	*Rogāre*
appellāre	*ēvolāre*	*mūtāre*	*rogitāre*
apportāre	*excitāre*	*nārrāre*	*salūtāre*
appropin-	*exclāmāre*	*natāre*	*salvāre*
quāre	*excōgitāre*	*nāvigāre*	*sānāre*
arāre	*excruciāre*	*necāre*	*secāre*
armāre	*excūsāre*	*negāre*	*servāre*
bālāre	*exīstimāre*	*nōmināre*	*signāre*
cantāre	*exōrnāre*	*numerāre*	*significāre*
cēnāre	*explānāre*	*nūntiāre*	*spectāre*
certāre	*expugnāre*	*occultāre*	*spērāre*
cessāre	*exspectāre*	*oppugnāre*	*spīrāre*
circumdare	*fatīgāre*	*optāre*	*stāre*
clāmāre	*flāre*	*ōrāre*	*suscitāre*
cōgitāre	*gubernāre*	*ōrdināre*	*turbāre*
commemo-	*gustāre*	*ōrnāre*	*ululāre*
rāre	*habitāre*	*ōscitāre*	*verberāre*
comparāre	*iactāre*	*palpitāre*	*vetāre*
computāre	*ignōrāre*	*parāre*	*vigilāre*
cōnstāre	*illūstrāre*	*perturbāre*	*vītāre*
conturbāre	*imperāre*	*pīpiāre*	*vocāre*
convocāre	*implicāre*	*plōrāre*	*volāre*
cōpulāre	*interpellāre*	*portāre*	*vorāre*
cruciāre	*interrogāre*	*postulāre*	*vulnerāre*
cubāre	*intrāre*	*pōtāre*	
cūrāre	*invocāre*	*praestāre*	

Deponent verbs

admīrārī	*fārī*	*luctārī*	*tumultuārī*
arbitrārī	*hortārī*	*minārī*	*versārī*
comitārī	*fābulārī*	*mīrār ī*	
cōnārī	*imitārī*	*ōsculārī*	
cōnsōlārī	*laetārī*	*precārī*	

2nd Conjugation
Inf. pres. act. *-ēre*, pass. *-ērī*

abstinēre	favēre	merēre	retinēre
appārēre	flēre	miscēre	rīdēre
audēre	frīgēre	monēre	rubēre
augēre	gaudēre	mordēre	salvēre
carēre	habēre	movēre	sedēre
cavēre	horrēre	nocēre	silēre
cēnsēre	iacēre	oportēre	solēre
complēre	impendēre	pallēre	studēre
continēre	implēre	pārēre	stupēre
dēbēre	invidēre	patēre	suādēre
decēre	iubēre	permovēre	sustinēre
dēlēre	latēre	persuādēre	tacēre
dērīdēre	libēre	placēre	tenēre
dētergēre	licēre	possidēre	tergēre
dēterrēre	lūcēre	pudēre	terrēre
dissuādēre	lūgēre	remanēre	timēre
docēre	maerēre	removēre	valēre
dolēre	manēre	respondēre	vidēre

Deponent verbs

cōnfitērī	intuērī	verērī
fatērī	tuērī	

3rd Conjugation

Inf. pres. act. *-ere*, pass. *-ī*
1. Ind. pres. pers. 1 sing. *-ō, -or*

abdūcere	canere	dēfendere	expōnere
accēdere	carpere	dēmere	extendere
accendere	cēdere	dēscendere	fallere
accidere	cernere	dēserere	fīdere
accumbere	cingere	dēsinere	figere
accurrere	claudere	dēsistere	flectere
addere	cōgere	dētrahere	fluere
adiungere	cognōscere	dīcere	frangere
admittere	colere	dīligere	fremere
adnectere	cōnfīdere	dīmittere	fundere
advehere	coniungere	discēdere	gerere
agere	cōnscendere	discere	ignōscere
alere	cōnsīdere	disiungere	impōnere
animadvertere	cōnsistere	dīvidere	imprimere
āmittere	cōnstituere	dūcere	inclūdere
appōnere	cōnsūmere	ēdūcere	incolere
apprehendere	contemnere	effundere	induere
arcessere	contrahere	ēlīdere	īnflectere
ascendere	convertere	ēligere	īnfluere
aspergere	coquere	emere	īnscrībere
āvertere	corrigere	ērubēscere	īnstruere
bibere	crēdere	ērumpere	intellegere
cadere	crēscere	ēvolvere	invehere
caedere	currere	excurrere	iungere
laedere	perdeere	reddere	statuere
legere	pergere	redimere	sternere
lūdere	permittere	redūcere	submergere
mergere	petere	regere	sūmere
metere	plaudere	relinquere	surgere
metuere	pōnere	remittere	tangere
minuere	poscere	repōnere	tollere
mittere	praepōnere	reprehendere	trādere
neglegere	prehendere	requiēscere	trahere
nōscere	premere	requīrere	tremere
nūbere	prōcēdere	resistere	ūrere
occidere	prōcurrere	retrahere	vehere
occīdere	prōmere	rumpere	vēndere
occurrere	prōmittere	scindere	vertere
ostendere	quaerere	scrībere	vincere
parcere	quiēscere	serere	vīsere
pāscere	recēdere	sinere	vīvere
pellere	recognōscere	solvere	
percurrere	recumbere	spargere	

Deponent verbs

colloquī	lābī	persequī	revertī
complectī	loquī	proficīscī	sequī
cōnsequī	nāscī	querī	ūtī
fruī	oblīvīscī	reminīscī	

2. Ind. pres. pers. 1 sing. *-iō, -ior*

abicere	*cōnspicere*	*iacere*	*rapere*
accipere	*cupere*	*incipere*	*recipere*
adicere	*dēspicere*	*interficere*	*sapere*
afficere	*efficere*	*parere*	*surripere*
allicere	*effugere*	*percutere*	*suscipere*
aspicere	*ēicere*	*perficere*	*suspicere*
aufugere	*ēripere*	*prōicere*	
capere	*facere*	*prōspicere*	
cōnficere	*fugere*	*quatere*	

Deponent verbs

ēgredī	*morī*	*patī*	*prōgredī*

4th Conjugation
Inf. pres. act. *-īre*, pass. *-īrī*

advenīre	*exaudīre*	*oboedīre*	*scīre*
aperīre	*exhaurīre*	*operīre*	*sentīre*
audīre	*fīnīre*	*pervenīre*	*servīre*
circumsilīre	*haurīre*	*prōsilīre*	*vāgīre*
convenīre	*invenīre*	*pūnīre*	*venīre*
cūstōdīre	*mollīre*	*reperīre*	*vestīre*
dēsilīre	*mūnīre*	*revenīre*	*vincīre*
dormīre	*nescīre*	*salīre*	

Deponent vebs

largīrī	*opperīrī*	*mentīrī*	*orīrī*
partīrī			

Vocabulary by Chapter

I. Imperium Rōmānum
nōmina
fluvius
imperium
īnsula
ōceanus
oppidum
prōvincia
grammatica
capitulum
exemplum
grammatica
littera
numerus
singulāris
pēnsum
plūrālis
syllaba
vocābulum
adiectīva
duo
Graecus
Latīnus
magnus
mīlle
multī
parvus
paucī
prīmus
Rōmānus
secundus
sex
tertius
trēs
ūnus
verba
est
sunt
praepositiōnēs
in
coniunctiōnēs
et
sed

quoque
adverbia
nōn
vocābula interrogātīva
-ne?
ubi?
num?
quid?

II. Familia Rōmāna
nōmina
ancilla
domina
dominus
familia
fēmina
fīlia
fīlius
liber
līberī
māter
pāgina
pater
puella
puer
servus
titulus
vir
grammatica
fēminīnum
genetīvus
masculīnum
neutrum
adiectīva
antīquus
centum
cēterī
duae
meus
novus
tria
tuus
coniunctiōnēs

-que
vocābula interrogātīva
cuius?
quae?
quī?
quis?
quot?

III. Puer Improbus
nōmina
nōmen
mamma
persōna
scaena
grammatica
accūsātīvus
nōminātīvus
verbum
adiectīva
improbus
īrātus
laetus
probus
verba
audit
cantat
dormit
interrogat
plōrat
pulsat
respondet
rīdet
venit
verberat
videt
vocat
pronomina
eam
eum
hīc
mē
quae
quam

293

quem
qui
tē
adverbia
iam
vocābula interrogātīva
cūr?
coniunctiōnes
neque
quia
alia
ō!

IV. Dominus et Servī
nōmina
baculum
mēnsa
nummus
pecūnia
sacculus
grammatica
imperātīvus
indicātīvus
vocātīvus
adiectīva
bonus
decem
novem
nūllus
octō
quattuor
quīnque
septem
suus
vacuus
verba
abest
accūsat
adest
discēdit
habet
imperat
numerat
pāret
pōnit
salūtat
sūmit
tacet
pronōmina
eius
is
adverbia
rūrsus
tantum
coniunctiōnes
quod

alia
salvē

V. Vīlla et Hortus
nōmina
aqua
ātrium
cubiculum
fenestra
hortus
impluvium
līlium
nāsus
ōstium
peristȳlum
rosa
vīlla
grammatica
ablātīvus
adiectīva
foedus
pulcher
sōlus
verba
agit
amat
carpit
dēlectat
habitat
pronōmina
is, ea, id
adverbia
etiam
praepositiōnes
ab
cum
ex
sine

VI. Via Latīna
nōmina
amīca
amīcus
equus
inimīcus
lectīca
mūrus
porta
saccus
umerus
via
grammatica
praepositiō
locātīvus
āctīvum
passīvum

adiectīva
duodecim
fessus
longus
malus
verba
ambulat
intrat
it eunt
portat
timet
vehit
adverbia
ante
autem
itaque
nam
post
prope
quam
tam
praepositiōnes
ā
ad
ante
apud
circum
inter
per
post
procul ab
prope
vocābula interrogātīva
unde?
quō?

VII. Puella et Rosa
nōmina
lacrima
mālum
oculus
ōsculum
ōstiārius
pirum
sōlum
speculum
grammatica
datīvus
adiectīva
fōrmōsus
plēnus
verba
adit
advenit
aperit
claudit

currit
dat
es
exit
exspectat
inest
lacrimat
tenet
terget
vertit
pronōmina
cui
eī
haec
hic
hoc
iīs
illīc
sē
adverbia
immō
praepositiōnēs
ē
coniunctiōnēs
et...et
neque...neque
alia
nōnne?

VIII. Taberna Rōmāna
nōmina
ānulus
collum
digitus
gemma
līnea
margarīta
ōrnāmentum
pretium
prōnōmen
sēstertius
taberna
tabernārius
adiectīva
alius
gemmātus
medius
nōnāginta
octōgintā
pecūniōsus
quantus
quārtus
tantus
vīgintī
verba
abit

accipit
aspicit
clāmat
cōnsistit
cōnstat
convenit
emit
mōnstrat
ōrnat
ostendit
vēndit
pronōmina
ille
adverbia
nimis
satis
coniunctiōnēs
aut

IX. Pāstor et Ovēs
nōmina
arbor
caelum
campus
canis
cibus
clāmor
collis
dēns
herba
lupus
modus
mōns
nūbēs
ovis
pānis
pāstor
rīvus
silva
sōl
terra
timor
umbra
vallis
vestīgium
grammatica
dēclīnātiō
adiectīva
albus
niger
ūndēcentum
verba
accurrit
bālat
bibit
dēclīnat

dūcit
errat
ēst edunt
iacet
impōnit
lātrat
lūcet
petit
quaerit
relinquit
reperit
ululat
pronōmina
ipse
adverbia
suprā
procul
suprā
praepositiōnēs
sub
alia
dum
ut

X. Bēstiae et Hominēs
nōmina
āēr
āla
anima
animal
aquila
asinus
avis
bēstia
cauda
deus
fera
flūmen
folium
homō
lectus
leō
mare
mercātor
nīdus
nūntius
ōvum
pēs
petasus
pila
piscis
pullus
pulmō
rāmus
vōx
grammatica

īnfīnītīvus
adiectīva
crassus
ferus
mortuus
perterritus
tenuis
vīvus
verba
ascendere
audēre
cadere
canere
capere
facere
lūdere
movēre
natāre
necesse est
occultāre
parere
potest possunt
spīrāre
sustinēre
vīvere
volāre
vult volunt
pronōmina
nēmō
coniunctiōnes
ergō
quod
alia
cum
enim

XI. Corpus Hūmānum
nōmina
auris
bracchium
capillus
caput
cerebrum
color
cor
corpus
crūs
culter
frōns
gena
iecur
labrum
manus
medicus
membrum

ōs
pectus
pōculum
sanguis
vēna
venter
viscera
adiectīva
aeger
hūmānus
noster
ruber
sānus
stultus
verba
aegrōtāre
appōnere
arcessere
dētergēre
dīcere
dolēre
fluere
gaudēre
horrēre
iubēre
palpitāre
posse
putāre
revenīre
sānāre
sedēre
sentīre
spectāre
stāre
tangere
adverbia
bene
male
modo
praepositiōnes
dē
īnfrā
super
coniunctiōnes
atque
nec

XII. Mīles Rōmānus
nōmina
arcus
arma
avunculus
bellum
castra
cognōmen

dux
eques
equitātus
exercitus
fīnis
fossa
frāter
gladius
hasta
hostis
impetus
lātus
metus
mīles
mīlia
nōmen
pars
passus
patria
pedes
pīlum
praenōmen
pugnus
sagitta
scūtum
soror
vāllum
versus
grammatica
adiectīvum
comparātīvus
adiectīva
altus
armātus
barbarus
brevis
fortis
gravis
levis
trīstis
vester
verba
dēfendere
dīvidere
expugnāre
ferre
fugere
iacere
incolere
metuere
mīlitāre
oppugnāre
pugnāre
coniunctiōnēs
ac

praepositiōnēs
contrā

XIII. Annus et Mēnsēs
nōmina
aequinoctium
aestās
annus
autumnus
diēs
faciēs
fōrma
glaciēs
hiems
hōra
īdūs
imber
initium
kalendae
lacus
lūna
lūx
māne
mēnsis
merīdiēs
nix
nōnae
nox
saeculum
stēlla
tempus
urbs
vēr
vesper
grammatica
indēclīnābilis
superlātīvus
adiectīva
aequus
calidus
clārus
decimus
dīmidius
ducentī
duodecimus
exiguus
frīgidus
nōnus
obscūrus
octāvus
postrēmus
quīntus
septimus
sexāgintā
sextus
tōtus

trecentī
trīgintā
ūndecim
ūndecimus
verba
erat, erant
illūstrāre
incipere
nōmināre
operīre
velle
adverbia
item
māne
nunc
quandō
tunc
coniunctiōnēs
igitur
vel

XIV. Novus Diēs
nōmina
calceus
gallus
nihil
parentēs
rēgula
rēs
stilus
tabula
toga
tunica
vestīmentum
grammatica
participium
adiectīva
alter
apertus
clausus
dexter
neuter
nūdus
omnis
pūrus
sinister
sordidus
togātus
verba
afferre
cubāre
excitāre
frīgēre
gerere
induere
inquit

lavāre
mergere
poscere
solēre
surgere
valēre
vestīre
vigilāre
pronōmina
mēcum
mihi
sēcum
tēcum
tibi
uterque
adverbia
adhūc
deinde
hodiē
nihil (also noun)
prīmum
quōmodo
praepositiōnēs
praeter
coniunctiō
an
vocābula interrogatīva
uter?
alia
valē

XV. Magister et Discipulī
nōmina
discipulus
domī
iānua
lectulus
lūdus
magister
malum
sella
tergum
virga
adiectīva
īnferior
malus
posterior
prior
sevērus
tacitus
vērus
verba
cōnsīdere
dēsinere
es
estis

exclāmāre
licēre
pūnīre
recitāre
reddere
redīre
sum
sumus
prōnomina
ego
nōs
tū
vōs
adverbia
quid?
nōndum
statim
tum
praepositiōnēs
antequam
coniunctiōnēs
at
nisi
sī
vērum

XVI. Tempestās
nōmina
altum
flūctus
fulgur
gubernātor
merx
nauta
nāvis
occidēns
oriēns
portus
locus
ōra
puppis
septentriōnēs
tempestās
tonitrus
vēlum
ventus
grammatica
dēpōnēns
adiectīva
āter
contrārius
īnferus
maritimus
serēnus
situs
superus

tranquillus
turbidus
verba
appellāre
cernere
complectī
cōnārī
cōnscendere
cōnsōlārī
ēgredī
fierī fit fīunt
flāre
gubernāre
haurīre
iactāre
implēre
īnfluere
interesse
intuērī
invocāre
lābī
laetārī
loquī
nāvigāre
occidere
opperīrī
orīrī
proficīscī
sequī
servāre
turbāre
verērī
adverbia
iterum
paulum
praetereā
semper
simul
vērō
vix
coniunctiōnēs
sīve
praepositiōnēs
propter

XVII. Numerī Difficiles
nōmina
as
dēnārius
respōnsum
adiectīva
absēns
centēsimus
certus
difficilis
doctus

duodēvīgintī
facilis
incertus
indoctus
industrius
largus
nōngentī
octingentī
piger
prāvus
prūdēns
quadrāgintā
quadringentī
quattuordecim
quīndecim
quīngentī
quīnquāgintā
rēctus
sēdecim
septendecim
septingentī
septuāgintā
sescentī
trēdecim
ūndēvīgintī
verba
cōgitāre
computāre
dēmōnstrāre
discere
docēre
interpellāre
largīrī
laudāre
nescīre
oportēre
partīrī
prōmere
repōnere
reprehendere
scīre
tollere
pronōmina
quisque
adverbia
aequē
numquam
postrēmō
prāvē
quārē
rēctē
saepe
tot
ūsque
coniunctiōnēs

quamquam

XVIII. Litterae Latīnae
nōmina
apis
calamus
cēra
charta
epistula
erus
ferrum
māteria
mendum
mercēs
papȳrus
zephyrus
grammatica
adverbium
cōnsonāns
sententia
vōcālis
adiectīva
dūrus
frequēns
impiger
mollis
quālis
rārus
tālis
turpis
varius
verba
addere
animadvertere
comparāre
coniungere
corrigere
deesse
dēlēre
dictāre
efficere
exaudīre
imprimere
intellegere
iungere
legere
premere
scrībere
signāre
significāre
superesse
pronōmina
īdem, eadem, idem
quisque, quaeque, quodque
adverbia
bis

deciēs
ita
quater
quīnquiēs
quotiēs
semel
sexiēs
sīc
ter
totiēs

XIX. Marītus et Uxor
nōmina
adulēscēns
amor
columna
coniūnx
dea
domus
dōnum
flōs
forum
marītus
mātrōna
pulchritūdō
signum
tēctum
templum
uxor
virgō
grammatica
praesēns
praeteritum
adiectīva
beātus
dignus
dīves
gracilis
magnificus
māior
māximus
melior
minimus
minor
miser
optimus
pauper
pēior
pessimus
plūrēs
plūrimī
verba
augēre
convenīre
minuere
mittere

opus esse
ōsculārī
possidēre
remittere
pronōmina
mī
ūllus
adverbia
cotīdiē
ergā
minus
plūs
tamen

XX. Parentēs
nōmina
colloquium
cūnae
domō
fīliola
fīliolus
gradus
īnfāns
lac
mulier
nūtrīx
officium
sermō
silentium
somnus
adiectīva
aliēnus
futūrus
necessārius
parvulus
ūmidus
verba
advehere
alere
carēre
colloquī
cūrāre
dēbēre
decēre
dīligere
fārī
manēre
nōlle
occurrere
pergere
postulāre
revertī
silēre
vāgīre
adverbia
crās

magis
mox
rārō

XXI. Pugna Discipulōrum
nōmina
bōs
causa
cornū
cruor
genū
humī
humus
porcus
pugna
solum
sordēs
tabella
vestis
grammatica
imperfectum
perfectum
adiectīva
angustus
candidus
falsus
indignus
mundus
validus
verba
āiō
cognōscere
cōnspicere
crēdere
dubitāre
excūsāre
fallere
fuisse
mentīrī
mūtāre
nārrāre
vincere
pronōmina
aliquid
aliquis
adverbia
interim
coniunctiōnes
postquam

XXII. Cavē Canem
nōmina
aurum
cardō
catēna
faber

foris
iānitor
imāgō
lignum
līmen
pallium
tabellārius
grammatica
supinum
adiectīva
aureus
ferōx
ferreus
ligneus
verba
accēdere
admittere
arbitrārī
cavēre
cēdere
cūstōdīre
dērīdēre
fremere
monēre
mordēre
pellere
prehendere
prōcēdere
recēdere
removēre
resistere
retinēre
rogitāre
rumpere
salīre
scindere
sinere
solvere
terrēre
tremere
vincīre
pronōmina
iste
adverbia
anteā
forās
forīs
nuper
posteā
prius
quīn
scīlicet
sīcut
tandem

XXIII. Epistula Magistrī
nōmina
clāvis
comes
factum
laus
litterae
prōmissum
pudor
signum
verbera
vultus
adiectīva
integer
pallidus
plānus
superior
verba
āvertere
comitārī
continēre
dēbēre
dīmittere
fatērī
inclūdere
īnscrībere
merēre
negāre
pallēre
perdere
prōmittere
pudēre
rubēre
salūtem dīcere
solvere
trādere
pronōmina
quidnam?
quisnam?
adverbia
antehāc
fortasse
herī
hinc
illinc
posthāc
umquam
praepositiōnēs
ob

XXIV. Puer Aegrōtus
nōmina
dolor
latus
os
sonus

strepitus
tumultus
grammatica
plūsquamperfectum
adiectīva
aegrōtus
cruentus
impār
laevus
pār
subitus
verba
convertere
cupere
flēre
frangere
ignōrāre
mīrārī
nōscere
patī
percutere
recumbere
coniunctiōnēs
etsī
praepositiōnēs
iūxtā
adverbia
aliter
certō
cēterum
continuō
dēnuō
intus
prīmō
subitō
valdē

XXV. Thēseus et Mīnōtaurus

nōmina
aedificium
agnus
auxilium
cīvis
cōnspectus
cupiditās
currus
exitus
expugnātiō
fābula
fīlum
glōria
labyrinthus
lītus
moenia

mōnstrum
mora
mors
nārrātiō
nex
rēx
saxum
taurus
adiectīva
complūrēs
cupidus
humilis
mīrābilis
parātus
saevus
terribilis
timidus
verba
aedificāre
coepisse
cōnstituere
dēscendere
dēserere
interficere
maerēre
necāre
oblīvīscī
occīdere
patēre
pollicērī
prōspicere
regere
trahere
vorāre
adverbia
brevī
forte
hūc
ibi
illūc
ōlim
quotannīs

XXVI. Daedalus et Īcarus

nōmina
ars
carcer
cōnsilium
fuga
ignis
lacertus
lībertās
multitūdō
nātūra
opus
orbis

paenīnsula
penna
grammatica
cāsus
gerundium
adiectīva
audāx
cautus
celer
īnfimus
ingēns
līber
propinquus
reliquus
studiōsus
summus
temerārius
verba
aberrāre
accidere
cōnficere
cōnsequī
cōnsūmere
dēspicere
effugere
estō
ēvolāre
excōgitāre
figere
imitārī
invenīre
iuvāre
levāre
mollīre
perficere
persequī
quatere
revocāre
suspicere
ūrere
vidērī
pronōmina
quisquam
coniunctiōnēs
sīn
praepositiōnēs
trāns
adverbia
deorsum
haud
paene
quidem
quoniam
sūrsum
tamquam

vērum

XXVII. Rēs Rūsticae
nōmina
ager
agricola
arātrum
calor
colōnus
cōpia
cūra
falx
frīgus
frūgēs
frūmentum
grex
īnstrūmentum
labor
lāna
negōtium
ōtium
pābulum
patientia
pecus
praedium
precēs
regiō
rūs
sēmen
ūva
vīnea
vīnum
vītis
adiectīva
amoenus
fertilis
gravidus
immātūrus
inhūmānus
mātūrus
neglegēns
nēquam
patiēns
rudis
rūsticus
siccus
suburbānus
trīcēsimus
urbānus
verba
arāre
cēnsēre
cingere
colere
crēscere
exīstimāre

invehere
labōrāre
metere
neglegere
nocēre
ōrāre
pāscere
prōdesse
prohibēre
prōicere
quiēscere
rapere
rigāre
serere
spargere
ūtī
pronōmina
quīdam
praepositiōnēs
abs
circā
prae
prō
coniunctiōnēs
nē
-ve
adverbia
dēnique
parum
tantum

XXVIII. Perīcula Maris
nōmina
animus
dictum
fāma
fretum
libellus
mundus
nāvicula
pecūlium
perīculum
phantasma
potestās
praedō
prīnceps
tībīcen
tranquillitās
turba
vigilia
vorāgō
adiectīva
attentus
caecus
claudus
cōnstāns

immortālis
mortālis
mūtus
perīculōsus
quadrāgēsimus
salvus
surdus
tūtus
ūniversus
verba
admīrārī
adōrāre
apprehendere
cessāre
disiungere
ēicere
ēvolvere
extendere
habērī
impendēre
mālle
memorāre
morī
nāscī
oboedīre
perīre
persuādēre
pervenīre
rēgnāre
rogāre
salvāre
servīre
spērāre
suscitāre
tumultuārī
versārī
vītāre
coniunctiōnēs
velut
adverbia
potius
utrum

XXIX. Nāvigāre
Necesse Est
nōmina
beneficium
cantus
carmen
delphīnus
dīvitiae
dorsum
fēlīcitās
fidēs
fidicen

fortūna
fundus
fūr
fūrtum
iactūra
invidia
laetitia
lucrum
maleficium
nāvigātiō
piscātor
rēmus
salūs
spēs
trīstitia
tyrannus
vīta
adiectīva
celsus
fallāx
fēlīx
ignārus
ignōtus
maestus
mīrus
nōbilis
nōtus
pretiōsus
rapidus
vēlōx
verba
abicere
abstinēre
adicere
aestimāre
afficere
allicere
āmittere
appārēre
appropinquāre
cōnfitērī
dēsilīre
dēspērāre
dēterrēre
dētrahere
dōnāre
ēripere
expōnere
fīnīre
invidēre
parcere
permittere
permovēre
perturbāre
precārī

querī
recognōscere
redūcere
remanēre
secāre
stupēre
suādēre
subīre
surripere
pronōmina
nōnnūllī
sēsē
adverbia
frūstrā
inde
nōnnumquam
prōtinus
quasi
repente

XXX. Convīvium
nōmina
argentum
balneum
bonum
calida
carō
cēna
cocus
convīva
convīvium
culīna
famēs
genus
holus
hospes
iter
lībertīnus
medium
mel
merum
minister
nux
sāl
sitis
trīclīnium
vās
adiectīva
acerbus
acūtus
argenteus
bīnī
dīligēns
dulcis
glōriōsus
īmus

inexspectātus
iūcundus
merus
molestus
singulī
tardus
ternī
verba
accubāre
accumbere
apportāre
aspergere
cēnāre
complēre
contrahere
coquere
ēligere
exhaurīre
exōrnāre
fruī
fundere
gustāre
līberāre
miscēre
nūntiāre
parāre
perferre
placēre
pōtāre
praeesse
prōferre
recipere
requiēscere
salvēre iubēre
sternere
vīsere
praepositiōnēs
circiter
adverbia
dēmum
diū
equidem
paulisper
prīdem
sānē

XXXI. Inter Pōcula
nōmina
crux
fidēs
iniūria
iūs
iuvenis
lēx
memoria
mōs

mūnus
nūgae
parricīda
poena
pōtiō
praemium
rūmor
scelus
senex
supplicium
adiectīva
asinīnus
avārus
clēmēns
crūdēlis
dēbilis
ēbrius
fīdus
fugitīvus
impatiēns
īnfēlīx
īnfīdus
iniūstus
invalidus
iūstus
nōnāgēsimus
praesēns
sapiēns
scelestus
vetus
verba
abdūcere
auferre
aufugere
cōnfīdere
cruciāre
ēducāre
fābulārī
fīdere
ignōscere
interpellāre
latēre
ōdisse
optāre
retrahere
statuere
vetāre
pronōmina
quidquid
quisquis
praepositiōnēs
cōram
super
adverbia
aliquantum

funditus
ideō
namque
nimium/nimis
priusquam
quamobrem
quantum

XXXII. Classis Rōmāna
nōmina
amīcitia
amphitheātrum
audācia
classis
condiciō
cursus
gēns
grātia
incola
inopia
pīrāta
poēta
populus
servitūs
talentum
victor
victōria
vīrēs
vīs
voluntās
adiectīva
adversus
cārus
commūnis
cūnctus
ēgregius
grātus
inermis
īnfēstus
internus
mercātōrius
mūtuus
nūbilus
proximus
superbus
vīlis
verba
adiuvāre
armāre
contemnere
dēsistere
dissuādēre
ēdūcere
flectere
meminisse
minārī

offerre
percurrere
praeferre
praepōnere
redimere
referre
rēmigāre
reminīscī
repugnāre
submergere
tuērī
coniunctiōnēs
neu
seu
adverbia
aliquandō
aliquot
dōnec
etiamnunc
intereā
ubīque
utinam

XXXIII. Exercitus Rōmānus
nōmina
aciēs
aetās
agmen
amnis
caedēs
cohors
ēnsis
gaudium
imperātor
lēgātus
legiō
legiōnārius
ōrdō
pāx
proelium
ratis
rīpa
stipendium
studium
valētūdō
virtūs
vulnus
adiectīva
arduus
citerior
dēnī
dīrus
horrendus
idōneus

incolumis
mīlitāris
ōtiōsus
posterus
prīvātus
pūblicus
quaternī
quīnī
rīdiculus
sēnī
trīnī
ulterior
ūnī
verba
adiungere
caedere
circumdare
cōgere
commemorāre
convocāre
cōpulāre
dēsīderāre
effundere
ērumpere
excurrere
fatīgāre
fore
hortārī
īnstruere
mūnīre
praestāre
prōcurrere
prōgredī
properāre
studēre
trānsferre
trānsīre
vulnerāre
pronōmina
plērīque
praepositiōnēs
citrā
secundum
ultrā
adverbia
citrā
diūtius
etenim
ferē
praecipuē
prīdiē
quamdiū
secundum
tamdiū
ultrā

XXXIV. De Arte Poēticā
nōmina
anus
arānea
aurīga
bāsium
cachinnus
certāmen
circus
cōmoedia
dēliciae
fātum
gladiātor
gremium
ingenium
lucerna
lūdus
mēns
nīl
nota
ocellus
odium
opera
opēs
palma
passer
prīncipium
ratiō
rēte
rīsus
scalpellum
sinus
spectātor
tenebrae
testis
theātrum
grammatica
dactylus
dipthongus
epigramma
hendecasyllabus
hexameter
iambus
pentameter
spondēus
trochaeus
versiculus
adiectīva
ācer
bellus
circēnsis
dubius
geminus
gladiātōrius
iocōsus

mellītus
misellus
niveus
perpetuus
poēticus
scaenicus
sērius
tenebricōsus
turgidus
ultimus
venustus
verba
accendere
affirmāre
certāre
circumsilīre
conturbāre
dēvorāre
ēlīdere
ērubēscere
excruciāre
favēre
implicāre
laedere
libenter
libēre
lūgēre
nūbere
ōscitāre
pīpiāre
plaudere
prōsilīre
requīrere
sapere
coniunctiōnēs
dummodo
adverbia
dein
interdum
plērumque

XXXV. Ars Grammatica
nōmina
admīrātiō
affectus
īra
Mūsa
ōrātiō
sacerdōs
scamnum
grammatica
appellātīvum (nōmen)
cāsus
causālis (coniūnctiō)
comparātiō
coniugātiō

coniūnctiō
cōpulātīva (coniūnctiō)
disiūnctīva (coniūnctiō)
explētīva (coniūnctiō)
īnflectere
interiectiō
optātīvus (modus)
positīvus (gradus)
proprium (nōmen)
quālitās
quantitās
ratiōnālis (coniūnctiō)
significātiō
speciēs

synōnymum
adiectīva
inconditus
similis
verba
adnectere
dēmere
explānāre
luctārī
mentiōnem facere
ōrdināre
praepositiōnēs
adversum
cis

adverbia
dumtaxat
forsitan
proptereā
quāpropter
quidnī
sīquidem
tantundem
interiectiōnēs
attat
eia
ēn
euax
papae

Latin English Vocabulary

A

ā/ab/abs *prp* +*abl* from, of, since, by
ab-dūcere take away, carry off
ab-errāre wander away, stray
ab-esse ā-fuisse be absent/ away/distant
ab-icere throw away
ab-īre -eō -iisse go away
abs *v.* ā/ab/abs
absēns -entis *adi* absent
abs-tinēre keep off
ac *v.* atque/ac
ac-cēdere approach, come near
accendere -disse -ēnsum light, inflame
ac-cidere -disse happen, occur
ac-cipere receive
ac-cubāre recline at table
ac-cumbere -cubuisse lie down at table
ac-currere -rrisse come running
accūsāre accuse
ācer -cris -cre keen, active, fierce
acerbus -a -um sour, bitter
aciēs -ēī *f* line of battle
acūtus -a -um sharp
ad *prp* +*acc* to, toward, by, at, till
ad-dere -didisse -ditum add
ad-esse af-fuisse (+*dat*) be present, stand by
ad-hūc so far, till now, still
ad-icere add
ad-īre -eō -iisse -itum go to, approach
ad-iungere join to, add

ad-iuvāre help
ad-mīrārī admire, wonder at
admīrātiō -ōnis *f* wonder, admiration
ad-mittere let in, admit
ad-nectere -xuisse -xum attach, connect
ad-ōrāre worship, adore
adulēscēns -entis *m* young man
ad-vehere carry, convey (to)
ad-venīre arrive
adversus/-um *prp* +*acc* toward, against
adversus -a -um contrary, unfavorable
aedificāre build
aedificium -ī *n* building
aeger -gra -grum sick, ill
aegrōtāre be ill
aegrōtus -a -um sick
aequē equally
aequinoctium -ī *n* equinox
aequus -a -um equal, calm
āēr -eris *m* air
aestās -ātis *f* summer
aestimāre value, estimate
aetās -ātis *f* age
affectus -ūs *m* mood, feeling
af-ferre at-tulisse al-lātum bring (to, forward, about)
af-ficere affect, stir
af-firmāre assert, affirm
age -ite +*imp* come on! well, now
ager -grī *m* field
agere ēgisse āctum drive, do, perform
agmen -inis *n* army on the march, file
agnus -ī *m* lamb

agricola -ae *m* farmer, peasant
ain' you don't say? really?
āiō ais ait āiunt say
āla -ae *f* wing
albus -a -um white
alere -uisse altum feed
aliēnus -a -um someone else's
ali-quandō once
ali-quantum a good deal
ali-quī -qua -quod some
ali-quis -quid someone, something
ali-quot *indēcl* some, several
aliter otherwise
alius -a -ud another, other
aliī...aliī some...others
allicere -iō -ēxisse -ectum attract
alter -era -erum one, the other, second
altum -ī *n* the open sea
altus -a -um high, tall, deep
amāns -antis *m* lover
amāre love
ambulāre walk
amīca -ae *f* girlfriend
amīcitia -ae *f* friendship
amīcus -ī *m* friend
amīcus -a -um friendly
ā-mittere lose
amnis -is *m* river
amoenus -a -um lovely, pleasant
amor -ōris *m* love
amphitheātrum -ī *n* amphitheater
an or
ancilla -ae *f* female slave, servant
angustus -a -um narrow

anima -ae *f* breath, life, soul
anim-ad-vertere notice
animal -ālis *n* animal,
living being
animus -ī *m* mind, soul
annus -ī *m* year
ante *prp +acc, adv* in front
of, before
anteā before, formerly
ante-hāc formerly
ante-quam before
antīquus -a -um old,
ancient, former
ānulus -ī *m* ring
anus -ūs *f* old woman
aperīre -uisse -rtum open,
disclose
apertus -a -um open
apis -is *f* bee
ap-pārēre appear
appellāre call, address
ap-pōnere place (on), serve
ap-portāre bring
ap-prehendere seize
ap-propinquāre
(+*dat*) approach, come
near
Aprīlis -is (mēnsis) April
apud *prp +acc* beside, near,
by
aqua -ae *f* water
aquila -ae *f* eagle
arānea -ae *f* spider, cobweb
arāre plow
arātor -ōris *m* plowman
arātrum -ī *n* plough
arbitrārī think, believe
arbor -oris *f* tree
arcessere -īvisse -ītum send
for, fetch
arcus -ūs *m* bow
arduus -a -um steep
argenteus -a -um silver, of
silver
argentum -ī *n* silver
arma -ōrum *n pl* arms
armāre arm, equip
armātus -a -um armed
ars artis *f* art, skill
as assis *m* as (copper coin)
a-scendere -disse climb, go
up, mount
asinīnus -a -um ass's
asinus -ī *m* ass, donkey

a-spergere -sisse -sum
sprinkle, scatter (on)
a-spicere look at, look
at but
āter -tra -trum black, dark
atque/ac and, as, than
ātrium -ī *n* main room, hall
attentus -a -um attentive
audācia -ae *f* boldness,
audacity
audāx -ācis *adi* bold,
audacious
audēre ausum esse dare,
venture
audīre hear, listen
au-ferre abs-tulisse
ablātum carry off, take
away
au-fugere run away, escape
augēre -xisse -ctum
increase
Augustus -ī
(mēnsis) August
aureus -a -um gold-, *m* gold
piece
aurīga -ae *m* charioteer,
driver
auris -is *f* ear
aurum -ī *n* gold
aut or
aut...aut either...or
autem but, however
autumnus -ī *m* autumn
auxilium -ī *n* help,
assistance
auxilia -ōrum *n pl* auxiliary
forces
avārus -a -um greedy,
avaricious
ā-vertere turn aside, avert
avis -is *f* bird
avunculus -ī *m* (maternal)
uncle

B
baculum -ī *n* stick
bālāre bleat
balneum -ī *n* bath,
bathroom
barbarus -a -um foreign,
barbarian
bāsium -ī *n* kiss
beātus -a -um happy
bellum -ī *n* war
bellus -a -um lovely, pretty

bene well
beneficium -ī *n* benefit,
favor
bēstia -ae *f* beast, animal
bēstiola -ae *f* small animal,
insect
bibere -bisse drink
bīnī -ae -a two (each)
bis twice
bonum -ī *n* good, blessing
bonus -a -um good
bōs bovis *m/f* ox
bracchium -ī *n* arm
brevī *adv* soon
brevis -e short

C
cachinnus -ī *m* laugh,
guffaw
cadere cecidisse fall
caecus -a -um blind
caedere cecidisse
caesum beat, fell, kill
caedēs -is *f* killing,
slaughter
caelum -ī *n* sky, heaven
calamus -ī *m* reed, pen
calceus -ī *m* shoe
calidus -a -um warm, hot, *f*
hot water
calor -ōris *m* warmth, heat
campus -ī *m* plain
candidus -a -um white,
bright
canere cecinisse sing (of),
crow, play
canis -is *m/f* dog
cantāre sing
cantus -ūs *m* singing, music
capere -iō cēpisse
captum take, catch,
capture
capillus -ī *m* hair
capitulum -ī *n* chapter
caput -itis *n* head, chief,
capital
carcer -eris *m* prison
cardō -inis *m* door pivot,
hinge
carēre +*abl* be without, lack
carmen -inis *n* song, poem
carō carnis *f* flesh, meat
carpere -psisse-
ptum gather, pick, crop
cārus -a -um dear

castra -ōrum *n pl* camp
cāsus -ūs *m* fall, case
catēna -ae *f* chain
cauda -ae *f* tail
causa -ae *f* cause, reason
gen (/meā) +causā for the sake of
cautus -a -um cautious
cavēre cāvisse cautum beware (of)
cēdere cessisse go, withdraw
celer -eris -ere swift, quick
celsus -a -um tall
cēna -ae *f* dinner
cēnāre dine, have dinner
cēnsēre -uisse -sum think
centēsimus -a -um hundredth
centum a hundred
cēra -ae *f* wax
cerebrum -ī *n* brain
cernere crēvisse discern, perceive
certāmen -inis *n* contest, fight
certāre contend, fight
certē certainly, at any rate
certō *adv* for certain
certus -a -um certain, sure
cessāre leave off, cease
cēterī -ae -a the other(s), the rest
cēterum *adv* besides, however
cēterus -a -um remaining
charta -ae *f* paper
cibus -ī *m* food
cingere cīnxisse cīnctum surround
-cipere -iō -cēpisse -ceptum
circā *prp* +acc round
circēnsēs -ium *m pl* games in the circus
circēnsis -e of the circus
circiter about
circum *prp* +acc round
circum-dare surround
circum-silīre hop about
circus -ī *m* circle, orbit, circus
cis *prp* +acc on this side of
citerior -ius *comp* nearer
citrā *prp* +acc on this side of

cīvis -is *m/f* citizen, countryman
clāmāre shout
clāmor -ōris *m* shout, shouting
clārus -a -um bright, clear, loud
classis -is *f* fleet
claudere -sisse -sum shut, close
claudus -a -um lame
clausus -a -um closed, shut
clāvis -is *f* key
clēmēns -entis *adi* mild, lenient
cocus -ī *m* cook
coep- *v.* incipere
cōgere co-ēgisse -āctum compel, force
cōgitāre think
cognōmen -inis *n* surname
cognōscere -ōvisse -itum get to know, recognize
cohors -rtis *f* cohort
colere -uisse cultum cultivate
collis -is *m* hill
col-loquī talk, converse
colloquium -ī *n* conversation
collum -ī *n* neck
colōnus -ī *m* (tenant-)farmer
color -ōris *m* color
columna -ae *f* column
comes -itis *m* companion
comitārī accompany
com-memorāre mention
commūnis -e common
cōmoedia -ae *f* comedy
com-parāre compare
com-plectī -exum embrace
com-plēre -ēvisse -ētum fill, complete
com-plūrēs -a several
com-putāre calculate, reckon
cōnārī attempt, try
condiciō -ōnis *f* condition
cōn-ficere make, accomplish
cōn-fidere +dat trust
cōn-fitērī -fessum confess
con-iungere join, connect
coniūnx -iugis *m/f* consort,

wife
cōn-scendere -disse mount, board
cōn-sequī follow, overtake
cōn-sīdere -sēdisse sit down
cōnsilium -ī *n* advice, decision, intention, plan
cōn-sistere -stitisse stop, halt
cōn-sōlārī comfort, console
cōnsonāns -antis *f* consonant
cōnspectus -ūs *m* sight, view
cōn-spicere catch sight of, see
cōnstāns -antis *adi* steady, firm
cōn-stāre -stitisse be fixed, cost
cōnstāre ex consist of
cōn-stituere -uisse -ūtum fix, decide
cōn-sūmere spend, consume
con-temnere -mpsisse -mptum despise, scorn
con-tinēre -uisse -tentum contain
continuō *adv* immediately
contrā *prp* +acc against
con-trahere draw together, wrinkle
contrārius -a -um opposite, contrary
con-turbāre mix up, confound
con-venīre come together, meet
convenīre (ad/+dat) fit, be fitting
con-vertere turn
convīva -ae *m/f* guest
convīvium -ī *n* dinner-party
con-vocāre call together
cōpia -ae *f* abundance, lot
cōpulāre join, connect
coquere -xisse -ctum cook
cor cordis *n* heart
cōram *prp* +abl in the presence of
cornū -ūs *n* horn
corpus -oris *n* body

cor-rigere -rēxisse -rēctum correct
cotīdiē every day
crās tomorrow
crassus -a -um thick, fat
crēdere -didisse +*dat* believe, trust, entrust
crēscere -ēvisse grow
cruciāre torture, torment
crūdēlis -e cruel
cruentus -a -um blood-stained, bloody
cruor -ōris *m* blood-stained, bloody
crūs -ūris *n* leg
crux -ucis *f* cross
cubāre -uisse -itum lie (in bed)
cubiculum -ī *n* bedroom
culīna -ae *f* kitchen
culter -tri *m* knife
cum *prp* +*abl* with
cum *coniūnctiō* when, as
cum prīmum +*perf* as soon as
cūnae -ārum *f pl* cradle
cūnctus -a -um whole, *pl* all
cupere -iō -īvisse desire
cupiditās -ātis *f* desire
cupidus -a -um (+*gen*) desirous (of), eager (for)
cūr why
cūra -ae *f* care, anxiety
cūrāre care for, look after, take care
currere cucurrisse run
currus -ūs *m* chariot
cursus -ūs *m* race, journey, course
cūstōdīre guard

D
dare dedisse datum give
dē *prp* +*abl* (down) from, of, about
dea -ae *f* goddess
dēbēre owe, be obliged
dēbilis -e weak
decem ten
December -bris (mēnsis) December
decēre be fitting, become
deciēs ten times

decimus -a -um tenth
dēclīnāre decline, inflect
de-esse dē-fuisse (+*dat*) be missing, fail
dē-fendere -disse -ēnsum defend
de-inde/dein afterward, then
dēlectāre delight, please
dēlēre -ēvisse -ētum delete, efface
dēliciae -ārum *f pl* delight, pet
delphīnus -ī *m* dolphin
dēmere -mpsisse -mptum remove
dē-mōnstrāre point out, show
dēmum *adv* at last, only
dēnārius -ī *m* denarius (silver coin)
dēnī -ae -a ten (each)
dēnique finally, at last
dēns dentis *m* tooth
dē-nuō anew, again
deorsum *adv* down
dē-rīdēre laugh at, make fun of
dē-scendere -disse go down, descend
dē-serere -uisse -rtum leave, desert
dēsīderāre long for, miss
dē-silīre -uisse jump down
dē-sinere -siisse finish, stop, end
dē-sistere -stitisse leave off, cease
dē-spērāre lose hope, despair (of)
dē-spicere look down (on), despise
dē-tergēre wipe off
dē-terrēre deter
dē-trahere pull off
deus -ī *m, pl* deī/diī/dī god
dē-vorāre swallow up, devour
dexter -tra -trum right, *f* the right (hand)
dīcere -xisse dictum say, call, speak
dictāre dictate
dictum -ī *n* saying, words
diēs -ēī *m (f)* day, date

dif-ficilis -e, *sup* -illimus difficult, hard
digitus -ī *m* finger
dignus -a -um worthy
dīligēns -entis *adi* careful, diligent
dīligere -ēxisse -ēctum love, be fond of
dīmidius -a -um half
dī-mittere send away, dismiss
dīrus -a -um dreadful
dis-cēdere go away, depart
discere didicisse learn
discipulus -ī *m* pupil, disciple
dis-iungere separate
dis-suādēre advise not to
diū, *comp* diūtius long
dīves -itis *adi* rich, wealthy
dīvidere -īsisse -īsum separate, divide
dīvitiae -ārum *f pl* riches
docēre -uisse doctum teach, instruct
doctus -a -um learned, skilled
dolēre hurt, feel pain, grieve
dolor -ōris *m* pain, grief
domī *loc* at home
domina -ae *f* mistress
dominus -ī *m* master
domum *adv* home
domus -ūs *f, abl* -ō house, home
dōnāre give, present with
dōnec as long as
dōnum -ī *n* gift, present
dormīre sleep
dorsum -ī *n* back
dubitāre doubt
dubius -a -um undecided, doubtful
du-centī -ae -a two hundred
dūcere -xisse ductum guide, lead, draw, trace
uxōrem dūcere marry
dulcis -e sweet
dum while, as long as, till
dum-modo provided that, if only
dumtaxat only, just
duo -ae -o two

duo-decim twelve
duo-decimus -a -um twelfth
duo-dē-trīgintā twenty-eight
duo-dē-vīgintī eighteen
dūrus -a -um hard
dux ducis *m* leader, chief, general

E
ē *v.* ex/ē
ēbrius -a -um drunk
ecce see, look, here is
ēducāre bring up
ē-dūcere bring out, draw out
ef-ficere make, effect, cause
ef-fugere escape, run away
ef-fundere pour out, shed
ego mē mihi/mī I, me, myself
ē-gredī -ior -gressum go out
ēgregius -a -um outstanding, excellent
ē-icere throw out
ē-līdere -sisse -sum omit, elide
ē-ligere -lēgisse -lēctum choose, select
emere ēmisse ēmptum buy
ēn look, here is
enim for
ēnsis -is *m* sword
eō *adv* to that place, there
epigramma -atis *n* epigram
epistula -ae *f* letter
eques -itis *m* horseman
equidem indeed, for my part
equitātus -ūs *m* cavalry
equus -ī *m* horse
ergā *prp +acc* toward
ergō therefore, so
ē-ripere -iō -uisse -reptum snatch away, deprive of
errāre wander, stray
ē-rubēscere -buisse blush
ē-rumpere break out
erus -ī *m* master

esse sum fuisse futūrum esse/fore be
ēsse edō ēdisse ēsum eat
et and, also
et...et both...and
et-enim and indeed, for
etiam also, even, yet
etiam atque etiam again and again
etiam-nunc still
et-sī even if, although
ē-volāre fly out
ē-volvere -visse -lūtum unroll
ex/ē *prp +abl* out of, from, of, since
ex-audīre hear
ex-citāre wake up, arouse
ex-clāmāre cry out, exclaim
ex-cōgitāre think out, devise
ex-cruciāre torture, torment
ex-currere -rrisse -rsum run out, rush out
ex-cūsāre excuse
exemplum -ī *n* example, model
exercitus -ūs *m* army
ex-haurīre drain, empty
exiguus -a -um small, scanty
ex-īre -eō -iisse -itum go out
ex-īstimāre consider, think
exitus -ūs *m* exit, way out, end
ex-ōrnāre adorn, decorate
ex-plānāre explain
ex-pōnere put out/ashore, expose
ex-pugnāre conquer
ex-pugnātiō -ōnis *f* conquest
ex-spectāre wait (for), expect
ex-tendere -disse -tum stretch out, extend
extrā *prp +acc* outside

F
faber -brī *m* artisan, smith
fābula -ae *f* story, fable, play
fābulārī talk, chat

facere -iō fēcisse factum make, do, cause
faciēs -ēī *f* face
facile *adv* easily
facilis -e, *sup* -illimus easy
factum -ī *n* deed, act
fallāx -ācis *adi* deceitful
fallere fefellisse falsum deceive
falsus -a -um false
falx -cis *f* sickle
fāma -ae *f* rumor, reputation
famēs -is *f* hunger, famine
familia -ae *f* domestic staff, family
fārī speak
fatērī fassum admit, confess
fatīgāre tire out, weary
fātum -ī *n* fate, destiny, death
favēre fāvisse +*dat* favor, support
Februārius -ī (mēnsis) February
fēlīcitās -ātis *f* good fortune, luck
fēlīx -īcis *adi* fortunate, lucky
fēmina -ae *f* woman
fenestra -ae *f* window
fera -ae *f* wild animal
ferē about, almost
ferōx -ōcis *adi* fierce, ferocious
ferre tulisse lātum carry, bring, bear
ferreus -a -um of iron, iron
ferrum -ī *n* iron, steel
fertilis -e fertile
ferus -a -um wild
fessus -a -um tired, weary
-ficere -iō -fēcisse -fectum
fīdere fīsum esse +*dat* trust, rely on
fidēs -eī *f* trust, faith, loyalty
fidēs -ium *f pl* lyre
fidicen -inis *m* lyre-player
fīdus -a -um faithful, reliable
fierī factum esse be made, be done, become, happen

fīgere -xisse -xum fix, fasten
fīlia -ae *f* daughter
fīliola -ae *f* little daughter
fīliolus -ī *m* little son
fīlius -ī *m* son
fīlum -ī *n* thread
fīnīre limit, finish
fīnis -is *m* boundary, limit, end
flāre blow
flectere -xisse -xum bend, turn
flēre -ēvisse cry, weep (for)
flōs -ōris *m* flower
flūctus -ūs *m* wave
fluere -ūxisse flow
flūmen -inis *n* river
fluvius -ī *m* river
foedus -a -um ugly, hideous
folium -ī *n* leaf
forās *adv* out
foris -is *f* leaf of a door, door
forīs *adv* outside, out of doors
fōrma -ae *f* form, shape, figure
fōrmōsus -a -um beautiful
forsitan perhaps, maybe
fortasse perhaps, maybe
forte *adv* by chance
fortis -e strong, brave
fortūna -ae *f* fortune
forum -ī *n* square
fossa -ae *f* ditch, trench
frangere frēgisse frāctum break, shatter
frāter -tris *m* brother
fremere -uisse growl
frequēns -entis *adi* numerous, frequent
fretum -ī *n* strait
frīgēre be cold
frīgidus -a -um cold, chilly, cool
frīgus -oris *n* cold
frōns -ontis *f* forehead
frūgēs -um *f pl* fruit, crops
fruī +*abl* enjoy
frūmentum -ī *n* corn, grain
frūstrā in vain
fuga -ae *f* flight
fugere -iō fūgisse run away, flee

fugitīvus -a -um runaway
fulgur -uris *n* flash of lightning
fundere fūdisse fūsum pour, shed
funditus *adv* to the bottom, utterly
fundus -ī *m* bottom
fūr -is *m* thief
fūrtum -ī *n* theft
futūrus -a -um (*v.* esse) future
tempus futūrum future

G

gallus -ī *m* cock, rooster
gaudēre gavisum esse be glad, be pleased
gaudium -ī *n* joy, delight
geminus -a -um twin
gemma -ae *f* precious stone, jewel
gemmātus -a -um set with a jewel
gena -ae *f* cheek
gēns gentis *f* nation, people
genū -ūs *n* knee
genus -eris *n* kind, sort
gerere gessisse gestum carry, wear, carry on, do
glaciēs -ēī *f* ice
gladiātor -ōris *m* gladiator
gladiātōrius -a -um gladiatorial
gladius -ī *m* sword
glōria -ae *f* glory
glōriōsus -a -um glorious, boastful
gracilis -e slender
gradus -ūs *m* step, degree
Graecus -a -um Greek
grammatica -ae *f* grammar
grātia -ae *f* favor, gratitude
gen (/meā) + **grātiā** for the sake of
grātiam habēre be grateful
grātiās agere thank
grātus -a -um pleasing, grateful
gravida *adi f* pregnant
gravis -e heavy, severe, grave
gremium -ī *n* lap

grex -egis *m* flock, herd, band
gubernāre steer, govern
gubernātor -ōris *m* steersman
gustāre taste

H

habēre have, hold, consider
habitāre dwell, live
hasta -ae *f* lance
haud not
haurīre -sisse -stum draw (water), bail
herba -ae *f* grass, herb
herī yesterday
heu o! alas!
heus hey! hello!
hic haec hoc this
hīc here
hiems -mis *f* winter
hinc from here, hence
hodiē today
holus -eris *n* vegetable
homō -inis *m* human being, person
hōra -ae *f* hour
horrendus -a -um dreadful
horrēre bristle, stand on end, shudder (at)
hortārī encourage, urge
hortus -ī *m* garden
hospes -itis *m* guest, guest-friend
hostis -is *m* enemy
hūc here, to this place
hūmānus -a -um human
humī *loc* on the ground
humilis -e low
humus -ī *f* ground

I

iacere -iō iēcisse iactum throw, hurl
iacēre lie
iactāre throw, toss about
iactūra -ae *f* throwing away, loss
iam now, already
iānitor -ōris *m* doorkeeper
iānua -ae *f* door
Iānuārius -ī (mēnsis) January
ibi there
-icere -iō -iēcisse -iectum

īdem eadem idem the same
id-eō for that reason
idōneus -a -um fit, suitable
īdūs -uum *f pl* 13th/15th (of the month)
iecur -oris *n* liver
igitur therefore, then, so
ignārus -a -um ignorant, unaware
ignis -is *m* fire
ignōrāre not know
ignōscere -ōvisse +*dat* forgive
ignōtus -a -um unknown
ille -a -ud that, the one, he
illīc there
illinc from there
illūc there, thither
illūstrāre illuminate, make clear
imāgō -inis *f* picture
imber -bris *m* rain, shower
imitārī imitate
im-mātūrus -a -um unripe
immō no, on the contrary
im-mortālis -e immortal
im-pār -aris *adi* unequal
im-patiēns -entis *adi* impatient
im-pendēre +*dat* threaten
imperāre +*dat* command, order, rule
imperātor -ōris *m* (commanding) general
imperium -ī *n* command, empire
impetus -ūs *m* attack, charge
im-piger -gra -grum active, industrious
im-plēre -ēvisse -ētum fill, complete
im-plicāre -uisse -itum enfold
impluvium -ī *n* water basin
im-pōnere place (in/on), put
im-primere -pressisse -pressum press (into)
im-probus -a -um bad, wicked
īmus -a -um *sup* lowest
in *prp* +*abl* in, on, at
prp +*acc* into, to, against
in-certus -a -um uncertain

in-cipere -iō coepisse coeptum begin
in-clūdere -sisse -sum shut up
incola -ae *m/f* inhabitant
in-colere inhabit
incolumis -e unharmed, safe
inconditus -a -um unpolished, rough
inde from there, thence
index -icis *m* list, catalogue
in-dignus -a -um unworthy, shameful
in-doctus -a -um ignorant
induere -uisse -ūtum put on (clothes)
indūtus +*abl* dressed in
industrius -a -um industrious
in-ermis -e unarmed
in-esse be (in)
in-exspectātus -a -um unexpected
īnfāns -antis *m/f* little child, baby
īn-fēlīx -īcis *adi* unlucky, unfortunate
īnferior -ius *comp* lower, inferior
īnferus -a -um lower
Īnferī -ōrum *m pl* the underworld
īnfēstus -a -um unsafe, infested
īn-fidus -a -um faithless
īnfimus -a -um *sup* lowest
īn-fluere flow into
īnfrā *prp* +*acc* below
ingenium -ī *n* nature, character
ingēns -entis *adi* huge, vast
in-hūmānus -a -um inhuman
in-imīcus -ī *m* (personal) enemy
in-inimīcus -a -um unfriendly
initium -ī *n* beginning
iniūria -ae *f* injustice, wrong
in-iūstus -a -um unjust, unfair
inopia -ae *f* lack, scarcity

inquit -iunt (he/she) says/said
inquam I say
īn-scrībere write on, inscribe
īnscrīptiō -ōnis *f* inscription
īn-struere -ūxisse -ūctum draw up, arrange
īnstrūmentum -ī *n* tool, instrument
īnsula -ae *f* island
integer -gra -grum undamaged, intact
intellegere -ēxisse -ēctum understand, realize
inter *prp* +*acc* between, among, during
inter sē (with) one another
inter-dum now and then
inter-eā meanwhile
inter-esse be between
inter-ficere kill
interim meanwhile
internus -a -um inner, internal
inter-pellāre interrupt
inter-rogāre ask, question
intrā *prp* +*acc* inside, within
intrāre enter
intuērī look at, watch
intus *adv* inside
in-validus -a -um infirm, weak
in-vehere import
in-venīre find
in-vidēre +*dat* envy, grudge
invidia -ae *f* envy
in-vocāre call upon, invoke
iocōsus -a -um humorous, funny
ipse -a -um himself
īra -ae *f* anger
īrātus -a -um angry
īre eō iisse itum go
is ea id he, she, it, that
iste -a -ud this, that (of yours)
ita so, in such a way
ita-que therefore
item likewise, also
iter itineris *n* journey, march, way
iterum again, a second time

iubēre iussisse
  iussum order, tell
iūcundus -a -um pleasant,
  delightful
Iūlius -ī (mēnsis) July
iungere iūnxisse
  iūnctum join, combine
Iūnius -ī (mēnsis) June
iūs iūris *n* right, justice
iūre justly, rightly
iūstus -a -um just, fair
iuvāre iūvisse iūtum help,
  delight
iuvenis -is *m* young man
iūxtā *prp +acc* next to,
  beside

K

kalendae -ārum *f pl* the 1st
  (of the month)
kalendārium -ī *n* calendar

L

lābī lāpsum slip, drop, fall
labor -ōris *m* work, toil
labōrāre toil, work, take
  trouble
labrum -ī *n* lip
labyrinthus -ī *m* labyrinth
lac lactis *n* milk
lacertus -ī *m* (upper) arm
lacrima -ae *f* tear
lacrimāre shed tears, weep
lacus -ūs *m* lake
laedere -sisse -sum injure,
  hurt
laetārī rejoice, be glad
laetitia -ae *f* joy
laetus -a -um glad, happy
laevus -a -um left
lāna -ae *f* wool
largīrī give generously
largus -a -um generous
latēre be hidden, hide
Latīnus -a -um Latin
lātrāre bark
latus -eris *n* side, flank
lātus -a -um broad, wide
laudāre praise
laus laudis *f* praise
lavāre lāvisse lautum wash,
  bathe
lectīca -ae *f* litter, sedan
lectulus -ī *m* (little) bed
lectus -ī *m* bed, couch

lēgātus -ī *m* envoy, delegate
legere lēgisse lēctum read
legiō -ōnis *f* legion
legiōnārius -a -um
  legionary
leō -ōnis *m* lion
levāre lift, raise
levis -e light, slight
lēx lēgis *f* law
libellus -ī *m* little book
libenter with pleasure,
  gladly
liber -brī *m* book
līber -era -erum free
līberāre free, set free
libēre: libet +*dat* it pleases
līberī -ōrum *m pl* children
lībertās -ātis *f* freedom,
  liberty
lībertīnus -ī *m* freedman
licēre: licet +*dat* it is
  allowed, one may
ligneus -a -um wooden
lignum -ī *n* wood
līlium -ī *n* lily
līmen -inis *n* threshold
līnea -ae *f* string, line
lingua -ae *f* tongue,
  language
littera -ae *f* letter
lītus -oris *n* beach, shore
locus -ī *m* place
loca -ōrum *n pl* regions,
  parts
longē far, by far
longus -a -um long
loquī locūtum speak, talk
lūcēre lūxisse shine
lucerna -ae *f* lamp
lucrum -ī *n* profit, gain
luctārī wrestle
lūdere -sisse -sum play
lūdus -ī *m* play, game,
  school
lūgēre -xisse mourn
lūna -ae *f* moon
lupus -ī *m* wolf
lūx lūcis *f* light, daylight

M

maerēre grieve
maestus -a -um sad,
  sorrowful
magis more
magister -trī

m schoolmaster, teacher
magnificus -a -um
  magnificent, splendid
magnus -a -um big, large,
  great
māior -ius *comp* bigger,
  older
Māius -ī (mēnsis) May
male *adv* badly, ill
maleficium -ī *n* evil deed,
  crime
mālle māluisse prefer
malum -ī *n* evil, trouble,
  harm
mālum -ī *n* apple
malus -a -um bad, wicked,
  evil
mamma -ae *f* mummy
māne *indēcl n*,
  adv morning, in the
  morning
manēre mānsisse remain,
  stay
manus -ūs *f* hand
mare -is *n* sea
margarīta -ae *f* pearl
maritimus -a -um sea-,
  coastal
marītus -ī *m* husband
Mārtius -ī (mēnsis) March
māter -tris *f* mother
māteria -ae *f* material,
  substance
mātrōna -ae *f* married
  woman
mātūrus -a -um ripe
māximē most, especially
māximus -a -um biggest,
  greatest, oldest
medicus -ī *m* physician,
  doctor
medium -ī *n* middle, center
medius -a -um mid, middle
mel mellis *n* honey
melior -ius *comp* better
mellītus -a -um sweet
membrum -ī *n* limb
meminisse +*gen/
  acc* remember, recollect
memorāre mention
memoria -ae *f* memory
mendum -ī *n* mistake, error
mēns mentis *f* mind
mēnsa -ae *f* table
mēnsa secunda dessert

mēnsis -is *m* month
mentiō -ōnis *f* mention
mentīrī lie
mercātor -ōris *m* merchant
mercātōrius -a -um
  merchant-
mercēs -ēdis *f* wage, fee,
  rent
merēre earn, deserve
mergere -sisse -sum dip,
  plunge, sink
merīdiēs -ēī *m* midday,
  noon, south
merum -ī *n* neat wine
merus -a -um pure, neat,
  undiluted
merx -rcis *f* commodity, *pl*
  goods
metere reap, harvest
metuere -uisse fear
metus -ūs *m* fear
meus -a -um, *voc* mī my,
  mine
mīles -itis *m* soldier
mīlitāre serve as a soldier
mīlitāris -e military
mīlle, *pl* mīlia -ium
  n thousand
minārī +*dat* threaten
minimē by no means, not
  at all
minimus -a -um
  sup smallest, youngest
minister -trī *m* servant
minor -us *comp* smaller,
  younger
minuere -uisse -ūtum
  diminish, reduce
minus -ōris *n, adv* less
mīrābilis -e marvelous,
  wonderful
mīrārī wonder (at), be
  surprised
mīrus -a -um surprising,
  strange
miscēre -uisse mixtum mix
misellus -a -um poor,
  wretched
miser -era -erum unhappy,
  miserable
mittere mīsisse
  missum send, throw
modo only, just
modo...modo now...now
modus -ī *m* manner, way

nūllō modō by no means
moenia -ium *n pl* walls
molestus -a -um
  troublesome
mollīre make soft, soften
mollis -e soft
monēre remind, advise,
  warn
mōns montis *m* mountain
mōnstrāre point out, show
mōnstrum -ī *n* monster
mora -ae *f* delay
mordēre momordisse -sum
  bite
morī mortuum die
mors mortis *f* death
mortālis -e mortal
mortuus -a -um (< morī)
  dead
mōs mōris *m* custom, usage
movēre mōvisse
  mōtum move, stir
mox soon
mulier -eris *f* woman
multī -ae -a many, a great
  many
multitūdō -inis *f* large
  number, multitude
multō +*comp* much, by far
multum -ī *n, adv* much
mundus -ī *m* world,
  universe
mundus -a -um clean, neat
mūnīre fortify
mūnus -eris *n* gift
mūrus -ī *m* wall
Mūsa -ae *f* Muse
mūtāre change, exchange
mūtus -a -um dumb
mūtuus -a -um on loan
mūtuum dare/
  sūmere lend/borrow

N
nam for
-nam ...ever?
namque for
nārrāre relate, tell
nārrātiō -ōnis *f* narrative
nāscī nātum be born
nāsus -ī *m* nose
natāre swim
nātūra -ae *f* nature
nātus -a -um (< nāscī) born

XX annōs nātus 20 years
  old
nauta -ae *m* sailor
nāvicula -ae *f* boat
nāvigāre sail
nāvigātiō -ōnis *f* sailing,
  voyage
nāvis -is *f* ship
-ne ...? if, whether
nē that not, lest, that
nē...quidem not even
nec *v.* ne-que/nec
necāre kill
necessārius -a -um
  necessary
necesse est it is necessary
negāre deny, say that...not
neglegēns -entis
  adi careless
neglegere -ēxisse -ēctum
  neglect
negōtium -ī *n* business,
  activity
nēmō -inem -inī no one,
  nobody
nēquam *adi indēcl, sup*
  nēquissimus worthless,
  bad
ne-que/nec and/but not,
  nor, not
n....n. neither...nor
ne-scīre not know
neu *v.* nē-ve/neu
neuter -tra -trum neither
nē-ve/neu and (that) not,
  nor
nex necis *f* killing, murder
nīdus -ī *m* nest
niger -gra -grum black
nihil/nīl nothing
nimis too, too much
nimium too much
nimius -a -um too big
nisi if not, except, but
niveus -a -um snow-white
nix nivis *f* snow
nōbilis -e well known,
  famous
nocēre +*dat* harm, hurt
nōlī -īte +*īnf* don't...!
nōlle nōluisse be unwilling,
  not want
nōmen -inis *n* name
nōmināre name, call
nōn not

nōnae -ārum *f pl* 5th/7th (of
  the month)
nōnāgēsimus -a -um
  ninetieth
nōnāgintā ninety
nōn-dum not yet
nōn-gentī -ae -a nine
  hundred
nōn-ne not?
nōn-nūllī -ae -a some,
  several
nōn-numquam sometimes
nōnus -a -um ninth
nōs nōbīs we, us, ourselves
nōscere nōvisse get to
  know, *perf* know
noster -tra -trum our, ours
nostrum *gen* of us
nota -ae *f* mark, sign
nōtus -a -um known
novem nine
November -bris
  (mēnsis) November
nōvisse (< nōscere) know
novus -a -um new
nox noctis *f* night
nūbere -psisse *+dat* marry
nūbēs -is *f* cloud
nūbilus -a -um cloudy
nūdus -a -um naked
nūgae -ārum *f pl* idle talk,
  rubbish
nūllus -a -um no
num …? if, whether
numerāre count
numerus -ī *m* number
nummus -ī *m* coin, sesterce
numquam never
nunc now
nūntiāre announce, report
nūntius -ī *m* messenger,
  message
nūper recently
nūtrīx -īcis *f* nurse
nux nucis *f* nut

O
ō o!
ob *prp +acc* on account of
oblīvīscī -lītum *+gen/
  acc* forget
ob-oedīre *+dat* obey
obscūrus -a -um dark
occidēns -entis *m* west

oc-cidere -disse fall, sink,
  set
oc-cīdere - disse -sum kill
occultāre hide
oc-currere -rrisse
  +dat meet
ōceanus -ī *m* ocean
ocellus -ī *m* (little) eye
octāvus -a -um eighth
octin-gentī -ae -a eight
  hundred
octō eight
Octōber -bris
  (mēnsis) October
octōgintā eighty
oculus -ī *m* eye
ōdisse hate
odium -ī *n* hatred
of-ferre ob-tulisse
  oblātum offer
officium -ī *n* duty, task
ōlim once, long ago
omnis -e all, every
opera -ae *f* effort, pains
operīre -uisse -ertum cover
opēs -um *f pl* resources,
  wealth
oportēre: oportet it is right,
  you should
opperīrī -ertum wait (for),
  await
oppidum -ī *n* town
op-pugnāre attack
optāre wish
optimus -a -um *sup* best,
  very good
opus -eris *n* work
opus est it is needed
ōra -ae *f* border, coast
ōrāre pray, beg
ōrātiō -ōnis *f* speech
orbis -is *m* circle, orbit
orbis terrārum the world
ōrdināre arrange, regulate
ōrdō -inis *m* row, rank,
  order
oriēns -entis *m* east
orīrī ortum rise, appear
ōrnāmentum -ī
  n ornament, jewel
ōrnāre equip, adorn
os ossis *n* bone
ōs ōris *n* mouth
ōscitāre gape, yawn
ōsculārī kiss

ōsculum -ī *n* kiss
ostendere -disse show
ōstiārius -ī *m* door-keeper,
  porter
ōstium -ī *n* door, entrance
ōtiōsus -a -um leisured, idle
ōtium -ī *n* leisure
ovis -is *f* sheep
ōvum -ī *n* egg

P
pābulum -ī *n* fodder
paene nearly, almost
paen-īnsula -ae *f* peninsula
pāgina -ae *f* page
pallēre be pale
pallidus -a -um pale
pallium -ī *n* cloak, mantle
palma -ae *f* palm
palpitāre beat, throb
pānis -is *m* bread, loaf
pap*rus -ī *f* papyrus
pār paris *adi* equal
parāre prepare, make ready
parātus -a -um ready
parcere pepercisse
  +dat spare
parentēs -um *m pl* parents
parere -iō peperisse give
  birth to, lay
pārēre (*+dat*) obey
parricīda -ae *m* parricide
pars -rtis *f* part, direction
partīrī share, divide
parum too little, not quite
parvulus -a -um little, tiny
parvus -a -um little, small
pāscere pāvisse
  pāstum pasture, feed,
  feast
passer -eris *m* sparrow
passus -ūs *m* pace (1.48 m)
pāstor -ōris *m* shepherd
pater -tris *m* father
patēre be open
patī passum suffer,
  undergo, bear
patiēns -entis *adi* patient
patientia -ae *f* forbearance,
  patience
patria -ae *f* native country/
  town
paucī -ae -a few, a few
paulisper for a short time

paulō +*comp, ante/post* a little

paulum a little, little

pauper -eris *adi* poor

pāx pācis *f* peace

pectus -oris *n* breast

pecūlium -ī *n* money given to slaves

pecūnia -ae *f* money

pecūniōsus -a -um wealthy

pecus -oris *n* livestock, sheep, cattle

pedes -itis *m* foot-soldier

pēior -ius *comp* worse

pellere pepulisse pulsum push, drive (off)

penna -ae *f* feather

pēnsum -ī *n* task

per *prp* +*acc* through, by, during

per-currere -rrisse -rsum run over, pass over

per-cutere -iō -cussisse strike, hit -cussum

per-dere -didisse -ditum destroy, ruin, waste

per-ferre carry, endure

per-ficere complete, accomplish

pergere per-rēxisse proceed, go on

perīculōsus -a -um dangerous, perilous

perīculum -ī *n* danger, peril

per-īre -eō -iisse perish, be lost

peristȳlum -ī *n* peristyle

per-mittere allow, permit

per-movēre move deeply

perpetuus -a -um continuous, permanent

per-sequī follow, pursue

persōna -ae *f* character, person

per-suādēre -sisse +*dat* persuade, convince

per-territus -a -um terrified

per-turbāre upset

per-venīre get to, reach

pēs pedis *m* foot

pessimus -a -um *sup* worst

petasus -ī *m* hat

petere -īvisse -ītum make for, aim at, attack, seek, ask for, request

phantasma -atis *n* ghost, apparition

piger -gra -grum lazy

pila -ae *f* ball

pīlum -ī *n* spear, javelin

pīpiāre chirp

pīrāta -ae *m* pirate

pirum -ī *n* pear

piscātor -ōris *m* fisherman

piscis -is *m* fish

placēre +*dat* please

plānē plainly, clearly

plānus -a -um plain, clear

plaudere -sisse (+*dat*) clap, applaud

plēnus -a -um (+*gen/abl*) full (of)

plērī-que plērae- plēra-most, most people

plērumque mostly

plōrāre cry

plūrēs -a *comp* more

plūrimī -ae -a *sup* most, a great many

plūs plūris *n, adv* more

pōculum -ī *n* cup, glass

poena -ae *f* punishment, penalty

poēta -ae *m/f* poet

poēticus -a -um poetical

pollicērī promise

pōnere posuisse positum place, put, lay down

populus -ī *m* people, nation

porcus -ī *m* pig

porta -ae *f* gate

portāre carry

portus -ūs *m* harbor

poscere poposcisse demand, call for

posse potuisse be able

possidēre -sēdisse possess, own

post *prp* +*acc, adv* behind, after, later

post-eā afterward, later

posterior -ius *comp* back-, hind-, later

posterus -a -um next, following

posthāc from now on, hereafter

post-quam after, since

postrēmō *adv* finally

postrēmus -a -um *sup* last

postulāre demand, require

pōtāre drink

potestās -ātis *f* power

pōtiō -ōnis *f* drinking, drink

potius rather

prae *prp* +*abl* before, for

praecipuē especially, above all

praedium -ī *n* estate

praedō -ōnis *m* robber, pirate

prae-esse (+*dat*) be in charge (of)

prae-ferre prefer

praemium -ī *n* reward, prize

prae-nōmen -inis *n* first name

prae-pōnere +*dat* put before/in charge of

praesēns -entis *adi* present

prae-stāre -stitisse furnish, fulfill

praeter *prp* +*acc* past, besides, except

praeter-eā besides

praeteritus -a -um past

prāvus -a -um faulty, wrong

precārī pray

precēs -um *f pl* prayers

prehendere -disse -ēnsum grasp, seize

premere pressisse pressum press

pretiōsus -a -um precious

pretium -ī *n* price, value

prīdem long ago

prī-diē the day before

prīmō *adv* at first

prīmum *adv* first

prīmus -a -um first

prīnceps -ipis *m* chief, leader

prīncipium -ī *n* beginning

prior -ius first, former, front-

prius *adv* before

prius-quam before

prīvātus -a -um private

prō *prp +abl* for, instead of
probus -a -um good, honest, proper
prō-cēdere go forward, advance
procul far (from), far away
prō-currere -rrisse -rsum run forward, charge
prōd-esse prō-fuisse +*dat* be useful, do good
proelium -ī *n* battle
profectō indeed, certainly
prō-ferre bring forth, produce
proficīscī -fectum set out, depart
prō-gredī -ior -gressum go forward, advance
pro-hibēre keep off, prevent
prō-icere throw (forward)
prōmere -mpsisse -mptum take out
prōmissum -ī *n* promise
prō-mittere promise
prope *prp +acc, adv* near, nearly
properāre hurry
propinquus -a -um near, close
proprius -a -um own, proper
propter *prp +acc* because of
propter-eā therefore
prō-silīre -uisse spring forth
prō-spicere look out, look ahead
prōtinus at once
prōvincia -ae *f* province
proximus -a -um *sup* nearest
prūdēns -entis *adi* prudent, clever
pūblicus -a -um public, State-
pudēre: pudet mē (+*gen*) I am ashamed (of)
pudor -ōris *m* (sense of) shame
puella -ae *f* girl
puer -erī *m* boy
pugna -ae *f* fight
pugnāre fight
pugnus -ī *m* fist

pulcher -chra -chrum beautiful, fine
pulchritūdō -inis *f* beauty
pullus -ī *m* young (of an animal)
pulmō -ōnis *m* lung
pulsāre strike, hit, knock (at)
pūnīre punish
puppis -is *f* stern, poop
pūrus -a -um clean, pure
putāre think, suppose

Q

quadrāgēsimus -a -um fortieth
quadrāgintā forty
quadrin-gentī -ae -a four hundred
quaerere -sīvisse -sītum look for, seek, ask (for)
quālis -e what sort of, (such) as
quālitās -ātis *f* quality
quam how, as, than
quam +*sup* as...as possible
quam-diū how long, (as long) as
quam-ob-rem why
quamquam although
quandō when, as
quantitās -ātis *f* quantity, size
quantum -ī *n* how much, (as much) as
quantus -a -um how large, (as large) as
quā-propter why
quā-rē why
quārtus -a -um fourth
quārta pars fourth, quarter
quasi as, like, as if
quater four times
quatere -iō shake
quaternī -ae -a four (each)
quattuor four
quattuor-decim fourteen
-que and
querī questum complain, grumble
quī quae quod who, which, he who
quī quae quod (...?) what, which
quia because

quid *n* (*v.* quis) what, anything
quid *adv* why
quī-dam quae- quod- a certain, some
quidem indeed, certainly
nē quidem not even
quidnī why not
quid-quam anything
neque/nec quidquam and nothing
quid-quid whatever, anything that
quiēscere -ēvisse rest
quiētus -a -um quiet
quīn why not, do...!
quīn-decim fifteen
quīn-gentī -ae -a five hundred
quīnī -ae -a five (each)
quīnquāgintā fifty
quīnque five
quīnquiēs five times
Quīntīlis -is (mēnsis) July
quīntus -a -um fifth
quis quae quid who, what
quis quid (sī/num/nē...) anyone, anything
quis-nam quid-nam who/ what ever?
quis-quam anyone
neque/nec quisquam and no one
quis-que quae- quod- each
quis-quis whoever, anyone who
quō *adv* where (to)
quod (= quia) because, that
quod *n* (*v.* quī) what, which, that which
quō-modo how
quoniam as, since
quoque also, too
quot *indēcl* how many, (as many) as
quot-annīs every year
quotiēs how many times

R

rāmus -ī *m* branch, bough
rapere -iō -uisse -ptum tear away, carry off
rapidus -a -um rushing, rapid
rārō *adv* rarely, seldom

rārus -a -um rare
ratiō -ōnis *f* reason
ratis -is *f* raft
re-cēdere go back, retire
re-cipere receive, admit
recitāre read aloud
re-cognōscere recognize
rēctus -a -um straight, correct
rēctā (viā) straight
re-cumbere -cubuisse lie down
red-dere -didisse -ditum give back, give
red-imere -ēmisse -ēmptum ransom
red-īre -eō -iisse -itum go back, return
re-dūcere lead back, bring back
re-ferre rettulisse bring back, return
regere rēxisse rēctum direct, guide, govern
regiō -ōnis *f* region, district
rēgnāre reign, rule
rēgula -ae *f* ruler
re-linquere -līquisse -lictum leave
reliquus -a -um remaining, left
re-manēre remain, stay behind
rēmigāre row
re-minīscī +*gen/acc* recollect
re-mittere send back
re-movēre remove
rēmus -ī *m* oar
repente suddenly
reperīre repperisse repertum find
re-pōnere put back
re-prehendere blame, censure
re-pugnāre fight back, resist
re-quiēscere rest
re-quīrere -sīvisse -sītum seek, ask
rēs reī *f* thing, matter, affair
re-sistere -stitisse +*dat* halt, resist

re-spondēre -disse -sum answer
respōnsum -ī *n* answer
rēte -is *n* net
re-tinēre -uisse -tentum hold back
re-trahere pull back, bring back
re-venīre come back
revertī -tisse -sum return, come back
re-vocāre call back, revoke
rēx rēgis *m* king
rīdēre -sisse -sum laugh, make fun of
rīdiculus -a -um ridiculous
rigāre irrigate
rīpa -ae *f* bank
rīsus -ūs *m* laughter, laugh
rīvus -ī *m* brook
rogāre ask, ask for
rogitāre ask (repeatedly)
Rōmānus -a -um Roman
rosa -ae *f* rose
ruber -bra -brum red
rubēre be red, blush
rudis -e crude, rude
rūmor -ōris *m* rumor
rumpere rūpisse ruptum break
rūrī *loc* in the country
rūrsus again
rūs rūris *n* the country
rūsticus -a -um rural, rustic, farm-

S

sacculus -ī *m* purse
saccus -ī *m* sack
sacerdōs -ōtis *m/f* priest, priestess
saeculum -ī *n* century
saepe often
saevus -a -um fierce, cruel
sagitta -ae *f* arrow
sāl salis *m* salt, wit
salīre -uisse jump
salūs -ūtis *f* safety, well-being
salūtem dīcere +*dat* greet
salūtāre greet
salvāre save
salvē -ēte hallo, good morning
salvēre iubēre greet

salvus -a -um safe, unharmed
sānāre heal, cure
sānē certainly, quite
sanguis -inis *m* blood
sānus -a -um healthy, well
sapere -iō -iisse be wise, have sense
sapiēns -entis *adi* wise
satis enough, rather
saxum -ī *n* rock
scaena -ae *f* scene, stage
scaenicus -a -um theatrical
scalpellum -ī *n* scalpel, surgical knife
scamnum -ī *n* stool
scelestus -a -um criminal, wicked
scelus -eris *n* crime
scīlicet of course
scindere scidisse scissum tear, tear up
scīre know
scrībere -psisse -ptum write
scūtum -ī *n* shield
sē sibi himself
secāre -uisse -ctum cut
secundum *prp* +*acc* along
secundus -a -um second, favorable
sed but
sē-decim sixteen
sedēre sēdisse sit
sella -ae *f* stool, chair
semel once
sēmen -inis *n* seed
semper always
senex senis *m* old man
sēnī -ae -a six (each)
sententia -ae *f* opinion, sentence
sentīre sēnsisse sēnsum feel, sense, think
septem seven
September -bris (mēnsis) September
septen-decim seventeen
septentriōnēs -um *m pl* north
septimus -a -um seventh
septin-gentī -ae -a seven hundred
septuāgintā seventy
sequī secūtum follow

serēnus -a -um clear,
　cloudless
serere sēvisse satum sow,
　plant
sērius -a -um serious
sermō -ōnis *m* talk,
　conversation
servāre preserve, save
servīre +*dat* be a slave,
　serve
servitūs -ūtis *f* slavery
servus -ī *m* slave, servant
ses-centī -ae -a six hundred
sēsē himself
sēstertius -ī *m* sesterce
　(coin)
seu *v.* sī-ve/seu
sevērus -a -um stern, severe
sex six
sexāgintā sixty
sexiēs six times
Sextīlis -is (mēnsis) August
sextus -a -um sixth
sī if
sīc in this way, so, thus
siccus -a -um dry
sīc-ut just as, as
signāre mark, seal
significāre indicate, mean
significātiō -ōnis
　f meaning, sense
signum -ī *n* sign, seal,
　statue
silentium -ī *n* silence
silēre be silent
silva -ae *f* wood, forest
similis -e similar, like
simul together, at the same
　time
simul atque +*perf* as soon as
sīn but if
sine *prp* +*abl* without
sinere sīvisse situm let,
　allow
singulī -ae -a one (each),
　each
sinister -tra -trum left, *f* the
　left (hand)
sinus -ūs *m* fold (of toga)
sī-quidem seeing that, since
sitis -is *f* thirst
situs -a -um situated
sī-ve/seu or, or if
s. ... s. whether...or
sōl -is *m* sun

solēre -itum esse be
　accustomed
solum -ī *n* soil, ground,
　floor
sōlum *adv* only
sōlus -a -um alone, lonely
solvere -visse
　solūtum untie, discharge,
　pay
nāvem solvere cast off, set
　sail
somnus -ī *m* sleep
sonus -ī *m* sound, noise
sordēs -ium *f pl* dirt
sordidus -a -um dirty,
　mean, base
soror -ōris *f* sister
spargere -sisse -sum scatter
speciēs -ēī *f* appearance,
　aspect, sort
spectāre watch, look at
spectātor -ōris *m* spectator
speculum -ī *n* mirror
spērāre hope (for)
spēs -eī *f* hope
-spicere -iō -spexisse
　-spectum
spīrāre breathe
stāre stetisse stand
statim at once
statuere -uisse -ūtum fix,
　determine
stēlla -ae *f* star
sternere strāvisse
　strātum spread
stilus -ī *m* stylus
stipendium -ī *n* soldier's
　pay, service
strepitus -ūs *m* noise, din
studēre +*dat* devote oneself
　to
studiōsus -a -um
　(+*gen*) interested (in)
studium -ī *n* interest, study
stultus -a -um stupid,
　foolish
stupēre be aghast
suādēre -sisse +*dat* advise
sub *prp* +*abl/acc* under,
　near
sub-īre -eō -iisse go under,
　undergo
subitō *adv* suddenly
subitus -a -um sudden
sub-mergere sink

sub-urbānus -a -um near
　the city
sūmere -mpsisse -mptum
　take
summus -a -um
　sup highest, greatest
super *prp* +*acc* on (top of),
　above
prp +*abl* on, about
superbus -a -um haughty,
　proud
super-esse be left, be in
　excess
superior -ius *comp* higher,
　upper, superior
superus -a -um upper
supplicium -ī *n* (capital)
　punishment
suprā *prp* +*acc, adv* above
surdus -a -um deaf
surgere sur-rēxisse rise,
　get up
sur-ripere -iō -uisse
　-reptum steal
sūrsum up, upward
suscitāre wake up, rouse
su-spicere look up (at)
sus-tinēre support, sustain,
　endure
suus -a -um his/her/their
　(own)
syllaba -ae *f* syllable

T

tabella -ae *f* writing-tablet
tabellārius -ī *m* letter-
　carrier
taberna -ae *f* shop, stall
tabernārius -ī
　m shopkeeper
tabula -ae *f* writing-tablet
tacēre be silent
tacitus -a -um silent
talentum -ī *n* talent
tālis -e such
tam so, as
tam-diū so long, as long
tamen nevertheless, yet
tam-quam as, like
tandem at length, at last
tangere tetigisse
　tāctum touch
tantum -ī *n* so much
alterum tantum twice as
　much

tantum *adv* so much, only
tantun-dem just as much
tantus -a -um so big, so great
tardus -a -um slow, late
tata -ae *m* daddy
taurus -ī *m* bull
tēctum -ī *n* roof
temerārius -a -um reckless
tempestās -ātis *f* storm
templum -ī *n* temple
tempus -oris *n* time
tenebrae -ārum *f pl* darkness
tenebricōsus -a -um dark
tenēre -uisse -ntum hold, keep (back)
tenuis -e thin
ter three times
tergēre -sisse -sum wipe
tergum -ī *n* back
ternī -ae -a three (each)
terra -ae *f* earth, ground, country
terrēre frighten
terribilis -e terrible
tertius -a -um third
testis -is *m/f* witness
theātrum -ī *n* theater
tībiae -ārum *f pl* flute
tībīcen -inis *m* flute-player
timēre fear, be afraid (of)
timidus -a -um fearful, timid
timor -ōris *m* fear
titulus -ī *m* title
toga -ae *f* toga
togātus -a -um wearing the toga
tollere sus-tulisse sublātum raise, lift, pick up, remove, take away
tonitrus -ūs *m* thunder
tot *indēcl* so many
totiēs so many times
tōtus -a -um the whole of, all
trā-dere -didisse -ditum hand over, deliver
trahere -āxisse -actum drag, pull
tranquillitās -ātis *f* calmness
tranquillus -a -um calm, still

trāns *prp +acc* across, over
trāns-ferre transfer, transport
trāns-īre -eō -iisse -itum cross, pass
tre-centī -ae -a three hundred
trē-decim thirteen
tremere -uisse tremble
trēs tria three
trīcēsimus -a -um thirtieth
trīclīnium -ī *n* dining-room
trīgintā thirty
trīnī -ae -a three
trīstis -e sad
trīstitia -ae *f* sadness
tū tē tibi you, yourself
tuērī tūtum guard, protect
tum then
tumultuārī make an uproar
tumultus -ūs *m* uproar
tunc then
tunica -ae *f* tunic
turba -ae *f* throng, crowd
turbāre stir up, agitate
turbidus -a -um agitated, stormy
turgid(ul)us -a -um swollen
turpis -e ugly, foul
tūtus -a -um safe
tuus -a -um your, yours
tyrannus -ī *m* tyrant

U
ubi where
ubi prīmum *+perf* as soon as
ubī-que everywhere
ūllus -a -um any
nec/neque ūllus and no
ulterior -ius *comp* farther, more distant
ultimus -a -um *sup* most distant, last
ultrā *prp +acc* beyond
ululāre howl
umbra -a *f* shade, shadow
umerus -ī *m* shoulder
ūmidus -a -um wet, moist
umquam ever
nec/neque umquam and never
ūnā *adv* together
unde from where

ūn-dē-centum ninety-nine
ūn-decim eleven
ūndecimus -a -um eleventh
ūn-dē-trīgintā twenty-nine
ūn-dē-vīgintī nineteen
ūnī -ae -a one
ūniversus -a -um the whole of, entire
ūnus -a -um one, only
urbānus -a -um of the city, urban
urbs -bis *f* city
ūrere ussisse ustum burn
ūsque up (to), all the time
ut like, as
ut + coni that, in order that, to
uter utra utrum which (of the two)
uter-que utra- utrum- each of the two, both
ūtī ūsum *+abl* use, enjoy
utinam I wish that, if only…!
utrum…an …or…? whether…or
ūva -ae *f* grape
uxor -ōris *f* wife

V
vacuus -a -um empty
vāgīre wail, squall
valdē strongly, very (much)
valē -ēte farewell, goodbye
valēre be strong, be well
valētūdō -inis *f* health
validus -a -um strong
vallis -is *f* valley
vāllum -ī *n* rampart
varius -a -um varied, different
vās vāsis *n, pl* -a -ōrum vessel, bowl
-ve or
vehere vēxisse vectum carry, convey, *pass* ride, sail, travel
vel or
velle volō voluisse want, be willing
vēlōx -ōcis *adi* swift, rapid
vēlum -ī *n* sail
vel-ut like, as
vēna -ae *f* vein
vēn-dere -didisse sell

venīre vēnisse ventum come

venter -tris *m* belly, stomach

ventus -ī *m* wind

venustus -a -um charming

vēr vēris *n* spring

verbera -um *n pl* lashes, flogging

verberāre beat, flog

verbum -ī *n* word, verb

verērī fear

vērō really, however, but neque/nec vērō but not

versārī move about, be present

versiculus -ī *m* short verse

versus -ūs *m* line, verse

versus: ad...versus toward

vertere -tisse -sum turn

vērum but

vērus -a -um true, *n* truth

vesper -erī *m* evening

vesperī *adv* in the evening

vester -tra -trum your, yours

vestīgium -ī *n* footprint, trace

vestīmentum -ī *n* garment, clothing

vestīre dress

vestis -is *f* clothes, cloth

vestrum *gen* of you

vetāre forbid

vetus -eris *adi* old

via -ae *f* road, way, street

vīcēsimus -a -um twentieth

victor -ōris *m*, *adi* conqueror, victorious

victōria -ae *f* victory

vidēre vīdisse vīsum see, *pass* seem

vigilāre be awake

vigilia -ae *f* night watch (I-IV)

vīgintī twenty

vīlis -e cheap

vīlla -ae *f* country house, villa

vincere vīcisse victum defeat, overcome, win

vincīre -nxisse -nctum tie

vīnea -ae *f* vinyard

vīnum -ī *n* wine

vir -ī *m* man, husband

vīrēs -ium *f pl* strength

virga -ae *f* rod

virgō -inis *f* maiden, young girl

virtūs -ūtis *f* valor, courage

vīs, *acc* vim, *abl* vī force, violence, power

viscera -um *n pl* internal organs

vīsere -sisse go and see, visit

vīta -ae *f* life

vītāre avoid

vītis -is *f* vine

vīvere vīxisse live, be alive

vīvus -a -um living, alive

vix hardly

vocābulum -ī *n* word

vōcālis -is *f* vowel

vocāre call, invite

volāre fly

voluntās -ātis *f* will

vorāgō -inis *f* abyss, whirlpool

vorāre swallow, devour

vōs vōbīs you, yourselves

vōx vōcis *f* voice

vulnerāre wound

vulnus -eris *n* wound

vultus -ūs *m* countenance, face

Z

zephyrus -ī *m* west wind

Grammatical Terms

LATIN	ABBREVIATIONS	ENGLISH
ablātīvus (cāsus)	*abl*	ablative
accūsātīvus (cāsus)	*acc*	accusative
actīvum (genus)	*āct*	active
adiectīvum (nōmen)	*adi*	adjective
adverbium -ī *n*	*adv*	adverb
appellātīvum (nōmen)		appellative
cāsus -ūs *m*		case
comparātiō -ōnis *f*		comparison
comparātīvus (gradus)	*comp*	comparative
coniugātiō -ōnis *f*		conjugation
coniūnctiō -ōnis *f*	*coni*	conjunction
coniūnctīvus (modus)	*coni*	subjunctive
datīvus (cāsus)	*dat*	dative
dēclīnātiō -ōnis *f*	*dēcl*	declension

LATIN	ABBREVIATIONS	ENGLISH
dēmōnstrātīvum (prōnōmen)		demonstrative
dēpōnentia (verba)	*dēp*	deponent
fēminīnum (genus)	*f, fēm*	feminine
futūrum (tempus)	*fut*	future
futūrum perfectum (tempus)	*fut perf*	future perfect
genetīvus (cāsus)	*gen*	genitive
genus (nōminis/verbī)		gender/voice
gerundium -ī *n*/ gerundīvum -ī *n*		gerund/gerundive
imperātīvus (modus)	*imp, imper*	imperative
imperfectum (tempus praeteritum)	*imperf*	imperfect
indēclinābile (vocābulum)	*indēcl*	indeclinable
indēfīnītum (prōnōmen)		indefinite
indicātīvus (modus)	*ind*	indicative
īnfīnītīvus (modus)	*īnf*	infinitive
interiectiō -ōnis *f* interjection		
interrogātīvum (prōnōmen)		interrogative
locātīvus (cāsus)	*loc*	locative
masculīnum (genus)	*m, masc*	masculine
modus (verbī)		mode
neutrum (genus)	*n, neutr*	neuter
nōminātīvus (cāsus)	*nōm*	nominative
optātīvus (modus)		optative
pars ōrātiōnis		part of speech
participium -ī *n*	*part*	participle
passīvum (genus)	*pass*	passive
perfectum (tempus praeteritum)	*perf*	perfect
persōna -ae *f*	*pers*	person
persōnāle (prōnōmen)		personal
plūrālis (numerus)	*pl, plūr*	plural
plūsquamperfectum (tempus praet.)	*plūsqu*	pluperfect
positīvus (gradus)	*pos*	positive
possessīvum (prōnōmen)		possessive
praepositiō -ōnis *f*	*prp, praep*	preposition
praesēns (tempus)	*praes*	present
praeteritum (tempus)	*praet*	preterite, past tense
prōnōmen -inis *n*	*prōn*	pronoun
proprium (nōmen)		proper name
relātīvum (prōnōmen)	*rel*	relative
singulāris (numerus)	*sg, sing*	singular
superlātīvus (gradus)	*sup*	superlative
supīnum		supine
tempus (verbī)		tense
verbum	*vb*	verb
vocātīvus (cāsus)	*voc*	vocative